D0025366

CONTRIBUTIONS IN
AMERICAN HISTORY

SERIES EDITOR
STANLEY I. KUTLER
University of Wisconsin

NEGROES AND THE
GREAT DEPRESSION

NEGROES AND THE GREAT DEPRESSION

The Problem of Economic Recovery

Raymond Wolters

CONTRIBUTIONS IN AMERICAN HISTORY
Number Six

Greenwood Publishing Corporation
WESTPORT, CONNECTICUT

Copyright © 1970 by Raymond Wolters

All rights reserved. No portion of this book may be
reproduced, by any process or technique, without the
express written consent of the author and publisher.

Library of Congress Catalog Card Number: 78-95510
SBN: 8371-2341-0

Greenwood Publishing Corporation
51 Riverside Avenue, Westport, Conn. 06880
Greenwood Publishers Ltd.
42 Hanway Street, London, W.1., England

Printed in the United States of America

Contents

Acknowledgments

An earlier draft of this study was prepared as a doctoral dissertation in history at the University of California, Berkeley, and I am grateful to my adviser, Charles Sellers, for valuable criticism and wise counsel. I also want to thank Herbert Aptheker, Milton Cantor, August Meier, Wilson Record, Stephen Salsbury, and Ronald Takaki for suggestions that have prompted me to effect some important modifications. I am especially indebted to my wife Mary for several perceptive readings and valuable editorial assistance. The University of Delaware provided funds that enabled me to do some field research and to have the manuscript typed.

Introduction

WHEN Franklin D. Roosevelt was inaugurated as President of the United States on March 4, 1933, the economic life of the nation was at a standstill. Agricultural prices were less than half what they had been four years earlier, industrial production had declined by more than half, and more than twelve million workers were unemployed. During the years of the Great Depression, Negroes were the most disadvantaged major group in American society; it is commonplace but nevertheless accurate to say that they were the first fired and the last hired. Black people naturally hoped that the economic policies of the new administration would be constructed in such a way as to assist their recovery.

The first two sections of this study consist of an analysis of the manner in which Negroes were affected by the two major pieces of recovery legislation which the Roosevelt administration sponsored in the spring of 1933, the Agricultural Adjustment Act and the National Industrial Recovery Act. Although these were only two of the many proposals enacted into law during the hectic Hundred Days, they formed the very heart of the new administration's attempt to revive the economy. Other aspects of the New Deal program have been discussed briefly when they were an outgrowth of the original economic recovery program, as was the case with the Farm Security Administration (FSA), the Public Works Administration (PWA), and the Works Progress Administration (WPA).

In any study such as this there are difficult decisions to make concerning what should be included and what must be excluded. In this study I have not presented a comprehensive account of the New Deal and the Negro but have focused on *the problem of economic recovery*. Hence I have ignored the government's relief and welfare programs, not because I want to slight their importance in helping black people survive the depression but because relief and welfare were considered to be temporary expedients to tide the unemployed over until recovery had been achieved.[1] My concern is with the manner in which Negroes were affected by and responded to macro-economic plans to revive the economy to the point where prosperity would be self-sustaining.

In my analysis of the economic recovery program, I have given detailed attention to the special problems of black farmers and workingmen, and I have argued that definite measures for the protection of black people were needed if they were to benefit from the recovery programs. Unfortunately, the New Deal had no fixed policy with regard to the protection of black people. Each department and administrative agency established its own procedure for handling Negro problems, and often the fate of the black man depended on the extent to which the dominant personalities in various offices were sensitive or indifferent to the special needs of Negroes. Some New Deal economic recovery agencies did implement policies that ensured fair treatment for black people; this was particularly true of the Farm Security Administration, the Public Works Administration and, to a lesser extent, the Works Progress Administration. In part, the racial sensitivity of these agencies can be attributed to the fact that their chief administrative officers, Will Alexander, Harold Ickes, and Harry Hopkins, had strong convictions concerning the need for racial justice. Each of these administrators appointed knowledgeable men to specially created positions as "advisers" on the problems of Negroes, and each of them used the power of the central administration in Washington to force local authorities to grant government benefits to needy citizens regardless of race.

On the other hand, the leaders of the Agricultural Adjustment Administration and the National Recovery Administration were not willing to make the efforts needed to secure racial justice. They refused to appoint specialists to keep them posted on Negro problems, and they did not take steps to ensure the distribution of government benefits among Negroes. As a result, most of the AAA and NRA benefits did not trickle down to the masses of black workers and farmers.

Yet the Negro's failure to receive a fair share of the AAA and NRA benefits was not solely the result of the racial insensitivity and/or prejudice of some prominent officials; it resulted primarily from the fact that Negroes were weak and poorly organized, lacking in political and economic power. The New Deal was essentially an attempt to solve the nation's economic problems democratically, but such a "democratic" system usually gives the greatest benefits to those who are best organized. Since most Negro workers were not affiliated with strong unions and were not organized in tightly disciplined pressure groups, they inevitably gained little.

During the early years of the Roosevelt administration, the major Negro betterment organizations attempted in various ways to influence New Deal policy. Conferences were arranged in which black leaders consulted with government officials concerning the special problems of Negroes; members of protest organizations such as the National Urban League and the National Association for the Advancement of Colored People (NAACP) deluged government officials with letters and telegrams demanding fair treatment for Negroes in the recovery program; representatives of the Joint Committee on National Recovery diligently attended the NRA's Code Hearings and did what they could to eliminate any provisions detrimental to Negro workers; the major Negro betterment groups launched campaigns of agitation and education aimed at bringing the facts concerning the plight of the Negro in the national recovery program to public attention; and race leaders from all walks of life joined together to emphasize the need for Negro advisers at every level of government. Negro leaders assumed that somehow the calling of attention to the inconsistencies between the New Deal's egalitarian rhetoric and its frequently discriminatory practical effects would educate the public mind and bring relief. They were convinced that the function of protest groups was to protest and that their job was to expose and condemn discrimination wherever it appeared. Walter White, the executive secretary of the NAACP, stated the credo of the professional Negro agitator when he declared that his job was "to get the facts on discrimination and then to protest morning, noon and night to those in authority." "Only those who continue to raise a racket in season and out . . . are going to escape being given the rawest of deals."[2]

Although Negro leaders and organizations occasionally

were successful in securing relief from flagrant discrimination, they were not able to compel the Roosevelt administration to structure its economic recovery program so that a fair portion of the government benefits would seep down to the masses of black farmers and workers. While Negro leaders appealed for fair policies on grounds of equity and justice, their requests were seldom granted because almost invariably they conflicted with the claims of better organized and more powerful white groups. Recognizing that in a democracy conflicts of interest are generally resolved in favor of the stronger of two competing groups, many black leaders of the 1930s concluded that it was the Negro's weakness that allowed the government to neglect his interests. A. Philip Randolph, the president of the Brotherhood of Sleeping Car Porters, stated a point of view that was widely shared in the black leadership community when he declared that "True liberation can be acquired and maintained only when the Negro people possess power; and power is the product and flower of organization—organization of the masses, the masses in the mills and mines, on the farms, in the factories."[3] W. E. B. Du Bois was convinced that "the campaign of appeal for social justice has reached . . . its limits" and that "power is now needed to reinforce appeal." In his view, the power realities of American society made it necessary for black leaders to promote "such intensified class and race consciousness as will bring irresistible force rather than mere sentimental and moral appeal to bear on the motives and actions of men for justice and equality. . . . Unless the Negro unites for the intelligent guidance of his economic and industrial interests, he is going to be left out of the New Deal and the future reorganization of society."[4]

Yet Negroes of the depression decade could not agree on the best method for organizing black power and advancing the cause of economic recovery. While admitting that agitation, education, and appeals to conscience usually did not produce immediate results, most of the established leaders believed that an accurate picture of conditions was the essential prerequisite for corrective action, and they continued to place primary emphasis on publicity and protest. Others believed that white racism was so deeply rooted that appeals to conscience would have no short-run effect, and while not advocating a cessation of protest, many agreed with Du Bois's contention that Negroes should accept the fact that segregation would exist for the foreseeable future and should make the most of the situation by cooperatively organizing their already separate Negro nation-within-the-nation so that blacks could do for themselves what whites were unwilling to do. An even larger number agreed with the NAACP's treasurer, Mary White Ovington, that "one thing is sure. The Negro is at the complete mercy of the white man. He has no power, and he cannot attain power unless he can find some white group to join and assist. By himself, he will get the leavings."[5] Believing that a weak minority group in a democratic country could obtain strength only by allying itself with a portion of the majority, many Negro leaders concluded that primary emphasis should be placed on a campaign to foster biracial trade unionism and to make black and white workers recognize that they had common problems and common enemies. Still others refused to accept protest, self-help, or biracial trade unionism as viable solutions to the black man's economic problems and decided that the only hope for the future lay in organizations whose avowed aim was revolution.

By 1935 most articulate Negroes had concluded that government officials had paid insufficient attention to the special problems of Negroes and that the New Deal recovery program had failed to improve significantly the economic condition of the black masses. Thereafter, the focal point of Negro thinking about economic recovery shifted away from the question of how to influence government programs directly and centered instead on the way in which black people could best organize themselves as a powerful interest group that no government could afford to ignore. I have followed this shift in the focus of Negro thought, and the third and final section of this study assesses the nature of Negro economic thinking by considering in some detail the changing strategies and tactics of the nation's major Negro betterment organization, the NAACP. Thus within the limits of the problem of economic recovery, I have described and analyzed three major areas: (1) the manner in which Negroes fared (in terms of the actual consequences for the Negro population at large) under the New Deal's original economic recovery program; (2) the efforts of the major Negro betterment organizations to influence the New Deal; and (3) the controversy within the NAACP over proper strategy in a time of economic crisis.

The story of Negroes and economic recovery is essentially dual, at once a part of general American national history and simultaneously an experience in itself. Thus, my account is bifocal—telling both what white government officials believed and did about the Negro and what Negroes were thinking and doing about the government and economic recovery, even though the two did not define the problem in the same terms and were not always addressing themselves to the same aspects of the question. Too much of our written Negro history has been presented simply as an extension of white history— white attitudes and policies toward blacks, with the Negroes as passive creatures to whom things happen. The real need is for a biracial history that takes both perspectives into account and shows how blacks and whites considered the same problem in substantially different terms.

NOTES

1. The reader who is interested in the relations between Negroes and the relief agencies will want to consult several other studies, most of which have not been published. The most comprehensive work is that of Allen Kifer, "The Negro and the New Deal" (Ph.D. dissertation, University of Wisconsin, 1961), a good account of the way Negro problems were handled by the Civilian Conservation Corps (CCC), the National Youth Administration (NYA), the writers' and actors' projects of the WPA, and the resettlement communities of the Department of Interior, the Federal Emergency Relief Administration, the Resettlement Administration, and the Farm Security Administration. John A. Salmond has also discussed the CCC experience, "The Civilian Conservation Corps and the Negro," *Journal of American History*, 52 (June, 1965):75-88. Joseph H. B. Evans prepared a perceptive manuscript, "The Negroes' Part in the Resettlement Administration" (typescript in National Urban League Files). Frank G. Davis wrote his doctoral dissertation in economics on "The Effect of the Social Security Act on the Status of the Negro" (Ph.D. dissertation, State University of Iowa, 1939). John P. Davis prepared an extensive and interesting study of "The Negro and TVA: A Report to the NAACP" (n.d.) NAACP Files. Richard Sterner's *The Negro's Share* (New York: Harper and Brothers, 1943) has more detail on the relations between Negroes and the WPA and PWA than I have considered advisable to present here, and Sidney Baldwin's *Poverty and Politics* (Chapel Hill: University of North Carolina Press, 1968) discusses the policies and personnel of the Farm Security Administration at great length. By focusing on the problem of economic recovery and by slighting the government's relief and welfare programs, I have concentrated attention on some of the New Deal's more discriminatory agencies and perhaps have obscured the fact that some of the welfare policies of the Roosevelt administration were remarkably fair. This welfare alleviated the distress of many black men and women, and it was largely in thanks for this aid that many Negroes in the 1930s began to vote for the Democratic party for the first time. This realignment in black partisan identification—the breaking loose from traditional loyalty to the Republican party and the subsequent and tenacious loyalty to the urban Democratic coalition—was one of the more important political develop-

ments of the New Deal era, but it was not integrally related to the problem of economic recovery.

2. Walter White to Frances Williams, 2 June 1934, NAACP Files; NAACP Press Release, 1 July 1934, NAACP Files.

3. A. Philip Randolph, "The Crisis of the Negro and the Constitution," *Official Proceedings of the Second National Negro Congress,* pamphlet (1937) in NAACP Files.

4. W. E. B. Du Bois to Will W. Alexander, memorandum on the Economic Condition of the American Negro in the Depression, 20 November 1934, National Archives, Record Group 96 (hereafter cited as NA RG);| Du Bois, "The Negro and Social Reconstruction," typescript (1936) in WEBD collection, Amistad Foundation, Fisk University, p. 78; Du Bois to Harry E. Davis, 19 July 1934, NAACP Files.

5. Mary White Ovington to Roy Wilkins, 19 February 1934, NAACP Files.

PART ONE

Agricultural Recovery and the Negro Farmer

1

The Need for
Agricultural Adjustment

The Purchasing Power Theory

DURING the first four years of the Great Depression the economic position of the American farmer steadily deteriorated. Unlike some industrial producers who were able to minimize losses by restricting production and maintaining price levels, farmers continued to produce surpluses, and consequently farm prices fell drastically. The Department of Agriculture reported that in 1933 farm production was only 6 percent below that in 1929, but prices had fallen by more than 60 percent. On the other hand, to take one example of industrial production during these years, the production of farm implements declined by more than 80 percent, while the price level fell only 6 percent. The overall parity index—the

3

ratio of agricultural prices to the prices of other commodities—plummeted from 90 to 50 (with 1910-1914 as 100). The farmer was caught in the pinch of a price scissors; while the prices of the goods he produced declined sharply, the prices of the items he had to purchase remained relatively stable.[1]

Many New Deal officials believed that the economic difficulties of the depression were due in large part to an uneven distribution of income, which made it difficult for farmers to purchase the goods produced in other sectors of the economy. Henry A. Wallace, the Secretary of Agriculture, lamented that farm income had declined so sharply. "Before the war," he wrote, "the farm population—30 per cent of the total—received 15 per cent of the total national income; at the bottom of the deflation in 1933, the farm population, now 25 per cent of the total, received only 7 per cent of the national income." Wallace believed that economic recovery would not be possible unless effective action were taken to increase the farmers' income. Speaking before the members of the Senate Committee on Agriculture and Forestry, he said: "The Administration accepts as a fundamental principle the view that restoration of the farmers' buying power is an essential part of the program to relieve the present economic emergency."[2]

Other New Dealers also went on record in support of the thesis that farm operators must receive a larger share of the national income if general prosperity were to be restored. M. L. Wilson, an agricultural economist from Montana State College and one of the chief architects of the Roosevelt administration's farm program, reminded the members of the House Committee on Agriculture that the economic machinery of the country was at a standstill. "Now, different theories could be advanced as to what might push us off dead center," but it was Wilson's judgment that "an increase in the purchasing power of agriculture would probably do it more effectively and more easily than could be done otherwise." Mordecai Ezekiel, one of Secretary Wallace's economic advisers, prepared a lengthy memorandum in which he advanced the thesis that over half of the existing unemployment was due to the decline in farm buying-power. "One can roughly say," Ezekiel maintained, "that of every 100 men now out of work in the cities 60 have lost their jobs because of the reductions in rural buying power . . . Restoring the income for farmers is an essential step toward starting industry and trade moving once more." George N. Peek, the nation's best-known advocate of farm price parity and the first administrator of the Agricultural Adjustment program, maintained that if farmers received an equitable income their money would find its way into the cities "in the form of orders for shoes, clothing, and a thousand and one industrial products . . . Purchasing power placed in the hands of the people on the farm is certain to be used. Like a blood transfusion for a dying man, it circulates through the arteries of our economic body and brings a new vitality." In his first inaugural address, President Roosevelt himself called for "definite efforts to raise the value of agricultural products and with this the power to purchase the output of our cities."[3]

The Agricultural Adjustment Act was the Roosevelt administration's major legislative attempt to implement its belief that equitable purchasing power for agriculture must be restored if general prosperity were to be achieved. The preamble to the legislation declared that the act would "relieve the existing national emergency by increasing agricultural purchasing power," and the general goal was defined as the reestablishment of "prices to farmers at a level that will give agricultural commodities a purchasing power with respect to articles farmers buy equivalent to the purchasing power of agricultural commodities in the base period . . . 1909 . . . [to] 1914."[4]

In its attempt to stimulate a general increase in farm purchasing power, the Agricultural Adjustment Act authorized a wide range of governmental activity, including marketing agreements, trade treaties, commodity loans, and cheaper credit facilities. But the most important aspect of the new agricultural program involved the establishment of an Agricultural Adjustment Administration (AAA), which was given authority to sponsor acreage and production control. The Adjustment Act authorized the AAA to disburse "benefit payments" to individual farmers who voluntarily pledged not to grow a crop on more than an agreed on percentage of their acreage. Of course those farmers who did not choose to sign the production control contracts would gain from the general price increase that was expected to result from restricted production, but it was thought that the benefit payments would be large enough to enable cooperating farmers to show a still greater profit. The government was to obtain the funds for these benefit payments by levying a special excise tax on the processors of agricultural commodities (for example, the mill where cotton fiber was converted into fabric).

Ultimately consumers would have to assume the cost of the farm subsidies. Prices of farm commodities would be higher because of crop reduction and because most of the processors would pass along the cost of the new tax (or, after the processing tax was declared unconstitutional in 1936, the cost of the subsidy would be passed along to the general public in the form of higher federal taxes). Some critics maintained that the new program would not increase net purchasing power but would merely transfer existing purchasing power from urban consumers to rural producers. Yet Secretary Wallace insisted that the new agricultural program would not take unfair advantage of consumers. In his view, the new program merely forced consumers to pay a "fair exchange value" and prevented them from taking unfair advantage of abnormally low farm prices; in the final analysis, he believed, the parity concept would serve as a protection for the consumer, since the Adjustment Act instructed the president to terminate the benefit payments as soon as parity prices had been restored. Other defenders of the administration reminded critics that the Agricultural Adjustment Act was an integral part of the whole recovery structure. They insisted that the restoration of farm income would help to stimulate general recovery by providing more jobs in industry, transportation, and commerce, thus giving consumers the funds with which to pay higher farm prices.[5]

The Economic Status of the Negro Farmer

According to the 1930 census, 56 percent of the total Negro population lived in rural areas, and about 40 percent of Negro wage earners were engaged in some form of agricultural work. Ninety-seven percent of these colored farmers lived in the South, but less than 20 percent of them owned their land. Roughly 70 percent stood at the bottom of the agricultural ladder as wage hands, sharecroppers, and share tenants, while another 10 percent were little better off as cash tenants.[6] Any attempt to describe how Negro farmers were affected by the Roosevelt administration's agricultural policies must focus on the extent to which these landless farmers shared the benefits of the recovery program.[7]

Contemporary studies of southern agriculture revealed that most sharecroppers lived in abject poverty, and systematic investigations of farm income revealed that Negro tenants and wage hands were in even more desperate economic straits than were whites. In his 1934 study of 646 cotton plantations, T. J. Woofter discovered that "for all tenure classes, the net income was much less for Negroes than for whites, the average Negro income being about 73 per cent of the white." Negro sharecroppers were found to have an average income of $295 per year as compared with $417 for white sharecroppers; the Negro cash renter averaged $307, the white $568; the Negro wage hand averaged $175, the white $232. In some areas, economic conditions were even worse: thus, Arthur Raper discovered that the average income of all black families in Georgia's Green and Macon counties was less than $200 in 1934; and a 1931 church survey of 112 black tenants in Alabama revealed that only two managed to earn more than $100 in the course of the year.[8]

Statistical information such as this convinced the leaders of the NAACP that there were two distinct agricultural problems. Admitting that a larger share of the total national income should go to agriculture, they also insisted that the economic conditions of the various subgroups in the farm population were strikingly different and maintained that special precautions should be taken to ensure that those farmers who were most in need would share in the government benefit program. The association declared that "the natural desire of Negro citizenry of this country is that the New Deal administration shape its course in such a way as to bring relief to those elements of the national population which have suffered most. They hope that the slogans of the new administration will have meaning for black farmers as well as for white farmers."[9]

Yet the AAA program was concerned only with total farm

income; the Adjustment Act did not refer to any maldistribution of income within agriculture. Partly for this reason, the
program was approved by the House of Representatives after
only two days of debate. Nobody in the House questioned the
manner in which the program would affect the working classes
which were affiliated with commercial agriculture. The Senate
debated the merits of the program at greater length and
devoted several days to a consideration of the probable effects
on farmers in general, as well as on consumers, processors, and
manufacturers. But little attention was given to the adverse
effect that the program might have on the lower classes of
farmers. None of the Senators appeared to be alarmed about
the possibility that the acreage reduction program might
displace thousands of tenant farmers, sharecroppers, and hired
hands.[10]

The Cotton Programs

Agricultural poverty was particularly acute in the Cotton
Belt, where the great majority of Negro farmers were employed. Cotton, which had been selling for eighteen cents per
pound in 1929, was bringing less than six cents in the spring of
1933. Gross farm income from cotton and cottonseed had
fallen by more than two-thirds, from $1,470,000,000 in
1928-1929 to $464,329,000 in 1932-1933. In addition, thirteen
million bales—enough to meet the demand for an entire
year—were already on hand; another bumper crop was
expected in 1933, and this promised to drive the price still
lower. Henry Wallace accurately observed that "the crisis in
cotton" was "one of the principal reasons for the adoption of
the Agricultural Adjustment Act."[11]

It was clear that the AAA would have to resort to extraordinary measures if it were to succeed in its announced goal of raising cotton prices and the purchasing power of cotton farmers. At first the New Deal's agricultural experts were reluctant to sponsor an active campaign aimed at the destruction of a growing crop; such action, Secretary Wallace admitted, contradicted the soundest instincts of human nature and was "a shocking commentary on our civilization." Yet after considering the alternatives, the agricultural planners decided that crop destruction was the only feasible means of preventing another bumper harvest. Accordingly, the AAA's 1933 cotton contract offered government benefits of $7 to $20 per acre to those farmers who would agree to plow up from 25 to 50 percent of their cotton acreage.[12] Available evidence indicates that farmers actually destroyed more than four million bales, about one-fourth of the potential crop. Partly as a result of this program, cotton was selling for 9.4 cents per pound on December 1, 1933, as compared with 5.7 cents a year earlier. The United States Department of Agriculture estimated that gross income from cotton and cottonseed increased from $431 million in 1932 to $670 million in 1933, and additional government benefit payments to cooperating farmers amounted to $162 million. Since the general cost of living increased by only 3 percent in 1933, the relative economic position of cotton farmers was substantially improved.[13]

The AAA's cotton contract provided that government benefits should be paid only to landowners, but supplementary instructions advised landowners to distribute the payments among their tenants according to the interest of each in the crop. It was expected that sharecroppers would receive one-half of the payment, share tenants two-thirds to three-fourths, and cash tenants the entire amount. The AAA could require landowners to show receipts for payments distributed to tenants, and it was provided that all benefits would be suspended if a landowner refused to distribute government money to his tenants.[14]

The idea that government benefit money should be given only to landowners originated in the AAA's cotton section. The men of the cotton section were primarily responsible for the administration of the reduction program, and they knew that the task of processing more than one million contracts with landowners would strain their administrative resources to the limit. Without a substantial increase in the size of their staff, it would have been impossible for them to process the additional million contracts which might have been made with tenants and sharecroppers. The principal leaders of the cotton section also knew that the crop reduction program would certainly fail if it did not receive the voluntary support of a substantial majority of southern landowners. Cully Cobb, the head of the section, and his two assistants, E. A. Miller and W. B. Camp, were southerners and were familiar with southern traditions. (Cobb was a Tennessee farm boy who was educated at Mississippi A. and M. and had served as assistant director of extension in Mississippi, while Miller and Camp had also been associated with southern agricultural colleges.) They knew that many southern landlords would oppose any government program that proposed to give tenants, especially black tenants, an independent source of income. The men of the cotton section claimed that they were not opposed to social reform, and in their own way they were concerned about the welfare of tenants and croppers. But they were convinced that the best way to improve the tenants' position was by rehabilitating the southern economy through crop control. They maintained that anything that jeopardized the necessary landlord cooperation would militate against the tenants' own best interests, and they pointed out that everyone in the South suffered when the cotton farmer was forced to accept a disastrously depreciated price for his crop. On the other hand, they claimed that the entire South would benefit if the AAA succeeded in raising farm prices. Tenants and croppers, black and white, were an integral part of the economic structure of the South, and as such they would profit from any general rehabilitation of the southern economy. Of course the practice of paying government money to one private citizen as trustee for another was, as Alger Hiss, an attorney in the AAA's legal division, pointed out, "contrary to the traditional method of handling government funds" and offered virtually limitless opportunities for graft and deception. Yet the practice was officially condoned because the ranking administrators in the New Deal's agricultural agencies believed that nothing should be permitted to stand in the way of securing a large sign-up.[15]

By 1934-1935 the AAA was no longer requesting that farmers plow up their crops but instead was asking them to keep about 40 percent of their land out of production, and thus it was necessary to make some changes in the method of payment. After much discussion it was finally decided that in return for taking land out of production farmers were to receive "rental payments" of 3.5 cents for each pound of cotton not produced and additional "parity payments" of "not less than one cent per pound." The practice of dispensing all benefits through the landowners was to continue.[16]

When the farm operator owned his own land, no problem arose concerning the payment of government benefits. But most cotton farms were operated by tenants, and in these cases the AAA had to decide how much of the payment the landlord

should distribute to the tenants. The 1934-1935 cotton contract resolved this problem by providing that cash tenants
were to receive the entire amount of both rental and parity
payments; sharecroppers and other tenants would receive
none of the rental payment and from one-half to three-quarters of the parity payment, the exact amount depending on the
extent of their interest in the crop; farm laborers were to
receive no money from the government. Under this arrangement a sharecropper would receive one-half cent for each
pound of cotton not produced, while the landowner would
receive four cents per pound.[17]

Thus, southern sharecroppers, who as a group were among
the nation's poorest citizens, were to receive only one-ninth of
the government's 1934-1935 benefit payments. This was a
considerably smaller portion than the fifty-fifty division of the
1933 plow-up payments and much less than the share that
AAA was distributing to tenants who were producing other
crops. Several government officials acknowledged that this
eight-to-one ratio was inequitable, and yet it was generally
felt, as one AAA study put it, that southern landlords "could
not be induced to sign the contract if they were not given a
larger share of the rental benefits than landlords received in
the case of the other acreage reduction contracts."[18]

In the South it was the more prosperous farmers associated
with the American Farm Bureau Federation who had demanded the reduction program. These farmers were concerned primarily with increasing their income, and while it is
true that many of them had a paternalistic interest in
improving conditions for tenants, they had no desire to change
the established southern order. Like Cully Cobb and the men
in the cotton section, the leaders of the Farm Bureau believed
that the tenants' position could be improved most by rehabil-

itating the southern economy, thereby making it possible for prosperity to trickle down to the farm workers.

The Farm Bureau was in a position to obtain concessions from the new administration because it was politically influential and had delivered a substantial number of votes to President Roosevelt in the 1932 election. After his inauguration, the president invited the Farm Bureau's leaders to consult with him concerning the shape of the New Deal's agricultural program, and it soon became apparent that these farm leaders heartily approved of AAA's major outlines; indeed, they were so pleased with the new program that, as one student has observed, they were "prone to claim credit for the early New Deal farm program. Over and over in the years to follow, Farm Bureau leaders reiterated the theme: It was our program, and the president had the good sense to adopt it." The rhetoric of the Farm Bureau may have been less accurate as a statement of fact than as a statement of belief, but it is significant as an indication that the bureau considered the Roosevelt agricultural policies eminently satisfactory. Writing to a fellow farm leader in 1936, Edward Asbury O'Neal, the president of the Farm Bureau, confided that "more than any other Secretary of Agriculture I have ever known, Secretary Wallace has conferred and advised with the farm organizations' leaders, particularly the Farm Bureau."[19]

For the purposes of this study, it is important to note that the Farm Bureau did not represent all groups of farmers. In some states, as in Louisiana, Negroes were not permitted to become members of the state federation; in other states, such as Mississippi, Negroes were allowed as members but were not permitted to vote; in still other states, such as Alabama, the state federation encouraged Negro membership, but each county was permitted to handle the colored members as it thought best. The result was that by 1939 there were only fifteen thousand black members of the Farm Bureau. The bureau represented primarily the interests of the more well-to-do commercial farmers, and it provided only incidental representation for the poverty-stricken Negro sharecroppers who were not well organized and had little political influence.[20]

It should also be noted that southern congressmen, because of their long seniority, had come to hold many key committee chairmanships, and the Roosevelt administration believed that it needed the support of these congressmen if its economic-recovery programs were to be enacted into law. Most of these southern politicians were willing to support the New Deal; they were loyal to the Democratic party, and they knew that their sectional economy was desperately in need of federal aid. But most of them also shared the conventional attitudes of their section; they fervently believed in the necessity of maintaining the traditional caste and class structure. And yet the Roosevelt administration—with its promise of a New Deal for the forgotten man—inevitably threatened to subvert the status quo.[21] Roosevelt believed that he would lose the support of these southerners if his administration made any direct attempt to reform traditional racial and class patterns, and consequently, as Frank Freidel has observed, in certain respects the president "was willing to modify or water down the New Deal in its practical operation in the South . . ." On several occasions Roosevelt told Walter White, the secretary of the NAACP, that he had "to get legislation for the entire country passed by Congress. If I antagonize the Southerners who dominate Congressional committees through seniority, I'd never be able to get bills passed." [22]

There were other factors that also influenced the final

decision concerning the division of payments, but the character of the farm lobby and the power of the southern Congressmen within the Democratic party were the two factors most responsible for the cotton landlords' receiving such a large share of the government benefit payments.[23] Mordecai Ezekiel correctly assessed the situation when he reminded Secretary Wallace that "there can be no question that the farm owners, constituting less than half of those engaged in agriculture, have been the dominant element in the preparation and administration of AAA programs. . . . In certain commodities, notably cotton, this has resulted in their receiving the lion's share of the benefits." No one within the AAA was specifically responsible for representing the interests of the sharecroppers and tenant farmers during the hours of deliberation over the cotton contract. Alger Hiss and others in the legal division did what they could to include certain legal protections in the contracts, but in the final analysis they had little effect on policy decisions and their recommendations were overruled.[24]

NOTES

1. Gardiner C. Means, *The Corporate Revolution in America* (New York: Collier Books, 1962), pp. 77-96; Mordecai Ezekiel and Louis H. Bean, *Economic Bases for the Agricultural Adjustment Act* (Washington, D.C.: U. S. Department of Agriculture, 1933), pp. 4, 7-8; Edwin G. Nourse, Joseph S. Davis, and John D. Black, *Three Years of the Agricultural Adjustment Administration* (Washington, D.C.: The Brookings Institution, 1937), p. 21; Arthur M. Schlesinger, Jr., *The Coming of the New Deal* (Boston: Houghton Mifflin Company, 1959), pp. 35-36.

2. Henry A. Wallace, *New Frontiers* (New York: Reynal and Hitchcock, 1934), p. 116. See also U.S., Congress, Senate, *Hearings before the Senate Committee on Agriculture and Forestry*, 73rd Cong., 1st sess., 25 March 1933, p. 128.

3. U.S., Congress, House, *Hearings before ·the House Committee on Agriculture,* 72nd Cong., 2nd sess., 16 December 1932, pp. 140, 361; Ezekiel and Bean, *Economic Bases for the AAA,* pp. 8-13, 65-67; George N. Peek, "Progress on All Fronts," *New York Times,* 12 November 1933, p. 1; F. D. Roosevelt, *Public Papers and Addresses of Franklin D. Roosevelt,* ed. Samuel I. Rosenman (New York: Random House, 1938-1950), 2:13.

4. U. S., *Statutes at Large,* 48:31.

5. For an example of this criticism, see "The Parity Plan," *Nation,* 18 January 1934, p. 54. Defenders of the New Deal insisted that the transfer of funds from city to farm would help to stimulate recovery. They maintained that business was essentially "a continuing process of shifting funds from person to person . . . Prosperity results from a brisk or accelerating tempo in this process." Assuming that the well-to-do did not spend their money as quickly as the lower orders, the New Deal planners concluded that insofar as farm subsidy payments were derived from progressive taxes "it would seem that such funds . . . were moved from a position of sluggish activity to one where they moved at high velocity." This rationale would not apply to the period before 1936, when funds were secured via the retrogressive processing tax. Even after 1936 the stimulative effect was minimal. See Nourse, Davis, and Black, *Three Years of the AAA,* pp. 430-435.

6. In rural towns, wage hands were generally employed by the day or by the week. On the cotton plantations, however, they were employed by the year; that is, the landlord furnished a cabin on the condition that the worker be available at all times, but the wage hand was paid only for the days he actually worked. Sharecroppers, like wage hands, had only their labor to offer. It was necessary for the landowner to supply them with food, clothing, work animals, and farm equipment. The cropper did all the work necessary to produce a crop and was generally paid one-half of the crop's value. Cash tenants owned their own farm equipment and work animals. They paid a fixed cash rent for their land and kept all the profits from the farm enterprise. Share tenants owned some of the necessary farm equipment, and for the use of the land and the necessary additional tools they paid the landlord one-half to one-fourth of their crop.

7. U. S., Bureau of the Census, *Fifteenth Census of the United States, 1930* (Washington, D.C.: U. S. Government Printing Office, 1931-1934). The 1930 census figures were summarized by Clark Foreman, "What Hope for the Rural Negro?" *Opportunity* 12 (April, 1934):105-106. See also Olive Stone, "The Present Position of the Negro Farm Population: The Bottom Rung of the Farm Ladder," *Journal of Negro Education* 5 (January, 1936): 20-31; J. Phil Campbell, "The Government's Farm Policies and the Negro Farmer," *Journal of Negro Education* 5 (January, 1936): 32-34.

8. T. J. Woofter, "The Negro and Agricultural Policy" (Carnegie-Myrdal

Manuscripts, 1940) pp. 56-57; Richard Sterner, *The Negro's Share* (New York: Harper & Brothers, 1943), pp. 62-67; Arthur F. Raper, *Preface to Peasantry* (Chapel Hill: University of North Carolina Press, 1936), p. 56; and Norman Thomas, "Victims of Change," *Current History* 42 (April, 1935):39. Charles Johnson, Edwin Embree, and Will W. Alexander reported that as of 1930 "Negroes no longer make up the bulk of the cotton tenants . . . In the decade from 1920 to 1930, white tenants in the cotton states increased by 200,000 families—approximately a million persons. During the same decade Negro tenants decreased by 2,000 families as a result of mass movements to cities . . . Increasingly, therefore, the problems of the rural South in general, and of cotton tenancy in particular, are those of native white families more than of Negroes." See Charles Johnson, Edwin Embree, and Will W. Alexander, *The Collapse of Cotton Tenancy* (Chapel Hill: University of North Carolina Press, 1935), pp. 4-5.

Nevertheless, 80 percent of Negro farmers were tenants, while less than 50 percent of the whites were tenants. Gunnar Myrdal has warned against drawing false conclusions from the fact that more than 60 percent of the total number of tenants were white. "It does not follow . . . that white tenancy is more serious than Negro tenancy. Rather it is the other way around. We have seen that Negroes, more than whites, are concentrated in the lower tenure groups, and that in each tenure group Negroes are economically much weaker than whites." Gunnar Myrdal, *An American Dilemma* (New York: Harper & Brothers, 1944), p. 243.

9. NAACP Press Release, June, 1934, NAACP Files.

10. David Conrad has written a good account of the congressional debates and hearings, *The Forgotten Farmers: The Story of Sharecroppers in the New Deal* (Urbana, Ill.: University of Illinois Press, 1965), pp. 24-36.

11. Statistical information concerning economic conditions in the Cotton Belt has been summarized by H. I. Richards, *Cotton Under the Agricultural Adjustment Act* (Washington, D.C.: The Brookings Institution, 1934) pp. 63-105; Thomas A. Rousse, *Government Control of Cotton Production* (University of Texas Bulletin no. 3538, 8 October 1935), pp. 85-86; and Wallace, *New Frontiers*, pp. 172-174.

12. Cooperating farmers who did not need all their government benefit money at once could choose to be paid in cotton options. Under the option plan, the farmer would receive from $6 to $12 in cash for each acre not planted plus an option to purchase an amount of government-owned cotton equal to that destroyed at six cents per pound. Since the price of cotton rose to more than nine cents in 1933 and to twelve cents in 1934, farmers who chose to take this option generally earned more than those who accepted the larger cash payments.

13. Wallace, *New Frontiers*, pp. 171, 174-175. Despite the plow-up, farmers actually harvested 13,147,262 bales of cotton, slightly more than the 13,000,002 bales produced in 1932. If the entire acreage of cotton

planted in 1933 had been harvested, the market probably would have been inundated with a record-breaking crop of more than 17 million bales. The Department of Agriculture and the AAA made several studies of the economic effects of the cotton reduction programs. The conclusions of these studies have been summarized by Richards, *Cotton Under the AAA*, pp. 63-105; and *Statistical Abstract of the United States, 1934* (Washington, D.C.: Government Printing Office, 1934), p. 290.

14. Richards, *Cotton Under the AAA*, p. 45.

15. Conrad, *Forgotten Farmers*, pp. 45-46, 52-54, 56-57; Oscar Johnston to Chester Davis, memorandum, 26 January 1935, National Archives, Record Group 145; Cully Cobb to Victor Christgau, memorandum, 8 September 1934, NA RG 145; Alger Hiss to Jerome Frank, memorandum, 26 January 1935, NA RG 145; John Gilland Brunini, "The Negro's New Deal," *Commonweal*, 12 January 1934, pp. 293-295.

16. Cotton Acreage Reduction Contract for 1934-1935, NA RG 145. Government benefit payments were based on the estimated yield of the land kept out of cotton production. A five-year base period, 1928-1932, was adopted for the establishment of all acreage and production quotas. Under the 1934-1935 contract, payments were limited to a maximum of $18 per acre kept out of production.

17. Ibid.

18. Mordecai Ezekiel to Henry Wallace, memorandum, 5 February 1936, NA RG 16. Calvin B. Hoover pointed out that "this method of dividing benefit payments between landlords and sharecroppers . . . differs from the method of division of benefit payments in the wheat and corn-hog contracts where few sharecroppers are involved. It also differs from the method of division used in the tobacco contract by the terms of which the sharecropper obtains a part of the rental payment as well as the parity payment. In these contracts the division of the benefit payment between landowners and tenants is in proportion to their interest in the crop. Thus a sharecropper in the tobacco contracts receives one-half of the benefit payments instead of one-ninth as in the case of the cotton contracts." Calvin B. Hoover, "Human Problems in Acreage Reduction in the South," NA RG 145.

19. Christiana McFadyen Campbell, *The Farm Bureau and the New Deal* (Urbana, Ill.: University of Illinois Press, 1962), pp. 56, 103.

20. Ibid., pp. 24-26, 101. Grant McConnell has also discussed the relation between the Farm Bureau and the AAA; see Grant McConnell, *The Decline of Agrarian Democracy* (Berkeley and Los Angeles: University of California Press, 1953), pp. 66-83.

21. Ironically, southern loyalty to the Democratic party was based largely on the belief that this "white man's party" must remain supreme if the horrors of black rule were to be avoided. The Democratic party in the North, however, needed Negro support and openly appealed for black votes. Thus, good southern Democrats occasionally found their allegiance to white supremacy conflicting with their allegiance to party. On one occasion,

for example, Cully Cobb was assigned to meet Mrs. Frederick Douglass Patterson, the wife of the president of Tuskegee Institute, and persuade her to support President Roosevelt. Cobb was instructed to call her "Mrs.," but the head of the cotton section declared that he had never "Missussed" a colored woman in his life, "and I don't intend to start now." Cobb was then told that if he could not be polite, the meeting would have to be postponed, and the Democratic party might suffer the consequence of losing a good many votes. Cobb then announced, "Well for the purposes of this meeting she's 'Mrs.,' but not another damn time!" Donald Hughes Grubbs, "The Southern Tenant Farmers' Union and the New Deal" (Ph.D. dissertation, University of Florida, 1963), pp. 137-138.

22. Frank Freidel, *F.D.R. and the South* (Baton Rouge: Louisiana State University Press, 1965), pp. 36, 66; Walter White, *A Man Called White* (New York: The Viking Press, 1948), p. 169; idem, "Roosevelt and the Negro," typescript, n.d., NAACP Files. Roy Wilkins of the NAACP has also commented on Roosevelt's dependence on the support of southern congressmen: "Now the Southerners of course formed the backbone of the Roosevelt foreign policy and a good many of his domestic policies—the alphabet agencies and so on. The Southerners went along with the New Deal, except on the Negro question. So Roosevelt wasn't going to endanger either his foreign policy or his domestic policy by bending over backwards doing favors for the Negroes—and it will be found in the record of Franklin Roosevelt that he was no special friend of the Negro...." Roy Wilkins, Columbia University Oral History Project, pp. 98-99.

23. Some defenders of the cotton reduction program maintained that the AAA was actually doing the sharecropper a favor by giving him a small portion since this would reduce the danger that landlords would evict tenants in order to get a larger share of the payment. Yet tenants could have been protected against eviction if the reduction contracts had provided that no payments would be made to landlords who evicted any of their tenants. Other defenders of the AAA justified the contracts by pointing out that a reduction in acreage did not reduce the landlord's capital investment in land or his fixed expenses such as taxes, while it did substantially reduce the amount of labor required of the sharecropper. It should be remembered, however, that while the sharecropper's labor was reduced in 1934, he usually was not able to spend his spare time in gainful employment. If the landlord was entitled to compensation for the land he was not allowed to use, then, in equity, the sharecropper was entitled to compensation for the labor he was not allowed to use. The fact that the 1934-1935 benefit payments were primarily rental payments for land withdrawn from cultivation reveals a great deal about the class biases of those who controlled the AAA's cotton programs. See Richards, *Cotton Under the AAA*, p. 138; Hoover, *Human Problems in Acreage Reduction in the South*, NA RG 145.

24. Mordecai Ezekiel to Henry Wallace, memorandum, 5 February 1936, NA RG 16.

2

Special Problems

DESPITE the inequitable division of payments, the tenant who received both the market price for his cotton and his allotted share of the government benefit payments stood to profit from the AAA's cotton reduction program. Consider the case of a sharecropper who had been tending forty-five acres with an average yield of two hundred pounds of lint cotton per acre. At the depth of the depression in 1932, when cotton was selling for about six cents per pound, he would have received $270 for his half of the crop. According to the 1934 contract, the cropper would have had to reduce his acreage by about 40 percent, but by 1934 the price of cotton had risen to slightly more than twelve cents per pound, causing the dollar value of his smaller crop to rise to $324. In addition, the cropper would receive $18 as a parity payment from the government. Thus his gross income would have increased from $270 to $342, or by 27 percent. Even after making allowance for the rise in the general cost of living, the tenant was left with a substantial increase in net income, and officials in the Department of Agriculture frequently maintained that the rise in the dollar value of cotton was the best measure of the success of the reduction program. Assistant Secretary Paul Appleby, for example, assured the NAACP that "the situation of all cotton producers is infinitely better now [1935] than it was in 1932" because "this doubling in value of the South's chief crop and that particular crop in which colored people are most interested...has had a far-reaching favorable effect." Yet it should be apparent that the income of the sharecropper, who received only one-ninth of the government benefit payment, did not increase as much as the income of the landowner. While the income of the sharecropper on our hypothetical forty-five-acre farm was rising by 27 percent (from $270 to $342), the income of the landlord rose by 73 percent (from $270 to $468).[1]

However, tenants—and especially black sharecroppers— were plagued by a number of special problems, and they frequently did not fare as well as the information tabulated here would suggest. Many tenants, particularly the Negro sharecroppers who worked on the larger plantations, were not allowed to sell their crops. Instead the landlord did the selling and credited the tenants with the proceeds. Under these circumstances it was not unusual for the landlord to give the tenant credit for the cotton at the lowest price of the season when in fact the crop had been kept off the market until conditions were better and the price higher. There is no way of knowing how many landlords resorted to this type of chicanery, but many must have been tempted since economic conditions were so desperate. Moreover, there was nothing that the Negro tenant could do to prevent such chiseling. If he asked to see the accounts, the chances were that he would succeed only in infuriating the landlord. A lawsuit was out of the question, since it would have amounted to calling the white landlord a thief and, given the prevailing mores in many parts of the South, it was extremely dangerous for a Negro thus to challenge the integrity of his employer.[2]

Since the sharecropper had only his labor to invest in the production of the crop, it was necessary for the landlord to supply him with the other necessities—work animals, tools, fertilizer, food, and clothing. During the course of the year, these items were "furnished" to the sharecropper from the landlord's commissary, where prices usually were substantially higher than in independent stores. In addition, the tenant had to pay interest charges for the money advanced to him for the purchases. In most cases the charge for such money was a flat 10 percent, but since the credit was used for only three or four months the annual rate of interest was much higher—30 percent or more. Because of the high prices and the high interest charges, the commissary was often the most profitable operation on the plantation.[3]

After making the necessary deductions for the goods and the interest charges, the landlord gave the tenant his share of the profits. The tenant, particularly the Negro sharecropper, was at the mercy of the planter; he had to take the landlord's word concerning the price received for the cotton, the total amount of the advances, and the amount of the interest charges. From the planter's point of view, it was ideal if the tenant just managed to break even, and often accounts were managed in such a way that a tenant's cash income from the crop and his expenses at the commissary nearly balanced. One middle-class Negro gave this example: "A tenant may make ten bales of cotton, worth $750, for which his share would be $375, less his advances. The Negro has kept accounts and knows the advances to be, say, $100. The landlord or the overseer calls the tenant and tells him he did very well this year: he made $10. If the Negro offers a mild challenge, he is told, 'Do you mean to call me a liar?' This settles the discussion because to call a white man a liar is extremely dangerous for a Negro." The nature of the landlord-tenant relationship presented the landlord with great opportunities for fraud, and under these circumstances it is not surprising that many landlords took unfair advantage. After making a thorough investigation of tenant problems for the AAA, Professor Calvin B. Hoover of Duke University was forced to acknowledge that "there have been a considerable number of cases in which tenant farmers have not received the full amount specified by the...cotton contract." All too often, Hoover concluded, "whether the tenant received anything at all...depended upon the charitableness of the landlord."[4]

Any successful effort to improve the tenant's position had to provide relief from high credit charges. In this regard, the New Deal's Farm Credit Administration (FCA) provided relief for farm owners but was of little benefit to farm tenants and workers. Through the FCA, long-term, low-interest loans were available to farmers who could offer a first mortgage on farm realty as security; additional sources of credit were available for farmers' cooperative associations; and some six hundred local associations were established to provide short-term production credit.[5]

Since tenants and sharecroppers could not offer first mortgages on farm realty, they were not eligible for the FCA's long-term loans; but tenants could take advantage of the short-term production credit if they could offer security in the form of an unencumbered mortgage on chattel property or an unencumbered crop lien. Cash renters had relatively little difficulty in negotiating government loans, since there was no landlord lien on their crops. Most tenants did not own chattel property, however, and since landlords held first liens on the growing crops, they could block a tenant's application for production credit by refusing to waive the first lien. Of course, some landlords were willing to waive their liens, and in these cases the tenants were able to save substantial sums by purchasing feed, seed, and fertilizer at cash prices. Yet many owners were reluctant to do this, since it would deprive them of a share of their commissary profits, and others would waive their liens only if the tenants agreed to deliver the government checks to them. Thus, Arthur Raper observed several cases where the planter "took the money, deposited it to his own account, and issued cash back to the tenant as he thought it was needed. The planter usually charged him 8 to 10 per cent 'interest.' Thus the tenant paid double interest—6 per cent to the government for the money and an additional 8 to 10 per cent to the planter for keeping it for him." Still other planters used the 6 percent government loans to stock their own commissaries, enabling them to furnish tenants with goods at the customary inflated credit prices. In these cases, as Rupert Vance observed, the government found itself "an involuntary, if not an unsuspecting partner in usury."[6]

Yet there was little that the Farm Credit Administration could do for the sharecropper, since it insisted that it was not a relief agency. It hoped to alleviate the farmers' condition by extending cheap credit in a manner consistent with responsible business practices. Sound business required an unencumbered security for every loan granted but, as FCA people themselves acknowledged, this insistence on loan security materially impeded the FCA's effectiveness in reducing production credit charges for tenant farmers.[7]

The Farm Credit Administration, however, did make a genuine attempt not to be bound by traditional prejudices in its dealings with Negro farm *owners*. One indication of this intention to treat Negroes fairly was the decision to appoint Henry A. Hunt, the nationally prominent Negro president of Georgia's Fort Valley Industrial School, as assistant to the governor of the FCA and adviser on the special problems of Negroes. It was Hunt's responsibility to keep black farmers informed concerning their opportunities to secure government credit, and he also did what he could when Negroes complained of injustice on the part of local authorities. It is impossible to determine precisely how effective Hunt's office was, since the FCA records were not broken down by color, and it is not known what proportion of its loans were made to Negroes. But some local studies did indicate that Negro owners were receiving a fair share of the loans. Arthur Raper, for example, reported that in Georgia's Green and Macon counties, "Negroes contracted for approximately one-twentieth of the loans, a proportion which corresponds to their ownership of acreage." And when Rayford Logan of Atlanta University sent out inquiries to Negro extension workers and teachers, most replied that black farm owners in their districts encountered little difficulty in obtaining FCA loans.[8]

Of course, Negro landowners were not treated equally well in all areas of the South. Much depended on the attitude of the local committees which passed on their applications for government credit. One of the duties of these committees was to appraise the value of the farm property offered as security for the loan. Negroes were not allowed to serve on the committees, and white businessmen generally acted as appraisers. Thus in many cases the Negro farmer who wanted to save his farm had to go to the very men who held the mortgage, and under these circumstances it is not surprising that the Negro applicant occasionally received less than fair treatment. Rayford Logan reported in 1937 that "not a single Negro farmer in Arkansas was able to obtain a loan through the Farm Credit Administration," and he objected to what he called "the prejudiced machinations of white appraisers...who purposely refused to place a large enough appraisal on the land." He cited several examples of Negro farmers who lost "splendid farms" because the white appraisers themselves held the mortgages and wanted to foreclose.[9]

The distress caused by duplicity in the keeping of accounts and the charging of extravagant interest on loans often was compounded when the tenant did not receive even the small share of the benefit payment which the government recommended. The AAA practice of making all payments to landowners naturally presented great opportunities for additional deception. In most cases the landlord did not forward the government money to the tenant but simply credited the money to the tenant's account at the commissary. Sometimes this arrangement was satisfactory for the tenant. For example, one Mississippi sharecropper claimed that "when I plowed up my cotton I got $136 deducted from my account. It was really deducted, for I saw the statement itemized." But generally tenants were not so well informed; a more representative sharecropper claimed that he "plowed up six acres of my cotton last year, but I didn't get a cent from the government. Boss said it was credited to my account, but I don't know." Other tenants were given a small portion of the government payment in cash while the remainder was credited to their accounts. Only a very few sharecroppers received cash for the entire amount allotted for them. (After making an intensive study of 335 tenant households in Alabama, the Federal

Emergency Relief Administration reported that 86 percent of the Negro sharecroppers had paid a portion of their AAA money to their landlords, and 47 percent had been forced to do so. Forty-eight percent of the white croppers made such payments, and of these only 19 percent were forced.)[10]

Knowing that it would be easy for landlords to defraud tenants if they were permitted to use government checks for the purpose of canceling tenant debts at the commissary, Jerome Frank of the legal division proposed that the AAA should insist that fair prices were charged. He suggested that the AAA require landlords to fill out a detailed form specifying the price and quantity of goods they had advanced to their tenants. But the cotton section, which would have had to audit these itemized forms, objected to Frank's proposal on the grounds that it would result in a "colossal and expensive task" of administration and might provoke a "negative reaction" among planters. This dispute was forwarded to higher authorities within the AAA for a decision and, as had been the case with the controversy over indirect payments for tenants, the cotton section again prevailed. While the AAA did include a short formal statement reminding landlords that AAA's central purpose was to increase mass purchasing power and recommending that cash be distributed among tenants, it would not require itemized accounting of the prices and rates of interest charged at the plantation commissaries.[11]

The AAA's decision to delegate primary responsibility for the administration of the cotton reduction program to local authorities also militated against the interests of black sharecroppers. Some New Dealers believed that by combining centralized policy planning with decentralized administration they could solve the age-old problem of making democracy effective without creating a leviathan state, and they concluded that local administration would be the crowning glory of the AAA. President Roosevelt, for example, was to declare that the AAA was "a picture of economic democracy in action" because it was "administered locally by community committees selected by the farmers themselves." In some respects this promise of democracy was realized. In the Cotton Belt, black and white farmers—owners and tenants alike—were allowed, even encouraged, to vote for members of their local county and community committees, and this marked a significant stride forward along the road toward meaningful democracy. Even Ralph Bunche, who was then a young professor of political science at Howard University and a severe critic of many aspects of the New Deal, admitted that "the participation of Negroes in these elections and on equal basis with whites is of the utmost social significance in the South. That such activities will tend to bring about a recognition by both white and Negro producers of parallel economic interests would seem clear. Participation in these referenda has given to a great many Negroes in the South the first opportunity to cast a ballot of any kind that they have ever had. Moreover, it tends to accustom a great many whites to the practice of Negro voting."[12]

Yet this grass roots participation was more apparent than real. Negroes were not allowed to participate in the nomination of candidates, and throughout the South not a single Negro farmer served on a county committee. Eighty percent of the committeemen were white landowners, and most of the remainder were white cash renters. The composition of these committees is significant because they were responsible for adjudicating any complaints that arose. If a tenant believed that his landlord had given him an unfair acreage allotment or had illegally appropriated his government money, he was required to present his case before the county committee. Since the committees were composed of the landlord's own friends and associates, such complaints were rarely decided in favor of the tenant and often resulted in further harassment for the complainant.[13]

The AAA's cotton reduction program also jeopardized the job security of many tenants, causing some to be dismissed from their work and forcing others to accept lower level jobs. Put in the most simple terms, it would seem axiomatic that it was impossible to reduce cotton acreage by 40 percent without also reducing the need for labor in the cotton fields.[14] In addition, the 1934-1935 contracts, providing that landlords would not have to share parity payments with wage laborers, gave many owners an economic incentive for shifting from farming with sharecroppers and share tenants to farming with wage hands. Thus, if the hypothetical forty-five-acre farm mentioned above had been operated by a wage hand instead of a sharecropper, the owner would have received an additional $18 in government benefit money that otherwise would have gone to the cropper. Since many owners employed several score of croppers, this amounted to a considerable economic incentive, and one Mississippi Delta planter summed up the feelings of many when he announced in 1935, "Sure I'm going to shift to farming entirely by day labor next year. It's the only way a landlord can make money now."[15]

The leaders of the AAA knew that crop reduction might cause substantial unemployment among farm tenants, and thus special provisions were written into Paragraph 7 of the 1934-1935 cotton contracts, requiring that landowners "maintain on this farm the normal number of tenants and other employees" and that all tenants be permitted "to continue in the occupancy of their houses on this farm, rent free. . . ." Yet

Cully Cobb and his colleagues in the cotton section believed that these stringent requirements might antagonize many southern planters and jeopardize the chances for securing a large sign-up. Consequently, they proposed that the qualifying words *"insofar as possible"* be affixed to the requirement that landlords "maintain...the normal number of tenants." They also knew that it would be extremely difficult to force a landlord to keep an undesirable tenant, and therefore they proposed that tenants be permitted to "continue in the occupancy of their houses...*unless any such tenant shall so conduct himself as to become a nuisance or a menace to the welfare of the producer."* Again the legal division objected to the proposed qualifications of the cotton section; as attorney Alger Hiss pointed out, the additional phrases were vague, left the landlord with the prerogative of determining what was "possible" and who was a "nuisance," and made it impossible for the legal division to go to court and force a recalcitrant landlord to honor the protective sanctions of Paragraph 7. Nevertheless, Secretary Wallace and administrator Chester Davis again sided with the cotton section, and as a result the 1934-1935 cotton contracts, as finally drafted, expressed nothing but the AAA's hope that tenants would be treated fairly by the landowners.[16]

Beginning in 1934, observers in many sections of the South reported that landlords were evicting tenants and thereby were reducing their acreage in the easiest and most economical manner. Sociologist Gordon W. Blackwell reported that in eastern North Carolina tenant displacement was greater during the first three months of 1934 than it had been during the entire previous year. In the Arkansas delta, Dr. William B. Amberson, a nationally known physiologist, made a detailed study of more than five hundred tenant families and concluded that the AAA's cotton reduction program had caused more than 15 percent of these tenants to be driven from the land; "over the whole cotton belt," he estimated, "about one-third of the present rural unemployment can be directly referred to the reduction program." After observing the situation in two Georgia Black Belt counties, Arthur Raper concluded that "the landless farmers" were not helped by the New Deal's cotton programs but instead were "actually losing status. Many tenants are being pushed off the land while many others are being pushed down the tenure ladder, especially from cropper to wagehand status." Liberals throughout the country were beginning to fear that, as Norman Thomas put it, "a large army of unknown size has been driven off the cotton lands to swell the legions of unemployed in towns and cities."[17]

As a consequence of these ominous reports and the ensuing flood of protesting letters and telegrams, the AAA itself undertook several investigations of the displacement question. Local county committeemen were instructed to visit each farm under AAA contract to ascertain whether the contracting farmer had complied with the provisions of the cotton contract. Each landlord had to report the number of tenants, sharecroppers, and farm laborers on his land, and if there was any change from the number employed previously the landlord was required to offer an explanation. He also had to certify that he had allowed tenants to remain rent-free in the occupancy of their houses, in accordance with the provisions of Paragraph 7. Before the AAA would make final payment of government benefits, a representative of the county committee had to certify that he was "acquainted with the farm...and have examined and considered the representations made by the producer, and have found the statements made...to be correct to the best of my knowledge and belief."[18]

Yet AAA was aware of the local committees' pro-landlord biases and realized that their statements were not conclusive proof of compliance. Consequently, beginning in 1934 the central AAA administration in Washington also began to investigate the extent to which the provisions of Paragraph 7 had been violated. Various committees were established to review the reports from the field, and several surveys of conditions in local areas were made by administrators from Washington. These studies generally confirmed the local reports that there had been no large-scale displacement and that the press had exaggerated the number of tenants who had been forced to accept a lower status. Officials such as Henry Wallace placed great faith in the accuracy of these AAA reports, and Wallace frequently referred to them when replying to critics of the reduction program. When he wrote to Congressman Richard M. Kleberg, of Texas, for example, Wallace maintained that "a very careful investigation indicates that there has been practically no release of tenants because of the cotton program and that there has been little change in status. In most cases there are as many tenants on plantations as there were before the contracts were signed."[19]

Yet in retrospect it is clear that these optimistic conclusions were invalid. The administrators of the cotton reduction programs grossly underestimated the amount of tenant displacement—partly because they were forced to accept the validity of the figures given them by the landlord-dominated local committees and partly because of their natural reluctance to admit that AAA programs had aggravated tenant problems. But the full extent of tenant displacement could not be obscured indefinitely, and the 1940 census figures revealed that there were 192,000 fewer Negro and 150,000 fewer white tenants than there had been in 1930.[20]

Of course, the AAA cotton reduction program was not the only cause of tenant displacement during the 1930s. The availability of relief, the mechanization of agriculture, and the movement of population from city to countryside during the depression were three other factors that also undermined the tenant's position. Moreover, it should be remembered that there was considerable displacement prior to 1933 when low cotton prices forced the curtailment of the labor force. Yet the AAA cotton reduction program must be charged with responsibility for a significant amount of further displacement. It is clear that the cotton program gave landowners a strong economic incentive to replace tenants with wage labor. At the same time, there were only the legally unenforceable exhortations of Paragraph 7 to discourage owners from making such a change. As Gunnar Myrdal has written:

> Landlords have been made to reduce drastically the acreage for their main labor-requiring crops. They have been given a large part of the power over the local administration of this program. They have a strong economic incentive to reduce their tenant labor force, a large part of which consists of politically and legally impotent Negroes. Yet they have been asked not to make any reduction. It would certainly not be compatible with usual human behavior if this request generally had been fulfilled. Under the circumstances, there is no reason at all to be surprised about the wholesale decline in tenancy. Indeed, it would be surprising if it had not happened.[21]

NOTES

1. The cotton prices are based on figures taken from *The Yearbook of Agriculture, 1935* (Washington: U. S. Government Printing Office, 1935), p. 426, and the 40 percent reduction was about average for 1934. I have estimated the 1932 crop at 9,000 pounds and the 1934 crop at 40 percent

less, or 5,600 pounds. Nine thousand pounds at six cents per pound would come to $540, which would be divided equally by landlord and cropper, and thus the figure of $270 for 1932. A half share of 1934's 5,600 pounds at twelve cents per pound would come to $324, and in addition the sharecropper would be entitled to one-half cent parity payment for each of the 3,600 pounds not grown, or $18, bringing his total to $342. The landowner would receive the same parity payment plus $126 in rental payments (three and one-half cents per pound for each of the 3,600 pounds not grown), bringing his government benefit money to $144 and his total income to $468. This example is typical. After investigating a cross section of representative plantations, the Department of Agriculture reported that the increase in landlord income from 1932 to 1934 ranged from 74 to 100 percent, while sharecropper income increased by 27 percent. U.S., Department of Agriculture, memorandum, "Benefit Payments in the Cotton Reduction Program," April 1935, NA RG 16. The quotation is from Paul Appleby to Walter White, 6 March 1935, NA RG 145.

2. Addison T. Cutler and Webster Powell, "Tightening the Cotton Belt," *Harper's Magazine* 168 (February, 1934):308-318. Arthur Raper has given the following example of the fate that often awaited protesting tenants: "Three years ago, when a Negro moved from Uvalda, a small town in the Southern part of the county, he tried to get a settlement with his landlord who owed him some money. When the landlord would not settle, the Negro filed a suit against him. The Negro was severely flogged. None of the floggers were ever indicted." Arthur F. Raper, *The Tragedy of Lynching* (Chapel Hill: University of North Carolina Press, 1933), p. 201.

3. T. J. Woofter has pointed out that in the rural South, "The legal rate of interest is a fiction. Credit is used not for 12 months, but for from three to eight months, yet interest is charged at a flat rate as if the loan were used for the full year. The most common practice is to charge a flat 10 per cent. That is to say a loan of $100 will cost $10 regardless of whether the loan runs for three or eight months." T. J. Woofter, *Landlord and Tenant on the Cotton Plantation* (Washington, D.C.: Works Progress Administration, 1936), pp. 53, 64, 211-212.

4. John Dollard, *Caste and Class in a Southern Town* (Anchor Edition, 1957), (Garden City, New York: Doubleday and Company, 1957), p. 121; Harold Hofsommer, "The AAA and the Cropper," *Social Forces* 13 (May, 1935):494; Calvin B. Hoover, "Human Problems in Acreage Reduction in the South," NA RG 145.

5. U. S., *Statutes at Large*, 48:257; Arthur Schlesinger, Jr., *The Coming of the New Deal* (Boston: Houghton Mifflin Company, 1959), p. 45; Theodore Saloutos, *Agricultural Discontent in the Middle West, 1900-1939* (Madison: University of Wisconsin Press, 1951), pp. 469-470, 498.

6. Arthur F. Raper and Ira De A. Reid, *Sharecroppers All* (Chapel Hill: University of North Carolina Press, 1941), p. 42; Rupert Vance, as quoted by T. J. Woofter, "The Negro and Agricultural Policy" (Carnegie-Myrdal Manuscripts, 1940), p. 121.

7. Henry A. Hunt to Vera Williams, 30 August 1935, NA RG 183, Oxley File; Rexford G. Tugwell to Travis B. Howard, 25 July 1933, NA RG 16.

8. Hunt's office prepared a memorandum for Ralph Bunche explaining the "Purpose of the Negro Relations Section of the Farm Credit Administration." See Bunche, "Political Status of the Negro" (Carnegie-Myrdal Manuscripts) pp. 1403-1407; Arthur F. Raper, *Preface to Peasantry*, (Chapel Hill: University of North Carolina Press, 1936), p. 234; and Rayford Logan, "Negro Status Under the New Deal," *Sphinx* (May, 1937):39.

9. Ralph Bunche, "Report on the Needs of the Negro," typescript, Schomburg Library; John P. Davis, speech to the Twenty-fifth Annual Conference of the NAACP (1934), NAACP Files; Logan, "Negro Status Under the New Deal," p. 38.

10. Handwritten statements from tenants complaining about fraud and cheating by their landlords have been gathered together in folder 467, Solicitor's File, NA RG 16. The quotations are from Charles Johnson, Edwin Embree, and Will Alexander, *The Collapse of Cotton Tenancy* (Chapel Hill: University of North Carolina Press, 1935), p. 53. See also Richard Hofstadter, "Southeastern Cotton Tenants Under the AAA, 1933-1935" (Master's thesis, Columbia University, 1938), pp. 36-37; and Harold Hofsommer, "The AAA and the Cropper," *Social Forces* 13 (May, 1935):106.

11. Jerome Frank to D. P. Trent, memorandum, 5 November 1934, NA RG 145; Cully Cobb to Chester Davis, memorandum, 26 October 1934, NA RG 145; and David Conrad, *The Forgotten Farmers: The Story of Sharecroppers in the New Deal* (Urbana, Ill.: University of Illinois Press, 1965), pp. 72-74, 127.

12. F. D. Roosevelt, *The Public Papers and Addresses of Franklin D. Roosevelt*, ed. Samuel I. Rosenman (New York: Random House, 1938-1950), 5:419-420; Russell Lord, *The Wallaces of Iowa* (Boston: Houghton Mifflin Company, 1947), pp. 381-382; William Leuchtenburg, *Franklin D. Roosevelt and the New Deal* (New York: Harper & Row, 1963), pp. 86-87; Bunche, "Political Status of the Negro," p. 1059. The complicated election procedures have been described by H. I. Richards, *Cotton Under the Agricultural Adjustment Act* (Washington: The Brookings Institution, 1934), pp. 74-81.

13. Gunnar Lange, "Agricultural Adjustment Programs and the Negro" (Carnegie-Myrdal Manuscripts), pp. 22-25; Richards, *Cotton Under the AAA*, pp. 78-79; Hofstadter, "Southeastern Cotton Tenants," pp. 18-23; Conrad, *Forgotten Farmers*, p. 81; and Donald Hughes Grubbs, "The Southern Tenant Farmers' Union and the New Deal" (Ph.D. dissertation, University of Florida, 1963), p. 526. In one of the AAA's Commodity Information Series pamphlets the question was asked, "Where does the responsibility for the administration of the cotton program rest? Answer: The administration is primarily local, resting upon community and county

committees chosen by the cotton farmers." Howard Kester, *Revolt Among the Sharecroppers* (New York: Covici, Friede, 1936), p. 32. Yet Webster Powell and Addison Cutler reported that "in hundreds of counties we visited we did not find a single case where a sharecropper or a representative of the poorer ranks of farmers was put on the [local] committee." *Harper's Magazine* 168 (February, 1934):311. Election officials themselves acknowledged that Negro participation was strictly limited; thus one county officer of elections told Ralph Bunche, "Yes, they vote, but they don't know what it's all about and we take care that they don't. They vote like we say. The niggers are 17 to 1 in this part of the country, so we don't fool with them." Bunche, "Political Status of the Negro," p. 1066.

14. Though, to be sure, the labor requirements did not decline as much as the acreage, since by using fertilizer and planting rows closer together many farmers managed to increase the output of those acres still under cultivation. Despite the reduction in acreage devoted to cotton, the annual yield remained rather steady during the middle 1930s and increased in the last years of the decade. The demand for labor, of course, was related to the total size of the crop as well as to the number of acres under cultivation.

15. Woofter, *Landlord and Tenant*, p. 156. In Congress, Representative Malcolm Tarver of Georgia reported that he had received "hundreds of letters from constituents in my district who state that they have been refused the privilege of re-renting lands from landlords for the present year [1935] by reason of the fact that the landlords have decided to produce what cotton is allocated to their farms by themselves, and to use hired labor. . . ." Hofstadter, "Southeastern Cotton Tenants," p. 69.

16. Oscar Johnston to Chester Davis, memorandum, 26 January 1935, NA RG 145; Alger Hiss to Jerome Frank, memorandum, 26 January 1935, NA RG 145; Conrad, *Forgotten Farmers*, pp. 56-59; and Richards, *Cotton Under the AAA*, p. 112. The final text of Paragraph 7 read as follows: "The producer shall. . . endeavor in good faith to bring about the reduction of acreage contemplated in this contract in such a manner as to cause the least possible amount of labor, economic and social disturbance, and to this end, insofar as possible, he shall effect the acreage reduction as nearly ratable as possible among tenants on this farm; shall, insofar as possible, maintain on this farm the normal number of tenants and other employees; shall permit all tenants to continue in the occupancy of their houses on this farm, rent free, for the years of 1934 and 1935, respectively (unless any such tenant shall so conduct himself as to become a nuisance or a menace to the welfare of the producer); during such years [he] shall afford such tenants or employees, without cost, access to fuel [and] to such woodlands as he may designate; [he] shall permit such tenants the use of an adequate portion of the rented acres to grow food and feed crops for home consumption and for pasturage for domestically used livestock; and for such use of the rented acres [he] shall permit the reasonable use of work animals and equipment in exchange for labor." U. S., Department of Agriculture, *Cotton Contract, 1934-1935*, NA RG 145.

17. Gordon W. Blackwell, "The Displaced Tenant Farm Family in North Carolina," *Social Forces* 8 (October, 1934):65-79; William B. Amberson, "The New Deal for the Sharecroppers," *Nation*, 13 February 1935, pp. 185-187; Norman Thomas, *Plight of the Sharecroppers* (New York: League for Industrial Democracy, 1934), pp. 19-25; Raper, *Preface to Peasantry*, pp. 6-7; and Norman Thomas, "Victims of Change," *Current History* 42 (April, 1935):36.

18. Conrad, *Forgotten Farmers*, pp. 120-135; Richards, *Cotton Under the AAA*, pp. 150-151.

19. D. P. Trent to Henry Wallace, memorandum, 2 July 1934, NA RG 16; Report of the Adjustment Committee, 1 September 1934, NA RG 145; and Cully Cobb to Claude Barnett, 12 June 1935, NA RG 145. David Conrad and Donald Hughes Grubbs have discussed the operations of the AAA's investigating committees at some length: Conrad, *Forgotten Farmers*, pp. 120-135; Grubbs, "The Southern Tenant Farmers' Union," pp. 142-154. See also Richards, *Cotton Under the AAA*, pp. 146-148; Wallace to Richard M. Kleberg, 25 September 1934, NA RG 16.

20. U. S., Bureau of the Census, *Fifteenth Census of the United States, 1930* (Washington: U. S. Government Printing Office, 1931-1934); idem, *Census of Agriculture, 1935* (Washington: U. S. Government Printing Office, 1935); idem, *Sixteenth Census of the United States, 1940* (Washington: U. S. Government Printing Office, 1942-1943). The relevant information has been conveniently summarized and tabulated by Gunnar Myrdal, *An American Dilemma* (New York: Harper & Brothers, 1944), p. 253.

21. Myrdal, *American Dilemma*, p. 258.

3

NAACP Protest and
the AAA

Since 40 percent of the nation's Negro workers were employed as farm tenants and laborers, it was appropriate that the NAACP should concern itself with the problem of agricultural poverty. Yet, since the association's founding in 1910 it had been concerned primarily with protecting the Negro's civil liberties and had devoted only incidental attention to the economic conditions of the masses of black workers. Unfortunately, the tactics that were effective in courtroom disputes to secure civil liberties were not designed to cope with the problems of mass unemployment and poverty. With the increasing deterioration of the Negro's economic position during the early years of the Great Depression, the association was forced to reexamine its strategy and reorient its program in such a way as to place increased emphasis on the economic needs of the Negro masses. To be sure, the NAACP did not renounce its legal campaign against caste discrimination, but during the depression it began to insist that civil liberties and basic economic security must complement one another. "We are becoming convinced," the association declared in 1932, "that it is because we are poor and voiceless. . .that we are able to accomplish so little. . . .We are going to continue to agitate. . . .But we believe that what the Negro needs primarily is a definite economic program."[1]

Despite its rhetorical concern with economic issues, there is no evidence to indicate that the association's leaders seriously considered the manner in which the proposed cotton reduction program would affect black farmers. This lack of attention to the potential consequences of the AAA program is surprising in view of the fact that the NAACP for some time had acted as a "watchdog" over Negro rights. The association prided itself on being alert to any developments that might affect Negro interests adversely, but it did not scrutinize the AAA program, and it is significant that no one from the NAACP testified at the congressional hearings when the New Deal farm program was first considered.

However, when it became apparent that Negro tenant farmers were not receiving a fair share of the government benefit payments and that some previous difficulties had been aggravated by the AAA, the association took steps designed to protect the interests of black tenants. In the spring of 1934, the NAACP sent John P. Davis, a young Washington attorney, into the southern states to interview Negro sharecroppers concerning their grievances against the AAA. Davis learned that many tenants objected to the cotton program's eight-to-one ratio for distributing benefit payments, and others complained that they did not receive even the meager amount recommended by the AAA. Davis himself reported that while certain provisions of the cotton contract had been designed to prevent tenant displacement, there was definite evidence that the AAA's cotton program had caused Negro tenant evictions in the southeastern states. After concluding his investigation, Davis represented the NAACP at a special conference of AAA officials and presented specific proposals concerning the proper drafting of acreage reduction contracts and the administration of the program. He suggested that "payment of monies for the government rental of land . . . be made directly to persons entitled thereto," and he recommended that sharecroppers be given a larger share of the government money.[2] In another conference with AAA officials, Mary White Ovington, a founder of the association and a member of its board of directors for more than a quarter of a century, explained that the government farm program varied "according to the white people chosen to administer it, but always there is discrimination." In her view, "it would have been better to have had a dole, like the English, which would have been distributed from one source," and she insisted that conditions could not be improved "unless distribution of these benefits is given to federal officers." Yet Miss Ovington realized that such a concentration of power in Washington would offend many southern congressmen, and her hopes were dampened by the knowledge that "Roosevelt and the Democratic Party, concerned with continuing their power, . . . want to keep in with the politicians."[3]

Spokesmen for the NAACP also insisted that black farmers would receive more equitable treatment if qualified Negroes participated "in all phases of the administration of farm legislation both in national and local units. . . ." On several occasions, Secretary Walter White wrote to government officials requesting that some distinguished Negroes be appointed to advisory positions in the Department of Agriculture, and Assistant Secretary Roy Wilkins later recalled that "we spent all our waking hours working on it—to get Negroes into the government." Perhaps no one made this case more persuasively than Negro farm journalist Charles S. Brown, who reminded Secretary Wallace that "the American scheme of things promotes dual problems for the Negro farmer—those of agriculture and those of race." According to Brown, "honest solutions of all widespread national problems are compromised" because "too much attention is given to placating reactionary forces, who are wealthy and vocal." While admitting that "the lower rungs of the agricultural ladder are inarticulate and disorganized," Brown nevertheless insisted that this was not a sufficient excuse for "administrative abandonment," and he concluded that if the Department of Agriculture were truly interested in giving black farmers fair treatment it would immediately recognize the need to appoint certain officials as advisers on the special problems of Negro farmers. Pursuing the same line of argument, Rayford Logan pointed out that "when the landlords or their representatives were making the argument in favor of the new contract, there was no Negro in the Agricultural Adjustment Administration occupying any position as 'Negro adviser,' nor was there any white man acting as 'Adviser' on the economic status of Negroes in this organization. Hence the poor Negro tenants and sharecroppers had no one to argue their side of the case."[4]

Yet the Department of Agriculture steadfastly refused to appoint Negro advisers, maintaining, as Undersecretary Rexford G. Tugwell put it, that it was "unable to see what advantage there could be to Negro farmers in the appointment of a special assistant here in Washington." Henry Wallace went even further and claimed that the appointment of a special Negro adviser might seem "patronizing" or even "discriminatory," and he insisted that "the most progressive among our negro population...would prefer that the Department of Agriculture render to them the same service, through the same organizations, that is rendered to our entire rural population." To be sure, a few Negroes were appointed to positions in the department and its subsidiary administrations, but none of them served in advisory capacities. A Negro newspaperman from Chicago, Claude Barnett, became a "special assistant" in 1938, but he received no salary and spent very little time in Washington. When he did come to the Capitol in 1941, he was refused service when he tried to eat with a white companion in the department's lunchroom. In addition, the AAA employed at least three colored officials, James P. Davis, A. L. Holsey, and Mrs. Jennie B. Moton, but they were concerned primarily with publicizing the reduction programs among Negroes, and they did not have any influence when it came to effecting modification of policies.[5] Administration spokesmen frequently reminded critics that 239 Negroes were employed in the southern extension service as county agricultural agents, and another 186 as county home-demonstration agents, and that the work of most of these extension employees was directed by two Negro supervisors, T. M. Campbell of Tuskegee Institute in Alabama, and J. B. Pierce of Hampton Institute in Virginia. None of these extension workers, however, had any influence on policy decisions in Washington.[6]

Publicity had always played a vital role in the work of the NAACP, and it was to be expected that in its efforts to protect the interests of Negro tenants the association would continue to place great emphasis on publication. The national leaders of the NAACP devoted a good deal of their time to the production of educational propaganda, publishing a great many pamphlets and brochures in addition to the monthly *Crisis* and the *Annual Report*. Reports on the special problems of black tenant farmers were featured prominently in many of these publications, and the officers of the association also presented their case to the white public by writing articles for various national magazines and by undertaking lecture tours throughout the country. In addition, the NAACP operated its own press service, which the country's Negro newspapers relied on greatly and which was used occasionally by liberal white magazines and newspapers.[7]

The association also placed great faith in agitation and protest, and members of ths NAACP were instructed to "keep alert" concerning any discriminatory practices in the operation of the various New Deal programs. They were urged to "get the facts on discrimination and then to protest morning, noon and night to those in authority." Walter White stated the viewpoint of most of the association's members when he declared that "only by persistent, unyielding protest will we be heard and answered." Responding to White's call, several local chapters organized campaigns in which hundreds of letters were sent to government administrators demanding fair treatment for the Negro in the New Deal's agricultural programs.[8]

The resolutions of the NAACP's annual conferences, the speeches of its leaders, and the information released by the organization's press service all emphasized "the oppression suffered by the Negro—America's real 'forgotten man'—under the New Deal." The association condemned the "shameless and unrebuked stealing of government cheques made out to sharecroppers and tenant farmers," and chastized the federal government for "ignoring...complaints against maladministration, fraud and dishonesty." Walter White protested that the AAA program had caused the eviction of "more than 100,000 Negro and white sharecroppers and tenant farmers," and he personally urged President Roosevelt "to instruct AAA to hold up all payments until [the] present situation is straightened out." Benefit payments never were suspended, however, and John P. Davis reflected a growing disenchantment with the Roosevelt administration when he complained that the government had "failed absolutely to protect the equities of the tenant...and made it an easy matter for the cotton producer to defraud and cheat his tenants....Yet the administration in Washington—like Pontius Pilate—washes its hand of the whole matter and leaves it to the consciences of the white plantation owner of the South to see that justice is done." The delegates to the NAACP's annual conference in 1934 declared that "nearly six million Negroes dependent upon agriculture have found no remedy for their intolerable condition in this [AAA] program," and officers of the association continually reminded the New Deal's agriculture experts that there were more than one million gainfully employed southern Negroes engaged in the production of cotton and that economic recovery could not be achieved in the South unless this large group was "given just consideration in the setting up of the recovery machinery." Of course, Negroes acknowledged that the New Deal was not responsible for the system of tenancy, but they maintained that during the depression the system would have collapsed under the weight of its own inefficiency if the federal government had not rescued it with agricultural benefit payments. Roy Wilkins spoke for most of his colleagues when he demanded "that now, while the Government is pouring millions of dollars into the South, is the time for it to insist upon the correction of some of the evils of the plantation system as a condition of government aid."[9]

In addition to conferring with government officials and carrying on a determined campaign of publicity and agitation, the NAACP supported the cause of the Southern Tenant Farmers Union (STFU). Organized in Tyronza, Arkansas, in July of 1934, the STFU, like the NAACP, demanded "that rental and parity payments be made direct[ly] to tenants and sharecroppers by the Federal Government... [and] that the eviction from the land be stopped." By 1936, the union's membership had grown to more than thirty thousand tenant farmers—more than one-third of whom were Negroes. Noting the union's successful direction of a 1934 cotton-pickers strike, the biracial character of its organization, and the nature of its overall goals, the leaders of the NAACP came to believe that the association could work most effectively on behalf of southern Negro tenant farmers by supporting the work of the STFU. Walter White and Roy Wilkins knew that while the NAACP was influential in certain urban areas of the North, where protest and militancy could be employed with relative impunity, the organization could not act effectively in the rural South, where traditional respect for Negro economic and civil rights was notoriously weak.[10]

Insofar as the limited resources of the NAACP's budget permitted, the association contributed funds to help defray the expenses of the STFU. Walter White annually served as one of the sponsors of National Sharecroppers Week, a yearly fund-raising drive for the union, and also served as chairman of the committee which financed publication of Howard Kester's account of the union's activity. On several occasions Roy Wilkins attempted to persuade prominent Negro celebrities such as Marian Anderson and Roland Hayes to give benefit concerts for the union, and the association's national office encouraged its local branches to arrange fund-raising dinners and Dutch-treat cocktail parties for the union. When members of the STFU found themselves in court, as frequently was the case, the NAACP was one of several organizations that donated legal aid, and occasionally the association contributed funds to supplement the meager salaries of union officials, particularly Howard Kester. Walter White insisted that the NAACP pay expenses to enable union representatives to speak at the association's annual conferences of the 1930s, and White and Wilkins themselves made a point of attending the STFU conventions, where they were prominently featured as speakers. The total amount of contributions from the NAACP's national office to the STFU probably never exceeded a few hundred dollars in any year, but this was a significant sum from an organization that was short of money and had to keep its annual spending under $40,000.[11]

For many years the association had condemned the American labor movement for betraying the interests of the black worker by following discriminatory admission policies. Yet the NAACP maintained that fundamentally "the Negro as a worker has interests identical with those of white workers," and during the depression many of the NAACP's members, particularly the younger people, came to believe that the Negro could not make significant economic progress unless he allied himself with the white working class. Reflecting this new emphasis, Charles Houston, the NAACP's legal counsel, insisted that "the only thing left to do is to unite with the poor white man who is just as bad off as the Negro. . . . It will be hard. There will be suspicion and enmity at first. The minds of both the poor whites and the Negroes have been poisoned against each other, but the attempt must be made. The Negro must carry his case to the poor white. Together they can win against the forces which are seeking to exploit and keep them down. Separately they will lose and the other fellow will continue to win."[12]

The biracial policies of the STFU corresponded perfectly with the program of black and white working-class solidarity that Houston and other NAACP people recommended, and it was the union's racial egalitarianism that made support from the NAACP possible, even inevitable. STFU officials emphasized the common economic grievances of black and white tenants and attempted to unite all farm workers, regardless of color, in common opposition to their employers. Even in the Mississippi Delta, most STFU locals were thoroughly integrated, although segregated units were organized in a few towns where, as Donald Hughes Grubbs has written, "the whites were too strongly gripped by superstition to organize with people of a different color." Black men were employed as STFU organizers and were elected to union offices at all levels—the most prominent Negro official being Vice-President E. R. McKinney—and, as noted above, approximately one-third of the STFU's membership was black.[13]

Of course not all white sharecroppers were enthusiastic about the union's biracial policy, but they knew that if the STFU adopted a discriminatory admission policy it would ultimately be defeated because the planters would replace union members with Negroes. Lucien Koch, the director of Commonwealth College and a part-time organizer for the STFU, aptly described a prevailing attitude when he wrote that "the feeling of the whites for the Negroes is a strange mixture of a sense of superiority and at the same time a realization that without the strength of the Negroes they cannot hope to progress far."[14]

Yet while considerations of expediency motivated the STFU's decision to drop the color line, it is nevertheless true that the union made a significant attempt to alter deeply rooted southern prejudices and in the process created an egalitarian working-class solidarity that transcended mere opportunism. Union organizers repeatedly insisted that racial hatred was largely instigated by planters who fostered bitter feelings in the hope that the working force then would be divided along caste lines and thus unable to work effectively for common interests;[15] and they enjoyed considerable success in converting black and white croppers to this point of view. On one occasion, for example, a racially mixed group of rank and file members applauded wildly when a black sharecropper declared: "For a long time now the white folks and the colored folks have been fighting each other and both of us has been getting whipped all the time. We don't have nothing against one another but we got plenty against the landlord. The same chain that holds my people holds your people too. If we're chained together on the outside we ought to stay chained together in the union." Walter White was tremendously impressed by the STFU's success in educating workers on the race question, and he believed the union was "the most significant labor movement created in the United States in many years" because it had invaded the South and established an "unprecedented mixed union of white and colored tenant farmers and sharecroppers." Indeed, White believed that the STFU was "the only organization which has really done anything about sharecropping," and thus he concluded that the NAACP could best support the cause of southern Negro farmers by doing what it could to help the STFU.[16]

Most of the NAACP's activities on behalf of Negro tenant farmers proved to be ineffective. The association never succeeded in its attempts to have the AAA appoint knowledgeable colored men as advisers on the special problems of Negro farmers. And, as will be shown, its demands that larger payments be made directly to tenants were only partially met. Moreover, while the Southern Tenant Farmers Union did win occasional victories, the power of the union was broken after 1936, partly because it was almost impossible to bargain effectively with landlords whose economic position was so desperate that they could not survive without government subsidies and partly because of the landlords' ruthless opposition to the union.[17]

The NAACP's campaign of agitation and publicity, however, helped persuade a significant section of the public that the AAA's cotton reduction program had aggravated the sharecroppers' condition. By 1935, criticism of the cotton reduction program was widespread, and important segments of the liberal community were calling on the federal government to do more for landless farmers. The American Federation of Labor, for example, demanded a federal investigation of the "inhuman levels to which the workers employed in the cotton plantations have been reduced," and the Rosenwald Foundation appropriated $25,000 to finance a study of southern tenancy. When this study was published, it criticized the AAA's cotton reduction program, concluded that there were more than two million displaced individuals who were no longer needed as cotton tenants, and recommended that the federal government "buy up huge acreages of farm lands" for distribution to unemployed tenants and laborers at low prices and easy terms of payment.[18]

It is difficult to assess the importance of the NAACP in arousing the liberal community concerning the plight of the sharecropper. Walter White, Roy Wilkins, Charles Houston, and John P. Davis did take the tenant farmers' case to high officials in the Roosevelt administration; and, by their speeches throughout the country, their articles written for various journals, and their use of the NAACP press service, they helped to focus national attention on the manner in which the black sharecroppers' condition was aggravated by the AAA's cotton reduction program. However, the leaders of the NAACP were not alone in calling public attention to the plight of the sharecropper. Others, such as Norman Thomas, the leader of the Socialist party, Gardner Jackson, the AAA's assistant consumers' counsel, and particularly the leaders of the Southern Tenant Farmers Union also worked tirelessly to make their countrymen more sensitive to the special problems of tenant farmers. This cause was also supported by the liberal journals, particularly the *Nation* and the *New Republic*, which carried several accounts relating the difficulties of tenured farmers in the South, and the press coverage given by the Scripps-Howard newspaper chain, the *New York Times,* and several of the newsweeklies was also of great importance since these publications enjoyed wide circulation. In addition, many novelists used their skills to dramatize the misery of the tenant farmers and day laborers, the most important literary works being contributed by John Steinbeck, Erskine Caldwell, and James Agee and Walker Evans. The NAACP, then, was only one of the many groups responsible for arousing liberal opinion concerning the desperate conditions of southern farm tenants.[19]

NOTES

1. The reorientation of the NAACP's program and strategy is discussed at length in Part Three. The quotation is from "Address to the Country," Twenty-third Annual Conference of the NAACP, 1932, NAACP Files.

2. To dramatize his testimony, Davis brought a small group of Negro tenants from Alabama to the conference, but he never repeated this tactic because the identity of the black croppers was somehow revealed to the local sheriff in Alabama. During the early years of the New Deal, it was a standard AAA practice to refer complaints sent to Washington back to state AAA administrators, who then passed them on to county agents for adjustment. These agents in many cases informed the accused landlord of the proceedings, with the result that the complaint often ended in further injury and discomfiture to the complainant. There was a certain grim truth in the charge leveled by Harry Williams, the Negro president of the Alabama Sharecroppers Union: "Whenever the sharecroppers complained about not getting AAA checks their complaints were always sent back to the county officers by the government." On this point, see the following: John P. Davis, Report of the Executive Secretary of the Joint Committee on National Recovery, 16 March 1934, 1 June 1935, 19 June 1935, and 23 November 1935, NA RG 183, Oxley File. Also see the remarks of Robert Weaver, Minutes of the Fourth Meeting of the Interdepartmental Group Concerned with the Special Problems of Negroes, 1 June 1934, NA RG 48; Roy Wilkins to E. A. Miller, 30 March 1934, NA RG 145; Richard Hofstadter, "Southeastern Cotton Tenants Under the AAA, 1933-1935" (M.A. thesis, Columbia University, 1938), p. 62.

3. John P. Davis to Henry Wallace, 23 April 1934, NA RG 16 (Davis included a stenographic copy of the transcript of his interviews with various tenants); U. S., Congress, Senate, "Alleged Communistic Activities at Howard University," *Senate Miscellaneous Documents,* no. 217, 10016:44. Davis's official position was that of executive secretary of the Joint Committee on National Recovery, but the bulk of his salary was paid by the NAACP. The unusual administrative relations between the joint committee and the NAACP will be discussed in detail in Part Three. Mary White Ovington to Roy Wilkins, 19 February 1934, and 6 March 1934, NAACP Files; Ovington to William Pickens, 2 March 1934, NAACP Files; Ovington to J. E. Spingarn, Arthur B. Spingarn, Louis T. Wright, Walter White, Charles Houston, Juanita Jackson, memorandum, 18 November 1935, NAACP Files.

4. Resolutions of the Twenty-fifth Annual Conference of the NAACP, 1934, NAACP Files; Walter White to Henry Wallace, 21 February 1935, NA RG 16; White to Harry L. Brown, 15 September 1937, NA RG 16; White to Franklin D. Roosevelt, telegram, 31 August 1937, NA RG 16; Clark Foreman to Wallace, 2 January 1934, NA RG 16; W. J. Hale to Wallace, 24 June 1935, NA RG 16; Charles S. Brown to Wallace, memorandum, 9 November 1937, NA RG 16; Chester Davis to Foreman, 17 January 1934, NA RG 145; Rayford Logan, "Negro Status Under the New Deal," *Sphinx,* May, 1935, p. 21; Allen Kifer, "The Negro and the New Deal" (Ph.D. dissertation, University of Wisconsin, 1961), p. 144; White, "Report of the Secretary," 7 March 1935, NAACP Files.

5. As a matter of fact, very few Negroes were employed in Washington by the agricultural administrations, even in menial capacities. In 1939 the Department of Agriculture employed a total of fifty-two thousand men and women but only one thousand were Negroes. Reflecting the prevailing Negro exasperation, Rayford Logan complained that the AAA "has absolutely no Negro representation in it other than a few employed as messengers, porters and card punchers in the office of the Comptroller and these work at night over in the old Post Office Building. If there are any Negroes working in any of the offices of the Administration located in the South Building of the Agricultural Building, either as messengers or porters, they too must work at night, for I have spent every day for one week from three to four hours, walking up and down the different floors of the building on which are located the offices of the Agricultural Adjustment Administration and I have yet to see the first colored messenger—quite a contrast to the sight one sees over at the Department of Interior where the offices of the Public Works Administration are located. There one does see quite a large complement of Negro messengers." "Negro Status Under the New Deal," *Sphinx* (May, 1935):21. See also Kifer, "The Negro and the New Deal," p. 147.

6. Rexford G. Tugwell to Fred Hildebrandt, 4 August 1933, NA RG 16; Tugwell to W. F. Reden, 7 July 1933, NA RG 16; Henry Wallace to Fred Hildebrandt, 28 August 1933, NA RG 16; C. W. Warburton to Hildebrandt, 28 August 1933, NA RG 16; J. D. LeCron to Charles S. Brown, 16 December 1937, NA RG 16; Alfred D. Stedman to LeCron, memorandum, 10 December 1937, NA RG 16; Charles West to Mrs. J. F. Price, 17 September 1935, NA RG 48; John Blake to Cully Cobb, 24 April 1937, NA RG 145; W. S. Brown to Cobb, 25 May 1937, NA RG 145; A. P. Spender to Cobb, 28 June 1937, NA RG 145; W. H. Bell to Cobb, 16 July 1937, NA RG 145; Jennie B. Moton to Cobb, 20 July 1937, NA RG 145; Kifer, "The Negro and the New Deal," pp. 146-147.

7. For an interesting discussion of the NAACP's publicity apparatus during the 1930s, see the interview with George S. Schuyler in the Columbia University Oral History Project, pp. 391-393. See also Gunnar Myrdal, *An American Dilemma* (New York: Harper and Brothers, 1944), p. 827.

8. NAACP Press Release, 1 July 1934; Walter White to Abram Harris, 13 July 1934, NAACP Files.

9. NAACP Press Release, 1 July 1934; Resolutions of the Twenty-fifth, Twenty-sixth, and Twenty-seventh Annual Conferences of the NAACP, 1934, 1935, and 1936, NAACP Files; Walter White to Franklin D. Roosevelt, telegram, 18 February 1935, OF 2538, FDR Library; John P. Davis, Speech to the Twenty-fifth Annual Conference of the NAACP, 1934, NAACP Files; Roy Wilkins to Chester Davis, 28 May 1934, NA RG 145; Wilkins to Oscar Chapman, 21 May 1934, NAACP Files; *Pittsburgh Courier*, 25 March 1933; Ralph Bunche, "Report on the Needs of the

Negro," typescript, n.d., Schomburg Library, p. 23; White, "Report of the Secretary," 7 March 1935, NAACP Files.

10. The best account of the STFU is Donald Hughes Grubbs, "The Southern Tenant Farmers' Union and the New Deal" (Ph.D. dissertation, University of Florida, 1963). Another good brief account is that of David Conrad, *The Forgotten Farmers: The Story of Sharecroppers in the New Deal* (Urbana, Ill.: University of Illinois Press, 1965), chap. 5. The quotations are from Howard Kester, *Revolt Among the Sharecroppers* (New York: Covici, Friede, 1936), p. 72, and H. L. Mitchell, "Organizing Southern Sharecroppers," *New Republic,* 3 October 1934, pp. 217-218. See also Walter White to Leon Turner, 4 March 1938, NAACP Files; White to LeRoy Baxter, 11 March 1938, NAACP Files; and White to John Brophy, 24 March 1939, NAACP Files.

11. Walter White to Pauli Murray, 11 December 1939, NAACP Files; Harriet Young to White, 25 October 1938, NAACP Files; Freda Kirchway to White, 21 March 1938, NAACP Files; White to Reinhold Niebuhr, 14 August 1938, and 14 August 1939, NAACP Files; White to Leon Turner, memorandum, 6 April 1939, NAACP Files; Harriet Young to White, 9 December 1938, NAACP Files; Roy Wilkins to Branch Officers, memorandum, 16 March 1939, NAACP Files; NAACP Press Release, January, 1939, NAACP Files; *Twenty-seventh Annual Report of the NAACP,* 1936, p. 10, NAACP Files; Walter White to Arthur B. Spingarn, Hubert Delaney, Louis T. Wright, and Mary White Ovington, memorandum, 26 December 1935, NAACP Files; White, "Report of the Secretary," 4 April 1935, NAACP Files.

12. "Address to the Country," Twenty-third Annual Conference of the NAACP, 1932, NAACP Files; Charles H. Houston, Speech to the Twenty-fifth Annual Conference of the NAACP, 1934, NAACP Files.

13. Grubbs, "The Southern Tenant Farmers' Union," pp. 109-110, 117-118, 309-310, 400, 421-422, 428, 480; Kester, *Revolt Among the Sharecroppers,* pp. 20, 56; Lucien Koch, "The War in Arkansas," *New Republic,* 27 March 1935, p. 184; Ward Rodgers, "Sharecroppers Drop the Color Line," *Crisis* 42 (June, 1935):168-169, 178; Conrad, *Forgotten Farmers,* p. 95.

14. Lucien Koch, "The War in Arkansas," p. 184.

15. Organizer Howard Kester, for example, wrote that racial strife was "born of economic frustration of the poor white farmers who were crowded out of the rich bottom lands by the great planters. While they bore a deep resentment toward the planting aristocracy, the Negro became the object of their bitterness and scorn. The planting aristocracy, sensing the potential strength of the poor whites and the rising middle class, directed the grievances of these classes from themselves to the Negro masses who, in time, became the scapegoat for all the South's sins." Kester, *Revolt Among the Sharecroppers,* pp. 20, 56.

16. Ibid. Walter White to Leon Turner 4 March 1938, NAACP Files; White to LeRoy Baxter, 11 March 1938, NAACP Files; White to John

Brophy, 24 March 1939, NAACP Files; *Twenty-eighth Annual Report of the NAACP*, 1937, p. 13, NAACP Files.

17. For a good account of the economic plight of the landlords, see T. J. Woofter, *Landlord and Tenant on the Cotton Plantation* (Washington, D.C.: Works Progress Administration, 1936), pp. 65-86; and idem, "The Negro and Agricultural Policy" (Carnegie-Myrdal Manuscripts, 1940), p. 59. Donald Hughes Grubbs and David Conrad have written graphic accounts of the repression and terror that landlords directed at the STFU: Grubbs, "The Southern Tenant Farmers' Union," chaps. 12, 15, and 17; and Conrad, *Forgotten Farmers*, chap. 9. See also Kester, *Revolt Among the Sharecroppers*, pp. 81-85.

18. *Report of the Proceedings of the Fifty-fifth Annual Convention of the American Federation of Labor* (Washington, D.C., 1935), p. 588; Charles Johnson, Edwin Embree, and Will Alexander, *The Collapse of Cotton Tenancy* (Chapel Hill: University of North Carolina Press, 1935), p. 65 and passim.

19. M. S. Venkataramani, "Norman Thomas, Arkansas Sharecroppers, and the Roosevelt Agricultural Policies, 1933-1937," *Mississippi Valley Historical Review* 47 (September, 1960):225-246; Conrad, *Forgotten Farmers*, pp. 213, 246; Grubbs, "The Southern Tenant Farmers' Union," passim.

4

Agricultural Programs After 1935

THE response of the Roosevelt administration to the growing criticism of its cotton reduction program was threefold. First, between 1933 and 1935, an important group of government officials came to conclude that much of the criticism of the AAA was justified. Along with Jerome Frank and Alger Hiss, this pro-tenant group included Margaret Bennett, Lee Pressman, Francis Shea, and John Abt of the legal division, Paul Appleby and Mordecai Ezekiel of Secretary Wallace's staff, Frederick C. Howe and Gardner Jackson of the AAA's consumers' counsel, and Rexford G. Tugwell, the Undersecretary of Agriculture. These officials had never been satisfied with the tenant provisions of the cotton contracts, and by 1935 they were convinced that, bad as the provisions were, the AAA had not made an honest effort to enforce them. Yet when these pro-tenant administrators took action to ameliorate the sharecroppers' condition, and in the process seemingly threatened the existence of the southern caste and class system, they ran afoul not only of the influential southern congressmen but also of such New Deal stalwarts as Henry Wallace, Cully Cobb, and AAA administrator Chester Davis, who believed that economic recovery could be achieved without inaugurating any basic changes and that the condition of all farmers could be improved substantially without launching a frontal assault on traditional southern practices. This important factional confrontation ultimately led to the famous "purge" of 1935, wherein the most prominent members of the pro-tenant group were forced to resign from the New Deal's agricultural administrations. These events have been related in detail elsewhere and need not detain us here.[1] It should be noted, however, that while the pro-tenant liberals lost the important battle of 1935, several remained in government service and waged a significant battle to ensure that the 1936 and later cotton contracts would be rewritten so that tenants would receive a larger share of the government payments. Still another round in the struggle was touched off when President Roosevelt attempted to mollify critics by appointing a special committee to consider the problems of farm tenancy. When this committee submitted its report early in 1937, it pointed out that there had been a great decline in farm ownership and that a "large segment of the farm population has never reached a state of economic advancement where its members could even aspire to farm ownership." On the basis of the evidence in this report, the president sadly concluded that "the American dream of the family-size farm, owned by the family which operates it, has become more and more remote." To restore the reality of this dream, the committee and the president recommended "a program of land purchase by the Federal Government and disposition of the land under long-term contracts of sale to operating farmers."[2]

The 1936-1939 Cotton Contracts

When the provisions of the 1936 cotton contracts were discussed, even the men of the cotton section knew that tenants
would have to be allotted a larger share of the benefit
payments if unfavorable publicity were to be avoided. Tentative plans were drafted by which sharecroppers were to
receive approximately 25 percent of the government payment
instead of the 12 percent they had been getting. However, in
January of 1936 the Supreme Court intervened by declaring
the AAA's processing tax unconstitutional. A few weeks later
Congress managed to save the AAA by enacting new legislation which was designed to achieve the goal of crop reduction
without resorting to the unconstitutional processing tax. The
Soil Conservation and Domestic Allotment Act authorized the
AAA to pay bounties to farmers, not for restricting production
of commercial crops, but instead for retiring their acres to
soil-enriching pasture and woodland. Money for the program
was to be appropriated directly by Congress.[3]

The terms of the 1936 cotton contracts had to be revised in
accordance with the specifications of the Soil Conservation
Act, but this did not affect the decision that tenants should
receive a larger share of the benefit payments. The new
contract provided for "a single adjustment payment of not less
than 5 cents per pound on the average yield of lint cotton on
land withheld from cotton production." Landowners were to
receive 37.5 percent of this benefit payment; 12.5 percent was
to go to the person furnishing work, stock, and equipment,
while the remaining 50 percent was to be divided between
landlord and tenant according to the usual crop share. Thus,
tenant families were to receive at least 25 percent of the
government benefit money, and Holley, Winston, and Woofter

reported that the average payment to the three thousand southern tenant families in their sample increased from $11 in 1934 to $27 in 1937.[4]

In addition, John R. McCarl, the comptroller general of the United States, ruled in October of 1935 that the AAA would have to make separate payments to landlords and tenants. As was to be expected, the cotton section objected to McCarl's ruling, as it had earlier objected to Alger Hiss's similar recommendation, again maintaining that direct payments to tenants would provoke landlord opposition in the South. While the men of the cotton section admitted that the practice of making payments to the landlords as trustees for their tenants had not worked satisfactorily, they insisted that abuses could be eliminated if joint payments were made to landlord and tenant, with the provision that each would have to endorse the check before payment would be made. McCarl, however, refused to allow joint payments, and unlike Hiss he had the authority to enforce his decision. Henry Wallace claimed at the time that AAA complied with McCarl's ruling, that beginning in 1936 "a separate unencumbered check was issued to each person who participated in the plan and qualified for payment. No joint payees were designated nor was it permissible to assign these payments." But Wallace's statement was exaggerated. While the record of the AAA improved after 1935, the cotton section frequently ignored the comptroller general's decision and in fact continued to make joint payments. One indication of conditions that continued to prevail in certain parts of the South was given when it was reported that a crook named Smithers, posing as a lawyer or a county agent, traveled through the Arkansas delta promising to collect tenants' money for them—for a fee of half the payment.[5]

Yet increasing the tenant's share of the government money had the character of a double-edged sword, since it gave landlords a greater economic incentive for decreasing the number of tenants or lowering their status to wage laborers. The danger of eviction was particularly acute because the 1936-1939 cotton contracts significantly failed to improve on the inadequate security protections which had been written into Paragraph 7 of the 1934-1935 contracts. The 1936-1939 contracts provided that if landlords reduced the number of tenants on their farms the AAA might withhold a portion of the government payments so that the landlords would not receive any more government money than they would have received if the tenants had not been released. But the contracts also provided that benefit payments would not be curtailed when "sound management" demanded that landlords reduce the number of tenants. While the 1934-1935 contracts provided that landlords should "insofar as possible, maintain...the normal number of tenants," the 1936-1939 contracts permitted the county committees to allow landlords to keep fewer tenants than normal if it was "economically unpracticable" not to do so. Given the pro-landlord sympathies of the county committeemen, it was to be expected that thousands of landlords would take advantage of this opportunity and substitute casual day-labor for sharecropper labor, and available statistical evidence indicates that tenant displacement continued at an accelerated rate during the years from 1935 to 1940.[6]

The Farm Security Administration

The support which the Roosevelt administration gave in 1937 to Senator John Bankhead's legislative efforts to create a governmental agency that would help tenants and sharecroppers become independent small landowning farmers was another indication of the growing concern for landless farmers. Yet despite the fact that Bankhead's legislation was designed specifically to provide low-interest, long-term credit for farm tenants who could not otherwise obtain money for land purchase, most Negro leaders opposed the bill. When the legislation was first presented to Congress in 1935 it was examined closely by the leaders of the NAACP, who no doubt recalled the association's earlier negligence in failing to scrutinize the provisions of the proposed Agricultural Adjustment bill. And after carefully examining the proposed farm tenancy legislation, these leaders (Walter White, Roy Wilkins, John Davis, and Charles Houston) concluded that if the measure were passed without amendment it would do "more harm than good." Walter White, who served as the association's major spokesman in this area, insisted that the bill should contain a specific prohibition of discrimination, and he called for a provision that would ensure that "the total amount expended in the purchase of land or in administration in any given state should not be less for Negroes than the percentage of the Negro population." Even this, in his opinion, "would be inadequate in that in the deep South the discrimination against Negroes makes their need so much greater than that even of white sharecroppers and tenant farmers."[7]

In addition to an outright prohibition of racial discrimination and provision for proportional sharing of the benefits, the leaders of the NAACP believed that further safeguards were needed to prevent owners from taking advantage of increased demand by raising land prices. If land prices rose, they reasoned, many tenants would be forced to buy submarginal land or good land in such small quantities that it would not provide a decent living for a family. White believed that "some adequate safeguard should be included to prevent the foisting of submarginal, worthless land upon the purchasers," and he also declared that "there should be specific provisions guaranteeing farms of sufficient size and fertility to insure a decent standard of living for their occupants. . . ." In his view, there was also a need for "definite provisions limiting annual payments for interest and amortization which should not exceed 10 or 12 percent of the gross annual income," and he suggested that the price paid for land should be based on "the average of the valuation of such lands for taxation purposes. . . modified by the ratio of such valuation to real value as prevails in the vicinity." Unless such provisions were included, White feared that the Bankhead program "would primarily do nothing but 'bail out' landlords, insurance companies and banks who hold this land on defaulted mortgages." John Davis agreed with White and contended that the Bankhead bill was so loosely drawn that without amendments it could be used "for every purpose except for the benefit of sharecroppers and farm tenants." Davis believed that the land-poor plantation owner would reap the greatest advantage from the proposed legislation, since "his sub-marginal land will be taken off his hands for cash paid by tax payers all over the country." Doubtless recalling the AAA experience, he predicted that the farm tenancy program would divert funds taken from all taxpayers "to the use of the better-than-average citizen, while the classes needing aid most are forgotten." Persuaded by such arguments, the delegates to the NAACP's Twenty-sixth Annual Conference (1935) declared that they were "unalterably opposed to the present form of the Bankhead farm tenant corporation bill," and they demanded that "adequate safeguards be written into the bill before it is passed."[8]

The leaders of the NAACP also questioned the desirability of providing small homesteads so that tenants could realize "the American dream of the family-size farm, owned by the family which operates it." Walter White and John Davis knew that small farmers could not afford to purchase the expensive equipment necessary for successful farming, and they reminded the AAA that "the large plantation has an economic justification which we neglect at our peril." Davis pointed out that "the whole trend of the federal farm program is toward restricted production," and he concluded that even if a tenant received his own land he would be expected to grow only farm produce for his own consumption. "With only the smallest capital, if any,...with elemental farm equipment," and with "submarginal land which plantation owners are eager to be rid of," Davis believed that it would be impossible for the former tenant to do more than "scratch a meagre existence out of his small farm," and he feared that the net result of the program would be to tie unfortunate tenants and sharecroppers to inferior acreage on the periphery of the large plantations, thereby furnishing a permanent supply of cheap labor for plantation owners. Joining with other spokesmen for the tenants' cause, Davis and White suggested that "it would be helpful to authorize experiments in cooperative farming and marketing under Federal Government auspices." The government, they believed, should "undertake an educational campaign to dispel the romantic notions that still preail concerning the advantages of rugged individualism on the farm." [9]

The NAACP also objected to the Bankhead bill's provision that three-man committees be established in each county to choose those tenants who were most deserving of federal loans and most likely to repay the debt. Charles Houston believed that this provision would give the county committee "despotic power in selecting the beneficiaries of the Act," and Walter White reminded the Department of Agriculture that "experience has shown unmistakably that in a great many counties of the South, Negroes will be the victims of gross discrimination if such decisions are left wholly to local boards." The NAACP consequently recommended that the Farm Tenancy bill be amended in such a way as to provide for civil service administration. The association also insisted repeatedly that the AAA experience had demonstrated the need for qualified Negro advisers at every level of administration.[10]

Given the composition of the Congress and President Roosevelt's dependence on the support of southern representatives, it was generally recognized that these NAACP demands were not going to be implemented, and there were friends of the association who maintained that "unsatisfactory as we know it to be...the surest road to some improvement is to back the bill as it stands and bring all the pressure we can on the administrative agencies." For example, Edwin R. Embree, the president of the Rosenwald Foundation and the man who, according to W. E. B. Du Bois, was the philanthropist most sensitive to the special problems of Negroes, candidly warned Walter White that congressional support would not be forthcoming for any "bill which attempted in itself to set up proportional distribution between the races," and he urged the association to rely on the goodwill of such government administrators as "[Rexford G.] Tugwell and M. L. Wilson [who] are alert to the situation and prepared in spite of counter-pressures to see that the Negro is given a square deal in this new homesteading." The leaders of the association doubtless recognized the political realism of Embree's position, and yet they continued to insist that the farm tenancy legislation would be of no value to Negroes unless specific safeguards were included. In this regard, John Davis spoke for most of his colleagues when he recalled that "these very tenants and sharecroppers have come to their present sad plight under the policies of Messrs. Wallace and Tugwell thus far in the New Deal." Negro leaders insisted that if the supporters of the proposed legislation were sincere in their desire to aid Negro farm tenants, they could not oppose liberalizing amendments. "If the bill is intended to do what its proponents claim," Davis argued, "they will not oppose the amendments which simply make their aims more certain. If on the other hand, the real intention is to bail out landlords and leave the tenant high and dry we shall know it."[11]

A modified version of the Bankhead bill was enacted by Congress in July of 1937 when Congress authorized the establishment of the Farm Security Administration (FSA) with an appropriation of $10 million for fiscal 1938, $25 million for 1939, and $50 million annually thereafter which would be loaned to tenants on very liberal terms (3 percent interest each year with a forty-year period for amortization). In its final form the legislation did include two safeguards which resembled the NAACP's recommendations: no loan was to be made for the acquisition of any farm, "unless it is of such size as the Secretary [of Agriculture] determines to be sufficient to constitute an efficient farm management unit," and the secretary was authorized to continue the ventures in cooperative farming that had been directed by the Resettlement Administration prior to 1937.[12] As Edwin Embree had predicted, however, the other NAACP suggestions did not appear in the final form of the legislation.[13]

Yet the most important weakness of the farm tenancy legislation was not the absence of the NAACP's liberalizing amendments, but the very limited scope of the new program. The expenditure of several million dollars each year for the purchase of tenant homesteads was undoubtedly a step in the direction of abolishing farm poverty, but it is clear that the Bankhead program did not appropriate anything like the

amount of money needed to eliminate farm tenancy. Altogether there were some 670,000 Negro tenant farm families in
the cotton South (out of a total of about 1,600,000 southern
tenant families), but by June of 1940 the total number of FSA
tenant purchase loans to blacks and whites was less than ten
thousand. At this rate, it would have required several
centuries to provide farms for all the needy tenant families,
and there was a grain of truth in the view expressed by
Congressman William Lemke of North Dakota: "If ever a
mountain labored to produce a mouse this bill is it. We have
heard a lot of lip service that we are going to make farm
tenants farm owners. In the light of that lip service this bill is
a joke and a camouflage." Norman Thomas believed that the
Bankhead program was a wholly inadequate method for
meeting the sharecroppers' problems. "It is simply a gesture,"
he concluded, "by which the leading advocates of the Bill in
the Administration would like to divert attention from some
results of the AAA and in particular the enormous hypocrisy of
Section 7 of the cotton contracts." Administration spokesmen
themselves admitted that they could not begin "to extend
these loan privileges to anything like a sizeable number with
the funds available at the present time." As Assistant Secretary
of Agriculture Harry Brown candidly put it, there were
"nearly three million farm tenants in the United States, and
the nine and a half million dollars in the present fiscal year
[1938] means that we can reach only about two thousand to
twenty-five hundred." In 1939, the FSA received 149,972 applications but made only 7,000 loans, and in 1942 there were
more than 175,000 applications for 8,000 available loans.[14]

Limited though its resources were, the Farm Security Administration did provide badly needed aid for thousands of
individual farm tenants. Altogether the FSA developed more

than a dozen different programs, but Negroes were helped most by three forms of assistance: tenant purchase loans, rehabilitation loans, and the construction of resettlement communities.

FSA tenant purchase loans were granted to tenant farmers who had no other source of credit, in order that they might have an opportunity to purchase their own family-size farm. The local FSA administration committee chose from among many applicants, and preference was given to those borrowers who could make a down payment or who had previously demonstrated managerial ability. Since the program was administered locally, since Negro tenants tended to be poorer than whites, and since Negroes generally had less managerial experience, these procedures would seem to have handi-capped the Negro loan applicant. Yet southern Negroes, who constituted 23.8 percent of the entire southern population, received 21 percent of all the tenant purchase loans made in the South during the 1930s. Given the prevailing mores, this was a remarkably equitable division, but it should be remem-bered that 40 percent of the South's non-landowning farmers were Negroes and that the grand total of tenant purchase loans to black farmers during the decade was only 1,919.[15]

Title II of the farm tenancy legislation authorized the FSA to continue the rehabilitation loan program which had been inaugurated by the Federal Emergency Relief Administration (FERA) in 1933 and which had been continued under the auspices of the Resettlement Administration from 1935 to 1937. Under the authority of this title, FSA loaned money to needy farm families—not for the purchase of land, but to help the families rehabilitate themselves through the purchase of livestock, farm equipment, and supplies. This title also authorized relief grants to enable poverty-stricken farm families to purchase the food and clothing necessary to carry on. For the most part the rehabilitation program provided relief for indigent sharecroppers and tenants, but an attempt was also made to provide corrective instruction which would enable "destitute farm families...to become self-supporting and independent of emergency relief aid."[16]

This rehabilitation program extended aid to some 854,000 families during the years from 1935 to 1940 and without question was the FSA's most extensive activity. Particularly relevant to this study is the fact that Negro borrowers constituted almost as large a percentage of the FSA's rehabilitation clientele (23 percent) as they did of the general farm population. Yet as Richard Sterner has pointed out, even this was an unsatisfactory measure of participation "because Negroes are found in such large proportions among the low income farmers whom the program is designed to assist.... While more than one out of five needy white farm families was currently assisted by the program, only one out of nine of the comparable colored families was given such assistance." Moreover, the dollar value of the loans and grants to white clients was slightly larger than that to Negroes.[17]

Congress also authorized the FSA to continue the community projects which had been established before 1937 by the Subsistence Homesteads Division of the Department of Interior, the Rural Rehabilitation Division of the FERA, and the Resettlement Administration. The story of the development of these communities is interesting because it throws light on a dilemma which Americans have faced on several occasions in the nineteenth and twentieth centuries. Since the beginnings of commercial agriculture some farmers have regarded their land strictly as a business proposition, while others have looked on the land primarily as an arcadian refuge from the "corruption" of urban commercial life. During periods of prosperity, American farmers have generally regarded their land as an economic resource, a means for securing wealth. But during periods of economic distress, as Paul Johnstone has observed, many farmers have lost "faith in the bright new world that only recently offered blessings hitherto undreamed of.... Thus every panic, every depression, every modern social crisis of major proportion—along with producing plans for making a wholly new, unprecedented, and Utopian world—has brought forth schemes for returning to the real or imagined order of the past."[18]

Paradoxically, the New Deal community program appealed both to "agrarians" who wanted to escape from the evils of commercial agriculture by taking refuge in a neo-Jeffersonian world of yeoman proprietors, and to daring social innovators who were convinced that commercial agriculture could succeed in the future only if large numbers of farmers renounced competitive individualism and joined together in cooperative community activities. The result of this unlikely alliance was the establishment of some one hundred urban and rural communities. Given the traditional individualism of American farmers and the contradictory motives of those who supported the new communities, it was inevitable that these projects would become controversial. The new communities became the center of a fierce ideological conflict between individualists and collectivists, between farmers who wanted to escape from commercial agriculture and those who thought they could earn larger profits by participating in cooperative ventures. An analysis of these ideological clashes would be beyond the scope of this study, but it is appropriate to focus attention here on the extent to which Negroes participated in the new community programs.[19]

When the community program was inaugurated in 1933, it was assumed that Negroes would be included. Clark Foreman, Secretary of Interior Harold Ickes's adviser on the economic status of Negroes, participated in the early policy discussions of the National Advisory Committee on Subsistence Homesteads, and Bruce Melvin, a rural sociologist, was given special responsibility for planning projects which would accommodate Negroes, Indians, and Mexican Americans. In January of 1934, Eleanor Roosevelt, who was especially interested in the new community projects, invited a group of Negro leaders to the White House to discuss the special problems involved in providing projects for Negroes.[20]

During the two years of its existence, the Division of Subsistence Homesteads began work on 31 communities, completed 691 houses, and began construction of 1,369 additional homes, but none of these homes was to be occupied by Negroes. The division claimed that "numerous protests on the part of white citizens against colored locations have been one of the major contributing causes of failure." For example, when the nationally known communitarian Ralph Barsodi proposed to establish a Negro community in Dayton, Ohio, 1,100 citizens signed a petition requesting that the project not be constructed because it would lead to the integration of the public schools and a depreciation of property values. Other projects intended for Indianapolis, Indiana, and Petersburg, Virginia, were abandoned when the white people of these cities vigorously protested against the establishment of Negro communities. A project at Helena, Arkansas, was rejected when the local white citizens insisted that the homes for Negroes be built for less money than the homes for whites.[21]

Yet the New Deal's community planners remained sensitive to the needs of Negroes. Early in 1935 the Division of

Subsistence Homesteads decided that something concrete had to be done, and in March it announced that "no new projects for whites would be constructed until a substantial beginning had been made on communities for Negroes." Plans were then begun for the first Negro project, Aberdeen Gardens, near Newport News, Virginia, and it was hoped that eventually about 10 percent of the new homesteaders would be black. But before the division could make any progress toward achieving this goal, President Roosevelt, in May of 1935, transferred responsibility for the community projects to the newly created Resettlement Administration.[22]

The Resettlement Administration and its successor, the Farm Security Administration, made a good deal more progress in developing projects for Negroes. Aberdeen Gardens was opened in August of 1936 and provided facilities for 158 Negro families. During the next four years plans were developed for thirteen additional communities in which Negroes would live, and eighteen standard (not community) rehabilitation projects were also established for Negroes. Altogether by June of 1940 some 1,400 Negro families were living on thirty-two FSA homestead projects in the South, constituting about one-fourth of the total number of families on southern homestead projects.[23]

Thus, the available statistical information indicates that the southern Negro's share of the FSA's tenant purchase loans, rehabilitation loans and resettlement projects was roughly equal to the percentage of Negroes in the entire southern population. Although one could argue, as Walter White and others did, that even this share was inadequate because the Negro's needs were so much greater and because Negroes composed such a large part of the non-landowning class, it is nevertheless a tribute to the fair-mindedness of the FSA's administrators that Negroes participated to such a large extent. It appears that Edwin Embree was correct when he told Walter White that certain officials in Washington had become "alert to the situation and...prepared in spite of counter-pressures to see that the Negro is given a square deal...." [24]

The agitation of groups such as the NAACP was partially responsible for the sensitivity of the FSA's officials to the special problems of Negro tenants. Equally important was the fact that Will W. Alexander was chosen as the first administrator of the Farm Security Administration. Unlike most of the New Deal's agricultural officials, Alexander held strong convictions concerning the need for interracial justice and cooperation. Born in Morrisville, Missouri, educated at Vanderbilt University and Southern College, and ordained as a Methodist minister, Alexander had served from 1931-1935 as president of New Orleans' colored Dillard University. During 1934 and 1935 he was a member of the Rosenwald Foundation's Committee on Minority Groups in Economic Recovery and co-author of the foundation's important report on the manner in which cotton tenants were affected by the AAA. He had served as executive director of the Committee on Interracial Cooperation, chairman of the Social Science Research Council's Committee on Race Studies, a trustee for five southern Negro colleges, and from 1935 to 1937 as Rexford Tugwell's assistant in the Resettlement Administration.

During his service as deputy administrator of the Resettlement Administration, Alexander was constantly plagued by the special problems of Negro tenants. To keep himself informed concerning these special difficulties he hired a Negro, Joseph H. B. Evans, to serve as his administrative assistant, and when Alexander left Resettlement to become the head of Farm Security he took Evans with him. During the next few years other advisers on Negro problems were added to the FSA's central office staff in Washington, and especially important advisory roles were assumed by Mrs. Constance E. H. Daniel and by George S. Mitchell. Moreover, by 1941, each of the three southern regional directors had a colored assistant to advise him concerning the special problems of black tenants. Negroes shared in the FSA benefits to the extent they did only because the Washington and regional offices exerted great pressure on the local authorities to grant benefits to needy farmers regardless of race.[25]

NOTES

1. David Conrad and Donald Hughes Grubbs have written the best accounts of the purge in the AAA. See Conrad, *The Forgotten Farmers: The Story of Sharecroppers in the New Deal* (Urbana: University of Illinois Press, 1965), pp. 194-218, and Grubbs, "The Southern Tenant Farmers' Union and the New Deal" (Ph.D. dissertation, University of Florida, 1963), pp. 155-226. Other useful accounts have been written by Arthur Schlesinger, Jr., *The Coming of the New Deal* (Boston: Houghton Mifflin Company, 1959), pp. 74-81; Russell Lord, *The Wallaces of Iowa* (Boston: Houghton Mifflin Company, 1947), pp. 393-409; Bernard Sternsher, *Rexford Tugwell and the New Deal* (New Brunswick: Rutgers University Press, 1964), pp. 194-208; Gilbert C. Fite, *George Peek and the Fight for Farm Parity* (Norman: University of Oklahoma Press, 1954), pp. 258-266.

2. U. S., Congress, House, "Report of the President's Committee on Farm Tenancy," *House Miscellaneous Documents,* 75th Cong., 1st sess., 10126:iii, 2, 11.

3. U. S., *Statutes at Large,* 49:1148.

4. H. I. Richards, *Cotton Under the Agricultural Adjustment Act* (Washington, D.C.: The Brookings Institution, 1934), pp. 54-55; Edwin G. Nourse, Joseph S. Davis, and John D. Black, *Three Years of the Agricultural Adjustment Administration* (Washington, D.C.: The Brookings Institution, 1937), p. 349; T. J. Woofter, "The Negro Agricultural Worker" (Carnegie-Myrdal Manuscripts, 1940), p. 86; Gunnar Lange, "Agricultural Adjustment Programs and the Negro" (Carnegie-Myrdal

Manuscripts), pp. 34-35; William Holley, Ellen Winston, and T. J. Woofter, *The Plantation South* (Washington, D.C.: Government Printing Office, 1936), p. 44; Grubbs, "The Southern Tenant Farmers' Union and the New Deal," pp. 361-363. Sharecroppers received an even more favorable payment division in the 1938 contract, which provided that cotton landlords should split benefits equally with croppers (as was the case in other crops and as had been the case for cotton in 1933).

5. Conrad, *The Forgotten Farmers: The Story of Sharecroppers in the New Deal*, pp. 199-201; Richards, *Cotton Under the AAA*, p. 55; Grubbs, "The Southern Tenant Farmers' Union," pp. 361-362; Henry Wallace to J. R. McCarl, draft of letter, 2 November 1935, NA RG 16; Chester Davis to McCarl, 28 October 1935, NA RG 145; and Wallace to W. D. McFarlane, 27 March 1937, NA RG 16.

6. Gunnar Myrdal, *An American Dilemma* (New York: Harper & Brothers, 1944), p. 257; Conrad, *Forgotten Farmers*, p. 202; and Lange, "AAA Programs and the Negro," pp. 36-37. The relevant statistical information in U. S., Bureau of the Census, *Fifteenth Census of the United States* (1930), the *Sixteenth Census of the United States* (1940), and the *Census of Agriculture: 1935* has been conveniently summarized by Myrdal, *American Dilemma*, p. 253.

7. Walter White to Edwin R. Embree, 12 April 1935, NAACP Files; Ward Rodgers to the NAACP, memorandum, April, 1935, NAACP Files. I have quoted from the comment which White penciled in the margin of this memo.

8. Walter White to William Rosenwald, 30 August 1935, NAACP Files; White, as quoted by Benjamin Marsh in a speech at the Cosmos Club, 20 April 1935, NAACP Files; White to Winifred Chapel, 15 July 1935, NAACP Files; John P. Davis to White, memorandum, April, 1935, NAACP Files; Davis, as quoted by Marsh in a speech at the Cosmos Club, 20 April 1935, NAACP Files; Resolutions of the Twenty-sixth Annual Conference of the NAACP (1935), NAACP Files; and Joint Committee on National Recovery, memorandum on Bankhead Farm Tenant Homes Act, 23 February 1935, NA RG 183, Oxley File.

9. Walter White, John Davis, Gardner Jackson, Rupert Vance, Norman Thomas, Howard Kester, Jeanette Rankin, Thomas Amlie, and Vito Marcantonio to Paul Appleby, memorandum, 12 November 1936, NA RG 16; Joint Committee on National Recovery, memorandum on Bankhead Farm Tenant Homes Act, 23 February 1935, NA RG 183, Oxley File; and John P. Davis, "Report of the Executive Secretary of the Joint Committee on National Recovery," 1 June 1935, NA RG 183, Oxley File.

10. Charles Houston to Will Alexander, 9 February 1937, NAACP Files; Mark Ethridge to Walter White, 20 September 1937, NAACP Files; White to Ethridge, 22 September 1937, NAACP Files; White to Frederick Douglass Patterson, 24 September 1937, NAACP Files; Thurgood Marshall to W. F. Reden, 11 September 1937, NAACP Files; and White to Editors (Virginius Dabney, Mark Ethridge, James Chappell, Douglas

Southall Freeman, Max Stern, Jonathan Daniels, P. B. Young, Robert L. Vann, C. B. Powell, Robert S. Abbott, and Carl Murphy), 7 September 1937, NAACP Files; NAACP office memorandum, "What Others Say about the Negro and the Farm Tenant Board," 30 October 1937, NAACP Files; White to Franklin D. Roosevelt, telegram, 31 August 1937, NA RG 16; White to Henry Wallace, telegram, 31 August 1937, NA RG 16; Harry L. Brown to White, 10 September 1937, NA RG 16; White to Brown, 15 September 1937, NA RG 16.

11. Edwin R. Embree to Walter White, 16 April 1935, NAACP Files; White to Mark Ethridge, 22 September 1937, NAACP Files; White to William Rosenwald, 30 August 1935, NAACP Files; John P. Davis to White, memorandum, April, 1935, NAACP Files; NAACP office memorandum, "Data on the Bankhead Bill," n.d. [1935], NAACP Files; George Streator to E. Franklin Frazier, Abram Harris, and W. E. B. DuBois, memorandum, [1934], W. E. B. DuBois Papers (hereafter cited as WEBD Papers).

12. U.S., *Statutes at Large*, 50:522. Sidney Baldwin's *Poverty and Politics: The Rise and Decline of the Farm Security Administration* (Chapel Hill: University of North Carolina Press, 1968) is a thoroughly researched, perceptive, and comprehensive account of the FSA.

13. In one important respect the final draft of the legislation was distinctly inferior to the program which Senator Bankhead had first presented to Congress in 1935. When it was originally presented, the Bankhead bill proposed to establish a federal agency which would purchase land for resale to tenants. Yet the final form of the legislation made no provision for government land purchase but merely authorized the establishment of a Farm Security Administration which would loan money to individual tenants. The expenditure of several million dollars each year for the purchase of tenant homesteads would have forced land prices upward regardless of whether the expenditures were made directly by a government agency or by individual farmers. If a government agency was the major buyer and landowners in one area were demanding unreasonable prices, however, the agency could make purchases in another community. Because individual tenants had no such independence, they were more likely to have to pay inflated prices. For a discussion of this point, see J. G. Maddox, "The Bankhead Jones Farm Tenant Act," *Law and Contemporary Problems* 4 (October, 1937):452; Grubbs, "The Southern Tenant Farmers' Union," pp. 546-551; Baldwin, *Poverty and Politics*, p. 181.

14. U. S., Congress, *Congressional Record*, 75th Cong., 1st sess., 81:6438. Yet Lemke added that he was "going to vote for this bill, because it is a toehold, in spite of the fact that it is camouflage and make-believe legislation." M. S. Venkataramani, "Norman Thomas, Arkansas Sharecroppers, and the Roosevelt Agricultural Policies, 1933-1937," *Mississippi Valley Historical Review* 47 (September, 1960): 240; Harry L. Brown to Walter White, 10 September 1937, NA RG 16; Baldwin, *Poverty and Politics*, p. 199.

15. Richard Sterner, *The Negro's Share* (New York: Harper & Brothers, 1943), pp. 305-307; T. J. Woofter, "The Negro and Agricultural Policy," p. 131; Baldwin, *Poverty and Politics*, pp. 196-197.

16. Clarence A. Wiley, "Settlement and Unsettlement in the Resettlement Administration Programs," *Law and Contemporary Problems* 4 (October, 1937):461; and Monroe Oppenheimer, "The Development of the Rural Rehabilitation Loan Program," *Law and Contemporary Problems* 4 (October, 1937): 473-488.

17. Sterner, *The Negro's Share*, pp. 298-300, 305, 421; Wiley, "Settlement and Unsettlement in the Resettlement Administration Program," p. 461; Oppenheimer, "The Development of the Rural Rehabilitation Loan Program," pp. 473-488; and Baldwin, *Poverty and Politics*, pp. 200-203.

18. Lord, *The Wallaces of Iowa*, p. 412.

19. Paul Conkin has written a good account of the New Deal's community program, *Tomorrow a New World* (Ithaca, N.Y.: Cornell University Press, 1959). See also Baldwin, *Poverty and Politics*, pp. 214-216.

20. Conkin, *Tomorrow a New World*, pp. 101, 200; and Clarence Pickett, *For More than Bread* (Boston: Little, Brown & Co. 1953) pp. 48-49. The Negroes present at the White House conference were: John Hope, president of Atlanta University, Robert Moton, president of Tuskegee Institute, Charles S. Johnson of Fisk University, Walter White of the NAACP, and Charles C. Spaulding, president of the North Carolina Mutual Life Insurance Company.

21. Conkin, *Tomorrow a New World*, pp. 129, 201; Rayford Logan, "Negro Status Under the New Deal," *Sphinx*, May, 1935, p. 28; Logan, "Negro Status Under the New Deal," *Sphinx*, February, 1937, p. 38; H. S. Hawkes, William C. Milloway, and Bryan Cooper to Ralph Barsodi, 2 April 1934, NAACP Files; George Edmund Haynes, "The Negro and National Recovery: Part Five—Subsistence Homesteads and the Negro," NAACP Files; J. LeRoy Dukes to Department of Agriculture, 16 November 1937, NA RG 16; John P. Davis, Report of the Executive Secretary of the Joint Committee on National Recovery, 21 February 1934, and 16 March 1934, NA RG 183, Oxley File.

22. Allen Kifer, "The Negro and the New Deal" (Ph.D. dissertation, University of Wisconsin, 1961), p. 161. See also Conkin, *Tomorrow a New World*, p. 129.

23. Sterner, *The Negro's Share*, pp. 307-308, 423. Allen Kifer has written a detailed account of conditions in three Negro community projects: Aberdeen Gardens, Virginia, Tillery, North Carolina, and Gee's Bend, Alabama, "The Negro and the New Deal," pp. 164-201.

24. Edwin R. Embree to Walter White, 16 April 1935, NAACP Files.

25. Kifer, "The Negro and the New Deal," pp. 208-209; Sterner, *The Negro's Share*, p. 300; and Ralph Bunche, "Political Status of the Negro," (Carnegie-Myrdal Manuscripts), pp. 1309-1403. In two respects, even the

FSA refused to insist on equal treatment for Negroes. The FSA employed a large staff of farm and home supervisors, but despite the fact that more than 20 percent of the FSA's southern clients were Negroes, only seventy-two of the more than seven thousand employees appointed in the South were Negroes. The FSA also refused to strike out against segregation. Though no formal declaration was made restricting homesteaders for certain projects according to race, FSA did decide that in practice applicants for rehabilitation communities would have to be selected "according to the sociological pattern of the community." In effect this meant that in certain areas FSA established segregated projects. These segregated developments naturally aroused opposition from integrationist groups such as the NAACP. At its Twenty-fifth Annual Conference (1934), the members of the association called on black and white Americans "to resist to the utmost any and all forms of segregation and discrimination in the federal government." The NAACP insisted particularly that "in the establishment of subsistence homesteads...there be none to which Negro citizens are denied solely on the ground of color." John P. Davis complained bitterly that despite the community programs' optimistic goal of creating a new and better society, its plans were so myopic that "it can only see for the next fifty years, Negro ghettoes, separate and apart from white communities." On this point, see Conkin, *Tomorrow a New World*, p. 200; Resolutions of the Twenty-fifth Annual Conference of the NAACP (1934), NAACP Files; NAACP Press Release, 30 June 1935, NAACP Files; Report of the Executive Secretary of the Joint Committee on National Recovery, 16 March 1934, NA RG 183, Oxley File. In certain parts of his very good study of the FSA, Sidney Baldwin has implied that the agency's leaders should not have compromised with race discrimination and should have concerned themselves more with the problems of the most impoverished tenants rather than with a carefully selected elite that was likely to make a good showing on loan collection records. Such an emphasis doubtless would have been more in keeping with FSA's moral commitment to deal with hard-core poverty; but, as Baldwin himself notes, any disruption of the Southern caste and class system would have sacrificed FSA's political capital and jeopardized the life of all its programs. Sidney Baldwin, *Poverty and Politics*, chaps. 7, 8, and 9, and especially pp. 196-197, 200-201, 217, 218, 255, and 279.

Summary

Official spokesmen for the Roosevelt administration maintained that general economic prosperity could not be restored unless the farm population were prosperous enough to purchase a substantial portion of the goods produced in other sectors of the economy. Time and again they insisted that the farmers' buying power would have to be increased if economic recovery were to be achieved. Consequently, the Congress provided an Agricultural Adjustment program to "relieve the existing national emergency by increasing agricultural purchasing power."

When the Agricultural Adjustment program was inaugurated, the 500,000 wealthiest farmers, constituting about 8 percent of the total number, received 40 percent of the national agricultural income while the bottom 50 percent of the farm population received less than 15 percent of the total farm income. There were more than three million farm families that received less than $1,000 per year. It would seem that an administration which believed that farm operators must receive a larger share of the national income would have taken steps to ensure that those farmers who were most in need would share the benefits of the government's new agricultural program.

Southern Negro farm tenants and wage laborers were the most impoverished major group of farm workers in the United States. They naturally hoped that the new agricultural program would be constructed in such a way as to bring relief to them. Yet the Roosevelt administration allowed both the formulation and administration of its cotton program to be controlled by those who were particularly sensitive to the power of southern congressmen and landowning farmers. As a consequence, the politically impotent Negro tenant farmers did not receive a fair share of the AAA benefits, and the desperate condition of many was aggravated when employers discovered that they could farm their reduced acreage with less labor and evicted farm operators by the thousand.

After 1935, the federal government made some commendable attempts to relieve the condition of the non-landowning farm operators. The FSA in particular was scrupulously fair in its treatment of Negro farmers. However, the scope of the FSA program did not compare with that of the AAA. While 192,000 Negro farm tenants were displaced during the 1930s, the FSA provided fewer than 2,000 tenant purchase loans to Negroes and resettled only 1,400 Negro families in its community projects. Reinhold Niebuhr has correctly observed that "There is no more striking irony in modern politics than the fact that the provisions of the Agricultural Adjustment Administration, designed to alleviate the condition of the American farmer, should have aggravated the lot of the poorest of our farmers, the southern sharecroppers."[1]

NOTES

1. Reinhold Niebuhr, Foreword to Howard Kester's, *Revolt Among the Sharecroppers*, (New York: Covici, Friede, 1936), p. iv.

PART TWO

Industrial Recovery and the Black Worker

5

The Need for Industrial Recovery

Purchasing Power and the NRA

ECONOMIC indices from 1933 suggest that conditions in industry were just as desperate as those in agriculture. The Federal Reserve Board estimated that manufacturing production had declined by more than half, from an index figure of 120 in 1929 to 57 in 1933, and other estimates, such as that of the *New York Times'* weekly index of business activity, reinforced this appraisal. Gross national product declined by almost 30 percent, from $104 billion to $75 billion, and the total value of all commodities at current prices fell even more, from $38 billion to $17 billion. According to the Bureau of Labor Statistics, more than twelve million workers were unemployed in March of 1933, and other organizations such as the

American Federation of Labor and the Labor Research Association placed the figure much higher. Altogether, about one-fourth of the total number of American wage and salary earners were entirely without work, and millions more were working only part-time. Under these circumstances it was apparent that the great objectives of the Roosevelt administration necessarily would be to increase national production and put more men to work. The problem was all the more pressing because it was generally recognized that the administration's attempts to stimulate agricultural recovery would increase the cost of farm products. Unless there was a parallel stimulation of industrial activity, a crushing burden would fall on the already hard-pressed urban population.[1]

Many New Dealers believed that the prosperity of the 1920s had been undermined and the depression initiated largely because advances in technology and organization enabled the nation to increase its production enormously while the demand for products remained relatively stable. During the 1920s, productivity per worker grew steadily, increasing by more than 40 percent, but contemporary studies showed that wages and salaries did not grow in proportion to the increase in production. While some prominent Americans maintained that there was no serious maldistribution of wealth, economist Paul Douglas of the University of Chicago calculated that eleven million American families earned less than the $1,500 per year which he believed was necessary to support minimum standards of health and decency. And the famous Brookings Institution study, *America's Capacity to Consume*, estimated that the nation's richest 631,000 families received a larger income than the 16,000,000 families at the bottom of the economic scale. Studies such as these indicated that whole sections of the population did not share the prosperity of the

1920s and consequently were not able to help the nation consume its increasing output.[2]

Believing that in the modern world most goods are produced for sale, many New Dealers concluded that the volume of production and the level of employment could be increased by expanding the total amount of purchasing power. Maintaining that underconsumption or lack of demand was one of the major causes of the economic decline, they insisted that the government, in the interest of general recovery, should take decisive steps to increase the wages of the working class. They reasoned that workers would spend their increased purchasing power and that consequently manufacturers would have to expand operations. This expansion of production would give employment to yet more workers, who in turn would increase the aggregate level of spending and create a demand for still more production and employment. Thus, it was hoped, the vicious spiral of deflation would be broken and the salutary spiral of economic recovery inaugurated.[3]

Knowing that purchasing power could be increased most effectively by supplementing the wages of the nation's lowest paid workers, the New Deal planners breathed new life into the generation-old struggle for minimum wage legislation. Further, it was thought that work for the unemployed could be created by limiting the number of hours worked by those already employed. The major obstacle in the way of implementing such a strategy was that during the depression few businessmen could afford the increased production costs that higher wages and shorter hours would entail. Even if nine out of every ten employers in a given field agreed with the New Dealers' analysis of the need for more purchasing power, there was always the danger that one producer would attempt to capture a larger share of the market for himself by reducing costs and underselling his competitors. Thus, when the Cotton Textile Institute agreed not to work women at night, 15 percent of the manufacturers refused to comply, and the agreement broke down. In this manner, businessmen of the lowest character often were able to set the standards for entire industries. "Cutthroat competition," Sidney Hillman of the Amalgamated Clothing Workers once observed, "makes the unscrupulous employer the leader in each industry and the rest willingly or otherwise follow."[4]

To raise wage and hour standards, then, it was necessary to find some way whereby *all* producers in an industry could be induced to observe better standards. Consequently, the New Deal planners began to consider the possibility of requiring licenses which would be issued only to businesses that complied with government-approved standards. To sweeten the pill of government regulation, the New Dealers pointed out that, in addition to the promise of economic recovery, there were certain immediate and definite advantages which would accrue if all employers observed the new standards. In the first place, by establishing standards of fair competition, scrupulous employers would no longer be at the mercy of ruthless competitors. Secondly, the establishment of standards offered the opportunity for businessmen to join together to eliminate certain unfair trade practices such as false advertising, discriminatory price-cutting, industrial espionage, and rebates. Finally, employers were to be invited to join together to determine fair production costs, which no one would be permitted to undercut. To alleviate any legal anxieties about such collaboration, the New Deal planners proposed to exempt such activities from the coverage of the nation's antitrust legislation.

Yet while believing that there was an urgent need to allow business cooperation for the purpose of outlawing long hours and low wages, the New Deal planners recognized that businessmen might use suspension of the antitrust laws and authorization not to sell below cost as an excuse for unnecessarily raising prices to the consumer. Hugh Johnson, who would become the first administrator of the Roosevelt administration's industrial recovery program, expressed the views of many New Dealers when he admitted that higher wages would lead to higher prices, but he warned that "if we do a thing like this and do not also put some control on undue price increases so that prices will not move up one bit faster than is justified by higher costs, the consuming public is going to suffer, the higher wages won't do any good, and the whole bright chance will just turn out to be a ghastly failure and another shattered hope."[5]

There was also the very real danger that large industrialists would take advantage of the opportunities presented by government-sponsored cooperation to make agreements for industrywide retrenchment. It was generally believed that during periods of recession some individual corporations could minimize short-run losses by restricting production, but the New Deal planners also knew that while such a policy might benefit the individual concerns, it would have disastrous effects on the economy as a whole. Such a policy inevitably would lead to the dismissal of workers and thus diminish further the purchasing power of the masses of people.[6]

The New Deal planners were aware of these dangers at the outset, but they felt there was no alternative but to gamble that businessmen would see that their own long-range self-interest demanded that they combine to establish fair wages and hours without at the same time agreeing to raise prices unduly or restrict production. The problem, as the New Dealers analyzed the situation, was to devise a method whereby prices could be raised enough to enable employers to provide decent wages and hours without raising them so much as to cancel out the increased purchasing power of the higher wages. Many NRA enthusiasts were convinced that such a method could be discovered, that prices need not rise as fast as wages. Paul Douglas, who served as a consultant for the NRA's Bureau of Economic Education, expressed these optimistic views when he declared that as a result of higher minimum wages "the increased monetary purchasing power in the hands of the workers would lead to an increased volume of purchases, and this should reduce overhead costs, which tend either to be constant or not to increase in the same ratio as output." Since total costs would not rise in the same proportion as wages, Douglas concluded that "a net increase in purchasing power should take place." Accepting this idea, President Roosevelt asked that "managements give first consideration to the improvement of operating figures by greatly increased sales to be expected from the rising purchasing power of the public." He reminded the nation's businessmen that "the aim of this whole effort is to restore our rich domestic market by raising its vast consuming capacity. If we now inflate prices as fast and as far as we increase wages, the whole project will be set at naught."[7]

With certain modifications and exceptions, these ideas were generally accepted by high officials in the new administration, and they were incorporated in the recovery program which Congress enacted on June 16, 1933. Noting the existence of "a national emergency productive of widespread unemployment and disorganization of industry," the National Industrial Recovery Act declared that the economy would be invigorated by "increas[ing] the consumption of industrial and agricultural products by increasing purchasing power." To effectuate this policy, the president was authorized to establish a National Recovery Administration (NRA) which would assume responsibility for organizing a system of industrial self-government under government supervision. The NRA was "to provide for the general welfare by promoting cooperative action among trade groups...under adequate governmental sanctions and supervision, to eliminate unfair competitive practices...to improve standards of labor, and otherwise rehabilitate industry." Whenever NRA found that "destructive wage or price cutting or other activities contrary to the policy of this [Act] are being practiced," it was authorized to license businesses which were complying with the national standards, and only those firms could "engage in or carry on any business in or affecting interstate or foreign commerce."[8]

The purpose of the recovery program was explained further in the speeches and congressional testimony of various New Deal officials closely associated with NRA. Testifying before the House Ways and Means Committee, Donald Richberg, who would soon be appointed assistant to the administrator of NRA, maintained that ruthless competition should not be permitted to undermine labor standards. He characterized the NRA as a "tremendous experiment," because by prescribing minimum standards which all employers in a given industry must observe, NRA encouraged business organizations "to get together to establish agreements that will promote fair competition, and primarily, from my point of view, fair competition as to labor; fair competition in wages and working conditions." Similarly, New York's Democratic Senator Robert F. Wagner, who was generally regarded as the leading congressional sponsor of the new legislation, maintained that there was an urgent need to outlaw sweatshops, long hours, and low wages. "The bill does not abolish competition," Wagner insisted, "it purifies and strengthens it." Competition would be retained, but it would be "competition on a high standard of efficiency rather than on a low standard of exploitation of labor." He predicted that NRA was "going to have not only a great economic effect by increasing purchasing power, but also a great social effect in giving the worker a wage which will permit him to live in decency." Hugh Johnson made the same point in his own colorful language when he explained that the NRA codes of fair practices would "eliminate eye-gouging and knee-groining and ear-chewing in business. Above the belt any man can be just as rugged and just as individual as he pleases." President Roosevelt explained:

> The Act proposes to our industry a great spontaneous co-operation to put millions of men back in their regular jobs. . . . The idea is simply for employers to hire more men to do the existing work by reducing the work-hours of each man's week and at the same time paying a living wage for the shorter week.
>
> No employer and no group of less than all employers in a single trade could do this alone and continue to live in business competition. But if *all* employers in each trade now bind themselves faithfully in these modern guilds—without exception—and agree to act together and at once, none will be hurt and millions of workers, so long deprived of the right to earn their bread in the sweat of their labor, can raise their heads again. The challenge of this law is whether we can sink selfish interest and present a solid front against a common peril.[9]

The Economic Status of the Urban Negro

Available statistics indicate that the position of urban

Negroes during the Great Depression was particularly desperate. Reports from Urban League investigators in 106 American cities revealed that "with a few notable exceptions...the proportion of Negroes unemployed was from 30 to 60 percent greater than for whites." The first reliable government statistics relating the "color or race" of families receiving relief pointed out that Negroes were "added to the relief rolls twice as frequently [in proportion to their number in the total 1930 population] by loss of private employment as whites, and are removed through finding places in private employment only half as frequently." In October of 1933 Negroes on relief comprised 17.8 percent of the total Negro population, whereas 9.5 percent of the non-Negro population was on relief. The Federal Emergency Relief Administration reported that in the nation's cities the proportion of all persons on relief was almost three times as high for Negroes (26.7 percent) as for whites (9.6 percent), and the Urban League declared that in some cities the situation was even worse: in Englewood, New Jersey, Negroes accounted for more than 90 percent of the relief cases though they comprised less than 20 percent of the population; in Detroit the 4 percent Negro population supplied one-quarter of the relief cases; and Negroes in St. Louis, only 9 percent of the total population, accounted for 60 percent of the relief cases.[10]

A number of factors were responsible for the preponderance of Negroes unemployed. When jobs were scarce, preference generally was given to white workers, and in some areas there was a tendency to dismiss Negroes in order to make jobs available for whites. The situation was complicated further because the largest concentrations of black industrial workers were in building construction and bituminous coal mining— two fields that were notoriously stagnant during the years of the Great Depression. In addition, many urban Negroes were employed as marginal, unskilled workers (almost 25 percent worked as household domestics), and often their services could be dispensed with most easily when the first distress of the depression was felt. Moreover, when technological innovation made certain jobs more attractive, Negroes frequently were replaced by white workers. When motor trucks were introduced in transportation, for example, many new "white men's jobs" were created out of old "Negro jobs." Even when black workers were not directly displaced by technological change, they often suffered indirectly. When the skill of a group of white workers was liquidated by an invention, they fell into the category of unskilled workers competing with Negro labor. Consequently, during the depression, Negroes discovered that they were no longer fighting to advance their position; rather they were struggling to avoid losses. T. Arnold Hill, the industrial secretary of the Urban League, assessed the situation correctly when he observed that "heretofore [the Negro's] employment problem has been chiefly one of advancement to positions commensurate with his ability. Today he is endeavoring to hold the line against advancing armies of white workers intent upon gaining and content to accept occupations which were once thought too menial for white hands."[11]

Because of their desperate economic plight, it was to be expected that many Negroes would rally in support of the new administration's program for economic recovery. Throughout the country, black citizens joined the gigantic parades and demonstrations which were organized in support of the NRA. In telegrams to President Roosevelt many Negro fraternal, business, and religious organizations pledged their "whole-hearted allegiance to the successful carrying through of this noble adventure." The Negro press generally supported the recovery program, believing, to cite the *Pittsburgh Courier* as an example, that "the National Recovery Act is destined to be a lifesaver to the colored American." *Opportunity*, the journal of the National Urban League, expressed attitudes that were widely held in the Negro community when it declared that "a minimum wage...and maximum hours of work...will be of immeasurable benefit to...black workers who are unskilled and confined to the lowest paid jobs in the industrial system."[12]

Yet the more perceptive Negro leaders recognized that black workers faced many problems in addition to those common to other American workers. They feared that while the new reforms might ameliorate the perilous condition of the population as a whole, they would not necessarily improve the position of black workers, because Negroes were affected by the factor of race as well as that of economic condition. In May of 1933 the delegates to the Rosenwald Foundation's Conference on the Economic Status of the Negro pointed out that definite measures for the recognition of colored labor would be needed if the recovery program were to benefit Negroes. They warned that "unless the claims of the Negro are definitely and persistently brought before [the recovery agencies] there is a real danger that he will be overlooked, and that the reorganization of industry may leave him in a worse position than before." Making the same point, the National Urban League prepared a special report for President Roosevelt, calling his attention to these special difficulties and requesting that the president personally take steps to ensure that Negroes would not be overlooked in the plans for economic recovery.[13]

Mr. Roosevelt claimed he was "very glad" to receive the

Urban League's "factual summary," and he asked Frances Perkins, the Secretary of Labor, to inform Eugene Kinkle Jones, the league's executive secretary, that he realized "the unfavorable economic position of the Negro, and the tremendous suffering which the present depression has brought to them." Miss Perkins went on to reassure Jones that the Roosevelt administration would "not forget the special problems of the more than ten million people who belong to your race." In another statement which was widely quoted in the Negro press, President Roosevelt himself assured C. C. Spaulding, the Negro president of the North Carolina Mutual Life Insurance Company, that "the entire recovery program of the administration has been planned from its initiation to aid the nation toward recovery by providing necessary assistance and regulatory measures for all persons without regard to race." Later, when a Negro reporter questioned Roosevelt concerning the effect that NRA would have on black workers, the president insisted that "the plan and spirit of the NRA is designed solely to give the average citizen greater returns for his labor and subsequent security for himself and his family. The elimination of inequalities and class distinctions are the underlying principles of the National Recovery Administration."[14]

NOTES

1. Irving Bernstein, *The Lean Years* (Boston: Houghton Mifflin Company, 1960), pp. 316-317; David A. Shannon, *Between the Wars: America, 1919-1941* (Boston: Houghton Mifflin Company, 1965), pp. 109-111; Raymond Moley, *After Seven Years* (New York: Harper & Brothers, 1939), p. 185; Leverett S. Lyon, *The National Recovery Administration* (Washington, D.C.: The Brookings Institution, 1939), p. 754; Arthur M. Schlesinger, Jr., *The Coming of the New Deal* (Boston: Houghton Mifflin Company, 1959), p. 87.

2. John K. Galbraith, *The Great Crash* (Boston: Houghton Mifflin Com-

pany, 1961), p. 180; Paul H. Douglas, *Wages and the Family* (Chicago: University of Chicago Press, 1925), pp. 5-6; Maurice Leven, Harold G. Moulton, and Clark Warburton, *America's Capacity to Consume* (Washington, D.C.: The Brookings Institution, 1934), p. 28 and passim; Simon Kuznets, *National Income and Its Composition, 1919-1938* (New York: National Bureau of Economic Research, 1941), pp. 216-217, 332-333, 352-353; Edwin G. Nourse, and associates, *America's Capacity to Produce* (Washington, D.C.: The Brookings Institution, 1934), passim; George Soule, *Prosperity Decade* (New York: Rinehart & Co., 1947), pp. 47-82; J. Joseph Huthmacher, *Senator Robert F. Wagner and the Rise of Urban Liberalism* (New York: Atheneum, 1968), pp. 193-194.

3. Leonard Ayres, *The Economics of Recovery* (New York: Macmillan Company, 1934), p. 95; Charles L. Dearing, Paul T. Homan, Lewis L. Lorwin, and Leverett S. Lyon, *The ABC of the NRA* (Washington, D.C.: The Brookings Institution, 1934), pp. 28-32.

4. Sidney Hilman, as quoted by Schlesinger, *The Coming of the New Deal*, p. 90.

5. Hugh Johnson, as quoted by Dearing, et al., *The ABC of the NRA*, p. 32.

6. For a good example of these apprehensions, see the confidential memorandum that Gardiner Means prepared for Henry Wallace. This memorandum was published in January, 1935, as *Senate Document*, no. 13, 74th Cong., 1st sess., under the title "Industrial Prices and their Relative Inflexibility." It has been reprinted in Means, *The Corporate Revolution in America* (New York: Collier Books, 1962), pp. 77-96.

7. Paul H. Douglas, "The Role of the Consumer in the New Deal," *The Annals of the American Academy of Political and Social Science* 172 (March, 1934):99; Franklin D. Roosevelt, as quoted by Lyon, *The NRA*, p. 758. My interpretation of the rationale behind the industrial recovery program differs from that given by Ellis W. Hawley in his fine monograph, *The New Deal and the Problem of Monopoly* (Princeton: Princeton University Press, 1966). Hawley acknowledges that some New Deal recovery planners placed primary emphasis on the need for more purchasing power, but he believes there was no consensus on this point. Other New Deal planners insisted that the depression was caused by excessive competition that destroyed profitable operations, undermined business confidence, and reduced the rate of investment. The solution, according to this view, lay in government measures to stop destructive competition, ensure reasonable profits, and thereby restore the business confidence that was thought to be an essential prerequisite for recovery. Hawley has brilliantly delineated the nuances of these two theories and has demonstrated that among the New Deal officials there was some confusion over the precise meaning of the recovery program. Yet it seems to me that much of this confusion can be explained in terms of the audiences to which the various explanations were offered. When addressing groups of businessmen, spokesmen for the Roosevelt administration tended to stress the need for legislation that

would suppress "chiseling" and "cutthroat competition" while providing simultaneously for price fixing, production control, and industrial leadership by "responsible and enlightened businessmen." When speaking to the general public, the administration emphasized the need for raising wages and spreading work while holding prices down and thereby increasing purchasing power. I have emphasized this second line of thinking, not because it represents the totality of New Deal thought with regard to recovery, but because, in my judgment, it represents the mainstream. To be sure, there were many crosscurrents within the administration, and at times the New Deal defies consistent explanation. Nevertheless, it seems to me that microscopic examinations of conflicting New Deal viewpoints tend to obscure the amount of consistency and direction that was present. Moreover, the New Dealers, when explaining their recovery program to Negroes, unabashedly spoke in terms of higher wages, shorter hours, and increased purchasing power, and later Negro disillusionment with the program can be understood properly only when we recall that Negroes had been assured that they would benefit from the program—not because they had been singled out for special consideration but because they preeminently belonged to the class whose condition the new program was designed to ameliorate.

8. U. S., *Statutes at Large*, 48:195.

9. U. S., Congress, House, *Hearing Before the House Committee on Ways and Means*, 73rd Cong., 1st sess., pp. 68-69, 105; Robert F. Wagner, as quoted by Dearing et al., *The ABC of the NRA*, pp. 12-13; Hugh Johnson, *The Blue Eagle* (New York: Doubleday, Doran and Company, 1935), p. 282; F. D. Roosevelt, "Presidential Statement on NIRA," in *The Public Papers and Addresses of Franklin D. Roosevelt*, ed. Samuel I. Rosenman (New York: Random House, 1938-1950), 2:252.

10. *Annual Report of the National Urban League, 1931*, pp. 10-11, Urban League Files; "How Unemployment Affects Negroes," typescript, Urban League Files; "Unemployment Status of the Negro," typescript, Urban League Files; Federal Emergency Relief Administration, *Unemployment Relief Census*, October, 1933, Urban League Files; "Negroes Out of Work," *Nation*, 22 April 1931, pp. 441-442.

11. T. Arnold Hill, "The Present Status of Negro Labor," *Opportunity* 7 (May, 1929):145; Charles S. Johnson, "Incidence Upon the Negroes," *American Journal of Sociology* 40 (May, 1935):737-745; idem, "Present Trends in the Employment of Negro Labor," *Opportunity* 7 (May, 1929):147; A. Philip Randolph, "The Economic Crisis of the Negro," *Opportunity* 9 (May, 1931):145-149; Gunnar Myrdal, *An American Dilemma* (New York: Harper & Brothers, 1944), p. 206; Soule, *Prosperity Decade*, pp. 170-178; Lawrence Oxley to Frances Perkins, 9 November 1935, NA RG 183, Oxley File; National Urban League, "Our Negro Working Population and National Recovery: A Special Memorandum Submitted to Franklin Delano Roosevelt," 4 January 1937, Urban League Files.

12. For one example of a mass Negro demonstration in favor of the NRA, see the account in the *Norfolk Journal and Guide*, 2 September 1933. A number of the telegrams have been collected in the President's Personal File (PPF) 1019, Franklin D. Roosevelt Library. The quotation is from "A Declaration of Faith in the Spirit of the National Recovery Act by the Colored Churches of the District of Columbia," typescript, 24 October 1933, PPF, FDR Library; *Pittsburgh Courier*, 8 July 1933; *Opportunity* 11 (July, 1933):199.

13. U. S., Department of Labor, "Washington Conference on the Economic Status of the Negro," *Monthly Labor Review* 37 (July, 1933):42-44; National Urban League, "A Special Memorandum on the Social Adjustment of Negroes in the United States," 15 April 1933, Urban League Files.

14. Frances Perkins to Eugene K. Jones, 27 April 1933, Urban League Files; Franklin D. Roosevelt to C. C. Spaulding, 5 July 1935, PPF 2667, FDR Library; *New York Age*, 7 July 1935; *Chicago Defender*, 7 October 1933.

6

Wages and Hours

The Case for a Racial Differential

TRADITIONALLY Negroes had encountered substantial difficulties in their attempts to find industrial employment, particularly in the South where many factory jobs were restricted for whites only. Yet even in the South many Negroes were employed in industry, though generally at lower wages than their white fellow workers. During the 1930s black workers played an important part in the manufacture of tobacco, and the majority of unskilled workers in the southern lumber, fertilizer, laundry, and iron and steel industries were Negroes. Moreover, because Negro wages tended to be lower than the wages of whites who were doing the same work, some employers in the predominantly white industries gave employment to Negroes in order to cut production costs.[1]

Many southern manufacturers believed that the presence of a cheap and plentiful supply of black labor was one of their primary assets and that without this advantage they could not succeed in their attempts to attract new businesses and investment capital. Consequently, some of them traveled to the NRA code hearings in Washington to testify in favor of a lower minimum wage for the South, and particularly for southern Negroes. These employers emphasized that it had been traditional to pay Negro workers less than whites, and they insisted that it would not be advisable to "disturb the economic conditions of the South." They feared that Negro agricultural laborers, who were receiving from thirty to sixty cents for a hard day's work, would become dissatisfied and unmanageable if a few black industrial workers received as much as $10 or $12 per week in NRA jobs. They insisted that Negro labor was needed on the farms and predicted that "the whole sociological condition" of predominantly agricultural areas would be upset by the payment of high wages to a few Negroes. As one southern businessman put it, "a negro makes a much better workman and a much better citizen, insofar as the South is concerned, when he is not paid the highest wage." Along with many others, he urged NRA "to come out immediately with the statement of a materially modified wage scale for unskilled colored labor."[2]

Several reasons were advanced to justify payment of a lower minimum wage to Negro workers. Many employers believed that the cost of living in the South was lower than in the North. William G. Anderson of the Bibb Manufacturing Company, Macon, Georgia, expressed this view when he suggested that a southern family of four could live on a food budget of $1.35 per week, and that by increasing the budget to $1.68 "such luxuries as meat, coffee, and sugar could be included." Senator Ellison D. "Cotton Ed" Smith of South Carolina expressed a similar opinion when he declared that "South

Carolina's living conditions are so kindly that it takes only 50 cents a day for one to live comfortably and reasonably, and up in the New England States it takes a dollar and a half a day." Moreover, many people believed that blacks could survive on less than whites, that, for example, they could live on a diet of fatback and corn, while white men could not.[3]

Negro leaders rejected the contention that it cost less to live in the South. This, they maintained, was a popular myth based on the prices of relatively few items, such as movie tickets or weekly wages of domestic servants. Walter White of the NAACP insisted that there were many hundreds of items and services bought during the course of a year, and he maintained that adequate comparisons could not be based on the prices of a few items. He pointed out that most of the evidence indicating the existence of a geographical differential in the cost of living came from comparing the costs of the items actually consumed by families of similar sizes, and he argued that such comparisons were invalid "since the goods and services one buys and the amount one spends for such goods and services are governed by the income one receives," not by the cost of the products.[4]

White believed that the only valid method for determining the existence of a regional differential in the cost of living would be to compare the cost of a specific list of goods in one area with the cost of similar or equivalent goods in another region. Studies made under the auspices of the Urban League and independent studies conducted by William Ogburn and his staff at the University of Chicago had indicated that there was only a slight regional variation in the cost of the important items on the family budget. White repeatedly called these studies to the attention of government officials who, partly as a result of his persistent prompting, undertook their own investigations which, when published in 1939, indicated that living costs in the South were only 3 percent lower than costs in the North. These studies convinced Negro leaders that the southern and Negro cost of living was not lower but rather that southerners lived differently and on a lower standard. If a laborer spent less in the South than in the North, it was because his wages were lower, not because it cost appreciably less to live in the South.[5]

Southern advocates of a differential wage also claimed that Negro labor was inefficient and that consequently business-men could not afford to pay black workers the same wages as whites. J. F. Ames of Montgomery, Alabama, prepared a study of "The Subnormal Negro and the Subnormal Code," in which he maintained that Negro labor was 30 percent less efficient than white. Charles H. Stone, a dyestuffs manufacturer from Charlotte, North Carolina, expressed the same point of view when he declared that white men were one-third more efficient than Negroes and announced that he would pay black workers twenty cents an hour and whites twenty-five and thirty cents. Accepting this reasoning, the Scripto Manu-facturing Company of Atlanta, Georgia, announced that it would continue its practice of having two wage scales—one for Negroes and the other for whites. In a special memoran-dum addressed "to all colored employees," the management explained:

> This company does not base wages on color but entirely on efficiency. . . . Our records show that the efficiency of colored help is only 50 per cent of that of white help in similar plants. . . . If the "false friends" of the colored people do not stop their propaganda about paying the same wages to colored and white employees this company will be forced to move the factory to a section where the minimum wage will produce the greatest production. Stop your "false friends" from talking you out of a job.[6]

Negro leaders hastened to point out that there was no conclusive evidence that black labor was less efficient than white. On the contrary, Negro economists such as Robert C. Weaver, who was then working as an adviser to Secretary of Interior Harold Ickes, and Lawrence Oxley, the adviser on Negro affairs in the Department of Labor, pointed out that "the assumption of lesser efficiency for Negroes has not been proved, and all the evidence we have about relative efficiency seems to refute the assertion." Weaver and Oxley contended that detailed studies made by the Chicago Commission on Race Relations, by the Detroit Bureau of Governmental Research, and by the Pennsylvania Department of Public Welfare presented statistical evidence indicating that the supposed superiority of white labor was a myth. With this evidence they concluded that "there is no reason for setting the wage for Negro labor below that for white workers." "Pleas for separate minimum wages for colored workers," Weaver suggested, "were not founded upon inferior colored efficiency but upon a traditional attitude toward Negro labor."[7]

The most telling and important argument for a lower minimum wage for Negroes was the contention that if black workers were not given such differential treatment they would be displaced by whites. Congressman J. Mark Wilcox of Florida stated the matter succinctly to his colleagues in the House of Representatives: "Many of our Northern friends may honestly think that by forcing a uniform wage scale upon the South they are doing the Negro a real service," he acknowledged. "But those who know the facts know that when employers are forced to pay the same wage to the Negro that is paid to the white man the Negro will not be employed. . . . This is just another instance of the well-intentioned but misguided interference of our uninformed neighbors in a

delicate racial problem." The *Atlanta Constitution* editorialized in a similar vein when it declared that the NRA's attempt
to fix a uniform minimum weekly wage was "prohibitive and
will deprive colored women of employment, and white labor
will be substituted." The *Thomasville* [Georgia] *Times-
Enterprise* spoke even more emphatically: "It is safe to say that
no store in town with delivery or porter service will sign an
agreement to pay that boy fourteen dollars per week. If he
[sic] does the messenger will be some white boy who will
work satisfactorily." Letters from several sections of the South
informed NRA administrators that, as Virginia attorney
Charles Kaufman put it, "differentials in wages and working
hours have kept the colored people in many jobs which would
otherwise have been filled by whites."[8]

Most Negroes realized that some black workers would lose
their jobs if a lower minimum wage were not established. Nevertheless, Negro leaders generally were opposed to any
legislation that seemed to brand black workers as inferior.
They recognized that the federal government's responsibility
for maintaining economic security was increasing, and, knowing that in the past the Negro's political, economic, and social
progress had been due, largely, to the aggrandizement of
federal power over states' rights, most black leaders favored
the growing centralization of power in Washington. It was
precisely because they recognized and welcomed the growing
importance of the federal government that Negro leaders
insisted that black workers should receive their full and fair
share of the government's benefits. Their opposition to the
proposed NRA wage differential was motivated in large part
by the belief that this was the entering wedge of a drive to
officially classify Negroes as inferiors who deserved only
substandard benefits from the federal government. The

NAACP, for example, predicted that "these codes will serve as standards for decades, if not generations," and the association declared that racial differentials would place a stigma of inferiority on Negroes "which it would take years of suffering and misery to work off."[9]

For some Negroes a second and equally important reason for opposition to the proposed wage differential was the growing belief that the black masses and the white working-men had a certain community of interests and that no effort should be spared in the attempt to effect an alliance between the black and white working classes. Robert Weaver, for example, believed that it would be better to keep the two races on a parity than to create so wide a difference in pay that antagonisms would be aroused; he objected to the differential primarily because "it would destroy any possibility of ever forming a strong and effective labor movement in the nation." Robert Russa Moton, the president emeritus of Tuskegee Institute, expressed a similar view when he declared that it would be better for Negroes to lose their jobs than to be "put down by organized labor and unorganized laborers as a group of strikebreakers and 'scabs.' " Making the same point, the delegates to the Urban League's 1933 convention resolved that they were "unalterably opposed to differential wage codes...based on the color of a worker's skin." Explaining this position, the delegates declared that "one cannot honestly and sincerely prosecute the cause of the Negro worker without recognizing the importance of collective bargaining.... We should see that the black laboring masses become innoculated with the labor point of view. No intelligent social program for the Negro can straddle this issue."[10]

Negroes knew that in the past it had been common to pay

black workers less than whites, but they believed that this
"traditional" policy had been an important cause of the
depression and that economic recovery could be achieved
only by increasing mass purchasing power. The standard
argument employed by the NAACP and the Urban League
emphasized that the nation desperately needed more spending power in the hands of every farmer and wage earner and
that if Negroes earned more money they would spend it, thus
fulfilling President Roosevelt's hopes for increased purchases
of commodities and food. Walter White and Roy Wilkins of
the NAACP directed personal appeals along these lines to "a
number of the more intelligent southern editors." Pointing out
that Negroes comprised from one-fourth to one-half of the
population in most southern states, they contended that it was
impossible for the white South to achieve prosperity unless it
was willing to permit southern Negroes to share in the
economic benefits. T. Arnold Hill of the Urban League made
a similar appeal; noting the New Dealers' arguments in favor
of increased purchasing power, Hill pointed out that "the
starvation wages received by Negroes have been directly
responsible for limiting the economic security of all workers,
as well as for contracting the market for consumer goods."[11]

A few white southerners accepted this reasoning. W. T.
Anderson, the editor of the *Macon Telegraph*, made a strong
plea for equal wages for Negroes. He noted that after
inaugurating a Negro news section the *Telegraph*'s income
from Negro subscriptions rose from $2,700 per year to $45,000,
and this increase in circulation naturally brought in additional
advertising from national accounts. Anderson believed that
"what the Negro has done for the *Telegraph* and Macon he
will do for Georgia—for the merchants and every other interest in this state, if he is given the chance." Those employers

who were urging a lower wage level for Negroes, he concluded, "are offering a dangerous proposal. If put into effect, it would undermine the President's program of economic recovery in the South, and at the same time would cut the foundations from under the feet of white workingmen." Making a similar point, Representative Maury Maverick of Texas maintained that "as far as I am concerned, if a black man does the same work as a white man, he ought to receive the same pay. I do not see anything terrible about this. I think Negroes should have economic justice. If a Negro makes good pay, he spends it—just like a white man. Purchasing power builds business, prosperity, and the Nation. If a Negro gets fair wages, he will spend, pay taxes, hire a doctor for his health, send his kids to school, be a better citizen, and contribute his part rather than being a burden."[12]

But, as Maverick's name suggests, these were minority sentiments. A letter to editor Anderson of the *Telegraph* summarized the majority viewpoint succinctly: "Your speeches and editorials on the greater things promised the South in the new deal are fine, and every word is gospel," the writer observed. "But when you talk about being fair and generous toward the Negro you are on an unpopular side, and you had better watch out." Negro leaders were convinced that the allegations concerning the cheaper cost of living in the South, the lower efficiency of colored workers, and the danger of job displacement were essentially rationalizations that masked the South's real reason for wanting a differential wage—race prejudice. "The truth of the matter," Roy Wilkins wrote, "is that the southerners want a lower wage scale because they do not wish Negroes to have wages equal to whites."[13]

The Fight for Equal Treatment

Southern employers did not advance convincing arguments in favor of a separate wage scale for black workers, but they were organized, powerful, and vocal, and therefore as the NRA's code hearings got underway the possibility of differential and inferior treatment for Negroes was very real. In theory the NRA codes were made democratically, with each interest group that would be affected by a proposed code having the right to speak at the public hearings held in Washington. But as a practical matter it was necessary to resolve the major issues at pre-hearing conferences between sponsoring groups of businessmen and labor union representatives, with an NRA administrator and his advisers acting as referees. Unfortunately for Negroes, the primary responsibility of these organized groups was to their own constituents, stockholders on the one hand and union members on the other, and neither was in a position to scrutinize the codes carefully from the standpoint of their effect on black workers.

It was also unfortunate that few NRA referees were willing to go out of their way in order to protect the unorganized Negro workers. On several occasions Clark Foreman of the Department of Interior reminded NRA officials that special precautions should be taken to protect colored workers. But these officials, according to Foreman, "were not prepared to look after the interests of Negroes, not only because of their unfamiliarity with the problems involved but also because they were hard pressed by the manufacturing interests in the South who, with political power, were determined to keep Negro labor cheap and amenable."[14]

NRA officials candidly acknowledged that the code-making process stacked the New Deal deck against the black worker. Speaking to a group of Negroes at Howard University, for example, A. Howard Meyers, the executive director of the Labor Advisory Board, declared that NRA was "fundamentally an effort to work out our economic problems on a democratic basis," but he went on to admit that such a "democratic" system usually gave the greatest benefits to those who were best organized. Because southern workers, white and black, were for the most part not affiliated with strong unions, he admitted that it was "inevitable that such groups gain little," and the only hope Meyers could see was for Negroes to organize in defense of their rights. Many Negroes agreed, and the *Pittsburgh Courier* spoke for them when it declared:

> Every major group of employers and employees is organizing to take full advantage of the New Deal and expedite the functioning of the National Recovery Act. Unfortunately the Negroes seem to be lagging behind, although there is no group in the country less organized and more in need of organization.
>
> Race prejudice and discrimination because of color have not ended and will not end because a few codes and agreements have been signed and adopted. With the best interests in the world, the National Administration cannot easily protect the Negro...from being discriminated against. ...We need and have long needed a well organized office in Washington to look after the interests of all Negroes regardless of locality.[15]

In the autumn of 1933 the Urban League attempted to step into this organizational breach. The league's national office distributed a *Handbook* that summarized the federal emergency legislation and told Negroes how to take advantage of the various programs, and 196 Emergency Advisory Councils were organized in thirty-two states and the District of

Columbia to advise blacks "concerning the ramifications of the various recovery services of the government" and aid those who had specific complaints. The league also encouraged its local branches throughout the country to send letters and telegrams to the president, cabinet members, and other government administrators demanding fair treatment for Negroes. Lester B. Granger of the national office stated the rationale behind these correspondence campaigns when he declared that the league was convinced that if it could establish through its local affiliates "a system which will produce on a week's notice thousands of letters and telegrams going to Washington, we can get a response which has not yet been forthcoming." As an example of the successful operation of these pressure tactics, Granger cited a case from Jackson, Mississippi. He maintained that the Mississippi administrators of the Works Progress Administration (WPA) had been helping local cotton producers get pickers at exploitative wages by closing down Negro WPA projects during the cotton-picking season. This practice was discontinued after Carrington Gill, of the Washington headquarters of WPA, received a flood of protesting mail from Jackson Negroes and telephone calls from the league's national office. On another occasion, the league protested against the boast of a Louisville, Kentucky, maître d' hôtel that he would never pay code wages to black workers and planned to discharge his entire staff of Negro waiters and replace them with whites. Under pressure from the league, the local NRA compliance director discussed the problems with the hotel management, and as a result the maître d' was dismissed and the Negro waiters retained. During 1933 and 1934 the league consistently filed such protests, and it believed that there was "no question but that Washington was moved to let down some of its restrictions because of the insistent campaign carried on by the organization." Granger was convinced that "any group in this country can get almost anything it wants. . . if only it applies enough pressure behind its request."[16]

The league's national office served as a medium through which Negroes could send their complaints about violations of the various emergency provisions with the hope that appropriate corrective action would be taken. Since the national office was located in New York City, however, it was difficult for it to act as an effective lobby for Negro interests at the NRA code hearings in Washington. Moreover, like many other social betterment organizations during the depression, the league lacked adequate financial resources. When Dr. Gustav Peck of the NRA informed the Urban League's T. Arnold Hill that the Recovery Administration "would be happy to have [the Urban League] cooperate with his office. . . on any matters touching Negro workers in connection with the codes," Hill had to decline the offer "because of lack of funds."[17]

During the summer of 1933 it became increasingly clear that a Washington-based organization was needed to advocate integration of Negroes into all phases of the national recovery program and to present effectively the Negroes' complaints against NRA. This task was undertaken by two young and well-educated Washington Negroes, John P. Davis, twenty-eight years old and a graduate of the Harvard School of Law, and Robert C. Weaver, a twenty-six-year-old Harvard Ph.D. As one observer has noted, Davis and Weaver had no money, organizational backing, or experience, but they possessed high intelligence, excellent education, and the faculty for making themselves seem ubiquitous. Calling themselves the Negro Industrial League, they appeared at several of the early NRA

Code Hearings, demanding fair treatment for Negroes and pointing to the specific code provisions that would adversely affect black workers.[18] Walter White of the NAACP and George Edmund Haynes of the Race Relations Department of the Federal Council of Churches brought the work of Davis and Weaver to the attention of other established Negro leaders, and in September of 1933, fifteen organizations joined with the Negro Industrial League to form the Joint Committee on National Recovery.[19]

Essentially the joint committee was an ad-hoc lobby formed by black leaders who feared that Negro interests were "in danger of serious impairment unless Negro organizations themselves become active and alert in opposition to discriminations as they appear." Davis expressed the organization's basic philosophy when he declared: "Wherever the Federal Government touches interracial life it should stand for the policy of interracial cooperation instead of separation.... Proposals to have the Federal Government set up or encourage separate Negro advisory councils in the Government, segregated subsistence-homestead settlements, different standards in public works and in public relief, different standards of wages and hours in industry, or any other Government measure that will place Negroes on a lower segregated status, should be opposed."[20]

The work of the joint committee closely paralleled the work of the emergency bureaus of the government. With regard to NRA, this meant that the scores of announcements and press statements that NRA released every day had to be studied. The proposed codes had to be scrutinized carefully to determine whether they contained any provisions detrimental to Negro employees. On analysis, the codes that seemed to have serious racial differentials were graded in terms of the number of Negro workers affected, the seriousness of the differential treatment, and the availability of factual material on which to base a case. According to Davis, "Those judged most important in these terms are set down for public appearance. Those next in importance are set down for written briefs and conferences with Government officials. The others are given such treatment as is possible. Sometime [sic] letters of protest will be written concerning them. Sometime [sic] the deputy administrator in charge of the code will be phoned. Sometime [sic] nothing is done." Altogether the joint committee appeared at more than one hundred public NRA code hearings. This was an outstanding performance inasmuch as after Robert Weaver resigned in order to become an adviser to Secretary of Interior Harold Ickes, the staff of the joint committee usually consisted of John Davis and a technical adviser, Rose M. Coe, and its annual budget was kept at about $5,000.[21]

Because its component groups were weak and disorganized, and because its finances were so meager, the joint committee had no real power. It was not nearly so effective in influencing the final form of the various codes as were the better organized businesses and trade unions. Under the circumstances perhaps it was inevitable that the committee would become a study group, primarily concerned with educating the public about "the inequitable status and treatment of Negro labor under the various Federal plans for national economic recovery." As such, it performed a valuable service and in the process helped to lay the foundation for a more effective Negro protest movement in the future. Yet despite its weakness, the joint committee did achieve one signal victory. Largely as a result of its agitation, the NRA decided that it would not be advisable to give the sanction of federal approval to lower wage and hour standards for black workers. In every case the requests of southern businessmen for racial differentials were denied.[22]

Displacement of Black Workers

Of course NRA's decision to prohibit racial differentials was not an unqualified victory for Negroes since, as friends and foes of the uniform scale had realized, equal wages under the NRA led to the displacement of many black workers. In this regard, however, it should be remembered that there had been a certain amount of displacement even during the prosperous 1920s. The pressure of unemployed whites desperately searching for any sort of work naturally increased during the first years of the depression, and even before the NRA experiment was inaugurated Negro leaders were reporting that white workers were being substituted in jobs customarily held by blacks. After traveling through the South, T. Arnold Hill reported that "colored janitors of white and Negro schools have been replaced by whites.... Coal wagons, on which a Negro would be employed to shovel the coal and a white man to drive, now make use of two whites, both of whom shovel." From Atlanta, social worker Forrester B. Washington submitted a similar report: "White men have taken over such positions as elevator operators, tradesmen, teamsters, expressmen, bill posting, city sanitary wagon drivers...stewards, cooks, waiters and bell boys in hotels, hospital attendants, mechanics at filling stations, delivery boys from drug stores, and not infrequently such domestic service employment as chauffeurs, maids, and all around domestics." J. A. Rogers, a columnist for the *Pittsburgh Courier,* remembered that when he made his first trip to the South in 1911 he was "very much struck by the seeming monopoly that the black man had on all the humbler kinds of work." Returning in the midst of the depression, he was "equally struck by the change in the color of those men now holding these jobs. These despised occupations have become respectable. They are white men's jobs." As early as 1931 the Urban League concluded that "there is abundant proof in reports from all sections of the country that many jobs Negroes once held are [now] being held by whites."[23]

There were several methods of displacing black workers. A few towns passed municipal ordinances prohibiting Negro competition in certain types of work. Tulsa, Oklahoma, and West Palm Beach, Florida, for example, authorized local statutes restricting black building mechanics to certain Negro sections of the city or to buildings inhabited by Negroes; some North Carolina towns followed Charlotte's example and enacted legislation prescribing that the services of Negro barbers should be confined to patrons of their own color; and in Houston, Texas, Negroes were legally prohibited from obtaining licenses that would have permitted them to sell garden vegetables and fish at the local farmers' markets.[24]

But legislation was rarely needed, largely because there were more effective, informal methods for displacing Negro workers. In several cities groups were organized with the frankly stated purpose of appealing to white race loyalty in order to deprive Negroes of jobs. One such organization, known as the Black Shirts, was especially active in Atlanta in the 1930s and had branches throughout the country. This group published a daily newspaper, the *Black Shirt,* held weekly parades, and claimed a membership of 21,000 in

Atlanta. The literature of the group advocated sending urban Negroes back to the farms, and it sent committees to white businessmen urging them to discharge Negro employees. Unemployed white laborers who were looking for jobs accompanied the committees when they made their rounds.[25]

It is difficult to assess the significance of racist organizations such as the Black Shirts. In most cities, as in Atlanta, the more moderate white people put an end to these groups as chartered organizations. But they were not able to destroy the spirit which was behind the movement, and Negroes were convinced that these groups continued to meet and operate secretly. T. Arnold Hill reported that white people repeatedly told him of "telephone calls to their homes demanding that they dismiss their colored help," and many employers were subjected to more direct harassment. It was not uncommon for houses that were painted by Negroes to be smeared overnight with warnings that jobs should be given to deserving whites.[26]

Although no systematic study of Negro displacement was ever made, it is clear that many employers capitulated before racist pressure. In Richmond, Virginia, the mayor declared that insofar as possible he would restrict employment on public works to white men and suggested that private employers "take the hint." In Columbia, South Carolina, white men replaced Negro maintenance laborers at the State House, and at the University of Mississippi Negro laborers were dismissed and whites hired in their place. Similar displacements occurred in the North, though not so frequently. The Urban League reported that one New York firm laid off twelve colored porters and replaced them with whites; three Pittsburgh dining rooms substituted white waitresses for Negro waiters; several Chicago department stores and one Detroit hotel dismissed their Negro employees and hired whites to take their places. There were many people in all sections of the country who believed that white men should be given favorable consideration when it came to the allocation of scarce jobs.[27]

Direct intimidation was a third method used to force Negroes to vacate jobs, and perhaps the most vicious example occurred in the southwestern division of Illinois Central Railroad. During the 1920s firemen's jobs on the railroad had been divided equally between Negroes and whites. During the early part of the depression, however, white firemen in the Louisiana division asked for a 5 percent reduction in the number of Negro firemen. This request was granted, but when the management refused to meet a later demand for an additional cut in the number of black employees the white firemen decided to take matters into their own hands. Vigilante groups were formed to warn black workers that if they did not resign they would suffer severe reprisals, and armed conflict erupted when most Negro workers refused to surrender their jobs. Some Negro firemen were lured from their engines with flares and then shot down; others were attacked in the engine cabs by white snipers. Altogether ten Negro railway employees were killed, and another eleven were wounded or shot at.[28]

Walter White of the NAACP believed that lynching was yet another way for white supremacists to intimidate Negroes and force them to leave their jobs. He noted that the number of lynchings had risen from eight in 1932 to twenty-eight in 1933, fifteen in 1934, and twenty in 1935. Moreover, White observed that in many cases the lynch mobs also attacked the stores of whites who employed Negroes. When one such case occurred in Marianna, Florida, the association sent Howard Kester of the STFU to investigate the circumstances. Kester reported that "while the feeling against Claude Neal [the victim] was certainly very great because of the crime which he was alleged to have committed [rape], the lynching was to a large extent a surface eruption. Beneath this volcanic eruption lay the pressing problem of jobs and bread and economic security. A very competent observer said to me: 'This lynching was a surface eruption. The basic cause of the lynching was economic. Here you put your finger on the sore spot. The lynching had two objects, first, to intimidate and threaten white employers of Negro labor and, secondly, to scare and terrorize Negroes so that they would leave the country and their jobs could be taken over by white men.' A white man with whom I talked observed: 'There are too many niggers and too many white people looking for the same job.' A clerk in a store said, 'A nigger hasn't got no right to have a job when there are white men who can do the work and are out of work.' "29

Of course these are extreme examples of vigilante action. Less extreme methods of intimidation were employed more often, but there is no way of ascertaining how many Negroes were threatened or suffered loss of property because they refused to give up their jobs. It can only be said that local branches of the NAACP and the Urban League reported that such cases occurred not infrequently.

Discriminatory legislation, racist pressures, and direct intimidation were not the only reasons for Negro displacement. Given the large number of unemployed white workers, it was inevitable that the NRA's decision to prohibit racial differentials would itself cause some further unemployment in the Negro community. There were some employers who hired black labor only because it was cheaper, and many of these employers dismissed their Negro workers rather than pay

NRA code wages. The day before the NRA code went into effect, for example, the Tri-State Manufacturing Company of Memphis, Tennessee, discharged fourteen black workers who had been working eight hours and forty-five minutes a day for $4.50 per week and hired white replacements at $12 per forty-hour week. A few days after the retail stores' code went into effect, Grant's Department Store in Greensboro, North Carolina, discharged a black employee with several years service and hired a white man in his place. And in New Castle, Pennsylvania, the Hotel Castleton released two black elevator girls and six bellmen, replacing them with whites.[30]

Still other employers of black labor simply could not afford to pay equal wages. In this regard, it should be remembered that those black workers who were able to find industrial employment tended to work for inefficient firms which used obsolete machinery. Because of their antiquated assembly lines, these marginal corporations generally had a smaller output per man-hour, and consequently they could not compete with the larger, more mechanized concerns unless they paid less for their labor. By dealing only with man-hours and not with units of production, the NRA placed these marginal firms at a severe competitive disadvantage; in effect, it forced small enterprisers to choose between modernizing and going out of business.

Many New Dealers believed that sweatshop operators had no right to exist. In his speech explaining the purposes of NRA, President Roosevelt laid down "the simple proposition ...that no business which depends for existence on paying less than living wages to workers has any right to continue in this country." Making the same point, W. Averell Harriman, who was then serving as an NRA administrative officer, declared that "the man who can hold his place in the competitive system only by working women and children for long hours at low wages has no right to survive." And Joel Berrall of NRA's Labor Advisory Board stated the matter succinctly when he explained that "those drafting minimum wage and maximum hour laws know that such laws imply economic death for thousands of submarginal enterprises. The drafting of such laws assumes that such economic surgery is necessary in a competitive economy in order to preserve the health of the larger body."[31]

Of course these sentiments were on a high moral plane, but this should not obscure the fact that the bankruptcy of marginal firms put many workers on the rolls of the unemployed and that the modernization of plant facilities often affected Negroes adversely. In Greensboro, Georgia, for example, twenty Negroes were employed by a local cotton textile mill. Before the NRA, the daily wage of workers in this mill was about seventy-five cents for a ten-hour day; afterward, wages ranged from $2 to $2.40 for an eight-hour day. The machinery in this mill was obsolete, and the firm had been able to compete with more modernized mills only because labor costs were so low. With the coming of the NRA the mill at Greensboro had three choices: to maintain employment, pay code wages, and operate at a loss; to ignore the NRA stipulations; or to install more productive machinery and pay code wages to fewer workers. Late in 1933 the mill decided to take the third alternative. After new machines were installed, the management calculated that the mill could produce the same amount of goods with twenty fewer workers, and the Negroes were released. Economic factors had dictated the installation of improved machinery at Greensboro; racial attitudes dictated the displacement of Negro employees first.[32]

Some textile mills chose to ask the NRA for a temporary

exemption from the requirement of paying the code minimum wage of $12 per week. A case in point involved the Reliance Manufacturing Company of Chicago, Illinois. This firm operated seventeen plants throughout the United States and employed seven thousand workers of whom some three hundred were Negroes. All of the black workers were employed by one of Reliance's subsidiaries, the Southland Manufacturing Company of Montgomery, Alabama. When the NRA's Cotton Textile Code went into effect, the Reliance Manufacturing Company asked for a temporary exemption for its Southland branch. The NRA granted the request in order to allow time for an investigation to determine if there were special circumstances which would justify such an exemption. Burton Oppenheim, the government investigator, could find no such circumstances, and consequently the NRA revoked the exemption and ordered Southland to pay $6,100 in back wages, the difference between the Cotton Textile Code minimum and the wages actually paid during the time of the exemption. Southland maintained that it could not remain in business if it had to pay the $12 minimum, and three months later it ceased operations, throwing the three hundred Negro employees out of work.[33]

The Southland case received wide publicity because of the participation of representatives of the Tuskegee Institute, who appeared at a second hearing asking that the closed plant be allowed to reopen at substandard wages. In his preliminary remarks before the NRA's Industrial Appeals Board, Mr. G. Lake Imes, secretary of the institute, spoke on behalf of the displaced workers. Imes declared that the minimum wage provision of the NRA's Cotton Textile Code was responsible for the Southland's decision to close and discharge its Negro employees. Assuming that the authors of the national recovery program had not intended to impose such a hardship on black workers, Imes appealed to the board to permit Southland to pay Negroes less than the code minimum "until such time as they can bring up the efficiency of the workers...to the point where...the workers themselves can earn the equivalent of the minimum requirements of the Code." Imes believed that this would enable the firm to reopen its plant. Such a dual code, he suggested, might be the only practical way of keeping hundreds and even thousands of Negroes from joining the army of unemployed. Mr. Herbert G. Mayer, the president of the Reliance Manufacturing Company, maintained that his testimony on behalf of substandard wages for Southland was also motivated by sincere concern for the workers "as people, as human beings and as individuals." "Unfortunately," he declared, the company was "in a position where the profit system is still in vogue, and I, as the representative of all our other workers, and of the two thousand or more stockholders that we have, can not afford to operate the Southland Manufacturing Company as a charitable institution..."[34]

When members of the board asked why Southland was not operating at a profit, Mayer stated that in his opinion "it must be on account of the characteristics of the people who have not had the experience and the background, *and their racial characteristics.*" This reasoning alarmed several members of the board, as well as the Negro observers present for the hearing. Rose Schneiderman of the Consumers Advisory Board pointed out that if an exemption were granted on the ground that Negro labor was inefficient, "within a couple of days the NRA will be deluged with appeals from all kinds of firms for the same kind of an exemption that these have." Clark Foreman of the Department of Interior believed that such an exemption would place a mark of inferiority on Negro labor and insisted that "we must not agree to a concession or arrangement that will throw such a stigma on them." John P. Davis maintained that Mayer had not presented any reputable evidence demonstrating that the workers at Southland were less efficient than other workers. Davis noted that Reliance was supporting its claim of inefficient Negro labor by comparing Southland with the firm's Bedford, Indiana, plant, but he pointed out that new "progressive line" machinery had been introduced at the Bedford plant but not at the Southland. Davis also presented information indicating that the rent cost per unit of production was higher at Southland than at any other Reliance subsidiary. Mary Anderson, the director of the Women's Bureau of the United States Department of Labor, noted that the Southland's black employees had been working at the plant for an average of six years, and she contended that these employees "should not have been retained by the firm for this length of time if they are as slow and inefficient as is claimed by the petitions." Burton Oppenheim of the NRA reported that his investigation had revealed that the Southland's black workers were as efficient as the white millhands at the neighboring Johnstone plant in Birmingham where machinery and overhead costs were similar. Oppenheim also challenged the Reliance's statement that it was in desperate financial condition, pointing out that the company in 1933 earned a profit of $750,000 on a gross business of $13 million. Partly as a result of this testimony, the Industrial Appeals Board denied Southland's petition for exemption.[35] Negro spokesmen had achieved a victory, but their happiness was tempered by the knowledge that three hundred black workers would remain without jobs.[36]

A third example of the manner in which NRA wage codes were responsible for Negro displacement occurred at the

Maid Well Garment Company of Forest City, Arkansas. The Maid Well Company employed 194 black seamstresses, but despite the fact that the NRA code required a $12 minimum weekly wage for seamstresses, the company continued to pay its Negro employees at the older rate of $6.16 per week. For several months the employees were reluctant to complain, knowing that the compliance board which was responsible for enforcement of the code was made up of members of the local chamber of commerce who were friendly to the company's management. Late in 1933, however, one intrepid but anonymous worker lodged a complaint with the Washington office of NRA. When the company learned that it was to be investigated, its response was immediate and severe. All 194 Negro workers were dismissed, the management claiming they were so inefficient that the company would certainly lose money if it were forced to pay code wages.

A long and protracted NRA code violation investigation, replete with several appeals and extending over a period of nine months, finally concluded that the Maid Well Company had indeed been violating the NRA's minimum wage code. Accordingly, in September of 1934 the Arkansas director of compliance entered orders for restitution of back wages of $5.84 for every week the black seamstresses had been employed during the NRA dispensation. However, the director ruled that payment should be postponed until the company's executive officer returned from Syria where he had been visiting his parents. But when the code violator finally did return in October of 1934, he refused to make restitution and instead destroyed the company's records thereby making it impossible for NRA to know how much was due in back wages. To get a decision on this point, NRA was forced to take the Maid Well management before the regional compliance board in Dallas, Texas, where it was ordered that the company must make payment of back wages in the amount of nearly $7,000. Before this order could be implemented, however, the Supreme Court, in May of 1935, declared NRA unconstitutional. The Negro seamstresses had been unemployed ever since the first complaint had been made eighteen months before, and they never did receive their back pay. Throughout this period of controversy, the Maid Well Company continued to sew the NRA's symbol of compliance, the Blue Eagle label, onto each of its cotton garments.[37]

Evading the NRA Codes

All workers in NRA industries, regardless of race, were supposed to receive the code minimum wage. In many cases, as we have seen, this standard minimum wage jeopardized the position of Negro workers, especially those employed by marginal business units. Yet it is important not to exaggerate the amount of displacement caused by NRA's refusal to enact a differential minimum wage. Many employers quickly discovered loopholes in the codes which enabled them to avoid paying regulation wages to black workers. Consequently, they continued to employ marginal black workers at the older, substandard rates for wages and hours.

Although the word "Negro" was not mentioned in any of the NRA codes, there were several provisions which enabled employers to pay white workers more than blacks. Some codes provided that certain jobs in an industry would be covered by NRA while other jobs would not, and these "occupational classifications" frequently were arranged so that minimum wage scales covered only that work which was generally performed by whites. Thus, there were more than thirteen thousand Negroes employed in American cotton mills, but the NRA's $12 weekly minimum wage for cotton textile workers would help few of these Negroes because more than eleven thousand of them were classified as "cleaners" and "outside employees," and the NRA code specifically excluded these two categories of workers from minimum wage-maximum hour benefits.[38]

The existence of such occupational classifications gave unscrupulous employers the opportunity to save money by reclassifying employees so that they would not be covered by the NRA codes. It is impossible to know how many of the 2,000 skilled Negro cotton textile mill operatives were reclassified, but John P. Davis was able to cite several examples of Negro "picker-tenders," an occupation classified within the pale of wage and hour regulations, who continued to do the same work but were classified as "sweepers" and "cleaners." Similar examples of differential classification can be cited in several other industries. In a Birmingham foundry there were two classifications of molders, with the black "molder's helper" receiving a lower wage than the white "molder." Even when the black "helper" taught the trade to a white man, the white was classified as the molder, received the higher rate of pay, and was addressed as "boss" by his instructor. In the Georgia Black Belt, shoe shine shops and barber shops managed to circumvent the NRA codes by telling their Negro bootblacks to inform all questioners that they were not hired by the owner of the shop but had rented the shoe shine equipment and were in business for themselves. In yet another instance a few Negroes were advanced to the rank of "executives" so that they could be exempted from code provisions. This practice of differential classification was particularly widespread in the South, but similar examples can be cited from other sections of the country. Thus, when A. Howard Meyers stopped at a northern hotel that was prominently displaying the NRA's Blue Eagle, he asked one of the black bellhops if this were an NRA hotel. "Oh yes sir, yes sir, this is an NRA hotel," the boy answered, "but we are not working here: we are only learning the business." Still another type of occupational classification affected black workers employed in certain types of factories. Thus workers in southern cotton oil mills—almost all of whom were Negroes— were classified as agricultural laborers and given a much lower wage than they would have received as industrial workers. The rationale was that they were processing agricultural products, but, as journalist George Schuyler has said, "nobody who has seen a cotton mill or a cotton gin would say that was agricultural. They're working on agricultural products, but they're using vast machinery and all of that, and it's actually an industrial job."[39]

Although none of the NRA codes contained a Negro differential, more than a hundred of them established geographical classifications that permitted the payment of lower minimum wages in the South than in other sections of the country. NRA officials maintained that they had to take account of the relative economic backwardness of the South, of its less skilled and less experienced working force, and of the normal desire of southern manufacturers to have the same advantages which the North enjoyed in its own industrial adolescence. They maintained that historical forces had brought about an uneven development of American industrial life, that wages in the South were lower than wages in the North before the depression, that any NRA attempt suddenly to eliminate these differences would make it difficult for many southern firms to compete with northern concerns. They knew that if labor costs were equal in all sections of the country, many of the less efficient businesses would be forced into bankruptcy, with a resulting increase in unemployment that would generate feelings of pessimism among businessmen. Rather than stimulating industry, such a condition would create a climate distinctly unfavorable to enterprise, investment, and employment.[40]

NRA officials such as Gustav Peck of the Labor Advisory Board also reminded Negroes of "the persistent rumblings of complaints that the minimum wages in codified industries are serving to displace colored workers by whites, because, under the social and economic conditions prevailing in the South, public opinion makes it necessary for employers to take on unemployed white workers for jobs formerly performed by colored workers at lower wages." Peck admitted that NRA did not have an entirely satisfactory answer to this problem, but his "honest judgment" was that it would be a "great mistake" to enforce a uniform minimum wage because "it would do harm to the economic life of the nation...and would be a disservice to colored workers."[41]

Most Negroes were not satisfied with these explanations. They maintained that all too frequently loose talk about the South's competitive disadvantage and the danger of Negro displacement was used by NRA as an excuse to keep the wages of black workers low. Leaders such as Walter White and John Davis believed that the possibility of displacement in many industries was extremely slight. White noted, for example, that Walter H. Pierce had told the delegates to the Forty-fifth Annual Convention of the Laundry Owners National Association that it would cost more than $35 to train each new laundry worker, and that even then new workers could not work quickly and would slow down assembly-line processing. White concluded that most laundry owners would not take up this expense merely to change the complexion of their workers, that they would not disrupt their business in order to keep Negro wages low. Yet the NRA held that the laundry code's low southern wage of fourteen cents per hour was necessary because of the danger of widespread Negro displacement. John Davis complained that NRA merely had repeated "all the quack arguments so familiar in the mouths of the bully-ragging industrialists at the code hearings."[42]

White and Davis also maintained that the presence of large numbers of black workers in certain industries influenced the final decision to permit geographical classification. They insisted that the geographical differential was really a racial differential because it applied disproportionately to Negroes. Noting that in most cases the NRA codes tended to narrow the difference in wages between the South and the rest of the country, White observed that this was not true for every industry and he maintained that the widest divergence was to be found in those industries where Negro workers comprised a large part of the total labor force. He warned Mrs. Roosevelt that the administration was letting itself be "led astray by those who for selfish reasons want to perpetuate a racial distinction which can only do harm to the country as a whole as well as to Negroes."[43]

To illustrate their position, Negro leaders pointed to the Codes of Fair Competition for the fertilizer industry. The Fertilizer Code provided for minimum wages of twenty-five cents per hour in the South, thirty-five cents per hour in the North and Midwest, and forty cents per hour on the Pacific Coast. Although the code made no mention of color or race in setting up these differentials, Negroes noted that three-quarters of the nation's fertilizer industry was located in the South and that from 85.8 percent to 96.9 percent of the fertilizer workers in southern states were Negroes. Relatively few Negroes were employed in fertilizer factories outside the South. Moreover, Negroes observed that southern wages in the fertilizer industry, where practically all the workers were colored, were only 60 percent of the code wage paid on the Pacific Coast. On the other hand, the southern wage in the cotton textile industry, where relatively few Negroes were covered by the codes, was 92.3 percent of the code wage paid outside the South.[44]

Negro leaders also observed that the NRA's geographical classifications were not consistent, that in some codes the lower minimum wages were provided for only nine "southern" states while in other codes the "South" included as many as seventeen states. John Davis believed that "the one common denominator in all these variations is the presence or absence of Negro labor. Where most workers in a given territory are Negro, that section is called South and inflicted with low wage rates. Where Negroes are negligible, the procedure is reversed." As an example he pointed to the fertilizer industry in Delaware, where nine of every ten workers were colored. "If the State of Delaware is placed in the North in 449 codes and given the higher wage rate applicable to the North," he asked, "why is it placed in the South in the fertilizer code and given the lower wage rate?" He believed that there was an economic Mason and Dixon line which shifted widely between codes and that these shifts were related to the proportion of Negroes in each industry. Walter White maintained that the differentials were only "thinly disguised as geographical," that in fact they worked "on a strictly racial basis." Roy Wilkins charged that "the recovery administrators have sanctioned discriminatory wage differentials and granted exemptions which, while not labelled on the basis of color, have nevertheless operated almost exclusively on that basis."[45]

Negroes insisted that the same type of discrimination was implicit in the NRA's code of fair competition for the iron and steel industry. Here the NRA established twenty-one districts and in nineteen of these districts the minimum wage for common laborers ranged between thirty-five and forty cents per hour. Yet in the southern and Birmingham districts, where Negroes comprised more than 80 percent of the common laborers, the code provided for minimum wages of twenty-five cents and twenty-seven cents per hour. In their campaign against this geographical differential in the iron and steel code, Negro protest leaders found an influential ally in the person of Secretary of Labor Frances Perkins. Secretary Perkins fought against the low wage rates for the two southern districts and openly charged that these rates had been determined by "the predominance of Negro labor in these districts." She reminded those present at the code hearing that the purchasing power of Negroes was "needed to provide different markets for the products of agriculture and industry." She contended that "a sound national industrial system cannot be based upon the capitalization of the colored laborers, and an increased wage that will not unfairly compete with the wage of the white laborer is essential to achieving this end." Yet even with the assistance of the secretary of labor, Negro groups were not able to prevent the enactment of the geographical differential in the iron and steel code.[46]

Eighteen approved codes contained yet another clause which some Negroes believed was included in order to permit racial discrimination. This clause provided that minimum wage scales for some classes of labor should be based on wages received as of a certain date in the past. William Pickens, the field secretary of the NAACP, characterized this as the "grandfather clause of the NRA" and maintained that it obviously perpetuated differential wages based on race. As written into the Building Contractors' Code, the "grandfather clause" provided that employers must pay a minimum wage of forty cents per hour, but wherever the minimum wage was less than forty cents per hour on July 15, 1932, it was provided that the code wage would be thirty cents. Since the vast majority of unskilled Negro workers had not been receiving more than forty cents they would receive the lower minimum wage. Many critics opposed this rather arbitrary method for determining a differential wage, but most of them were placated by the realization that even thirty cents represented a considerable improvement for the great majority of unskilled black construction workers.

Negroes were outraged, however, by the additional stipulation that the thirty-cent wage should not apply to employees whose rate of pay was "established for specific projects by competent governmental authority in accordance with... contracts now in force." They were convinced that this legal terminology was intended to apply to one particularly exploited group of black workers—those who were engaged in the construction of levees for the Mississippi Flood Control Project. They believed that the federal government had gone out of its way to ensure that those black field hands who had been recruited to work on the levees would not receive the thirty-cent minimum but would continue to be paid wages averaging ten cents per hour. Pickens complained that as a result of the "grandfather clause" these "starvation wages" were to be "preserved for the benefit of the contractors... and upheld by the strong arm of the State."[47]

In addition to the "occupational classifications," "geographical differentials," and the "grandfather clause of the NRA," it is necessary to consider the NRA's inadequate enforcement machinery in order to understand why so many employers were able to circumvent the minimum wage provisions. The responsibility for enforcing the codes was delegated to a special system of compliance agencies. When allegations of code violations were received, they were investigated by the NRA's compliance division and adjusted if possible. Those incapable of adjustment were taken before local compliance boards, but the authority of these boards was limited; they had no power to enforce their decisions. If the board determined that a code violation had occurred, however, it could recommend the removal of the NRA's emblem of compliance, the Blue Eagle, or it could threaten prosecution in civil courts.

This latter alternative was employed on a few occasions. For example, a Negro employee of the Marian and Koras Restaurant in Detroit won $68 in back pay when he convinced the court that he had not been receiving code wages. On another occasion a judge in Cleveland ruled that a local drugstore must pay $41 in back wages to a colored delivery boy who had been working for less than the code minimum. And in High Point, North Carolina, a Negro service station attendant was awarded $70 covering the difference between his $6 weekly wage and the minimum set by the code.[48]

But the NRA rarely resorted to prosecution in civil courts, largely because many NRA officials, including administrator Hugh Johnson, feared that the compliance provisions of the recovery program would be declared unconstitutional. Plagued by constitutional doubts and wishing to avoid a legal test case, NRA chose to prosecute only the most flagrant violations. Of the 155,000 cases investigated by the state offices of the compliance division, only some 1,500 reached NRA's litigation division, and only 564 of these were taken to court.[49]

Realizing the perils involved in seeking legal compulsion, General Johnson hoped that effective enforcement could be achieved by persuading the public to honor government-sponsored boycotts of code violators. "The Act," he declared, "was of such a nature to be absolutely unenforceable without a strong campaign of public opinion behind it." Accordingly, he launched one of the great experiments in the history of mass ballyhoo, featuring motorcades, mass meetings, brass bands, and various other devices considered likely to win public support for government-sponsored boycotts against NRA code violators. He hoped to convince the American housewife that "the Blue Eagle on everything that she permits to come into her home is a symbol of its restoration to security," that she should not deal with any "man or group of men who attempt to trifle with this bird."[50]

Unfortunately for the success of the recovery program, public opinion never rallied in support of the NRA. There were many reasons for this lack of popular support, but perhaps the most important factor was the prevalent desire to buy products at the lowest possible price, even if the low price was possible only because the producer exploited his labor. Two years after the Supreme Court declared the program unconstitutional, one careful investigator concluded that it was "doubtful whether the removal of a Blue Eagle ever injured any firm which was not supplying the Government."[51]

For a number of reasons, code enforcement was most inadequate when the complainants were Negroes. Local compliance boards were established in every community, but

Negroes rarely sat on these boards, even when black workers comprised the bulk of the industrial force. Most board members were chosen from among local employers or trade union officials. Especially in the South, these men were not particularly sympathetic when Negro workers alleged that they were receiving differential treatment. Consequently, Negro workers were reluctant to report code violations; as Ira DeA. Reid of the Urban League remarked, so far as they were concerned all too often the NRA "might just as well be administered by the Ku Klux Klan."[52]

Enforcement problems were particularly acute during the NRA's first year, when complaints sent to the national office frequently were referred back to local authorities. Given conditions in many sections of the country, this only worsened the position of the Negro complainant. The situation improved in 1934 when the recovery administration decided that complaints should be investigated by federal authorities. Yet this did not solve the problem because many federal investigators did not observe the established rule that neither the name nor the identity of the complainant should be revealed. When a South Carolina Negro lodged a complaint against a fertilizer plant, for example, an investigator for NRA visited the city where the complainant lived and asked him to come to the lobby of a white hotel. The workman came in overalls, and the NRA investigator proceeded to question him in the hotel lobby. Obviously the man was not free to give testimony; yet the investigator closed the case and reported that the company was complying with NRA regulations. Shortly afterward the complainant was dismissed from his job.[53]

Similar incidents occurred throughout the country, and several letters to NRA complained that, as Professor R. B. Parsons of the University of Tennessee described the situation in his state, "hundreds of employers are violating NRA codes. . . . I hear it on every hand. Many laborers are afraid to complain to the Compliance Boards because of the dominant Chamber of Commerce element on the boards. Of course there is some pretense of obeying the codes, especially as they deal with white laborers; but I have found no pretense of obeying codes where Negroes are concerned. . . ." After traveling through the South, Jesse O. Thomas, the southern field director of the Urban League, filed a similar report. He noted that many black workmen were afraid to give information concerning the extent to which the codes were being violated; they knew it might cost them their jobs if an employer discovered that violations had been reported to NRA authorities. Further, Thomas observed that "both the Negro employee and the white employer have very grave doubt as to the desire of the Government to compel compliance with the code." They knew that the federal government had permitted flagrant violation of provisions of the Fourteenth and Fifteenth Amendments to the federal Constitution, and they intuitively sensed that "if the government is powerless to enforce the provisions of these measures, it will be equally as powerless to enforce the provisions of these codes."[54]

Negro Representation Within NRA

During the two years of the NRA's existence, Negroes repeatedly insisted that some of the racial problems of the industrial recovery program could be solved if the government would appoint qualified Negroes to key positions in the administration. Noting that the problems of black labor were among the most difficult questions with which NRA had to deal, the major Negro organizations lobbied insistently for the appointment of a black economist to the Labor Advisory Board and repeatedly called for government field investigations of the manner in which Negroes were faring under the recovery program. Yet despite these repeated demands, the NRA never employed black advisers and refused to conduct any but the most cursory field studies. This seeming indifference to the condition of black labor aroused considerable resentment among articulate Negroes—more dissatisfaction, perhaps, than that kindled by any other New Deal recovery agency.[55]

There were a few New Deal officials who openly supported the demand for black representation on the Labor Advisory Board. Clark Foreman, the race relations adviser in the Department of Interior, pointed out to leading NRA officials that "the Negro press almost unanimously denounces the NRA for discrimination and unfairness to the Negro, and the sentiment against the NRA has become so great among the Negro group...that NRA is being understood by them as standing for 'Negro Removal Act.'" Foreman himself did not believe that NRA had done great harm to black workers; on the contrary, he was willing to concede that "the faults of the NRA have been over-estimated and insufficient attention has been given to the benefits which the Negro race has received as a result of NRA." Nevertheless, he thought it was "highly important" that NRA give some indication that it was devoting serious consideration to the special problems of black workers, and he thought "nothing would be more suitable or more effective in quieting the fears and misunderstandings among the group than the appointment of a first-class Negro to the Labor Advisory Board." Secretary of Labor Frances Perkins also did what she could in this regard, appointing Lawrence Oxley, her special assistant on Negro affairs, "as a liaison officer between the Department of Labor and the Labor Advisory Board for all questions which relate to negro labor." On several occasions Oxley made brief field trips to investigate cases of alleged maltreatment of Negro workers under the NRA, and he submitted memoranda to the NRA expressing a Negro point of view on various matters. Yet while Oxley did attend occasional NRA conferences his chief duties and responsibilities were with the Department of Labor, and he never exerted significant influence on NRA policy decisions.[56]

Despite this pressure, NRA refused to appoint a Negro representative to the staff of its Labor Advisory Board. Officials within the recovery administration evidently believed that A. Philip Randolph, Abram Harris, and Charles S. Johnson—the men whom Negroes most frequently proposed for an NRA position—were affiliated too closely "with Negro organizations which frequently gain newspaper attention for their criticism of the NRA."[57] Such men "with outside connections," one NRA offiice memorandum pointed out, "could be held under . . . control only with some diffiiculty."[58]

The leading offiicials within NRA wanted a Negro adviser who shared their point of view, if they were to have anyone at all, and consequently NRA planted trial balloon rumors to the effect that G. Lake Imes, the Tuskegee official who had come to public attention when he appealed for a Negro differential in the Southland Manufacturing Company case, would be appointed as a special adviser on Negro problems. The NAACP not surprisingly denounced this proposal. Roy Wilkins pointed out: "Mr. Imes is not an economist and lacks experience and training in the labor field. His appointment will be interpreted as acceptance by NRA of the policy of wage differentials for Negro workers as this is Imes' philosophy."

The association officially registered "unqualified opposition to [the] appointment of Imes because it will endanger the whole future of Negro industrial workers and place [the] stamp of government approval on [a] lower wage code for them on the basis of color."[59]

Wishing to avoid controversy, NRA dropped its plans for employing Imes and instead decided that attempts at mollifying Negro critics could be made most effectively by white NRA officials. Accordingly, Matthew Boyd, a staff official of the Labor Advisory Board, was given responsibility for making a study of the manner in which black workers were affected by the NRA. Boyd set about the task of collecting relevant information and wrote to various Negro leaders asking them to specify "any cases where Negro workers have been displaced in favor of white workers" and any cases where black workers were "told they must accept less than the code wages and say nothing about it or stand the consequences of losing their jobs entirely."[60]

Roy Wilkins of the NAACP hesitated before answering Boyd's request, pointing out that "the various Negro organizations, without exception, have not had and do not have the financial resources" necessary to carry on a thorough investigation of the condition of Negro workers under the NRA. Wilkins suggested that the government itself could "render the greatest service to the Negro worker and to the whole program of national recovery in the South by sending tactful but unbiased investigators on tour to discover, first, the extent of the displacement, and, second, the size of the differential wage payments." In the meantime, however, Wilkins was willing to keep Boyd posted concerning certain individual cases that came to the attention of local chapters of the NAACP. He reported, for example, that in St. Louis the

Con-Ferio Paint and Varnish Company "replaced 18 colored girls with whites as the salaries had increased to comply with the codes"; in Hartford, North Carolina, the Eastern Cotton Oil Company was "working colored men 72 hours a week—12 hours a day and paying them only 13 and ½ cents an hour"; at Meyer's Department Store in Greensboro, North Carolina, "all of the Negro porters are working shorter hours but they are not receiving the corresponding increase in salary," despite the fact that the manager of the store was the local director of NRA; and in Cincinnati "a large chain drug store refused to increase wages of colored girls doing the same work as white girls whose wages were increased."[61]

John P. Davis of the Joint Committee on National Recovery also supplied Boyd and the NRA with several specific instances of alleged code violations which affected Negro workers adversely. For example, under the NRA's code for the fertilizer industry the Royster Guano Company of Royster, South Carolina, should have paid its workers twenty-five cents per hour for a forty-hour week. Instead, according to the joint committee, the company worked its men for more than seventy hours each week at a salary of ten cents per hour. In Augusta, Georgia, the Southern Cotton Oil Company observed the standard eight-hour day, but allegedly paid its employees only seventeen and one-half cents per hour instead of the twenty-cent code minimum. In Garney, South Carolina, the Caroll Turner Saw Mill was accused of paying its men only fifteen cents an hour instead of the twenty-two cents prescribed by the code. The Clifton Mills of Clifton, South Carolina, and the Meritas Mill of Bibb City, Georgia, were charged with classifying men at machines as cleaners and paying them eighteen cents per hour instead of the thirty-cent code minimum. In Cincinnati, the Mably and Carew Department

Store took colored girls out of the rest rooms and offered them jobs as scrubwomen, giving the rest room jobs to whites. And Washington University in St. Louis was accused of dismissing many of its black workers and replacing them with whites.[62]

Boyd received what seemed to be an endless stream of similar reports from all sections of the country, and he was forced to admit that "there is a great deal of replacement going on and a larger amount of plain cheating on wages." As soon as he reached this conclusion, however, he was taken off the project and assigned to other work. Boyd's investigation was never completed, but the Division of Research and Planning released a hastily prepared report that concluded that "the replacement of Negro labor by white labor is a continuation of a process of long standing." This report noted that given the intense competition for available jobs a certain amount of displacement was inevitable, but it claimed that such displacement had been going on since the late 1920s and that NRA had not aggravated the situation. Taking a different tack, Arthur Raper, who prepared a second and more thoughtful NRA memorandum on black labor problems, argued that displacement had been kept to a minimum largely because there had been such widespread evasion of NRA provisions; since the codes were generally evaded and ignored, he claimed, many employers were able to keep their black workers—at the older subsistence wages.[63]

Within the entire NRA bureaucracy there was only one Negro professional worker, Miss Mabel Byrd, a graduate of the universities of Chicago and Oregon and a specialist in labor relations, who was employed for four months by the Division of Research and Planning to study the problems of Negro labor under the NRA. Unlike most NRA officials, Miss Byrd believed that the researches of her division had "pretty well established" the fact "that Negro labor is being displaced due directly to the payment of code wages and hours." Since this violated the purpose of NRA, Miss Byrd was anxious to develop some way in which displacement could be considered a technical violation of the codes. Accordingly, she asked the NRA's legal division for its opinion and was told that "it would be perfectly legal to include a provision in codes to the general effect that the discharge or displacement of Negroes due solely to the higher wages and shorter hours decreed by the codes is regarded as an unfair operation under the code." Miss Byrd then proposed that such a clause be added to all NRA codes, and she suggested further that clauses be added to the effect that service in the employment of a given establishment for a period of more than six months should be considered prima facie evidence of a worker's qualifications and efficiency.[64]

Such proposals, however, did not endear Miss Byrd to the ruling powers in NRA, and she was never able to function effectively. She and her secretary were organized as a special unit, ignored as much as possible, and were not invited to any of the staff meetings in their division. Miss Byrd hoped to be sent South as an investigator of code abuses, but her proposed investigation was canceled when high officials in the NRA decided they would be "playing with fire to send a northern trained Negro to the South, and certainly one trained in Chicago." Hugh Johnson believed that it would be simply "preposterous" to have a study of Negro labor made by a northern Negro. Late in 1933, Miss Byrd was informed that there was no work for her and that she would be relieved of her duties. Of course this dismissal only served to increase Negro dissatisfaction with the NRA. John Davis expressed the sentiments of many Negroes when he sarcastically pointed out that although Negroes had been requesting representation on the Labor Advisory Board "ever since the day the board was formed," nothing had been done, and as NRA entered its second year of operation there was not a single Negro employed "with a rank equal to that of a clerk."[65]

Miss Byrd's departure left the NRA without anyone specifically concerned with Negro problems and served to emphasize the recovery administration's indifference to the plight of the black worker. Some New Deal officials in other agencies, however, believed that the government should be on the alert to protect the special interests of Negroes. Secretary of Interior Harold Ickes, who had long been interested in questions of racial justice and had served as president of the Chicago branch of the NAACP during the 1920s, had particularly strong convictions in this regard. Because of his deep concern for Negroes and his awareness of their special problems, Ickes responded enthusiastically to suggestions that he appoint a special adviser to keep him informed concerning Negro matters. Believing that the appointment of a Negro counselor would infuriate the very segments of the white community that had to be placated, however, Ickes chose as his adviser Clark Foreman, a white liberal from Atlanta. This decision naturally provoked certain Negro leaders who, to take Roy Wilkins as an example, accused Ickes of "paternalism," declared that Negroes "bitterly resent having a white man designated by the government to advise them of their welfare," and suggested that the time had come "when Negroes of training and wide experience can interpret the problems of their race to the government." Secretary Ickes remained firm in his choice of Foreman, but to mollify his black critics and to satisfy Foreman, who saw considerable merit in the protest, Ickes did consent to the appointment of a Negro, Robert Weaver, as assistant to adviser Foreman.[66]

Foreman and Weaver were primarily concerned with the racial situation in the New Deal programs sponsored by the Department of the Interior. But, as Allen Kifer has observed, "because the Interior Department...participated in many New Deal programs involving more than one department, and because Secretary Ickes had a very broad view of the functions of the Interior Department and of the duties of a cabinet officer, Foreman and Weaver soon found themselves projected into almost every New Deal program." One of their first undertakings was the establishment, with the approval of Secretary Ickes and President Roosevelt, of a special inter-departmental committee on Negro affairs. They hoped that such a committee would enable them to exercise a degree of influence over the New Deal's various administrative agencies, and particularly that it would enable them to arouse the social conscience of the NRA. This interracial committee was chaired by a Negro, Robert L. Vann, the publisher of the *Pittsburgh Courier* and a recently appointed assistant to the attorney general. Other recently appointed black New Dealers also served on the committee: Henry Hunt, the assistant to the administrator of the Farm Credit Administration; Forrester B. Washington, a social worker from Atlanta who had taken a job with the FERA; and Eugene Kinkle Jones, who had taken a leave of absence from his duties as executive secretary of the National Urban League to serve as adviser to Secretary of Commerce Daniel C. Roper.[67] White representatives were sent by the Department of Labor, the Navy Department, the War Department, the Treasury, and by the Extension Service, the Agricultural Adjustment Administration, the National Recovery Administration, and the Tennessee Valley Authority.[68]

Little of a substantive nature was accomplished at the committee's first meeting, but a special subcommittee on labor was appointed. This subcommittee consisted of white representatives from the Department of Labor and NRA and three Negroes: Eugene Jones, Robert Weaver, and Forrester Washington. After more than two months of study they presented a report, noting that there was widespread violation of the NRA codes and that thousands of Negroes were not receiving regulation wages. As was to be expected, the "majority of complaints of violations of the NRA...came from employees in small concerns engaged in service occupations"; yet, while admitting that large corporations had more often complied with NRA regulations, the subcommittee maintained that "even these concerns...have not eliminated or significantly reduced the racial differential." Indeed, the subcommittee believed that evasion of NRA regulations was so widespread that there had been no decrease in the wage spread between white and black labor; on the contrary, it concluded that during the NRA period "the spread in total income...between southern white labor as a whole and southern Negro labor as a whole has been increased."[69]

On several occasions Foreman and Weaver reminded NRA of its responsibilities to colored workers, but they could find only one person in the NRA's Washington office who showed a willingness "to take up the cudgels for Negroes." This was Colonel R. A. Lea, an assistant administrator for industry; other officials in NRA seemed to regard Interior's suggestions as unwarranted intrusions. Of course, in the final analysis, there was little that the Department of Interior could do to force NRA to change its policies, and Foreman despondently reported to Ickes that the NRA's seeming lack of concern with the problems of black workers had "caused much dissatisfaction among Negroes, and the officials of the NRA have made no serious attempt to acquaint themselves with the problems of the Negro population and particularly with the problems of the Negro laboring population caused by the operation of the NRA."[70]

Although Negroes generally agreed that the NRA's record was one of neglect and indifference, most of them were careful not to attribute their problems to President Roosevelt. Professor Kelly Miller spoke for many black citizens when he observed, "If the Negro has any just complaints against the practical workings of the codes under the NRA, such discrepancies are due to the incidents of administration, and can in no wise be traceable to the thought or purpose of the Administration." T. Arnold Hill believed that the Negro's economic plight "could not justly be blamed on the New Deal," that the problem was "inherent in a vicious social system which has its roots extending 300 years back into the nation's economic history." The *Pittsburgh Courier* admitted that "the economic condition of the Negro workers has not improved on a par with that of white workers," but the paper contended that "only those blind to reality expected that."[71]

In his only recorded statement concerning the special problems of Negroes under the NRA, President Roosevelt apparently bowed to the power of southern industrialists. "It is not the purpose of this Administration," he declared, "to impair Southern industry by refusing to recognize traditional differentials." Some Negroes, such as George Streator, the managing editor of the *Crisis*, contended that the president's statement was a candid admission that the New Deal's "whole program for the Negro is absolutely empty of meaning." But Streator's remarks did not represent the mainstream of Negro opinion. The Republican *Chicago Defender* accurately reflected the mood of most Negroes when, less than a month after the president made his statement, it expressed "high admiration" for the "sincerity of President Roosevelt in his efforts to adjust a unified pay scale for the employees of various industries throughout the country." The *Defender* believed that the president was fighting gallantly "to carry out the spirit and intent of the National Recovery Act." Unfortunately, his best attempts were frustrated because "down in the South definite and extraordinary efforts are being put forth to nullify the economic intent and purpose of the NRA with respect to black citizens."[72]

While most Negroes were careful not to criticize the entire Roosevelt administration, they did not hide their hostility toward NRA and General Hugh Johnson. James Weldon Johnson, the noted poet and a former NAACP secretary, believed that while NRA did improve the status of some Negro workers, in most respects it had made matters worse for the race. Roy Wilkins maintained that "the harm which NRA has done black workers...far outweighs the good." The NAACP charged that in most cases the NRA "woefully failed to give sympathetic understanding to the many appeals presented to it on behalf of Negro citizens." Instead it showed a "decided tendency to single out black workers for differential treatment in the formulation of codes of fair competition" and "manifested indifference to complaints which have come to it of code violations affecting Negro workers." John P. Davis recalled that he had submitted lengthy, documented reports of code violations, but General Johnson "made no effort to seek the punishment of the offenders or to secure by impartial investigation the facts given him, although the offer was made to furnish him with complete details of each of a score of incidents cited." The NAACP condemned the recovery administration for its refusal "to name qualified Negro experts to positions of authority" and concluded that "the result of this discrimination has been the impoverishment of hundreds of thousands of black workers and a complete failure in remedying the serious condition of unemployment among Negro workers." When General Johnson resigned as administrator of NRA, the association's magazine, *Crisis,* observed: "There will be few tears shed by colored people. . . . From the day he took office until the day he resigned, General Johnson consulted with and took notice of every section of the industrial working population—except Negro Americans."[73]

Yet with regard to employment opportunities in the 1930s, Negro workers, ironically, may have benefited from the NRA's inability and unwillingness to enforce its wage and hour provisions. A series of disadvantageous cultural, economic, and educational factors compounded by the scarcity of complementary resources (especially capital) had led to chronically low productivity in many southern factories. Had the uniform wage and hour legislation been enforced, the previously existing geographical differential between North and South would have been effaced, with the result that higher production costs would have forced the less efficient southern firms into bankruptcy and left the more efficient northern concerns with a larger share of the market.

If northern enterprisers and workers had been able to force northern wages on the South, they would have denied employment to those southern workers who could not compete without differential consideration. Certainly many northern interests recognized that a uniform wage scale would retard the migration of industry to the low-wage South, and this helps to explain the strange alliance of northern conservatives and liberals in support of uniform wage and hour standards; conservatives such as the young Senator Henry Cabot Lodge of Massachusetts doubtless calculated that textile mills in their home states would profit if the inefficient factories of the South were forced to pay equal wages, and liberals such as John L. Lewis knew that unions could never be safe in Pennsylvania and Ohio so long as sweatshop conditions prevailed in West Virginia and Kentucky. Northern businessmen and workers stood to profit from the abolition of the wage differential, but this should not obscure the fact that equal wages tended to retard the migration of industries to the low-wage South and, as the Consumers' Advisory Board put it, "to increase unemployment among Southern Negroes and to close to them some of the all too few doors of opportunity now partially open to them."[74]

NRA and the Negro Consumer

Many New Dealers recognized at the outset of NRA that as labor costs increased businessmen would have to raise their prices. Hugh Johnson stated the matter succinctly when he told the nation, "Don't forget that nobody expects employers to pay the increased cost of re-employment. The consumer—as always—pays the bill. . . . It is inevitable that the employer will raise his prices and will himself pay nothing at all." Yet, it was clear that if prices rose more rapidly than the volume of wage and salary payments, there would be an actual curtailment rather than an expansion of purchasing power. The problem, then, was to devise a method whereby prices could be raised enough to enable employers to provide decent wages and hours without raising them so much as to cancel out the increased purchasing power of higher wages. Some government officials believed that NRA succeeded in achieving this goal. Thus, Dexter M. Keezer, the executive director of NRA's Consumers' Advisory Board, maintained that as of March, 1934, "The rise of dollar income has kept ahead of the rise in prices, which is perhaps the most important general test of the program." And Secretary of Labor Frances Perkins, relying on statistics collected by the Department of Labor, concluded that from June, 1933, to June, 1934, per capita weekly earnings of those employed in manufacturing increased 14 percent, while the cost of living increased less than 7 percent.[75]

During 1933 and 1934, however, a growing number of economists began to question the conclusions reached by Keezer and Perkins. Leverett S. Lyon and his associates at the Brookings Institution spoke for these skeptical economists when, after a careful study of the available information, they concluded that "for employees as a whole the NRA raised living costs in about the same proportion that it raised average hourly earnings." By 1934 even the NRA's own economists were deeply troubled by the prospect of higher prices canceling out additional purchasing power. Gardiner Means, a member of NRA's Consumers' Advisory Board, complained that "in case after case the price charged to the consumer has gone up...more than the increasing purchasing power paid out in production," and he predicted that "the New Deal would end in calamity" if this tendency to push prices up were not checked. Paul Douglas was in basic agreement; he noted that "the purpose of having prices raised to the ultimate consumer by more than the increased labor and raw material cost was not a part of the original intention," and he could "only regard it as an unhappy addition by the forces of industry."[76]

NRA was supposed to promote recovery by increasing the total real purchasing power of employees, and most writers who have considered the recovery program have attempted to determine whether it succeeded or failed in this objective. Accordingly, they have concentrated their attention on all workers, considered collectively, asking whether the rise in prices was extensive enough to cancel or curtail the increased purchasing power provided by the payment of code wages. It must be emphasized, however, that NRA affected particular ethnic, occupational, and geographical groups differently. There can be no doubt that NRA raised wage rates for some classes of employees by more than it raised living costs. On the other hand, it is clear that for some groups the cost of living was increased without a commensurate increase in income. Even Dexter Keezer, who contended that on balance NRA stimulated economic recovery by increasing total purchasing power, admitted that some groups and classes of workers were affected adversely. "Obviously," he wrote, "there is a considerable group or, at any rate, income-receiving interest which stands to lose in a program which calls for cost-raising and hence, in numerous instances, a price-raising process.... A very considerable body of consumers, or income-receiving interest, stands to lose, and it seems to me desirable to have that fact clearly faced and understood."[77]

In the United States of 1930, twenty-three of every two hundred persons gainfully employed were Negroes. Of these twenty-three, nine were engaged in some form of agricultural work, six were employed in industry, six earned their living as household employees, and the remaining two were engaged in trade, professions, or public service. A consideration of the manner in which these workers were affected by NRA must take account of the fact that there were no codes of fair competition, and consequently no government-sponsored increases in wages, for workers engaged in agriculture, domestic service, or the professions. Moreover, as we have seen, black workers employed in jobs supposedly covered by NRA often had to submit to a complicated system of exemptions that, in total effect, resembled a racial differential, or run the risk of displacement by unemployed whites. For most of these black workers the NRA meant an increase in the cost of living without a corresponding increase in wages. For some, such as the southern domestics who generally received about $2 for a sixty-hour work week, a small rise in the price level was sufficient to cause serious economic difficulties. In a sense, these Negro workers were "doubly exploited" because they did not receive the higher NRA wages but still had to pay higher prices for the necessities of life.

By 1934 virtually every Negro newspaper and magazine had complained of the rising cost of living and had criticized NRA for its failure to improve the position of black domestic, farm, and marginal workers who were so desperately in need of increased buying power. The *Chicago Defender* editorialized that it was "unable either to understand or appreciate a national program which increases the cost of every necessity while parallel with this program it reduces the purchasing power of the consumer." And the *Norfolk Journal and Guide* declared that NRA was defective because it

> does not reach down to the large body of farm and mill laborers or domestic servants. . . . As commodity prices rise—as part of the NRA plan—these people will have to pay more for their bread and meat and clothes and rent. . . . With all costs of living going up the living standards of Negro wage earners will necessarily be forced down, not only to the detriment of the Negro wage earner but to the detriment of business as a whole. . . . Recovery cannot be accomplished by bestowing all of the benefits of NRA upon white workers and crucifying Negro workers on an economic cross, merely because it has become customary . . . to take advantage.[78]

Negroes repeatedly reminded the administration of its statements to the effect that there could be "no recovery without increasing mass purchasing power," and argued further that "the existence of widespread Negro poverty must sooner or later contradict white prosperity." Roy Wilkins, for example, maintained that "the fortunes of the great laboring and middle classes as well as those of the farmers and industrialists cannot be improved if the fortunes of one-tenth of our citizens are ignored or impaired." John Davis warned that "the entire recovery program seems threatened by the failure intelligently and courageously to integrate Negro workers into the plan," and he concluded that "for either humanitarian or for the purely selfish reasons of the profit-seeker, NRA's first task was and is to guarantee to Negro industrial workers real wages sufficient to meet a decent standard of living over a definite period of time." The editor of the *Baltimore Afro-American* maintained that, in the final analysis, the New Deal was foundering "because it sought to stabilize living conditions for the middle groups and [left] the great mass of humble people at the bottom of the pyramid [to] wait for some future adjustment."[79]

By 1935, many Negroes were convinced that NRA was paying only lip service to the doctrine that economic recovery could be stimulated by increasing mass purchasing power. Walter White was convinced that if NRA had really been committed to the mass purchasing power formula it never would have permitted wages as low as the laundry code's fourteen cents per hour in the South. As he pointed out, "Even assuming 52 uninterrupted weeks of 45 hours each, Negro laundry workers ...would receive under the code an annual wage of only $327.60." Similarly, Robert Weaver believed that the minimum hourly wage of twenty-five and twenty-seven cents provided for steelworkers in the southern and Birmingham districts was too low, and he proposed a national minimum of forty cents per hour. And John Davis, noting that administration spokesmen had supported minimum wage legislation on the ground that it would raise excessively low wages, concluded that "special attention should be given to those workers whose wages are lowest." He reminded NRA authorities that the forces of organized labor and management which dominated the NRA code hearings would not make a special effort to protect unorganized black workers, and he maintained that consequently NRA should take on itself the responsibility for seeing that "Negro labor is openly and fairly dealt with in these codes." This, however, was not done, and, according to Davis, the consequence was that "the increased cost of living [carried] human misery in even greater quantities into the homes of every tenth man in the nation."[80]

NRA officials admitted that inequities existed, but they insisted that it was not fair for NRA to get "all the abuse for conditions far beyond its remote control." A. Howard Meyers, for example, emphasized that "while many of the complaints which the NRA has received from representatives of the Negro workers are directed against real injustices, they are complaints of inequities which have existed for generations, and the discredit for all of them should not be placed on the lap of NRA." Meyers pointed out that there was a "tremendous surplus of unemployed labor—black and white—in the South," and he reminded Negroes that given the intense competition for every available job it was inevitable that a certain number of black workers would be displaced. He insisted, however, that this displacement had been kept to an absolute minimum and, in any event, had begun long before NRA was created. Meyers also reminded Negroes of the seemingly insoluble dilemma that confronted the NRA: "On the one hand we are criticized for displacing Negroes with whites because we push wages too high. On the other hand we are criticized for allowing any differential at all."[81]

NRA officials also pointed out that it was difficult to generalize about the manner in which NRA affected Negro workers. To be sure, there were some employers who dismissed black workers rather than pay them the same wages as whites, and there were others who resorted to various sorts of chicanery to avoid paying code wages to Negroes. NRA officials, however, emphasized the existence of a third group of employers—those who were convinced that prosperity could be restored only by increasing the purchasing power of all wage earners—and NRA maintained that there were enough employers in this third class to warrant the conclusion "that the NRA has been of more benefit than harm to the Negro," that in most areas "the amount of wages going into the Negro community after the NRA was greater than before."[82]

Spokesmen for the administration further maintained that NRA "accomplished in one year what social reformers of every variety and breed for several generations had not been able to do." They believed that NRA was largely responsible for the irregular but nevertheless significant acceptance of the forty-hour week and minimum wage legislation; it had also speeded progress toward the elimination of child labor, had promoted collective bargaining "and the spread of the best labor standards hitherto prevailing only in our most advanced industrial states." Clark Foreman reminded Negroes that in the past "rugged individualism" had all too often led to "ragged individualism" for black workers, and he suggested that in the long run Negroes stood to benefit more than any other group from the government's surrender of the laissez-faire philosophy and its acceptance of responsibility for organizing and stabilizing industry "on a basis that would assure all citizens a decent living."[83]

Many Negroes were willing to admit that, when considered in long-range perspective, there was some merit in the NRA argument. Yet their economic plight was so desperate that they could not afford the luxury of considering what the long-range ramifications of NRA might be. They were utterly and immediately in need of higher wages and expanded employment opportunities. Some were willing to admit that "the Negro's present plight in its major aspects cannot justly be blamed on the NRA," but, as T. Arnold Hill noted, this was "cold comfort to the hard pressed Negro worker who is looking around today for some means of relief from his present intolerable situation." According to Hill, "Whether [the Negro's] plight began three years ago or three centuries ago, the fact is that [he] remains the most forgotten man in a program planned to deal new cards to the millions of workers neglected and exploited in the shuffle between capital and labor." It was Hill's view that "a government which is honest in its claim of a New Deal, and which wishes to improve the lot of the forgotten man, should protect those who are least protected." But, he concluded, "This has not been done. On the contrary, the will of those who have kept Negroes in economic disfranchisement has been permitted to prevail, and the government has looked on in silence and at times with approval. Consequently, the Negro worker has good reason to feel that his government has betrayed him under the New Deal."[84]

NOTES

1. For a discussion of lily-whiteism in industry, see Paul Norgren, "Negro Labor and Its Problems" (Carnegie-Myrdal Manuscripts), pp. 254-699; and Gunnar Myrdal, *An American Dilemma* (New York: Harper & Brothers, 1944), pp. 279-363.

2. The views of the southern manufacturers were made known at the various NRA code hearings. Complete transcripts of the relevant testimony are available at the National Archives, Record Group 9. For representative arguments from which the quotations used in this paragraph are taken, see the following: Horace L. Smith to Lester G. Wilson, 31 August 1933, NA RG 9; testimony of J. F. Ames, "Hearing on Application of Selma Manufacturing Company, Selma, Alabama, for Exemption from Code of Fair Competition for the Textile Bag Industry," 24 November 1933, NA RG 9; John E. Edgerton, "To Protect the South Against Discrimination," *Manufacturers Record* 103 (July, 1934):62; *Business Week*, 23 September 1933, pp. 9-10. Ludy Randolph Mason, the general secretary of the National Consumers' League, wrote a memorandum for President Roosevelt summarizing the arguments for and against a separate wage scale for Negro workers: "Objections to Minimum Wage Discrimination Against Negro Workers," PPF 1820, FDR Library. Another good summary of the various arguments was prepared by the NRA's Labor Advisory Board, "Territorial Differentials," [1934], in the correspondence files of Gustav Peck, NA RG 9.

3. Frank Freidel, *FDR and the South* (Baton Rouge: Louisiana State University Press, 1965) p. 58; *Newsweek*, 4 October 1937.

4. Walter White, "Cost of Living as a Basis for Determining Regional Wage Rates," typescript, n.d., NAACP Files.

5. Ibid.; William Ogburn, "Does It Cost Less to Live in the South?" *Social Forces* 14 (December, 1935): 211-214; U.S., Bureau of Labor Statistics, "Retail Prices of Food, May, 1934," *Monthly Labor Review* 39 (July, 1934): 175-183; White to Aubrey Williams, 1 March 1938, NAACP Files; Williams to White, 10 March 1938, NAACP Files; White to Frances Perkins, 21 December 1937, NAACP Files; White to Felix Frankfurter, 13 November 1937, NAACP Files; Frankfurter to White, 17 November 1937, NAACP Files; White to Editor of the *New York Herald Tribune*, 6 December 1937; Testimony of Walter White, "Code of Fair Competition for the Laundry Trade," NA RG 9.

6. J. F. Ames, "The Subnormal Negro and the Subnormal Code" (privately printed: Selma, Alabama, 1933); "Testimony of J. F. Ames," *Hearing on Application for Exemption from Code of Fair Competition for*

the Textile Bag Industry in the United States, 24 November 1933, NA RG 183, Oxley File; Horace Cayton and George Mitchell, *Black Workers and the New Unions* (Chapel Hill: University of North Carolina Press, 1939), pp. 437-438; H. E. Snow to Matthew Boyd, 27 January 1934, NA RG 9; T. Arnold Hill to Rose Schneiderman, 13 September 1933, NA RG 9; *Baltimore Afro-American,* 31 March 1934; Julian Harris, "South Is Fighting Equal Negro Pay," *New York Times,* 10 September 1933, p. 8.

7. U. S., Bureau of Labor Statistics, "Relative Efficiency of Negro and White Workers," *Monthly Labor Review* 40 (February, 1935): 335-338; Robert Weaver to Lawrence Oxley, 20 April 1934, NA RG 183, Oxley File; Lawrence Oxley, "The Negro Wage Differentials Under the Codes," typescript, n.d., NA RG 183, Oxley File.

8. U. S., *Congressional Record,* 75th Cong., 2nd sess., 82: 1404; *Atlanta Constitution,* 24 August 1933; *Thomasville Times-Enterprise,* 31 July 1933, as quoted by Jesse O. Thomas, "Will the New Deal Be a Square Deal for the Negro?" *Opportunity* 11 (October, 1933): 308-312; Charles Kaufman to Leo Wolman, 11 August 1933, NA RG 9.

9. NAACP Press Release, 25 August 1933, NAACP Files; Oxley, "Negro Wage Differentials Under the Codes," typescript, n.d., NA RG 183; W. E. B. Du Bois, notes for manuscript on the Negro and the New Deal, 1934, WEBD Papers; Kelly Miller, "Kelly Miller Says," *Norfolk Journal and Guide,* 7 December 1935.

10. Robert C. Weaver, "A Wage Differential Based on Race," *Crisis* 41 (August, 1934): 238; *Pittsburgh Courier,* 30 September 1933; Julian Harris, "Whites Oust Negroes Under NRA in South," *New York Times,* 27 August 1933, p. 6; Resolutions of the 1933 Convention of the National Urban League, Urban League Files; *Chicago Defender,* 14 October 1933; Ira DeA. Reid, "Black Wages for Black Men," *Opportunity* 12 (March, 1934): 75. See below, chapter 12, for an extended discussion of the NAACP's efforts to convince black and white workers that their economic problems were inextricably intertwined and could be solved only by biracial working class solidarity.

11. Walter White to Felix Frankfurter, 13 November 1937, NAACP Files. Among the southern editors with whom White and Wilkins corresponded were: Virginius Dabney of the *Richmond Times-Dispatch,* Jonathan Daniels of the *Raleigh News and Observer,* and George Fort Milton of the *Chattanooga News.* T. Arnold Hill, "An Emergency Is On!" *Opportunity* 11 (September, 1933): 280-281.

12. *Macon Telegraph,* 5 August 1933. Editor Jonathan Daniels of the *Raleigh News and Observer* expressed the same point of view on several occasions. See Jonathan Daniels, editorial, *Raleigh News and Observer,* 21 September 1933; ibid., 29 September 1933; ibid., 24-25 November 1933; U. S., *Congressional Record,* 75th Cong., 2nd sess., 82:1407.

13. Letter to W. T. Anderson, as quoted by Thomas, "Will the New Deal Be a Square Deal for the Negro?" p. 311; Roy Wilkins to Dorthea F. Nichols, 9 March 1938, NAACP Files.

14. Leverett S. Lyon, *The National Recovery Administration* (Washington, D.C.: The Brookings Institution, 1939), pp. 83-140; Clark Foreman to Harold Ickes, 13 December 1933, NA RG 48.

15. A. Howard Meyers, "The Negro Worker Under NRA," memorandum and speech notes, NA RG 9; *Pittsburgh Courier*, 12 August 1933.

16. National Urban League, *Annual Report for 1933*, (New York: National Urban League, 1933), p. 5; "The Urban League in Action," *Opportunity* 14 (May, 1936):158; *Pittsburgh Courier*, 26 August 1933; Charles Radford Lawrence, "Negro Organizations in Crisis," (Ph.D. dissertation, Columbia University, 1953), pp. 251-252; Ralph Bunche, "The Programs, Ideologies, Tactics and Achievements of Negro Betterment and Interracial Organizations" (Carnegie-Myrdal Manuscripts), pp. 228-229.

17. National Urban League, *Annual Report for 1933*, p. 5; T. Arnold Hill to Joel Berrall, 19 February 1934, NA RG 9.

18. Lawrence, "Negro Organizations in Crisis," p. 249; John P. Davis, "Report on the Joint Committee on National Recovery," *Senate Miscellaneous Documents*, no. 217, 74th Cong., 2nd sess., 10016: 38-49; idem, "Two Years with the Joint Committee of National Recovery, 1933-1935," pamphlet, NA RG 183, Oxley File; Walter White, "Report of the Secretary," 6 September 1933, NAACP Files; Roy Wilkins, interview, Columbia University Oral History Project, pp. 65-66.

19. Ultimately twenty-two groups affiliated with the Joint Committee on National Recovery: African Methodist Episcopal Church, African Methodist Episcopal Zion Church, Alpha Kappa Alpha Sorority, Alpha Phi Alpha Fraternity, Colored Methodist Episcopal Church, Delta Sigma Theta Sorority, Improved Benevolent and Protective Order of Elks of the Old World, National Association for the Advancement of Colored People, National Association of Colleges for Colored Youth, National Association of Colored Women's Clubs, National Baptist Convention, National Catholic Interracial Federation, National Housewives League, National Negro Bar Association, National Negro Business League, National Council of the Protestant Episcopal Church, National Technical Association, Negro Industrial League, Omega Psi Phi Fraternity, Public Affairs Committee of the National Young Women's Christian Association, Race Relations Department of the Federal Council of Churches of Christ in America, and the Women's Auxiliary of the National Baptist Convention.

The National Urban League was the only major Negro organization that refused to affiliate with the joint committee. The reasons for the league's refusal to cooperate will remain obscure until the league's correspondence files are open for inspection. It would not be surprising, however, if the leaders of the league had grave misgivings about the formation of a second organization devoted primarily to advancing the economic interests of black workers. After all, there was, in addition to the implied criticism of the league presented by the mere existence of a competitive group, the question of finances. There were only a certain number of philanthropists and foundations to which Negro groups could turn for assistance, and the league must have viewed with alarm the prospect of facing competition for the few dollars available to finance work aimed at improving the economic status of black workers. John P. Davis appears to have assessed the situation correctly: "I sent cordial letters to the Urban League...asking them to join us in our work. Responses to the appeal were vague and indefinite, and were met...by the announcement in the weekly press that an office had been set up in Washington by the Urban League. No such office has ever existed in Washington and does not now exist. ...I have on my desk this morning a letter from that group which amounts to a courteous refusal to even consider cooperation. The feeling seems to be that we would die a natural death because of inadequate financial support, and then the field will be left clear for others..."Davis to Frances Williams, September 11, 1933. NAACP Files.

20. Lawrence, "Negro Organizations in Crisis," pp. 249-250; Davis, "Report on the Joint Committee," p. 41; idem, "What Price National Recovery?" *Crisis* 40 (December, 1933): 271-272; Frances Williams to Roy Wilkins, 8 September 1933, NAACP Files; Williams to Davis, 8 September 1933, NAACP Files; Davis to Williams, 11 September 1933, NAACP Files.

21. Davis, "Report on the Joint Committee," pp. 41, 45-46; idem, "Summary of Work Already Accomplished and Suggested Next Steps in Program for the Joint Committee on National Recovery," confidential memorandum, 15 September 1933, NAACP Files; idem, "Two Years with the Joint Committee on National Recovery, 1933-1935," NA RG 183.

22. Davis, "Report on the Joint Committee," pp. 45-46; idem, "Two Years with the Joint Committee"; idem, "Report of the Executive Secretary of the Joint Committee on National Recovery," 9 February 1935, NA RG 183, Oxley File; Minutes of the Meeting of the Joint Committee on National Recovery, 21 February 1934, NA RG 183, Oxley File; "Summary of Work Already Accomplished and Suggested Next Steps," typescript, NAACP Files. I have searched through the National Archives in a vain effort to learn more about the NRA's final decision not to have a separate wage and hour standard for Negroes. The government records make no mention of this decision, however, and one would not know of it if Negro protest groups had not called attention to the matter. Since the protest groups were watchdogs over Negro rights and quick to call attention to any provisions that affected black people adversely, I regard their testimony concerning the absence of any specifically racial differential as conclusive. Yet the reasons for this decision remain a mystery. I suspect that NRA officials knew that important white interests could be placated by instituting the occupational and geographical classifications that are discussed in the fourth section of this chapter. Thus an avowedly racial differential was unnecessary and would serve only to further antagonize an important segment of the black community.

23. T. Arnold Hill, "Briefs from the South," *Opportunity* 11 (February,

1933):55; idem, "The Present Status of Negro Labor," *Opportunity* 7 (May, 1929): 145; Forrester B. Washington to Walter White, 27 February 1933, NAACP Files; J. A. Rogers, "Race Has Lost Jobs in South," *Pittsburgh Courier,* 22 August 1936; National Urban League, "How Unemployment Affects Negroes," 1931, Urban League Files.

24. Forrester B. Washington to Walter White, 27 February 1933, NAACP Files; Lawrence, "Negro Organizations in Crisis," pp. 118-124; *Charlotte News,* 22 January 1932; National Urban League, *The Forgotten Tenth,* pamphlet, Urban League Files.

25. Forrester B. Washington to Walter White, 27 February 1933, NAACP Files; NAACP Press Release, 27 October 1930, NAACP Files; *Time,* 8 September 1930, p. 17.

26. T. Arnold Hill, "Briefs from the South," p. 55.

27. Forrester B. Washington to Walter White, 27 February 1933, NAACP Files; H. A. Lett to White, 21 February 1933, NAACP Files; National Urban League, "How Unemployment Affects Negroes," 1931, Urban League Files; Lewis Caldwell, Jr., "What NRA Is Doing to the Race," *Chicago Defender,* 26 May 1934; *Chicago Defender,* 2 December 1933.

28. *Baton Rouge Morning Advocate,* 11 July 1934; *Baton Rouge State Times,* 12 July 1934; Hilton Butler, "Murder for the Job," *Nation,* 12 July 1933, p. 44; Cayton and Mitchell, *Black Workers and the New Unions,* pp. 439-445.

29. The statistics on lynching are taken from the *Annual Reports of the NAACP, 1930-1935.* Walter White to Arthur B. Spingarn, Hubert Delaney, Louis T. Wright, and Mary White Ovington, memorandum, 26 December 1935, NAACP Files. White sent Howard Kester's report to Henry Wallace, 26 November 1934, NA RG 16. Arthur Raper has presented detailed statistical information showing a positive correlation between economic adversity and the incidence of lynching in the Southern Cotton Belt. Arthur F. Raper, *The Tragedy of Lynching* (Chapel Hill: University of North Carolina Press, 1933), pp. 30-31.

30. Roy Wilkins to Matthew Boyd, 27 January 1934, NA RG 9; Boyd to Wilkins, 31 January 1934, NAACP Files; Monroe Work to Boyd, 3 February 1934, NA RG 9; D. H. Hunt to John Swope, 21 March 1934, NA RG 9; John P. Davis to Boyd, memorandum, 22 January 1934, NA RG 9; Abram Harris to Boyd, 4 December 1934, NA RG 9; Boyd to Phillips Russell, 31 January 1934, NA RG 9; Boyd to Lula Lewis, 30 January 1934, NA RG 9; Division of Research and Planning, "Report on Effect of NRA Codes Upon Negroes," 21 March 1934, NA RG 183; NAACP Press Release, 18 August 1933, NAACP Files.

31. F. D. Roosevelt, "Presidential Statement on NIRA," in *The Public Papers and Addresses of Franklin D. Roosevelt,* ed. Samuel I. Rosenman, 2:251; Arthur M. Schlesinger, Jr., *The Coming of the New Deal* (Boston: Houghton Mifflin Company, 1959), p. 170; Joel Berrall to R. L. Houston, memorandum, 10 September 1934, NA RG 9.

32. Arthur F. Raper, *Preface to Peasantry,* (Chapel Hill: University of North Carolina Press, 1936), pp. 238, 241.

33. Industrial Appeals Board of the National Recovery Administration, *Hearing on Petition of Southland Manufacturing Company of Montgomery, Alabama, for Exemption from Cotton Textile Code,* 8 October 1934, NA RG 9; memorandum to the Secretary and Commissioner of Labor Statistics, 23 October 1934, NA RG 183, Oxley File; *Baltimore Afro-American,* 13 October 1934; Allan A. Banks, Jr., "Wage Differentials and the Negro Under the NRA" (Master's thesis, Howard University, 1938), pp. 50-60.

34. "Testimony of G. Lake Imes," *Hearing on Petition of the Southland Manufacturing Company,* NA RG 9; Robert Russa Moton and G. Lake Imes, "Petition of the Tuskegee Normal and Industrial Institute addressed to the NRA Appeals Board," 18 September 1934, NA RG 183, Oxley File; "Testimony of Herbert C. Mayer," *Hearing on Petition of the Southland Manufacturing Company,* NA RG 9.

35. "Testimony of Herbert G. Mayer (italics added), Rose Schneiderman, Clark Foreman, John P. Davis, and Burton Oppenheim," *Hearing on Petition of the Southland Manufacturing Company,* NA RG 9: Mary Anderson to Lawrence Oxley, 9 October 1934, NA RG 183, Oxley File; U.S. Labor Advisory Board to the Secretary of Labor and Commissioner of Labor Statistics, memorandum, 23 October 1934, NA RG 183, Oxley File.

36. In March of 1935 the Industrial Appeals Board reversed itself and granted Southland an exemption from the minimum wage provisions of the Cotton Textile Code. The board's decision permitted Southland to pay its employees a minimum of $10 per week instead of the regulation $12, on provision that at least 50 percent of the workers would receive the $12 minimum and that this percentage would gradually be increased to 90.

Some Negroes hailed the exemption as the "opening wedge" in a drive to recover jobs. The *Norfolk Journal and Guide,* for example, observed that "in the last analysis, code provisions setting minimum wages are beneficial to the individual worker only if the workers are actually employed." John P. Davis and Walter White recognized the force of this argument and grudgingly endorsed the agreement. Yet the board's 1935 decision had no practical effect since less than two months later the Supreme Court declared the NRA unconstitutional. Industrial Appeals Board of the NRA, "Appeal of the Southland Manufacturing Company," NA RG 183; *Norfolk Journal and Guide,* 9 March 1935; Walter White to George Edmund Haynes, 6 October 1934, NAACP Files; Lawrence Oxley to Isador Lubin, memorandum, 12 April 1934; Gustav Peck to W. A. Harriman, 26 November 1934, and 11 December 1934, NA RG 9.

37. U. S., Congress, *Hearings before the Senate Finance Committee, Investigation of the National Recovery Administration,* 74th Cong., 1st sess. (testimony of John P. Davis at p. 2140 ff.); John P. Davis, "The Maid Well Garment Case," *Crisis* 41 (December, 1934): 356-357; idem, speech to the Twenty-fifth Annual Conference of the NAACP, 1934, NAACP

Files; Minutes of the Meeting of the Board of Directors, 11 March 1935, NAACP Files; Walter White, "Report of the Secretary," 7 March 1935, NAACP Files; John P. Davis, "Report of the Executive Secretary of the Joint Committee on National Recovery," 9 February 1935, and 1 June 1935, NA RG 183, Oxley File; *Pittsburgh Courier,* 16 June 1934; *Norfolk Journal and Guide,* 25 May 1935.

38. "Testimony of John P. Davis," *Code Hearing for the Cotton Textile Industry,* NA RG 9; John P. Davis and Robert C. Weaver, "Statement of the Negro Industrial League Concerning the Code of Fair Competition for the Cotton Textile Industry," 27 June 1933, NA RG 9; Walter White to Harold Ickes, 6 July 1933, NA RG 48; White to Franklin D. Roosevelt, 6 July 1933, NA RG 48; Roy Wilkins to Oscar Chapman, 21 May 1934, NAACP Files; Minutes of the Meeting of the Board of Directors, 10 July 1933, NAACP Files; *Norfolk Journal and Guide,* 3 March 1934.

39. "Testimony of John P. Davis," *Code Hearing for the Cotton Textile Industry,* NA RG 9; Banks, "Wage Differentials and the Negro Under NRA," p. 15; Raper, *Preface to Peasantry,* p. 239; Cayton and Mitchell, *Black Workers and the New Unions,* p. 100; A. Howard Meyers, "The Negro Worker Under NRA," *Journal of Negro Education* 5 (January, 1936): 48-49; Charles S. Johnson, "Incidence Upon the Negroes," *American Journal of Sociology* 40 (May, 1935): 739; George Schuyler, interview, Columbia University Oral History Project, pp. 391-392.

40. Gustav Peck, "The Negro Worker and the NRA," *Crisis* 41 (September, 1934): 262; Labor Advisory Board, "Territorial Differentials," typescript in office files of Gustav Peck, NA RG 9; Arthur F. Raper, "The Southern Negro and the NRA," typescript in NA RG 183, Oxley File; Lawrence Oxley, "The Negro Wage Differentials Under the Codes," typescript, NA RG 183, Oxley File.

41. Gustav Peck, "The Negro Worker and the NRA," p. 79.

42. "Testimony of Walter White," *Code Hearing for the Laundry Trade,* NA RG 9; White to Rose Marcus Coe, 22 November 1933, NAACP Files; White, "Report of the Secretary," 7 March 1935, NAACP Files; Mary Anderson, "Statement on the Proposed Code for the Laundry Trade," 23 November 1933, NA RG 183, Oxley File; John P. Davis, "NRA Codifies Wage Slavery," *Crisis* 41 (October, 1934): 299. Eleanor Roosevelt was impressed favorably by Davis's article and forwarded a copy to Donald Richberg of NRA. Richberg replied that "the problem of negro labor cannot be disposed of by any such generalizations as fill Mr. Davis' article and the economic considerations are constantly obscured by pure emotionalism. For example, the article refers to thirty thousand negro women in the laundry trade being condemned to a code wage of 14 cents an hour. The laundry industry competes with home workers and despite this outrageously low wage there was ample evidence presented to the effect that when laundry costs rose above the level of the cost of home work, the laundry workers lost their employment." Donald Richberg to Eleanor Roosevelt, 23 October 1934, NA RG 69; Eleanor Roosevelt to Walter

White, 8 January 1935, NA RG 69; White to Eleanor Roosevelt, 13 November 1934, NA RG 69.

43. *New York Times,* 9 January 1934, p. 1; *Pittsburgh Courier,* 20 January 1934; Walter White to Eleanor Roosevelt, 13 November 1934, NA RG 69.

44. Banks, "Wage Differentials and the Negro Under NRA," p. 30.

45. John P. Davis, speech to the Twenty-fifth Annual Conference of the NAACP (1934), NAACP Files; *New York Times,* 9 January 1934, p. 1; Lawrence Oxley to Frances Perkins, memorandum, 9 November 1935, NA RG 183; Roy Wilkins to Oscar Chapman, 21 May 1934, NAACP Files.

46. "Testimony of Frances Perkins," *Code Hearing for the Iron and Steel Industry,* NA RG 9; Roy Wilkins to Oscar Chapman, 21 May 1934, NAACP Files; *Chicago Defender,* 2 September 1933; Cayton and Mitchell, *Black Workers and the New Unions,* pp. 97-98.

47. William Pickens, "NRA—Negro Removal Act?" *World Tomorrow,* 28 September 1933, pp. 539-540; Pickens to J. E. Spingarn, 10 June 1934, WEBD Papers; Minutes of the Meeting of the Board of Directors, 12 September 1933, NAACP Files; NAACP Press Release, 8 September 1933, NAACP Files.

48. Allen Kifer, "The Negro and the New Deal" (Ph.D. dissertation, University of Wisconsin, 1961), p. 227; Roy Wilkins to Matthew Boyd, 27 January 1934, NA RG 9; John P. Davis to Boyd, memorandum, 22 January 1934, NA RG 9; *High Point Enterprise,* 5 October 1933.

49. Broadus Mitchell, *Depression Decade* (New York: Holt, Rinehart, 1947) p. 254.

50. Schlesinger, *The Coming of the New Deal,* pp. 108, 114.

51. C. F. Roos, *NRA Economic Planning* (Bloomington, Indiana: The Principia Press, 1937), p. 275.

52. Ira DeA. Reid, as quoted by Caldwell, "What the NRA Is Doing to the Race."

53. "Remarks of Robert Weaver," Minutes of the Fourth Meeting of the Interdepartmental Group Concerned with the Special Problems of Negroes, 1 June 1934, NA RG 48; John P. Davis, speech to the Twenty-fifth Annual Conference of the NAACP (1934), NAACP Files.

54. R. B. Parsons to Hugh Johnson, 12 December 1933, NA RG 9; Jesse O. Thomas, "The Negro Looks at the Alphabet," *Opportunity* 12 (January, 1934): 12-13.

55. Walter White, "Report of the Secretary," 6 September 1933, and 8 January 1934, NAACP Files; NAACP Press Release, 4 August 1933; George Edmund Haynes to Members of the Joint Committee on National Recovery, 4 October 1933, NAACP Files; "Report of the National Conference on the Special Problems of the Negro and Negro Youth," 1937, NA RG 48; National Urban League, "Our Negro Working Population and National Recovery: A Special Memorandum Presented to President Roosevelt," 4 January 1937, Urban League Files; XI chapter of Delta Sigma Sorority to Leo Wolman, telegram, 5 March 1934, NA RG 9; John

P. Davis to Rose Schneiderman, 23 October 1933, NA RG 9; Davis to Frances Perkins, 27 April 1934, NA RG 183, Oxley File.

56. Clark Foreman to Leo Wolman, 10 October 1933, NA RG 9; Foreman to Isadore Lubin, 5 December 1933, NA RG 9; Foreman to Ruth Stocking, 6 October 1934, NA RG 9; Frances Perkins to Wolman, 14 April 1934, NA RG 9; Lawrence Oxley to Perkins, memorandum, 9 November 1935, NA RG 183; John P. Davis to Perkins, 27 April 1934, NA RG 183.

57. Randolph was the president of the Brotherhood of Sleeping Car Porters; Harris was professor of economics at Howard University and a member of the board of directors of the NAACP; Johnson was professor of sociology at Fisk University.

58. Gustav Peck to Carroll, memorandum, 18 June 1934, NA RG 9.

59. Roy Wilkins to L. C. Marshall, telegram, 27 May 1935, NAACP Files; Charles Houston to Walter White, 23 May 1935, NAACP Files; *Chicago Defender*, 22 September 1934, and 8 June 1935.

60. Matthew Boyd to Lula Lewis, 30 January 1934, NA RG 9; Abram Harris to Boyd, 14 December 1934, NA RG 9; Boyd to Roy Wilkins, 23 January 1934, and 31 January 1934, NA RG 9; Wilkins to Boyd, 27 January 1934, NA RG 9; John P. Davis to Boyd, 22 January 1934, NA RG 9; *Baltimore Afro-American*, 20 January 1934.

61. Roy Wilkins to Matthew Boyd, 27 January 1934, NA RG 9; Boyd to Wilkins, 31 January 1934, NA RG 9; John P. Davis to Boyd, 22 January 1934, NA RG 9; Abram Harris to Boyd, 4 December 1933, NA RG 9; NAACP Press Releases, 18 August 1933, and 8 September 1933, NAACP Files.

62. John P. Davis to Matthew Boyd, 22 January 1934, NA RG 9; *Baltimore Afro-American*, 20 January 1934.

63. Matthew Boyd to Phillips Russell, 31 January 1934, NA RG 9; NRA Division of Research and Planning, "Report on Effect of NRA Codes Upon Negroes," 21 March 1934, NA RG 9; Monroe Work to Boyd, 3 February 1934, NA RG 9; Ralph N. Davis, "Conclusions from Survey in Alabama of the Effect of the Operations of the NRA Code on Negro Labor," n.d., NA RG 9; Mabel Byrd to Leo Wolman, memorandum, 17 November 1933, NA RG 9; Arthur F. Raper, "The Southern Negro and the NRA," typescript, NA RG 183, Oxley File.

64. Mabel Byrd to Leo Wolman, memorandum, 17 November 1933, NA RG 9.

65. Clark Foreman to Harold Ickes, 13 December 1933, NA RG 48. Minutes of the 18 September 1933 meeting of the Special Industrial Recovery Board. John P. Davis obtained a transcript of these minutes, and the record was published in the *Chicago Defender*, 23 December 1933. For more information on this meeting and the subsequent publication of the minutes see: Frances Perkins to Harold Ickes, 16 December 1933, NA RG 48; Ickes to Perkins, 2 January 1934, and 12 February 1934, NA RG 48; Clark Foreman to Ickes, 13 December 1933, NA RG 48; Frances Williams to Walter White, 20 December 1933, NAACP Files; Roy Wilkins to White,

28 December 1933, NAACP Files. With regard to Miss Byrd's termination at the NRA, see White to William Hastie, 5 December 1933, NAACP Files; Hastie to White, 7 December 1933, NAACP Files; John P. Davis and Rose M. Coe, "Negro Workers Under the NRA," typescript, n.d., NAACP Files; Cayton and Mitchell, *Black Workers and the New Unions*, p. 102. For more information indicating Hugh Johnson's insensitivity with regard to the problems of Negroes under the NRA, see Johnson to Nelson Nichols, 23 February 1934, NAACP Files; Nichols to Charles Houston, 24 February 1933, NAACP Files. The quotation from John Davis is from his "Statement...before the Complaint Hearing of the NRA," 28 February 1934, NA RG 183. In May of 1934 Dr. Abram Harris was appointed to a position on the NRA's Consumers' Advisory Board. However, Harris, busy with his duties as professor of economics at Howard University, member of the board of directors of the NAACP, and chairman of the association's important Committee on Future Plan and Program, was able to devote very little time to his NRA duties, and he resigned after serving for only four months.

66. Samuel Krislov and Allen Kifer have pointed out that the Rosenwald Foundation offered to pay the salary of any suitable candidate Secretary Ickes should name as adviser on Negro affairs in the Department of Interior. Samuel Krislov, *The Negro in Federal Employment: The Quest for Equal Opportunity* (Minneapolis: University of Minnesota Press, 1967) p. 24; Allen Kifer, paper read at the 1966 meeting of the Association for the Study of Negro Life and History; Roy Wilkins to Harold Ickes, telegram, 22 August 1933, NAACP Files; Walter White, "Report of the Secretary," 8 September 1933, NAACP Files; NAACP Press Releases, 18 August 1933, and 1 September 1933, NAACP Files; *Pittsburgh Courier*, 2 September 1933; *Chicago Defender*, 23 December 1933; Kifer, "The Negro and the New Deal," pp. 218-219.

67. Kifer, "The Negro and the New Deal," pp. 220-221. For an account of the activities of the adviser on Negro affairs, see the *Annual Report of the Secretary of Interior*, 1936, pp. 49-51. Harold Ickes to Will Marion Cook, 21 December 1936, NA RG 48; Robert Weaver to Rayford Logan, "The Negro and the New Deal," *Sphinx*, May, 1935, p. 3; Clark Foreman to Ickes, 22 December 1933, NA RG 48; Robert R. Moton to Ickes, 19 December 1933, NA RG 48; Ickes to Moton, 2 January 1934, NA RG 48; Minutes of the Interdepartmental Group Concerned with the Special Problems of Negroes, 7 February 1934, NA RG 48.

68. The members of this interdepartmental committee later became the nucleus of President Roosevelt's much publicized "Black Cabinet." I have not discussed the cabinet because it did not really begin operations until 1937 and 1938, long after most Negro leaders had lost confidence in the government's economic recovery program and had shifted their concern to organizational work within the black community. Moreover, the marginal effectiveness of the Black Cabinet was out of all proportion to the publicity it received. There are two good master's theses that tell the story of the

Black Cabinet in considerable detail: William J. Davis, "The Role of the Adviser on Negro Affairs and the Racial Specialists in National Administration" (Master's thesis, Howard University, 1940) and Jane Motz, "The Black Cabinet: Negroes in the Administration of Franklin D. Roosevelt" (Master's thesis, University of Delaware, 1964).

69. Subcommittee on Labor, "Report to the Interdepartmental Group Concerned with the Special Problems of Negroes," 18 April 1934, NA RG 48.

70. Clark Foreman to Harold Ickes, 13 December 1933, NA RG 48.

71. Kelly Miller, "Kelly Miller Says," *Norfolk Journal and Guide,* 2 December 1933; T. Arnold Hill, "The Plight of the Negro Industrial Worker," *Journal of Negro Education* 5 (January, 1936): 40; *Pittsburgh Courier,* 28 October 1933.

72. *Norfolk Journal and Guide,* 28 April 1934; *Chicago Defender,* 12 May 1934, 17 February 1934.

73. *New York Times,* 13 December 1933, p. 4; "No Permanent Slavery," *Crisis* 41 (November, 1934): 333; John P. Davis, speech to the Twenty-fifth Annual Conference of the NAACP (1934), NAACP Files; Davis to Leo Wolman, 9 February 1934, NA RG 9; A. Howard Meyers to Davis, 13 February 1934, NA RG 9; Resolutions of the Twenty-fifth Annual Conference of the NAACP (1934), NAACP Files; "Goodbye to General Johnson," *Crisis* 41 (November, 1934): 332.

Davis's charge of complete noncooperation was slightly exaggerated. Early in 1934, officials of the NRA's Labor Advisory Board agreed to a plan whereby the Joint Committee on National Recovery and the Labor Advisory Board would make a comprehensive study of the effects of the NRA on Negro labor. Four members of the staff of the Labor Advisory Board were to be assigned to this project, and for a short period they did work with John Davis and Rose Marcus Coe of the joint committee. Yet for reasons that I have not been able to discover, this cooperation broke down and the study was never completed. See John P. Davis, "Report on the Joint Committee on National Recovery," *Senate Miscellaneous Documents,* no. 217, 74th Cong., 2nd sess., 10016: 42; Davis to Gustav Peck, 23 January 1934, NA RG 9; Mildred Chisholm to C. F. Roos, memorandum, 2 March 1934, NA RG 9; T. Arnold Hill to Joel Berrall, 19 February 1934, NA RG 9; Berrall to Hill, 21 February 1934, NA RG 9; Hugh Johnson to Davis, 26 February 1934, NA RG 9; John P. Davis, "Report of the Executive Secretary of the Joint Committee," 16 March 1934, NA RG 183; Suzanne LaFollette, "A Message to Uncle Tom," *Nation,* 5 September 1934, pp. 265-266; *Pittsburgh Courier,* 27 January 1934, and 3 March 1934.

74. Edward D. W. Spingarn, "Shall There Be a Wage Differential Between North and South?", typescript, n.d., NAACP Files; Consumers' Advisory Board to W. L. O'Brien, memorandum, 30 June 1934, NA RG 183, Oxley File; Henry Simons, *Economic Policy for a Free Society* (Chicago: University of Chicago Press, 1948) pp. 121-159; H. H. Pixley,

"North-South Wage Differentials, 1929-1933," typescript, n.d., NA RG 9; Labor Advisory Board, "Territorial Differentials," typescript, n.d., correspondence files of Gustav Peck, NA RG 9; Arthur F. Raper, "The Negro and NRA," typescript in NA RG 183, Oxley File.

75. Hugh Johnson, as quoted by Lyon, *The NRA*, p. 759; Dexter M. Keezer, "The Consumer Under the National Recovery Administration," *Annals of the American Academy of Political and Social Science* 172 (March, 1934): 96; Frances Perkins, *The Roosevelt I Knew* (New York: The Viking Press, 1946), p. 208.

76. Lyon, *The NRA*, pp. 760, 796; Ellis W. Hawley, *The New Deal and the Problem of Monopoly*, (Princeton: Princeton University Press, 1966), pp. 80-81, 98-100; Gardiner Means, "The Consumer and the New Deal," *Annals of the American Academy of Political and Social Science* 173 (May, 1934): 11; Paul H. Douglas, "The Role of the Consumer in the New Deal," *Annals of the American Academy of Political and Social Science* 172 (March, 1934): 101-102.

In retrospect it is clear that despite NRA's formal prohibition of price fixing, many businessmen managed to inflate their prices by taking advantage of the regulation that products should not be sold below cost. Those who were familiar with corporation accounting practices had little difficulty in manipulating their cost statistics. Allowances for depreciation and obsolesence were subject to wide margins of uncertainty, and other items, such as salaries of executives and cost of materials, could occasionally be padded. As Paul Douglas observed, "To reject outright price fixing but to provide that goods shall not be sold below a definition of cost is...frequently to admit through the back door what has been denied admittance at the front." Moreover, it is clear that many producers took advantage of the system of government sponsored industrial cooperation to secure agreements for cutting production. (During the first months of NRA there was a sharp decline in production from an index figure of 101 in July, 1933, to 71 in November. Production then began to increase during the last two months of 1933 and the early months of 1934, reaching a high of 86 in May. But by September, 1934, the production index had fallen again to 71, thereby effacing all the gains that had been made during the first eighteen months of NRA. In February, 1935, NRA reported that while dividends and interest were 150 percent of their total in 1926, payrolls were only 60 percent of their 1926 level, and production had declined by about one-third.) This combination of high prices and low production naturally subverted the plan for increasing purchasing power. High prices diminished the purchasing power of everyone, and low production quotas made large-scale unemployment inevitable. Paul H. Douglas, "The Role of the Consumer in the New Deal," *Annals of the American Academy of Political and Social Science* 172 (March, 1934): 101-102; Basil Rauch, *The History of the New Deal* (New York: Capricorn Edition, 1963), pp. 128, 182.

77. Dexter M. Keezer, "The Consumer Under the National Recovery Administration," *Annals of the American Academy of Political and Social Science,* 172 (March, 1934): 88-89.

78. *Chicago Defender,* 23 March 1935; *Norfolk Journal and Guide,* 12 August 1933.

79. Roy Wilkins to Franklin D. Roosevelt, telegram, 20 August 1935, NAACP Files; *Chicago Defender,* 26 August 1935; U. S., Congress, Senate, *Hearings before the Senate Finance Committee, Investigation of the National Recovery Administration,* 74th Cong., 1st sess., p. 2140; Davis and Coe, "Negro Workers Under the NRA"; *Baltimore Afro-American,* 8 January 1938.

80. "Testimony of Walter White," *Code Hearings for the Laundry Trade,* NA RG 9; "Statement of the Negro Industrial League Concerning the Code of Fair Competition for the Lumber and Timber Products Industry," *Code Hearing for the Lumber Industry,* NA RG 9; "Testimony of John P. Davis," *Code Hearing for the Cotton Textile Industry,* NA RG 9.

81. A. Howard Meyers, "The Negro Worker Under NRA," typescript, n.d., NA RG 9; Lawrence Oxley to Isadore Lubin, memorandum, 24 October 1934, NA RG 183.

82. A. Howard Meyers, "The Negro Worker Under NRA," typescript, n.d., NA RG 9; Raper, "The Southern Negro and the NRA"; Jesse O. Thomas, "The Negro Looks at the Alphabet," *Opportunity* 12 (January, 1934): 12-14; Lucy Randolph Mason, "Objection to Minimum Wage Discriminations Against Negro Workers," 29 August 1933, typescript, PPF 1820, FDR Library.

83. Meyers, "The Negro Worker Under NRA"; Clark Foreman, "Negro Seen as Gainer in Recovery Deal," *New York Times,* 15 April 1934, p. 5; Foreman to Leo Wolman, 10 October 1933, NA RG 9; Lawrence Oxley to Isador Lubin, memorandum, 24 October 1934, NA RG 183; Raper, "The Southern Negro and the NRA."

84. T. Arnold Hill, "The Plight of the Negro Industrial Worker," *Journal of Negro Education* 5 (January, 1936): 40-47.

7

Section 7a and
the Black Worker

ACCORDING to President Roosevelt, the purpose of the
National Industrial Recovery Act was "to put people back to
work" at wages that would provide more than a bare living.
Roosevelt and his advisers believed that larger wage payments
would expand mass purchasing power and that this increased
demand would stimulate the volume of production and
thereby enable businessmen to reemploy workers they had
laid off. The crucial point in inducing recovery was thought to
be the expansion of purchasing power, and it was for this
reason that the administration's recovery bill required employers to "comply with the maximum hours of labor, minimum rates of pay, and other working conditions approved or
prescribed by the President."[1]

The Roosevelt administration believed that mass purchasing power could be expanded further if, in addition to the
wage and hour provisions, NRA actively encouraged the de-

velopment of trade unions which would protect the workers' interests. Several important New Deal advisers predicted that without the countervailing power of well-organized unions the excess supply of labor would put workers at a serious disadvantage when bargaining with employers, with the result that the wage earners' real income would not be large enough to sustain the mass purchasing power that would stimulate recovery. It was felt that by encouraging collective bargaining the government would enable workers to wrest higher wages from management and that the resulting increase in consumer spending would benefit the entire economy. Accordingly, Section 7a of the administration's National Industrial Recovery Act provided

> 1) that employees shall have the right to organize and bargain collectively through representatives of their own choosing, and shall be free from the interference, restraint or coercion of employers of labor, or their agents, in the designation of such representatives.
>
> 2) that no employee and no one seeking employment shall be required as a condition of employment to join any company union or to refrain from joining, organizing, or assisting a labor organization of his own choosing.[2]

Yet during the two years of NRA's existence there was great confusion and heated controversy concerning the exact meaning of Section 7a. The new legislation had affirmed the right of employees "to organize and bargain collectively through representatives of their own choosing" and, conversely, the obligation of employers not to interfere with this right. But it soon became apparent that there was much disagreement as to the meaning of collective bargaining "through representatives of their own choosing." Labor leaders such as John L. Lewis insisted that President Roosevelt wanted workers to join independent unions. On the other hand, businessmen who feared unionization noted that no provision had been made concerning the manner in which representatives were to be chosen. Many of them thought that by establishing company unions they could comply with the terms of Section 7a without losing any control over their businesses.[3]

Under these circumstances, direct conflict between labor and management concerning the correct interpretation of Section 7a was inevitable. Almost immediately, disputes broke out between workers who wanted independent unions and employers who were determined to avoid negotiation with outside organizations. Consequently, on August 5, 1933, President Roosevelt found it necessary to authorize the establishment of a National Labor Board (NLB) to help arbitrate differences and negotiate settlements. When disputes arose, the board generally recommended that free elections be held to determine the legitimate bargaining agent. The board assumed, though the doctrine was not explicitly stated for some months, that the organization chosen by a *majority* of workers was qualified to act as the bargaining agent for *all* workers. However, while the NLB was commissioned to make recommendations, it was powerless to enforce its decisions. If an employer refused to accept NLB recommendations for an election, the board could recommend nothing more than the ineffectual gesture of removing the NRA's symbol of compliance, the Blue Eagle. Theoretically, the NLB and its successor, the first National Labor Relations Board, also could ask the Department of Justice to inaugurate suits against recalcitrant bargainers, but judgments were not obtained in any of the thirty-three cases referred to the department between July 1, 1934, and March 1, 1935. Thus, almost from the beginning of the NRA it was apparent to many observers that Section 7a did not adequately safeguard labor's right to organize independent unions. The Recovery

Act had not established machinery for enforcing its collective bargaining provisions, and determined employers were able to avoid meaningful negotiation with outside unions.[4]

Historians and economists often have assumed that all wage earners would have benefited if the NRA had supported collective bargaining more enthusiastically and had provided adequate legislative protection of the workers' right to organize in independent unions. Yet insofar as Negro workers are concerned, this assumption is questionable. The great majority of Negro wage earners were members of the working class, but during the early years of the New Deal Negroes were rarely found in the ranks of organized labor. Altogether in 1930 there were at least nineteen independent unions which excluded Negroes from membership either by constitutional provision or by initiation ritual. An additional ten unions admitted Negroes to membership only in segregated auxiliary locals. Of course these were only the more blatant examples of union discrimination. Many unions prohibited Negro membership by tacit consent, while others permitted only token membership. Still others—perhaps a majority— discriminated against black workers in more subtle ways. While admitting that it was impossible to determine exactly the number of Negro trade union members, the NAACP felt it was "safe to say that there were in 1930 no more than 50,000 colored members of national unions," and half of these were members of the black Brotherhood of Sleeping Car Porters. These black union members represented about 3 percent of the 1,500,000 Negroes engaged in transportation, extraction of minerals and manufacturing in 1930 (compared with a figure of about 10 percent for all non-agricultural American workers).[5]

From its inception, the AFL showed little enthusiasm for the task of organizing unskilled, industrial workers. Indeed, some writers have interpreted the emergence of the AFL and the decline of the Knights of Labor in the late 1880s and early 1890s as the turning point which "marked the triumph of craft individualism over industrial brotherhood." Although the AFL occasionally issued statements concerning the need to organize the mass production industries, it had not made a major attempt in this direction since the abortive steel strike of 1919. During the 1920s, membership in the federation's largest industrial unions declined precipitously, and this reinforced the general impression that the federation represented only those skilled workers who composed the "aristocracy of labor." During the early years of the depression, several federal labor unions were chartered for the express purpose of organizing mass-production industries, but these federal unions were largely unsuccessful, and they did not receive enthusiastic support from AFL headquarters; Horace Cayton and George Mitchell expressed the skepticism of most Negroes when they noted that "the national office did nothing until its position became so paradoxical that some gesture was necessary to prevent a new union movement. . . ." [6]

Since a disproportionately large number of Negroes were either semiskilled or unskilled workers, it was inevitable that they would play a minor role in craft unions. Of the 825,000 Negroes employed in manufacturing industries in 1920, Spero and Harris calculated that only 16.6 percent were skilled workers; 67.9 percent were laborers, and 15.5 percent were semiskilled. The percentages for white workers were 32.4 skilled, 19.1 semiskilled, and 48.5 laborers. Thus, if skill was to be made the prerequisite for trade union membership, less than one-third of the Negro workers and only slightly more than half of the whites were eligible for organization. Statistics such as these convinced the Urban League that there was "little hope for the black worker so long as (the AFL) remains structurally a craft organization."[7]

The effects of race prejudice and the craft system of organization were compounded further by the large degree of independence which the AFL gave its constituent members. The AFL's official declarations that all workers should be organized without regard to race, creed, or color were ineffectual because authority in matters of membership and participation was left in the hands of the local union. Thus, while the AFL itself barred racial discrimination in union membership, the policy was of little significance because admission standards were set by the independent unions.[8]

However, Negro spokesmen believed that there was much that federation officials could have done in the way of informal persuasion to break down the pattern of racial discrimination. Unfortunately, it seemed to Negro leaders that the federation's constitutional difficulties were complicated by a fundamental unwillingness to persuade member unions to remove the Negro exclusion clauses from their constitutions. Ira DeA. Reid of the Urban League declared that "though the American Federation of Labor has uttered pronouncement upon pronouncement favoring the admission of Negro workers, that body has failed to convince the masses of Negro workers that it is rendering other than lip service to such expressed principles." W. E. B. Du Bois of the NAACP was even more emphatic: "The A. F. of L. has from the beginning of its organization stood up and lied brazenly about its attitude toward Negro labor," he proclaimed. "They have affirmed and still affirm that they wish to organize Negro labor when this is a flat and proven falsehood." T. Arnold Hill complained that the AFL had never "campaigned among its members for its idea of fair play reiterated in frequent resolutions."[9]

William Green, the president of the AFL, admitted that the federation's biracial ideals had not always been realized, but he reminded Negroes of the enormous problems faced by those who would change popular attitudes. He suggested that the AFL as a whole was not to be condemned because some of its affiliates discriminated against black workers, any more than a church should be condemned because all church members were not leading perfect lives. This explanation failed to satisfy most Negroes; indeed, many agreed with Elmer Carter, the editor of the Urban League's journal, *Opportunity*, who maintained that Green's reference to the church was singularly unfortunate. "For the church," Carter observed, "does not pursue a laissez-faire policy; it does not wait until its candidates are ready...as is the policy of the AFL. The church makes its candidates ready. It seeks them out, petitions, urges, pleads, cajoles, threatens; it goes into the far places where dwelleth the heathen and by every means of persuasion seeks to lure them under its enfolding mantle."[10]

The AFL's lack of enthusiasm for organizing mass-production workers and the fundamental inconsistency between the racial policies of the member unions and the affirmations of the parent body caused many Negroes to reject the assumption that all workers would benefit by increasing the power of organized labor. Roy Wilkins expressed views that were widely shared in the Negro community when he observed that "while Section 7a was a powerful weapon for the workers if they would use it and fight for the correct interpretation of it, we came shortly to realize...that while the American Federation of Labor was seizing upon Section 7a to carry on the most stupendous drive for membership in its history, it was doing little or nothing to include Negroes in the organizing." Jesse O. Thomas made the same point when he noted that "while Section 7a has greatly increased the security of labor in general, insofar as the different labor organizations thus benefited deny and exclude Negroes from their membership by constitutions or rituals, the position of Negro labor has been made less favorable." Thomas believed that in passing this legislation Congress had intended to benefit all workers; but because of the "unsportsman-like and anti-social attitude of the majority of the membership and heads of many of the unions and crafts, the position of Negroes has been made even more disadvantageous." Again W. E. B. Du Bois expressed a prevalent attitude most succinctly when he declared that "the most sinister power that the NRA has reinforced is the American Federation of Labor."[11]

Negro leaders were apprehensive about the prospect of AFL unions taking advantage of the encouragement and protection offered by Section 7a to organize workers and establish themselves as the sole representative of labor. In a special memorandum prepared for President Roosevelt, the Urban League warned of the dangers inherent in the new recovery legislation. The league pointed out that Section 7a did not explicitly accord protection "to minority groups of workers whom the union wishes, for racial or religious reasons, to exclude from employment." Consequently, there was the danger that after establishing itself as the sole collective bargaining agent, organized labor would demand that management discharge black employees. Such incidents had occurred in the past, and the league feared that the practice would become more serious in the immediate future when it was likely that union membership would become a necessary prerequisite for an increasing number of jobs.[12]

During the 1930s several examples of trade unions using their power to force the dismissal of black workers came to the attention of Negro leaders, an experience which under-

standably served to confirm their original pessimistic suspi-
cions. In Long Island City, New York, the Brotherhood of
Electrical Workers, Local No. 3, organized several electrical
supply shops, refused membership to the Negro workers
already employed there, and used its newly won power to
force the managements to discharge several dozen Negro
employees. In Manhattan, some locals of the Building Service
Employees' Union demanded that employers discharge Negro
workers and fill the vacancies with white unionists. As a result,
several hotels, restaurants, and office buildings were forced to
discharge Negro elevator operators and restaurant workers
and hire whites. In Milwaukee the Urban League reported
that the AFL affiliate had called a strike at the open-shop
Wehr Steel Foundry, but had not informed the Negro workers
in the plant. According to the league, "The blanket demand
made by the union was that the AFL be recognized. They did
not strike for higher wages, shorter hours or better working
conditions....After the plant was closed entirely, the specific
demand of the AFL union was dismissal of Negroes from the
plant." In St. Louis the depth of this anti-Negro sentiment was
strikingly illustrated when all the AFL men working on the
Homer Phillips Hospital (a $2 million hospital for blacks built
in the middle of a Negro neighborhood) walked off the job
and halted construction for two months in protest against the
General Tile Company's decision to employ a Negro as a tile
setter. Examples such as this naturally made other contractors
reluctant to hire black labor; they knew, as one independent
contractor observed, that if they did so they would run the
risk of having their white employees "suddenly become ill, or
have to take care of personal business, or for any number of
other fictitious reasons quit work." It was for this reason that
the building committee of the St. Louis board of education

would not allow black workers to do repair work on any of the city's seventeen colored schools. Other large contractors followed suit, and St. Louis's Negro mechanics were effectively barred from work on everything except small jobs.[13]

Roy Wilkins stated the viewpoint of many Negro leaders when he declared that all too often the AFL's strategy was to take advantage of Section 7a "to organize a union for all the workers, and to either agree with the employers to push Negroes out of the industry or, having effected an agreement with the employer, to proceed to make the union lily-white." The editor of the *Baltimore Afro-American* concluded that "unless the AFL is able to make its locals throughout the country open their doors to colored members in all crafts, it may be necessary for colored labor to organize and join in a country-wide fight on the union." And when Horace Cayton and George Mitchell interviewed Negro workers they discovered that resentment of the AFL was widely shared. One Homestead, Pennsylvania, steelworker told them that outside unions wanted Negroes to go out on strike with white workers, but that after the battle was won, the black worker would be made the victim and cast aside. Another steelworker in Cleveland told Cayton that the Negroes in his plant "have decided after studying that if labor organizations were to get a footing the colored would lose out. There are [a] few jobs that the colored hold which they [white union workers] would like to get; that is one reason why we have to fight against the labor organizations." According to the NAACP, most Negroes believed "that labor unions usually oppose the economic interests of Negroes. This follows from the fact that every union seeks to establish a closed-shop or as near a closed-shop as possible. Since American unions have largely excluded Negroes, the closed-shop has meant an arrangement under which there are no job opportunities offered black workers."[14]

Throughout the country and in a variety of ways, Negroes protested against the practice of union discrimination. Leaders such as Walter White urged the AFL "not only to make unequivocal pronouncement of opposition to any discrimination based on color but to take tangible steps to put the pronouncement into practice." Organizations such as the NAACP reminded the federation of the essential solidarity of interests of all labor and suggested that "there can and will be no industrial peace for white labor as long as black labor can be excluded from union membership." When the annual convention of the AFL met in San Francisco in 1934, local Negroes ringed the convention hall with pickets bearing signs proclaiming that "White Labor Cannot Be Free While Black Labor Is Enslaved," and that "White Unions Make Black Scabs." On the floor of the convention, A. Philip Randolph, the Negro president of the Brotherhood of Sleeping Car Porters, proposed that the AFL expel "any union maintaining the color bar." The resolutions committee rejected Randolph's motion on the ground that "the American Federation of Labor... cannot interfere with the autonomy of National and International Unions." However, the committee did accept an amendment authorizing the appointment of a five-member committee "to investigate the conditions of the colored workers of this country and report to the next convention."[15]

The AFL's Committee of Five to Investigate Conditions of the Colored Worker met in Washington on July 12, 1935, and heard the testimony of a number of witnesses familiar with the problems of Negro workers.[16] Specific examples of union discrimination were described by Reginald Johnson of the Urban League, Charles Houston of the NAACP, and A. Philip Randolph. In addition, several black workers appeared to tell of the difficulties they encountered when they tried to join union locals. In the course of his testimony, Houston informed the committee that a number of NAACP branches were "assembling data on discrimination against Negro workers in their cities" and urged that additional hearings be held in other sections of the country. Believing that sufficient information had been secured at the first and only hearing in Washington, however, President Green informed the NAACP that the federation had decided that additional regional hearings were not necessary. Ever suspicious, Walter White reminded Green that this refusal "to go further into this vitally important question will be construed as justification of the skepticism widely expressed of the sincerity of the American Federation of Labor's action."[17]

After concluding its hearings, the Committee of Five recommended a threefold plan: (1) that all international unions which discriminated against colored workers should take up the "Negro question at their next convention for the purpose of harmonizing constitution rules and practices to conform with the oft-repeated declarations of the AFL conventions on equality of treatment of all races within the trade union movement"; (2) that the AFL should issue no more charters to unions practicing discrimination; and (3) that the AFL begin an educational campaign "to get the white worker to see more completely the weaknesses of division and the necessity of unity between white and black workers to the end that all workers may be organized."[18]

The committee had been specifically instructed to report to the next convention, and if its recommendations had been accepted and implemented, significant internal reform of the AFL might have been achieved. The federation's executive council had grave reservations concerning the wisdom of the report, however, and President Green arranged for it to be submitted to the council rather than to the open convention.

At the same time the council also received a second report on the Negro question from one of its own members, George Harrison, the president of the exclusionist Railway Clerks. Harrison's report, advocating no action except "education," was considerably less forceful than the committee's recommendations. But because of its innocuousness, it was more to the liking of President Green and the council, who refused to release the committee's report and instead arranged for Harrison's inoffensive document to be presented to the convention. Even so, Harrison delayed his presentation until about 10:00 p.m. on the eleventh and last day of the 1935 convention. By then the delegates were exhausted and divided by the craft versus industrial union controversy (this was the convention which saw the final split in labor's ranks and the emergence of the CIO as an independent body) and were ready to accept any report that speeded progress toward adjournment.[19]

This sabotage of the committee's report by the AFL's executive council seemed to destroy the Negro's last hope for reform coming from within the federation. Writing to John L. Lewis, Walter White observed that "the recent hypocritical attitude of the American Federation of Labor in suppressing the report of the Committee...has destroyed the last vestige of confidence which Negro workers ever had in the AFL." The committee's chairman, John Brophy of the United Mine Workers, was even more outspoken. In a sharply worded letter of resignation, Brophy charged that the "maneuvering on the part of the executive council plainly indicated that [they] wanted the Committee of Five...to be merely a face saving device for the American Federation of Labor, rather than an honest attempt to find a solution of the Negro problem in the American labor movement."[20]

Given the record of AFL discrimination and the Negro's distrust of organized labor, it could be argued that colored workers were fortunate that Section 7a did not adequately safeguard labor's right to organize independent unions. Certainly many Negroes were convinced that their position would have been even more desperate if the Recovery Act had established effective machinery for enforcing its collective bargaining provisions. Moreover, while Negroes realized that company unions were not altogether satisfactory—that, especially during the NRA period, many employers had encouraged the organization of company unions as a defense against real collective bargaining—they understandably did not share the aversion which many white workers felt toward these management-controlled employee representation programs.[21]

Yet organized labor and large segments of the American liberal community believed that the proliferation of company unions was undermining the entire recovery program. Recalling the earlier argument that strong trade unions were needed in order to force management to increase mass purchasing power, the liberal-labor group maintained that NRA had failed to stimulate full recovery largely because ambiguities in the language of the recovery bill and the absence of enforcement powers had "enabled a minority of employers to deviate from the clear intent of the law and to threaten our entire program with destruction." Rallying behind the leadership of Senator Robert F. Wagner of New York, this group maintained that new legislation was needed to establish another labor board with the power to enforce its decisions and to prohibit employers from either dominating or supporting workers' organizations. Consequently, in March of 1934, Senator Wagner and his assistants began to work on a new bill that would "clarify and fortify the provisions of

Section 7a." As it finally emerged, the new legislation proposed to establish a strengthened National Labor Relations Board (NLRB) with the authority to investigate any disputes involving Section 7a, to order elections so that employees might choose their own representatives for collective bargaining with membership in the union chosen by the majority a mandatory prerequisite for continued employment, and the power to prohibit certain "unfair" employer practices such as company domination of the workers' organization. The legislation also provided that the NLRB was to be an independent administrative agency with the power to enforce its decisions.[22]

Negro leaders were not entirely out of sympathy with Senator Wagner's approach to collective bargaining. They approved of the requirement that certain conditions, among them free elections and majority choice, had to be fulfilled before a union could be certified as a legitimate bargaining agent. But Negro leaders also insisted that it was essential that the Wagner bill be amended so as to outlaw racial discrimination by unions. Without such an amendment, they reasoned, there was the very real danger that discriminatory unions again would use their power to restrict the Negro's economic opportunities. With such an amendment they would have, as Washington attorney William Hastie noted, "a strong weapon . . . for compelling unions to accept into membership all qualified employees."[23]

This demand for an antidiscrimination clause in the Wagner bill was widespread in the Negro community. T. Arnold Hill warned that "if the Wagner Bill passes in its present form, the power and influence of the labor movement will be greatly enhanced with the consequent danger of greater restrictions being practiced against Negro workers by organized labor."

Dean Kelly Miller of Howard University insisted that "every effort should be made to amend the Wagner Bill so as to safeguard the rights of the Negro.... Unless this is done it is easy to foretell the doom of the Negro in American industry." Roy Wilkins observed that the Wagner bill "rigidly enforces and legalizes the closed shop," and he noted that "the act plainly empowers organized labor to exclude from employment in any industry those who do not belong to a union." He thought it was "needless to point out the fact that thousands of Negro workers are barred from membership in American labor unions and, therefore, that if the closed shop is legalized by this act Negro workers will be absolutely shut out of employment." Harry E. Davis, a member of the NAACP's board of directors, summed up the sentiments of many Negroes when he observed that "it is not a 'closed' shop which is in the offing, but a 'white' shop."[24]

Negroes also pointed out that the Wagner legislation would require employers to rehire all striking employees after a settlement had been reached. According to the NAACP and the Urban League, this would jeopardize the position of strikebreakers who had been given employment while union men were off the job. While they "deplore[d] the necessity for strike-breaking," the Negro protest organizations maintained that "it is the one weapon left to the Negro worker whereby he may break the stranglehold that certain organized labor groups have utilized in preventing his complete absorption in the American labor market." The NAACP viewed the prospect of indirectly penalizing strikebreakers with particular alarm; it was convinced that "practically every important entry that the Negro has made into industries previously closed to him has been through his activity as a strikebreaker."[25]

While Congress was considering the Wagner bill, the

NAACP and the Urban League urged the inclusion of an amendment that would have denied the benefits of the legislation to any union which discriminated on the basis of race. Elmer Carter was sent to Washington, where he acted as the league's chief lobbyist, and T. Arnold Hill and Lester B. Granger prepared for the Senate Committee on Labor and Education a "Statement of Opinion" which summarized the league's objections to the unamended Wagner legislation. William Hastie prepared a similar document for the NAACP, and Walter White kept in close touch with Senator Wagner and his secretary, Leon Keyserling. From Keyserling, White learned that "The Act as originally drafted by Senator Wagner provided that the closed shop should be legal only when there were no restrictions upon members in the labor union to which the majority of workers belonged." But, according to Keyserling, "The American Federation of Labor fought bitterly to eliminate this clause and much against his will Senator Wagner had to consent to elimination in orde₁ to prevent scuttling of the entire bill."[26]

Negro spokesmen also presented their objections to the Wagner bill in correspondence to and informal conferences with labor leaders and government officials. Walter White, for example, wrote to William Green, specifically requesting Green's support for the proposed NAACP-Urban League amendment. Green, however, answered in an equivocal fashion that, in White's view, "boiled down, means precisely nothing." The NAACP secretary forwarded a copy of Green's reply to Senator Wagner "so that you may see how he dodges answering our specific question as to whether or not he and the American Federation of Labor will support a provision to eliminate discrimination by labor unions." White also wrote to President Roosevelt, reminding him that unions "with ill grace

can ask benefits for white labor while these unions discriminate against black labor," and he demanded that "full safeguards...be given to prevent this." "We rely on you," he
declared "to prevent [the] sacrifice of [the] Negro to Jim
Crow unionism." In the administration, Clark Foreman called
attention to "the fact that the American Federation of Labor
was being recognized more and more by government agencies
as the spokesman of labor—although quite commonly Negroes
are excluded from local unions belonging to the AFL."
Foreman maintained that "if we could assume, as had been
claimed, that Negro workers were better off under the company unions than under the AFL, the Administration should
be advised before sponsoring any measures which would
indirectly worsen the condition of the Negro." He suggested
that "whether or not the AFL or other labor organizations
were involved, the government should not do anything
against any element of the population or negotiate preferen-
tial agreements with any organization which discriminated
against certain elements of the population."[27]

The opposition to the proposed NAACP-Urban League
amendment was led by the American Federation of Labor
(though it is significant that the leaders of the emerging industrial unions of the CIO were not recorded in opposition). The
AFL maintained that recalcitrant employers would use these
amendments as an excuse to involve even nondiscriminatory
unions in costly litigation and thus delay the recognition of
that unions' right to bargain collectively with the employers.
Employing the rhetoric of working-class solidarity, the AFL
warned Negroes that they should not support legislation
which would impede the progress of trade unionism, "for in
the progress of honest trade unionism lies the future security
of all workers, of both minority and majority groups." Some

Negro leaders admitted that the AFL's position in this regard was not entirely without merit. Nevertheless, most concluded, as the Urban League did, that while "it is a dangerous thing for Negroes to request governmental interference in the internal security of unions, the least that Negroes can demand is that [the] government shall not protect a union in its campaign to keep them out of present and future jobs."[28]

Despite the essential validity of their arguments, Negroes suffered a defeat in 1935 when Congress passed and President Roosevelt signed the National Labor Relations (Wagner) Act without the NAACP-Urban League amendment. The reason for this was clear; the American Federation of Labor had more political power and influence than the two Negro protest organizations. Government officials candidly explained that "because there was no organization of Negroes, and therefore no one who could command the support of any considerable number of Negro workers, there was little likelihood of their gaining" special consideration. Negroes learned once again that insofar as labor was concerned the dominating forces in the government were, as Clark Foreman explained during the NRA's first year, "the industrialists and the AFL, both of whom are hostile to Negro labor, the former because they want to keep Negroes as a reserve of cheap labor, and the latter because they want to eliminate Negro competitive labor." Negro leaders had appealed for an amendment on grounds of equity and justice, but their request was not granted because it conflicted with the claims of better organized, more powerful white interests.[29]

NOTES

1. F. D. Roosevelt, "Presidential Statement on NIRA," in *The Public Papers and Addresses of Franklin D. Roosevelt* ed. Samuel I. Rosenman, 2:251; U. S., *Statutes at Large*, 48:195.

2. See the following for some representative examples of New Deal thinking with regard to collective bargaining: Hugh Johnson, *The Blue Eagle* (New York: Doubleday, Doran and Company, 1935), pp. 334-350; testimony of Donald Richberg, U. S., Congress, House, *Hearings Before the House Committee on Ways and Means*, 73rd Cong., 1st sess., pp. 68-69; testimony of Robert F. Wagner, ibid., p. 105. Irving Bernstein has written perceptively on the subject in *The New Deal Collective Bargaining Policy* (Berkeley and Los Angeles: University of California Press, 1950). The text of Section 7a is in U. S., *Statutes at Large*, 48:195.

3. Arthur M. Schlesinger, Jr., *The Coming of the New Deal* (Boston: Houghton Mifflin Company, 1959), chap. 9; Bernstein, *The New Deal Collective Bargaining Policy*, chaps. 3 and 4.

4. Schlesinger, *The Coming of the New Deal*, pp. 147-151, 400; Bernstein, *The New Deal Collective Bargaining Policy*, p. 87. In the Denver Tramway Case the NLB finally ruled that the majority principle should prevail in the choice of employee representatives. *New York Times*, 3 March 1934, p. 1.

5. Herbert Northrup, *Organized Labor and the Negro* (New York: Harper & Brothers, 1944), pp. 2-4; Sterling D. Spero and Abram L. Harris, *The Black Worker* (New York: Columbia University Press, 1931), pp. 58, 85-86; Bernstein, *The New Deal Collective Bargaining Policy*, p. 84; Herbert Hill, "Labor Unions and the Negro," *Commentary* 28 (December, 1959):482; NAACP office memorandum, "The Negro and Trade Unions," n.d., NAACP Files; National Urban League, *Negro Membership in American Labor Unions*, 1930 pamphlet, Urban League Files; Interdepartmental Group Concerned with the Special Problems of Negroes, "Report on Negro Labor," NA GR 48.

6. Spero and Harris, *The Black Worker*, p. 53; Norman Ware, *The Labor Movement in the United States, 1860-1895* (New York: D. Appleton and Company, 1929), passim. Irving Bernstein has written that union membership, which rose to slightly more than 5,000,000 in 1920, fell to less than 3,500,000 by 1930. By this later date, union members constituted only 10.2 percent of the 30,000,000 nonagricultural employees counted in the census, compared with 19.4 percent in 1920. "A significant feature of labor's decline in the 1920's is that it struck especially hard at organizations that were either wholly or predominately industrial in structure.... At the

same time many craft unions either held their own or made gains."
Membership in the largest industrial unions—the United Mine Workers,
the International Ladies Garment Workers, and the Amalgamated
Clothing Workers of America—declined from a total of about 670,000 in
1920 to 150,000 in 1930. Irving Bernstein, *The Lean Years* (Boston:
Houghton Mifflin Company, 1960), pp. 85-86, 335. See also Schlesinger,
The Coming of the New Deal, p. 138. Horace Cayton and George Mitchell,
Black Workers and the New Unions (Chapel Hill: University of North
Carolina Press, 1939), p. 125.

7. "The AFL and the Negro," *Opportunity* 7 (November, 1929):338;
Spero and Harris, *The Black Worker*, pp. 85-86.

8. Herbert Northrup has observed that "in a very real sense the
government of labor unions can be compared to the American federal system. Unions have their national, state, and local organizations as does the
government of our country. In the administration of programs of relief,
housing, industrial training, etc., Negroes receive the most equitable
treatment, as a rule, when the federal government administers the program directly...The same results are observable in matters of union
policy. Negroes almost invariably fare better when national officers assume
charge than they do when such questions as admissions or promotions are
left for the local leaders to handle." Northrup, *Organized Labor and the
Negro*, pp. 236-237.

9. Ira DeA. Reid, "Lily-White Labor," *Opportunity* 8 (June,
1930):170; W. E. B. Du Bois, "The A. F. of L.," *Crisis* 40 (December,
1933):292; T. Arnold Hill, "Letter to William Green," *Opportunity* 8
(February, 1930):56.

10. William Green to Elmer A. Carter, 7 November 1929, *Opportunity*
7 (December, 1929):381-382; "The President of the AFL Replies,"
Opportunity 7 (December, 1929):367.

11. Roy Wilkins to Horace Cayton, 30 October 1934, in Cayton and
Mitchell, *Black Workers and the New Unions*, pp. 413-414; Jesse O.
Thomas, "Negro Workers and Organized Labor," *Opportunity* 12 (Sep-
tember, 1934):278; W. E. B. Du Bois, "The A. F. of L.," *Crisis* 40 (Decem-
ber, 1933):292; W. E. B. Du Bois to Martha Adamson, 27 March 1936,
WEBD Papers.

12. Urban League memorandum, "Our Negro Working Population and
National Recovery," 4 January 1937, Urban League Files.

13. National Urban League, "Our Negro Working Population and
National Recovery, 4 January 1937, Urban League Files; Workers' Council
Bulletin 17, "Labor Relations Legislation and the Position of Negro
Minorities," 23 September 1937, NAACP Files; Charles Lionel Franklin,
The Negro Labor Unionist of New York (New York: Columbia University
Press, 1936), p. 241; *Chicago Defender*, 25 August 1934; Herbert Hill,
"Labor Unions and the Negro," *Commentary* 28 (December, 1959):483;
St. Louis Branch, National Urban League, "Report on Local Labor

Conditions, 1934," typescript, NAACP Files; John T. Clark to Donald Richberg, *Chicago Defender,* 31 March 1934; Interdepartmental Group Concerned with the Special Problems of Negroes, "Report on Negro Labor," NA RG 48; Thomas, "Negro Workers and Organized Labor," pp. 277-278; Lester B. Granger, "Negro Workers and Recovery," *Opportunity* 12 (May, 1934):153.

14. Roy Wilkins to Horace Cayton, 30 October 1934, in Cayton and Mitchell, *Black Workers and the New Unions,* pp. 413-414; *Baltimore Afro-American,* 19 April 1934; Cayton and Mitchell, *Black Workers and the New Unions,* p. 175; "The Negro and Trade Unions," typescript, n.d., in NAACP Files.

15. Walter White to William Green, telegram, *New York Times,* 4 October 1933, p. 4; Resolutions of the Twenty-fifth Annual Conference of the NAACP, 1934, NAACP Files; NAACP Press Release, 2 August 1935, NAACP Files; *Pittsburgh Courier,* 13 October 1934; *Report of the Proceedings of the Fifty-fourth Annual Convention of the American Federation of Labor* (Washington, D.C., 1934), pp. 330-332; Northrup, *Organized Labor and the Negro,* p. 11.

16. The members of the all-white Committee of Five were: John Brophy of the United Mine Workers, chairman; John E. Rooney of the Operative Plasterers and Cement Finishers; John Garvey of the Hod Carriers and Common Laborers; Jerry L. Hanks of the Journeyman Bargers; and T. C. Carroll of the Maintenance of Way Employees.

17. NAACP Press Releases, 12 July 1935, 19 July 1935, 26 July 1935, and 26 September 1935, NAACP Files; "Reports of the Executive Secretary of the Joint Committee on National Recovery," 19 June 1935 and 20 September 1935, NA RG 183.

18. *Report of the Proceedings of the Fifty-fifth Annual Convention of the American Federation of Labor* (Washington, D.C., 1935), p. 809; Northrup, *Organized Labor and the Negro,* p. 11.

19. "Report of the Executive Secretary of the Joint Committee on National Recovery," 23 November 1935, NA RG 183; Northrup, *Organized Labor and the Negro,* p. 12.

20. Walter White to John L. Lewis, 27 November 1935, NAACP Files; NAACP Press Release, 15 November 1935, NAACP Files.

21. See Spero and Harris, *The Black Worker,* chap. 7, and Cayton and Mitchell, *Black Workers and the New Unions,* pp. 61-63 and 171-175 for a good discussion of the relations between Negro workers and company unions. The attitudes of important Negro leaders in this regard are clearly stated in the following letters (in NAACP Files): Trevor Bowen to Roy Wilkins, 30 March 1934; Wilkins to Walter White, 21 March 1934; White to Franklin D. Roosevelt, 21 March 1934. See also Lloyd N. Bailer, "Negro Labor in the Automobile Industry" (Ph.D. dissertation, University of Michigan, 1943), passim.

22. J. Joseph Huthmacher, *Senator Robert F. Wagner and the Rise of Urban Liberalism* (New York: Atheneum, 1968), chaps. 5-10; National

Labor Relations Board, "Article by Senator Robert F. Wagner on Labor Unions," *Legislative History of the National Labor Relations Act, 1935* pp. 22-26; (Washington, D.C.: Government Printing Office, 1949); Bernstein, *The New Deal Collective Bargaining Policy,* chaps. 5-10. The bill Senator Wagner introduced in February, 1935, differed in some respects from the original 1934 version; most significantly, it emphasized the NLRB's position as a supreme court of labor relations by stressing the enforcement of labor's rights rather than the adjustment of differences, and by providing that all members of the board would represent the public (thus rejecting the earlier proposal to create a tripartite body with representation from management, labor, and the public). These changes were of considerable importance, but they did not affect black workers specifically and were not commented on by black leaders; indeed, Negro comment on the Wagner bill focused almost wholly on the 1934 measure. At first I suspected that some of the NAACP and Urban League files for 1935 had been misplaced, but Negro newspapers also ignored the revised 1935 bill, and I have concluded that black people decided they had stated their case and done what they could in 1934 and nothing further could be done in 1935. There is another interesting aspect to this, one that relates to the intra-NAACP factional struggle that is described at length in Chapter 12 below. Briefly, it is that the pro-labor forces within the association—those who thought that the economic problems of black and white workers were inextricably intertwined and could be solved only by biracial working-class cooperation—had become so strong by 1935 that the national officers decided to forego further criticism of trade unions.

23. William Hastie to Walter White, 27 March 1934, NAACP Files.

24. T. Arnold Hill to Walter White, 3 April 1934, NAACP Files; T. Arnold Hill, "Labor Marches On," *Opportunity* 12 (April, 1934):120-121; Kelly Miller, "Amend the Wagner Bill," *Norfolk Journal and Guide,* 31 March 1934; Roy Wilkins to NAACP office staff, memorandum, 23 March 1934, NAACP Files; Harry E. Davis to Walter White, 20 March 1934, NAACP Files.

25. NAACP office memorandum, "The Negro and Trade Unions," n.d., NAACP Files; Workers' Council Bulletin 17, "Labor Relations Legislation and the Position of the Negro Minorities," 23 September 1937, NAACP Files; National Urban League, "A Statement of Opinion on Senate Bill S2926," Urban League Files; Interdepartmental Group Concerned with the Special Problems of Negroes, "Report on Negro Labor," NA RG 48.

26. National Urban League, "A Statement of Opinion on Senate Bill S2926," Urban League Files. The proposed NAACP amendment read as follows: "Provided, however, that the term labor organization shall not include any organization, labor union, association, corporation, or society of any kind, which by its organic law or by any rule or regulation, or any practice excludes any employee or employees from membership in the organization or from equal participation with other employees by reason of race, creed or color." It should be noted that Senator Wagner supported the

NAACP's attempt to add an antidiscrimination clause to the Wagner bill. Robert F. Wagner to Walter White, telegram, 16 April 1934, NAACP Files; White to William Hastie, 28 March 1934, and 17 April 1934, NAACP Files.

27. Walter White to William Green, 17 April 1934, NAACP Files; Green to White, 2 May 1934, NAACP Files; White to Robert F. Wagner, 15 May 1934, NAACP Files. See also William Hastie to White, telegram, 29 March 1934, and White to Hastie, 15 May 1934, NAACP Files; White to Franklin D. Roosevelt, telegram, 21 March 1934, NAACP Files; Minutes of the Second Meeting of the Interdepartmental Group Concerned with the Special Problems of Negroes, 2 March 1934, NA RG 48.

28. The AFL arguments were summarized by the Urban League, Workers' Council Bulletin 17, "Labor Relations Legislation and the Position of the Negro Minorities," 23 September 1937, NAACP Files. The quotation attributed to the league is from this document.

29. Minutes of the Second Meeting of the Interdepartmental Group Concerned with the Special Problems of Negroes, 2 March 1934, NA RG 48; Clark Foreman to Harold Ickes, 13 December 1933, NA RG 48.

8

Title II of the NRA

Title II and the Purchasing Power Theory

Title II of the National Industrial Recovery Act provided for
the establishment of a Public Works Administration (PWA)
with an appropriation of $3.3 billion to finance construction of
"a comprehensive program of public works." As was the case
with the minimum wage and maximum hour provisions of
Title I and the labor provisions of Section 7a, this substantial
expenditure of government money for public works and
construction projects was expected to supplement the general
policy of stimulating economic recovery by increasing total
purchasing power.[1]

The relation between public spending and the more general
goals of the recovery program was stressed repeatedly, and
some New Dealers placed overwhelming emphasis on the
increase of national purchasing power which they thought
would result from the creation of new jobs on government

projects. To take one example, Raymond Moley, a special assistant to President Roosevelt, went so far as to declare that the NRA's wage-hour codes were "not primarily concerned with increasing production, but with spreading work and balancing production." In Moley's view the chief economic stimulus was to be provided by public works spending which would "pour money into the economy at a very rapid rate." Similarly, Hugh Johnson relied on PWA to "activate the heavy industries at once and thus increase the *total number of available purchasers.*" He viewed the codes of fair competition and the program for public spending as "complementary and necessary to each other"; economic recovery would not be achieved "unless Title I and Title II could move abreast in perfect coordination."[2]

General Johnson, however, was not given the opportunity to coordinate the two parts of the program. Knowing that the construction of public works offered great opportunities for graft and corruption, President Roosevelt believed it was essential that the spending campaign be supervised with the utmost care. Fearing that Johnson would be completely absorbed in the code-making process, that unscrupulous contractors might take advantage of the general's enthusiasm for public spending, and that no one man could administer both titles effectively, the president decided to place control of the public works program in the hands of Secretary of Interior Harold Ickes, a man who, in his own estimate, had "the negative and austere qualities which the handling of so much money requires."[3]

At the outset of his term as public works administrator, Ickes set for himself the ambitious goal of "administering the greatest fund for construction in the history of the world without scandal." Consequently, he proceeded with great caution—making time-consuming investigations to determine if there really was a need for the proposed projects and taking elaborate precautions to prevent the intrusion of graft and corruption. As a result, PWA was extraordinarily slow in getting under way. During the first six months only $110 million of the $3.3 billion appropriation was actually spent.[4]

Not all New Dealers were pleased with this circumspect handling of PWA money. Raymond Moley, for example, reproached Ickes for moving "at a snail's pace"; in Moley's view, "public works if they were to do any good, should have got under way with incredible speed—even at the risk of inefficiency and perhaps occasional dishonesty." He complained that "Ickes was so cautious that an absurdly small amount of money was spent on public works during that first crucial year, thus completely destroying any possibility of benefit from spending in the critical months when it might have helped." The president, however, did not share Moley's view. At a cabinet meeting in 1934, he noted that "a lot of people thought that all [Ickes] would have to do would be to shovel money out the window. There have been a good many complaints about the slowness of the public works and Harold's caution." But the president firmly supported the careful management of his PWA administrator because, as he put it, "There hasn't been even a minor scandal in public works and that is some record."[5]

In retrospect, it appears that, other than giving the nation a short-lived psychological boost, the NRA's largely ignored wage and hour codes did little to stimulate recovery. Had the codes been enforced, efficient and modernized firms would have been given a competitive advantage; less efficient businesses then would have been forced into bankruptcy, with a resulting increase in unemployment among those who had been working in marginal jobs. Spending for public works, on the other hand, offered the government the opportunity to pump purchasing power into the economy without jeopardizing any existing jobs. Hindsight indicates that a huge transfusion of dollars into the economy was desperately needed, and there was considerable merit to Moley's suggestion that if only the cautious Ickes had headed Title I and the impetuous Johnson the Public Works Administration, the New Deal's recovery program would have worked more effectively.[6]

PWA and the Negro

As members of the working class and with an unemployment rate more than double the national average, it would seem that Negro Americans stood to benefit more than any other group from the rapid expansion of employment that would have occurred if several billion dollars had been poured into the construction of public works. Had the spending program proceeded at the rate recommended by Moley and Johnson, it is quite possible that Negroes would have benefited—not because they were singled out for special consideration, but because they preeminently belonged to the group which would benefit most from a large-scale public works program. However, the administration of the AAA and NRA suggests that while certain programs might ameliorate the condition of the population as a whole, they would not necessarily improve the position of black workers, since Negroes were affected by the factor of race as well as that of class. Consequently, it can be argued that Negroes benefited from the president's decision to appoint Harold Ickes, a man who had long been particularly sensitive to the special needs of Negro workers, rather than the racially insensitive Hugh Johnson, to the post of public works administrator.

At any rate, PWA was more solicitous of the special needs of Negroes than any of the other industrial or agricultural agencies which were established in the spring of 1933. As has been pointed out above, Ickes was ever mindful of the special difficulties of colored workers and had appointed Clark Foreman and Robert Weaver as special advisers to keep him informed concerning Negro problems. In addition, local committees in charge of public works projects in particular areas were encouraged to have colored members who could keep them apprised of any special problems that developed. Although the authority of local Negro committeemen often was restricted—the nominal part which John Mitchell, the colored adviser in Richmond, Virginia, was expected to play became evident when it was revealed that he had been dead for six years—their appointment under pressure from the national administration betokened PWA's interest in committing the New Deal to working more generously with and for Negroes.[7]

The Public Works Administration had a dual purpose: the building of useful projects and the giving of employment to those in need of it. With regard to the first of these, most of the work was for projects that would benefit the entire population—roads, dams, post offices, government buildings—and there was, therefore, no way of determining the extent to which Negroes as such gained. As Ickes observed, all that could be said was that "they, like the rest of the American population, now have much better facilities in many lines than existed before."[8]

Ickes claimed, however, that PWA did not discriminate "against any project submitted by or for the benefit of

Negroes." "Every project coming before the PWA," he insisted, was "subjected to the same routine examination, regardless of the race, creed or color of the beneficiaries." Further, he pointed out that insofar as the color of the beneficiaries could be determined, Negroes had fared well under the PWA program. He reminded Negroes that the Veterans Hospital at Tuskegee, Alabama, built in 1923 at a cost of slightly more than $3 million was "the only outstanding project erected between 1900 and 1933 for Negroes...by the Federal Government." On the other hand, during the first three years of his administration of PWA, more than $13 million was expended for Negro schools and hospitals. While many Negroes had reservations about using government money to finance segregated facilities, most knew that it would be foolish to refuse such aid, and they gratefully accepted the projects as better than nothing at all.[9]

As far as Negroes were concerned, the brightest part of the PWA program was the decision to undertake the construction of government-aided, low-rent housing. In 1931, President Hoover's Committee on Negro Housing had reported that less than 50 percent of the buildings occupied by Negroes met modern standards. Consequently, as Robert Taylor observed in the *Crisis,* "No single social venture holds promise of such immediate benefits to the Negro, as that of a soundly conceived and ably administered public housing program." Ultimately, the PWA's Housing Division undertook the construction of forty-nine major housing projects in thirty-six cities. From the beginning, Negroes participated in the program; fourteen of the projects were for their exclusive occupancy, and seventeen others were for joint occupancy by Negroes and whites. Altogether one out of every four tenants housed by the PWA program was black. Moreover, the

policies established by PWA's housing division were continued under its successor, the United States Housing Authority, and of the 140,000 USHA-aided housing units under
contract in 1940, nearly a third were for Negro occupants.
Even a Negro as critical of other New Deal programs as
Rayford Logan was willing to admit that Negroes were given
fair consideration by the PWA's low-cost housing and slum
clearance programs.[10]

The second of PWA's two major purposes—the giving of
employment to the unemployed—presented greater problems
insofar as Negro workers were concerned. These difficulties
were presented in sharp outline at the construction of the $166
million Boulder Dam project at Lake Mead, Nevada. Early in
1932, William Pickens, the field secretary of the NAACP, had
investigated conditions at the dam and reported that none of
the three thousand workers employed was black. Pickens also
observed that Negroes were not permitted to live in the new
town of Boulder City, which the government had built
primarily as a residence for workers employed at the dam.
Pickens's findings were confirmed by Floyd Covington, the
secretary of the Los Angeles Urban League, and by a
committee of San Francisco investigators. Insistent demands
for an end to discrimination against black labor followed,
resulting finally in the hiring of thirty Negro workers shortly
before the national election of 1932. However, by early 1933
the number of Negro employees had dropped to eleven out of
a total of more than four thousand, and these Negroes were
still barred from Boulder City and had to live twenty-nine
miles away in Las Vegas. Roy Wilkins reported that "they
were transported to and from the dam in busses separately
from white workers, and on the job they were humiliated by
such petty regulations as separate water buckets."[11]

The Department of Interior was responsible for the construction of dams, and consequently the experience at Boulder was brought to the attention of Secretary Ickes. Shortly after taking office, he instituted an investigation which substantiated the NAACP-Urban League charges concerning the discrimination against Negro labor. But the investigation also revealed that while the department's agreement with the contractors specified that citizens of the United States, and especially war veterans, should be employed, the companies were not required to hire Negro labor. As a result, little could be done with regard to opening up jobs for Negroes at Boulder Dam. A later NAACP investigation reported that on April 20, 1934, there were only fifteen Negroes employed on the dam with an average total daily pay of $61 out of a total daily payroll of $21,674.[12]

Yet, Ickes was determined that the experience at Boulder Dam should not set a precedent for all public works projects. Consequently, on September 21, 1933, acting in his capacity as administrator of PWA, he issued an order to the effect that there should be "no discrimination exercised against any person because of color or religious affiliation." In making this announcement, Ickes felt that he was setting up a rule that would prevent discrimination. The ruling established no criteria for determining the existence of discrimination, however, and many contractors managed to comply by accepting token integration. Several informants wrote to PWA, complaining that in their areas, as Roy Wilkins described the situation in New York, "we have discovered some surprising attitudes on the part of construction firms who have erected post offices, court houses, parcel post buildings, etc. To illustrate what they consider 'no discrimination' we found that out of 122 bricklayers on a parcel post building, one was a

Negro. The firm handling this contract claims that it was not discriminating."[13]

To prevent discrimination effectively it was necessary to find some criterion which could be used to indicate when discrimination existed. Throughout the summer and fall of 1933 this problem was considered carefully by administrator Ickes and advisers Foreman and Weaver, and finally they decided to make public housing "the guinea pig for experimenting with developing techniques for assuring the employment of . . . Negro labor on public financed projects during a period of general unemployment." Public housing was chosen because the housing division of PWA was directly responsible for the construction of housing projects and was a party to the building contracts. Since experience had shown that a simple nondiscrimination clause was not effective, Robert Weaver suggested that the housing division include in the construction contracts a clause providing that failure to pay Negro workers a certain percentage of the total payroll would be considered evidence of discrimination. The value of this procedure, in his words, was that it did

> not correct an abuse after the project is completed—as is usually the case when Negroes' rights are being protected—but it set up a criterion which is *prima facie* evidence of discrimination. If the contractor does not live up to this requirement, it is accepted—until disproved—that he is discriminating against colored workers. Instead of Government's having to establish the existence of discrimination, it is the contractor's obligation to establish the absence of discrimination.[14]

Discrimination was presumed to exist wherever contractors failed to pay black workers a portion of the total payroll corresponding to about one-half of their percentage in the total labor force as revealed by the occupational census of

1930. Thus in Atlanta, where the occupational census showed that 24.4 per cent of skilled laborers were Negroes, public housing contractors were required to pay not less than 12 percent of their skilled payroll to Negroes; and in Montgomery, where 42 percent of skilled workers were colored, contractors were obliged to pay at least 21 percent of their skilled payroll to Negroes. Later, after the experiment was established, the housing division reduced the differential between the number of Negro skilled workers in the community and the percentage of the payroll which was required for skilled Negroes. Thus in Charleston, where 46 percent of the skilled work force was black, it was insisted that contractors pay at least 35 percent of their skilled wage bill to Negroes; in Washington contractors' payrolls were required to match the 12.5 percent which the census gave as the portion of skilled Negroes in the community, while New York contractors had to give not less than 3 percent of their skilled payroll to the 2.52 percent skilled Negro population. Where it was considered necessary, similar contractual provisions were written with regard to unskilled labor. Thus in Cincinnati, where the census reported that 71 percent of the common workers were black, contractors were expected to give no less than 80 percent of their unskilled payroll to Negroes; and in Detroit, where 45 percent of the unskilled workers were Negroes, contractors were compelled to pay at least 40 percent of their unskilled wage bill to black labor.[15]

By and large this technique proved to be an effective solution to a difficult problem. It was later adopted by the United States Housing Authority when it succeeded the housing division of PWA, and as of December, 1940, $2,250,000 or 5.8 percent of the total payroll to skilled workers on public housing projects in ninety-five cities had been paid to Negro artisans. Weaver could proudly note that "this represented a portion of the total skilled payroll larger than the proportion of Negro artisans reported in the occupational census of 1930."[16]

Yet this method of defining and enforcing nondiscrimination was not a sufficient solution to the Negro's unemployment problem. The objective of the minimum percentage clauses was to retain past occupational advances for Negroes in the middle 1930s—a period when there was intense competition for every available job and when the rate of unemployment for urban Negroes was almost three times as great as that for whites. The clauses, as Weaver himself frankly admitted, were "a device to regain lost ground; they were not designed to open new types of employment." He conceded that even the PWA effort was only a first step and that much remained to be done with regard to opening new jobs for Negroes and training them for new skills. But it was his view that "it would have been most unrealistic to have attempted to secure significant occupational gains for a minority group in a period when there was mass unemployment."[17]

WPA and the Negro

By an executive order dated May 6, 1935, certain functions of the PWA, along with some responsibilities of the Federal Emergency Relief Administration (FERA), were taken over by the Works Progress Administration (WPA) under the direction of Harry Hopkins. Fortunately for Negroes, Hopkins was sensitive to the special problems of colored citizens—though not to the same extent as Ickes. As administrator of various federal relief and work relief programs during the early months of the New Deal, Hopkins was forced to deal with several unsavory cases where prejudiced relief administrators discriminated against indigent black people. Realizing that he needed expert advice in situations such as these, Hopkins appointed Forrester B. Washington, a Negro social worker from Atlanta, to the specially created position of director of Negro work in FERA. Later other Negro advisers were added to the agencies under Hopkins' control: Alfred E. Smith was made administrative assistant and directed a staff of workers who were engaged in the adjustment of racial problems; John W. Whitten was appointed to the post of junior race relations officer; James Atkins served in the adult education division as a specialist in education among Negroes; Sterling Brown worked as an editor of Negro material in the Federal Writers Project; and T. Arnold Hill served for seven months as a consultant on white collar workers. In addition, several of Hopkins's white assistants, led by Aubrey Williams, a top aide in FERA, were also greatly concerned with the special difficulties of Negroes and did what they could to help resolve problems.[18]

While the WPA contracts never included such specific protection for Negro workers as those of the PWA's housing division, Hopkins after some hesitation did issue a celebrated administrative order proclaiming that "workers who are qualified by training and experience...shall not be discriminated against on any grounds whatever such as race, religion, or political affiliation." More important, the central administration repeatedly exerted pressure on local authorities to give jobs to needy workers regardless of race.[19]

Largely as a result of these determined efforts, the share of WPA jobs going to Negro workers during the late 1930s and early 1940s exceeded their proportion in the general population. WPA reported, to take one example, that at the end of April, 1941, about 16 percent of the 1,450,000 workers assigned to its projects were Negroes. "Thus," as Richard Sterner has observed, "the proportion of Negroes on WPA was higher than the proportion of nonwhites in the total population (10.2 per cent) or among all unemployed workers 14 years of age and over (12.5 per cent), according to the 1940 census." Nevertheless, Negro critics complained, with much merit, that even this share of WPA employment was inadequate because the Negro's needs were so much greater. Further, they pointed out that even a quarter of a million jobs on work relief utterly failed to meet the needs of the more than 600,000 Negro heads of families who were receiving relief as late as 1940 and the countless others who were in need but received no aid from the government. Yet it was only because of the fair-mindedness of the WPA's central administration and its willingness to exert pressure on local authorities that Negroes received as large a share of benefits as they did.[20]

The overall statistics should not obscure the fact that work relief practices varied widely, with the chance for securing government work often depending on factors such as the geographical location of the applicant. Northern Negroes were generally overrepresented on WPA rolls. In New York State, for example, the 4.5 percent Negro population supplied 18 percent of the WPA workers. In the southern and border states, on the other hand, black workers did not fare so well, though conditions varied from state to state and even from county to county within the same state. One comparison of southern counties having one or more cities with a population of at least ten thousand with counties having no such city revealed that it was particularly in the rural areas that Negroes had difficulty getting WPA jobs. In large southern cities, on the other hand, Negroes were well represented on the WPA rolls: in Baltimore the 19 percent Negro population supplied 53 percent of the WPA workers; Negroes in Norfolk comprised less than one-third of the total population but more than two-thirds of the WPA workers; and in New Orleans the Negro population of 30 percent furnished 56 percent of the WPA workers.[21]

WPA studies also revealed that male Negroes were more likely to receive work than females. This was partly due to the policy of giving government work to only one person in each family, usually the chief breadwinner. Negro men also stood a better chance because southern custom permitted black and white males to work on the same outdoor projects, while women's work, which was generally carried on indoors, was rigidly segregated. Moreover, white public opinion in parts of the South was opposed to government employment for Negro females since it competed with domestic service.[22]

The PWA-WPA wage policies underwent frequent changes during the 1930s, but generally there was a tendency for work relief wages to correspond with wage levels in the private labor market. In practice this meant that skilled workers would receive more than unskilled and that northern laborers would earn more than southern. Thus, to take the extremes of the 1935 scale as an example, unskilled workers in the rural South received $19 monthly for 130 hours of work while skilled technical workers in the urban north received as much as $94. While Negro leaders generally were reconciled to the inevitability of such differentials, they maintained that there was no justification for the great disparity in wages, and they particularly objected to WPA's decision that local work relief wages were to correspond to the prevailing wage scale of the section. The *Crisis* declared that "Mr. Roosevelt may not believe it and Mr. Hopkins may not want to admit it, but this means simply that the Negro workers on relief will go back to five and ten cents an hour—if that." Walter White pointed out that race prejudice would cause black workers in the South to be "uniformly classed as unskilled," and he accused the national administration of surrendering "to the demands of Governor Eugene Talmadge [of Georgia] and Southern officials." John P. Davis characterized the South's $19 rate as "coolie wages" which would affect "71.5 percent of the Negro working population but only 26 percent of the white working population." Yet in fairness to the work relief program, it must be noted that southern Negroes working on government projects frequently earned more than they would have received in private employment. This situation led to great apprehension in the white South and vigorous demands that government wages be scaled down to meet local standards. While the WPA was willing to compromise, and eventually did abandon its original thirty cent hourly minimum, it never accepted the $2 and $3 weekly wages that prevailed in large areas of the South.[23]

On the other hand, WPA attempted to placate the southern power structure by releasing Negro workers from government jobs at harvest time. This, of course, forced them to take low-paying, seasonal jobs in the fields. When the NAACP first protested against this procedure, administrator Hopkins firmly supported the local officials. He later reversed himself, however, ruling that WPA projects should not be suspended to provide labor for seasonal employment unless "actual employment at standard wages is available for workers thus released." Hopkins declared that it was "not the policy of the Works Progress Administration to take any action which will make an over supply of labor available for limited employment to depress going rates of wages or to force workers to accept substandard wages." Nevertheless, southern work relief administrators generally ignored this order and continued to provide large numbers of Negro wage hands during the harvest season. As a result, the standard wage for cotton picking in many areas of the South continued to hover around fifty cents per day.[24]

Negroes also complained about more specific abuses. For example, the NAACP charged that black women on work relief in South Carolina were forced to do road work and that female construction workers in Jackson, Mississippi, were supervised by armed guards. The *Chicago Defender* alleged that only three Negro workers were employed in the construction of the WPA's black Wendell Phillips High School in Chicago, and other Negro newspapers repeatedly printed similar allegations. The National Urban League charged that there was definite discrimination against Negro employees on the Triborough Bridge project in New York City, on the Inter-City Viaduct in Kansas City, and on all public construction in St. Louis. Jesse Thomas noted that southern newspapers such as the *New Orleans Times-Picayune* openly advertised WPA jobs for *white* workers, and Clark Foreman pointed out that while differentials were supposedly based on skill and geographical location, some southern newspapers openly offered whites higher WPA wages than Negroes who were doing the same work. The files of the NAACP are replete with similar examples, and Mary White Ovington of the board of directors summed up the feelings of most of the association's members when she wrote that "as to the Washington work relief,... it varies according to the white people chosen to administer it, but always there is discrimination." Even government officials such as Aubrey Williams were forced to admit that "most of the contentions are true." [25]

Yet it must be emphasized that, in spite of its local shortcomings, the PWA-WPA federal work relief program was more considerate of the special problems of Negroes and did more to help them weather the difficulties of the depression than any of the other economic recovery programs which were established in the spring of 1933. Although federal control of the low-rent housing program and of PWA-WPA projects in general has often been criticized, it is clear that Negroes were served best by federal, as opposed to state or local, control of projects. Indeed, it is understandable that many Negroes came to believe, as Rayford Logan did, that the black man benefited "from the New Deal in just the proportion that the federal government exercises direct control over [its] many ramifications." [26]

NOTES

1. U. S., *Statutes at Large*, 48:195.

2. Raymond Moley, *After Seven Years* (New York: Harper & Brothers, 1939), pp. 184-191; *New York Times*, 1 January 1934, p. 5; Hugh Johnson, *The Blue Eagle* (New York: Doubleday, Doran and Company, 1935), pp. 164, 200, 209-210 (italics in the original).

3. Frances Perkins, *The Roosevelt I Knew* (New York: The Viking Press, 1946), p. 275.

4. Arthur M. Schlesinger, Jr., *The Coming of the New Deal* (Boston: Houghton Mifflin Company, 1959), pp. 285-287.

5. Moley, *After Seven Years*, pp. 190-191; Harold L. Ickes. *The Secret Diary of Harold L. Ickes: The First Thousand Days* (New York: Simon and Schuster, 1953), p. 256.

6. Frank Freidel, *The New Deal in Historical Perspective* (Service Center for Teachers of History, Publication 25, 1959), p. 10; Ellis W. Hawley, *The New Deal and the Problem of Monopoly* (Princeton: Princeton University Press, 1966), p. 142.

7. Harold Ickes, message to Twenty-sixth Annual Conference of the

NAACP (1935), NAACP Files; John P. Davis to Nels Anderson, 1 August 1934, NA RG 69; Anderson to Davis, 6 August 1934, NA RG 69; Leslie Fishel, "The Negro and the New Deal Era," *Wisconsin Magazine of History* 48 (Winter, 1964-1965): 112-113; *Norfolk Journal and Guide,* 27 April 1935.

8. Ickes, message to Twenty-sixth Annual Conference of the NAACP; Ickes to Senator George McGill, 13 November 1936, NA RG 48; Harry Slattery to Frank S. Horne, 13 July 1936, NA RG 48.

9. Harold Ickes to Senator George McGill, 13 November 1936, NA RG 48.

10. Robert Taylor, "Low Cost Housing in America," *Crisis* 42 (March, 1935):86; John P. Murchison, "The Negro and Low Rent Housing," *Crisis* 42 (July, 1935):199-200; Robert C. Weaver, *The Negro Ghetto* (New York: Harcourt, Brace & Company, 1948), pp. 73-74; Charles Radford Lawrence, "Negro Organizations in Crisis," (Ph.D. dissertation, Columbia University, 1953), p. 213; Rayford Logan, "The Negro and the New Deal," *Sphinx* (December, 1936):33, 43. The NAACP formally expressed its appreciation of "the efforts of the Federal Government . . . to provide model residences for low-cost housing for the poor" and urged that "this program be continued, with special reference to the blighted areas in which Negro workers are forced to live." Resolutions of the Twenty-eighth Annual Conference of the NAACP (1937), NAACP Files.

11. William Pickens to Walter White, memorandum, 21 September 1936, NAACP Files; Roy Wilkins to Charles West, 18 May 1936, NAACP Files; Wilkins to Oscar Chapman, 21 May 1934, NAACP Files; Ralph Bunche, "Programs, Ideologies, Tactics and Achievements of Negro Betterment and Interracial Organizations" (Carnegie-Myrdal Manuscripts), pp. 94, 96.

12. Bunche, "Programs, Ideologies, Tactics," pp. 94-96.

13. Ickes, message to the Twenty-sixth Annual Conference of the NAACP; Ickes to Mr. Foley, memorandum, 30 October 1933, NA RG 48; Ickes to Walter White, 11 July 1933, NA RG 48; Ickes to Butler Wilson, 25 January 1934, NA RG 48; White to Ickes, 14 October 1933, and 20 October 1933, NA RG 48; Roy Wilkins to Harry Hopkins, 30 November 1934, NA RG 69. Senator Robert F. Wagner of New York also emphasized the need for an antidiscrimination clause in PWA contracts. On this point, see Wilkins to White, memorandum, 2 June 1933, NAACP Files; Robert F. Wagner to White, telegram, 26 May 1933, NAACP Files; White to Wagner, telegram, 26 May 1933, NAACP Files.

14. Robert Weaver, *Negro Labor: A National Problem* (New York: Harcourt, Brace, & Company, 1946), pp. 10-11; Robert Weaver, "An Experiment in Negro Labor," *Opportunity* 14 (October, 1936):298; Minutes of the Fourth Meeting of the Interdepartmental Group Concerned with the Special Problems of Negroes, 1 June 1934, NA RG 48. Most PWA projects were constructed by state or local governments, with the federal agency issuing loans and grants but not actually supervising construction.

15. Weaver, *Negro Labor*, pp. 295-298; Logan, "The Negro and the New Deal," pp. 43-44.

16. Weaver, *Negro Labor*, p. 12; Weaver to Lawrence Oxley, 22 June 1937, NA RG 183.

17. Weaver, *Negro Labor*, pp. 13-15. Weaver acknowledged that the technique of including minimum percentage clauses "almost lost its usefulness by being pushed too far." In 1940 he objected when there was a tendency to apply this method to an entirely different economic situation. "At the later date," he observed, "the demand for labor was expanding, and the need was not to retain past gains but to achieve new occupational advances. Fortunately, the proposals to apply minimum percentage clauses in such a period were not heeded and other more realistic devices, were developed."

18. Ralph Bunche, "Political Status of the Negro" (Carnegie-Myrdal Manuscripts), pp. 1393-1398; Alfred Edgar Smith, "New Deal Gives Negro Square Deal," in *WPA and the Negro*, 1937 pamphlet, NA RG 48; Clark Foreman to Harold Ickes, 20 February 1934, NA RG 48; Ickes to Harry Hopkins, 26 January 1934, and 3 February 1934, NA RG 48; Inter-departmental Group Concerned with the Special Problems of Negroes, "Report of the Agricultural Committee," NA RG 48; Mildred Chisholm to C. F. Roos, memorandum, 2 March 1934, NA RG 9.

19. Lawrence, "Negro Organizations in Crisis," pp. 251-252. Negroes naturally wondered if official statements against discrimination would have any real effect. John P. Davis, for example, chastised WPA for accepting the "unworkable thesis that to merely say there shall be no discrimination is tantamount to accomplishing its abolition." Yet WPA concluded that anything stronger than advice "would...put the Federal Administration in the position of forcing the hand of state and local administrators, especially in those communities where there would be a stubborn resistance. ...Far from allaying friction, such a move would operate to stir up the issue." George Edmund Haynes to Member Organizations, memorandum, 24 August 1934, NAACP Files; Nels Anderson to John P. Davis, 6 August 1934, NAACP Files; Davis, "Report of the Executive Secretary," 19 July 1935, NA RG 183.

20. Richard Sterner, *The Negro's Share* (New York: Harper & Brothers, 1943), pp. 239-241; Lester B. Granger, "A Statement on the Inadequacies of Present Relief," typescript, n.d., Urban League Files.

21. Sterner, *The Negro's Share*, pp. 239-246, 416.

22. Ibid., pp. 239-246.

23. "U. S. Adopts the Georgia Plan," *Crisis* 42 (January, 1935):17; *Norfolk Journal and Guide*, 1 June 1935; "The Surrender of the FERA," *Opportunity* 12 (December, 1934):360; Sterner, *The Negro's Share*, pp. 246-251; Logan, "The Negro and the New Deal" p. 34; Walter White to Harry Hopkins, telegram, 23 November 1934, NA RG 69; White to Franklin D. Roosevelt, telegram, 21 May 1935, NAACP Files; NAACP Press Release, 30 June 1935, NAACP Files; Resolutions of the Twenty-

sixth Annual Conference of the NAACP (1935), NAACP Files; John P. Davis, "Report of the Executive Secretary," 1 June 1935, NA RG 183.

24. Harry Hopkins to All State Emergency Relief Administrators, 19 November 1934, NA RG 69; FERA Press Release, 21 September 1934, NA RG 69; "The Surrender of the FERA," *Opportunity* 12 (December, 1934):360; Lester B. Granger, "That Work Relief Bill," *Opportunity* 13 (March, 1935):86.

25. *Norfolk Journal and Guide*, 6 May 1933; *Chicago Defender*, 16 February 1935; Logan, "The Negro and the New Deal," p. 34; Granger, "The Urban League in Action," *Opportunity* 14 (October, 1936):316; Jesse O. Thomas, "The Negro Looks at the Alphabet," *Opportunity* 12 (January, 1934):12-14; Urban League memorandum, "The Negro Working Population and National Recovery," 4 January 1937, typescript, Urban League Files; Jesse O. Thomas to Eugene K. Jones, 16 December 1933, NA RG 75; Clark Foreman to Harold Ickes, 20 February 1934, NA RG 48; Mary White Ovington to Roy Wilkins, 6 March 1934, NAACP Files; Aubrey Williams to Harry Hopkins, 30 November 1934, NA RG 69. There are several folders in the NAACP files containing correspondence relative to individual cases of discrimination under the New Deal. The Oxley Papers in NA RG 183 also contain much information along these lines.

26. Rayford Logan, "The Negro and the National Recovery Program," *Sphinx* (March, 1934):10.

Summary

BELIEVING that in the modern world most goods are produced for sale, the architects of the Roosevelt administration's industrial recovery program maintained that the volume of production and the level of employment could be increased by expanding mass purchasing power. Their strategy was to augment the buying power of industrial workers by increasing wages; concurrently, they proposed to reduce the number of hours in the standard workweek and to parcel out the surplus time among unemployed men and women. Of course industry could not take on more workers and pay higher wages without increasing its production costs, and it was expected that these additional costs would be passed along to the consumer in the form of higher prices. But this, it was thought, would not be detrimental since the consumer would have more money with which to make purchases.

Noting that the administration had supported minimum wage codes on the ground that they would raise excessively low wages, many Negroes believed that special consideration should have been given to those black workers who were the most impoverished major group of urban laborers. Yet this was not done; no minimum wage codes were drafted to protect domestic servants, and higher wages intended for black workers in code industries often were denied by employers who discovered that the codes could be evaded and ignored with impunity. Negro consumers were affected adversely, however, by the rise in the cost of living which occurred when businessmen passed along the higher cost of NRA wages for white workers.

During the New Deal period there were many employers who hired Negroes only because their labor was cheaper, and there were persistent reports to the effect that when these employers were forced to pay code wages they dismissed their black workers and hired whites. While there were such incidents, and some examples have been cited, it would seem that most employers discovered various loopholes that enabled them to avoid paying regulation wages to colored workers. Since the wage and hour codes were so widely ignored, NRA cannot be held responsible for most of the displacement of colored workers that occurred during the Great Depression. Of course it is true that thousands of Negroes lost their traditional jobs as barbers, cooks, bellboys, and waiters. This was unfortunate, but it was not primarily the result of the NRA's largely ignored minimum wage codes. It resulted from the economic pressure created by a great reservoir of unemployed workers, white and black, who were competing for every available job.

The public spending program authorized by Title II of the recovery bill did more for Negroes than the wage and hour codes, partly because it was administered by men who were particularly sensitive to the special problems of black workers and partly because public spending offered a practical way for the government to increase mass purchasing power without jeopardizing the jobs of marginal workers. The PWA-WPA constructed hundreds of badly needed Negro schools, recreation centers, and hospitals and thousands of low-cost rental apartments. In addition, it provided hundreds of thousands of jobs for Negro workers of every talent and skill. Yet when matched against the needs of the day, the resources of this program were so limited that it could do little more than initiate a mild beginning. While work relief provided badly needed aid for thousands of individual Negroes, it was not an adequate program for a time when the needy were numbered in the millions.

PART THREE

The NAACP in a Time of Economic Crisis

9

The Amenia Conference, 1933

As WE have seen, many Negro leaders hailed the inauguration of the New Deal's economic recovery program, thinking that its provisions for a minimum wage, maximum hours of work, and higher farm prices would be of great benefit to those black workers who were unskilled and confined to the lowest paid jobs in the economy. By 1934 and 1935, however, the predominant mood among articulate Negroes was one of skepticism. One black leader after another was forced to acknowledge that the New Deal program, as far as Negroes were concerned, was largely ineffectual.

Even before 1935 some of the younger black leaders had begun to look not to the government in Washington but to the Negro community itself for solutions to the difficult economic problems of the day. And as the younger generation of emerging black leaders looked at the Negro community, they became increasingly critical of the strategy and tactics of the major Negro betterment organizations, particularly the NAACP and the National Urban League, groups that, it was claimed, had not been able to formulate positive programs directed toward alleviating conditions of mass poverty and unemployment.

The most frequent complaint brought against the NAACP was the charge that its traditional insistence on political and civil liberties, while appropriate in the past, did not do enough to improve the desperate economic condition of the black masses. Correspondents from all sections of the country reminded the association's national officers that a considerable gulf existed between the thinking of the Negro leadership establishment and the attitudes of the black masses. For example, Ralph Bunche, then a young professor of political science at Howard University and a friend of the association's leaders, pointed out that "fights for civil rights—for the right of Negroes to serve on juries, for equal salaries for Negro teachers, for the admittance of Negroes to white colleges, and even for an anti-lynch bill—do not carry an appeal to the Negro in the mass which is designed to arouse him." Bunche admitted that efforts to secure "the full participation of Negroes in American political and civic life are vitally important," but he believed that civil rights meant much more to "the Negro middle class who boast relatively secure positions, homes, cars, and a glittering social life, and who resent any implication of inferiority, than they do to the downtrodden working mass." He sympathized with middle class Negroes who resented having to sit in a buzzard's roost to see *Gone with the Wind,* but he thought it was not surprising that most members of the black working class did not define the Negro problem in precisely the same terms. Letters such as this convinced Roy Wilkins that "among the liberals and radicals, both Negro and white, the impression prevails that the Association is weak because it has no economic program and no economic philosophy."[1]

Criticism of the association was particularly strong during the early 1930s when, in the wake of the Scottsboro case, the Communist party and front groups such as the League of Struggle for Negro Rights (LSNR) and the International Labor Defense (ILD) unreservedly criticized the elitist character of the NAACP and attempted to discredit the fundamental assumption that mere reform would enable Negroes to obtain justice under the existing form of American government. This criticism and competition were not without effect, and NAACP branch leaders such as those in Chicago warned the national office that "a large number of people feel that...the Association has grown weak and lost some of its aggressiveness... [that it] deserted the Scottsboro boys, that the ILD prepared and conducted a fine and manly defense and have [sic] been a real champion of Negro rights." In these circumstances, several influential leaders of the association came to believe that the NAACP was fighting for its organizational life; legal counsel Charles Houston, for example, acknowledged that the NAACP had become "topheavy with white-collar interests and attitudes," and admitted that programs had to be devised to give the organization "some strength on the industrial side."[2]

In an attempt to regain the confidence of the younger black leaders and to familiarize themselves with their attitudes toward reorganization of program and tactics, the NAACP's leaders in the spring of 1933 invited forty-three "young representatives of the colored race" to spend three days in conference at the Amenia, New York, estate of Joel E.

Spingarn, the president of the association and the chairman of its board of directors. According to W. E. B. Du Bois, the chairman of the planning committee, it was hoped that the young people would "discuss in a perfectly frank way and without publicity or limitations, the present situation of the American Negro and just what ought to be done." Stating the purpose of the conference even more explicitly, Roy Wilkins noted that "in 1910 the Association's program was regarded as radical." But, he asked, "How is the program regarded today? How should the program be changed or enlarged or shifted? . . ." Thirty-three men and women answered the call and gathered at Spingarn's estate in August of 1933. The average age of the delegates was thirty-two years, and almost all of them were, as the association claimed, "independent thinking Negroes of strong, honest character. . .not men who have just finished school, but rather those who have been out a few years and yet are not fixed in their ideas." Among the Amenia delegates were several young men who later would achieve considerable distinction in American life: United Nations undersecretary and Nobel laureate Ralph Bunche, economist Abram Harris, sociologists E. Franklin Frazier and Ira DeA. Reid, attorney Louis Redding, and literary critic Sterling Brown.[3]

A number of different ideas were expressed by the Amenia delegates. Some were outright revolutionaries, while others were liberal advocates of trade unionism. Some suggested voluntary segregation with group loyalty and nationalism, while others emphasized the need for interracial cooperation. But despite these differences, there was general agreement that the nation and the American Negro were at decisive turning points in history. According to the delegates, the "economic, political, and social values are rapidly shifting, and the very structure of organized society is being revamped." Because change was occurring so rapidly, the problem of analyzing the Negro's predicament and suggesting a way out was extremely difficult. Yet, there was general agreement that the NAACP's civil-libertarian program was, as Louis Redding put it, "inappropriate to the changed order impending." Some believed that "there should be a resolute decision to junk the old [Negro betterment] policies, followed by a clear-cut outlining of basically new philosophies or policies," while others insisted that the conferees should limit themselves to analyzing "the position of the Negro in a changing world and to suggest[ing] broad lines upon which future programs ought to be built." Whatever their emphases, however, all agreed that it was imperative that Negro betterment organizations develop "a new program suited to these times."[4]

One of the recurring themes of the conference concerned the need for Negro advisers at every level in government, and particularly in agencies whose programs affected large numbers of black workers. "In the process of reform," the delegates resolved, "the interests of the Negro cannot be adequately safeguarded by white paternalism in government. It is absolutely indispensable that in this attempt of the government to control agriculture and industry, there be adequate Negro representations on all boards and field staffs." Unless the government made "full and equal provision for the Negro," the delegates warned that "it cannot be effective in restoring economic stability."[5]

As the AAA and NRA experience demonstrated, there was much merit in the call for Negro advisers at every level in government. However, the Amenia delegates did not place excessive emphasis on this point. They seemed to recognize that while such advisers might occasionally secure relief from flagrant discrimination, they would not be able to compel the government to restructure its programs so that the benefits would seep down to the masses of black workers who stood on the bottom rung of the American economic ladder. They sensed that while Negro leaders might appeal for new policies on grounds of equity and justice, their requests would seldom be granted because almost invariably they would conflict with the claims of better organized and more politically powerful white groups.

Thus, the major emphasis of the Amenia delegates was on the need for power in the black community—power that could be used to reward or punish governments that were responsive or indifferent, as the case might be, to the needs of Negroes. In this vein, there was some discussion of the merits of Negro bloc voting and general agreement that "regardless of seeming class differences within the race, [Negroes] must unite more closely in the interests of the group's economic welfare." Intelligent bloc voting, however, depended on community organization, and according to several of the Amenia delegates, there were certain psychological factors that militated against effective organization of the black community. Meeting frustration and disappointment so frequently, it seemed that many Negroes had adapted by developing an eternal vigilance and distrust of others; they had learned never to trust anyone—black or white—and consequently they found it difficult to get together and cooperate for the attainment of common goals. It was to overcome this sense of hopeless isolation that delegates such as E. Franklin Frazier advocated "the conscious development of nationalistic sentiment." According the Frazier, Negroes would have to identify positively with their own culture and heritage before they could join together to attain the sort of organizational unity that politicians could not afford to ignore. Then, and only then, could Negroes engage in the disciplined bloc voting that would enable them to control the "balance of power" in American politics. The conference delegates resolved that "this point of view must be indoctrinated through the churches, educational institutions and other agencies working in behalf of the Negro," and President Spingarn later recalled that the young men and women of Amenia had considered "cultural nationalism for the American Negro as the most important thing for the Negro to aim at."[6]

But while most of the Amenia delegates believed that Negroes needed political strength, they insisted that organization of the black community for intelligent and disciplined voting would not be enough. A weak minority group in a democratic country could obtain real strength only by allying itself with a portion of the majority, and in their view the portion of the white community that was most likely to ally with Negroes in a common endeavor to improve the economic condition of the black working class was the American labor movement. Believing that only a well-organized, biracial trade union movement could wield sufficient power to *compel* management and government to deal fairly with the working class, the Amenia delegates called on Negro leaders to undertake a campaign to make the black worker "conscious of his relation to white labor and the white worker conscious that the purposes of labor, immediate or ultimate, cannot be achieved without full participation from the Negro worker." Of course such an effort would be difficult as long as organized labor was afflicted with the craft exclusiveness and racial prejudice that characterized so many of the AFL unions. Nevertheless, the young men and women of Amenia believed that there was an important distinction between a fundamentally sound principle (trade union organization) and an unsound policy (union discrimination), and they explicitly censured the older generation of black leaders for having "conspicuously failed in facing a necessary alignment between black and white labor." Enlightened Negro leaders, the delegates maintained, should do more than protest against union discrimination; they must also make every effort to create "a new labor movement," a movement that would "direct its immediate attention to the organizing of the great mass of workers both skilled and unskilled, black and white."[7]

It is hard to say whether the Amenia Conference fulfilled the expectations of its sponsors. President Spingarn had stated that the meeting was intended "to gather together a number of representatives of Negro youth, and others, under conditions of intimacy and privacy, and in beautiful surroundings, and to encourage informal discussion of the present status of the Negro, with the hope that a new programme suited to these times may result." Certainly the meeting fulfilled some of these purposes: everyone agreed that the weather and setting were lovely; the delegates did represent new trends in Negro thinking; the discussions were perfectly frank, and they enabled the established leaders to become acquainted at first hand with some of the younger people and their ideas. In a general way also, the broad outlines of a new program (Negro nationalism and biracial trade unionism) did emerge from the conference.[8]

Yet most of the established Negro leaders found it impossible to support the Amenia program. The NAACP had always been an interracial organization, and its leaders naturally had reservations about a program that placed great emphasis on racial pride. More important, the NAACP's repeated overtures to organized labor had consistently been rebuffed, and in 1932

the association's Twenty-third Annual Conference had officially declared it was impossible for Negroes to make "thoughtful
or advantageous alliance with white American labor because
of its intense race hatred." In addition, the New Deal's industrial recovery program was just beginning as the Amenia
delegates met, and there were many who hoped that the
government would succeed in its attempts to restore economic
stability. It was not until two years later, when most articulate
Negroes had lost faith in the national recovery program and
when the racially egalitarian and industrially organized new
unions of the CIO began to vie for leadership of the American
labor movement, that the NAACP was able to begin implementing the strategy of the Amenia delegates. Nevertheless,
the Amenia Conference was important because it underscored
the growing demand for a new economic emphasis in Negro
betterment policies and because it pointed the way toward the
strategy which the NAACP would begin to implement in
1935.[9]

NOTES

1. Bunche corresponded with the NAACP's leaders frequently, but I
have taken the quotation from a memorandum that he prepared for
Gunnar Myrdal in 1940. Ralph Bunche, "The Program, Ideologies, Tactics
and Achievements of Negro Betterment and Interracial Organizations"
(Carnegie-Myrdal Manuscripts), pp. 144-145. For a more guarded and
prosaic expression of the same views, see Bunche to Walter White, 12 February 1935, NAACP Files; Roy Wilkins to J. E. Spingarn, 23 May 1935,
NAACP Files.
2. The best discussion of the NAACP and the Communist party in
conflict is Wilson Record, *Race and Radicalism* (Ithaca: Cornell University
Press, 1964), pp. 52-83. On the Scottsboro case, see Dan T. Carter,
Scottsboro, a Tragedy of the American South (Baton Rouge: Louisiana
State University Press, 1969) passim. Robert L. Zangrando has also
commented perceptively on the NAACP's response to left-wing criticism in
"The Efforts of the National Association for the Advancement of Colored

People to Secure Passage of a Federal Anti-Lynching Law, 1920-1940"
(Ph.D. dissertation, University of Pennsylvania, 1963), pp. 251-263. See
also W. E. B. Du Bois, *Dusk of Dawn* (New York: Harcourt, Brace & Company, 1940), p. 299; Chicago branch of the NAACP to Roy Wilkins,
memorandum, 24 May 1933, NAACP Files; Charles Houston to Walter
White, 24 September 1934, and 25 November 1934, NAACP Files;
Houston to Wilkins, 22 May 1935, NAACP Files.

3. J. E. Spingarn, official letter of invitation to the Second Amenia Conference, 12 April 1933, NAACP Files; W. E. B. Du Bois to Walter White,
14 March 1933, NAACP Files; Roy Wilkins, Letter of invitation to the
Second Amenia Conference, 15 July 1932, NAACP Files; Minutes of the
Meeting of the Board of Directors, 14 March 1933, NAACP Files;
Wenonah Bond, "Impressions of the Second Amenia Conference,"
memorandum, J. E. Spingarn Papers, Howard University; "The Amenia
Conference," memorandum, 27 May 1933, Spingarn Papers, Howard University; W. E. B. Du Bois, "Youth and Age at Amenia," *Crisis* 40 (October,
1933):226-227. The association's Twenty-fourth Annual Conference, held
in Chicago in July of 1933, was something of a precursor to the Amenia
Conference. An entire session of this conference was devoted to a
discussion of "Shifting Lines of Attack to Meet the Needs of the Day," and,
according to Roy Wilkins, the purpose of the discussion was "to secure
frank opinions from the delegates as to the effectiveness of the methods
pursued by the NAACP and to secure first-hand advice from those who
believe that some change in methods is necessary." Criticism of the association and demands for change were clearly enunciated at this session, and
the consensus of the delegates was that the association's leaders were out
of touch with a significant segment of the black community. In the NAACP
Files, see Roy Wilkins to Mrs. F. Katherine Bailey, 6 June 1933, Wilkins
to Charles A. J. McPherson, 6 June 1933; memorandum from William
Pickens to Walter White, Roy Wilkins, and Mary White Ovington, 4 July
1933; John C. Bruce to Walter White, 20 July 1933; Marie Gray Baker to
White, 11 August 1933; Transcript of discussion on "Shifting Lines of
Attack to Meet the Needs of the Day," July, 1933, NAACP Files.

4. Wenonah Bond, "Impressions of the Second Amenia Conference";
"Findings of the Second Amenia Conference," August, 1933, NAACP
Files; "Report of the [Amenia] Publicity Committee," August, 1933,
NAACP Files; Louis Redding to Roy Wilkins, 2 September 1933,
NAACP Files; Wilkins to William N. Jones, 7 September 1933,
NAACP Files.

5. "Findings of the Second Amenia Conference," August, 1933, NAACP
Files; Du Bois, "Youth and Age at Amenia," pp. 226-227.

6. "Findings of the Second Amenia Conference," August, 1933, NAACP
Files; "Report of the [Amenia] Publicity Committee," August, 1933,
NAACP Files; E. Franklin Frazier to Walter White, 17 May 1934,
NAACP Files; Louis Redding to Roy Wilkins, 2 September 1933,
NAACP Files; Chairman of the Board of Directors of the NAACP to the

Secretary of the NAACP, memorandum, 10 January 1934, NAACP Files; Du Bois, "Youth and Age at Amenia," pp. 226-227. Abram Kardiner and Lionel Ovesey have discussed some of the psychological factors militating against effective cooperation within the Negro community, *The Mark of Oppression* (New York: W. W. Norton and Company, 1951), pp. 301-317.

7. "Findings of the Second Amenia Conference," August, 1933, NAACP Files; "Report of the [Amenia] Publicity Committee," August, 1933, NAACP Files; Elmer Carter to Roy Wilkins, 30 August 1933, NAACP Files; Du Bois, "Youth and Age at Amenia," pp. 226-227.

8. J. E. Spingarn to Mr. White and Dr. Du Bois, memorandum, 22 December 1932, NAACP Files.

9. Resolutions of the Twenty-third Annual Conference of the NAACP (1932), NAACP Files; Roy Wilkins to Horace Cayton, 30 October 1934, Cayton and Mitchell, *Black Workers and the New Unions* (Chapel Hill: University of North Carolina Press, 1939), pp. 413-414; W. E. B. Du Bois, *Dusk of Dawn*, pp. 299-302. No one placed greater faith in the New Deal than the association's president, J. E. Spingarn. Spingarn had begun his adult life as a member of the Republican party, "the party of Lincoln and Sumner." But he was soon disillusioned and came to the conclusion that the fight for Negro rights had to be made independently of either party. After 1912, he resigned from active participation in party politics and consistently refused to endorse candidates for political office. During the early New Deal years, however, Spingarn began to support the Roosevelt administration, and Henry Morgenthau, President Roosevelt's close friend and adviser, was invited to address the Amenia Conference. In 1936, Spingarn broke his long silence in political affairs and openly endorsed President Roosevelt's campaign for reelection. Spingarn statement on Franklin D. Roosevelt, 1936, NAACP Files; Elliott M. Rudwick, *W. E. B. Du Bois: A Study in Minority Group Leadership* (Philadelphia: University of Pennsylvania Press, 1960), pp. 272-274.

10

W. E. B. Du Bois and the Depression: Self-Help and Economic Recovery

AMONG the national leaders of the NAACP, none considered the proposals of the Amenia delegates more carefully than W. E. B. Du Bois, a founder of the association, the editor of its journal, the *Crisis,* and for twenty-four years a member of its board of directors. Like the young men and women who met at Spingarn's estate, Du Bois believed that the depression presented the NAACP with one of the greatest crises in its history. "War and [economic] chaos," he maintained, had made the association's traditional "negative plan of protest" anachronistic. The new conditions of mass poverty and unemployment demanded that the association become something more than a black civil liberties league and anti-lynching lobby; it was essential that the NAACP fashion "a positive program of construction and inspiration," a program that would place more emphasis on the economic betterment of the black masses.[1]

In his early years, Du Bois had believed that ignorance was the basic cause of the American race problem. On the one hand, there was the Negro's "racial ignorance and lack of culture," and on the other, there was the ignorance of whites who "did not know of or realize the continuing plight of the Negro." Accordingly, for fifteen years Du Bois devoted himself to the task of educating black students, first for two years as a professor of Greek and Latin at Wilberforce College in Ohio and then for thirteen years as a professor of social science at Atlanta University. And while teaching in these Negro colleges, Du Bois repeatedly addressed himself to the problem of white ignorance. In 1896 his Harvard doctoral dissertation, "The Suppression of the African Slave Trade," was published as the first volume in the new Harvard Historical Studies. Three years later, demonstrating the versatility for which he would become famous, Du Bois turned from history to sociology and wrote *The Philadelphia Negro*, a comprehensive account of social conditions in one black community. The publication of *The Souls of Black Folk*, in 1903, was of historic importance, in that it prophetically heralded a turn to protest and self-assertion as a major tactic in the struggle for Negro betterment. In 1909, Du Bois released his biography of *John Brown*, and the year 1911 saw the publication of his first novel, *The Quest for the Silver Fleece*. Other books followed regularly: *The Negro*, a short account of African history and culture, in 1915; *Darkwater*, a series of essays, in 1920; *The Gift of Black Folk* in 1924; another novel, *Dark Princess*, in 1928; and in 1935 a classic of revisionist historiography, *Black Reconstruction.* In addition, during his years at Atlanta University, Du Bois presided over and contributed to the famous Atlanta Conferences that prepared a series of studies on matters such as the health, religion, education, criminal and business activities of the Negro community. Indeed, at Atlanta, Du Bois established the most outstanding institute for Negro studies of his day, and he took justifiable pride in noting that "between 1896 and 1920 there was no study of the race problem in America made which did not depend in some degree upon the investigations made at Atlanta University." Moreover, Du Bois continued his educational activities after he left Atlanta in 1910 to become the NAACP's director of publications and research and the editor of its journal, the *Crisis.* He was attracted to the association largely because he perceived that its activities were of an educational nature. As he put it, the association was striving "by book and periodical, by speech and appeal, by various dramatic methods of agitation, to put the essential facts before the American people."[2]

Viewing the Negro problem from the midst of the Great Depression, however, Du Bois was convinced that his and the NAACP's earlier assumptions were in need of qualification. While many Negroes still were ignorant, Du Bois had come to the disconcerting conclusion that "white people on the whole are just as much opposed to Negroes of education and culture, as to any other kind, and perhaps more so." While the NAACP's unceasing agitation and unqualified demand for full manhood rights had led to some amelioration of the Negro's condition, progress had been uneven, and Du Bois believed that, on the whole, segregation and discrimination were more firmly entrenched in the 1930s than they had been when he began his work for racial betterment. (At the turn of tl century, to mention only one of the several examples he cited, "not a single hotel in Boston dared to refuse colored guests. Today there are few Boston hotels where colored people are received.") Consequently, Du Bois concluded that his earlier belief that "America would yield to clear reason and determined agitation" had been naive and mistaken. On the contrary, "to some extent the very agitation carried on in these years has solidified the opposition," and he concluded that it was not feasible to look for salvation from whites. "So far as they were ignorant of the results of race prejudice, we had taught them. ...There can be no doubt that Americans know the facts; and yet they remain for the most part indifferent and unmoved." While Du Bois believed the NAACP, through agitation, publicity, and legal action, should persist in its attack on white ignorance and insensitivity, it had become clear to him that full equality would not be achieved in the near future; he openly proclaimed that "no person born will live to see national and racial distinctions altogether abolished, and economic distinctions will last many a day."[3]

According to Du Bois, this white resistance to appeals to reason did "not mean that agitation does not pay"; but it did mean that "you cannot necessarily cash in quickly upon it." He had come to believe that, in addition to ignorance, there were "other and stronger and more threatening forces forming the founding stones of race antagonisms." Du Bois's own study of psychology, under William James at Harvard in the 1890s, had preceded the Freudian era. But during the depression he began "to realize that in the fight against race prejudice, we were facing not simply the rational, conscious determination of white folk to oppress us; we were facing age-long complexes sunk now largely to unconscious habit and irrational urge, which demanded on our part not only the patience to wait, but the power to entrench ourselves for a long siege against the strongholds of color caste." Admitting that some white Americans did not know of the Negro's plight and others were simply malevolent, Du Bois had come to believe that the prevailing insensitivity of whites was largely "the result of inherited customs and of those irrational and partly subconscious actions of men which control so large a proportion of their deeds." Attitudes and habits thus built up over the centuries could not be changed by a program that simply called on white folk to desist from certain practices and beliefs. Rather, the cause of racial betterment demanded "a long, patient, well-planned and persistent campaign."[4]

To wage any such campaign successfully, however, "the colored group must be financially able to afford to wait," and this would be difficult because the depression had dealt such a heavy blow to the Negro's already inadequate economic foundation. According to Du Bois, a major portion of the American economy was entering into a postcompetitive stage where it would be dominated by large corporations that commanded advanced technology and were relatively free from control by market forces. Acting in defiance of the law of supply and demand, these corporations were able to restrict output in time of depression and maintain prices, and thus black consumers, if they were to avoid exploitation, would have to join together in an organized countervailing power bloc. Moreover, with the advance of automation, Du Bois predicted that the vast demand for labor, a demand that had called black men to the nation, was coming to an end and that the future would see a surfeit of laborers, with most black workers finding only casual employment as migrant farm workers and sweatshop industrial hands. Under these circumstances, it was necessary for the NAACP to supplement its traditional work for black civil liberties and against lynching with a new emphasis on economic matters. In addition to protesting against certain aspects of the New Deal programs, it was necessary to develop a positive plan "in accordance with the definite economic needs of the Negro today." While the association properly focused attention on the weaknesses in the plans presented by others, Du Bois complained that it had nothing to offer "when it comes to positive constructive measures for ourselves." He was convinced that "unless the Negro unites for the intelligent guidance of his economic and industrial interests, he is going to be left out of the New Deal and the future reorganization of society." Black people had learned from bitter experience the futility of asking the New Deal for an equitable distribution of federal funds, "when we know perfectly well that any such honest attempt would wreck the Roosevelt administration, . . . an administration which bases its power on a political foundation of fifty [southern] congressional votes stolen from Negroes."[5]

Up to this point, Du Bois's thinking was not incompatible with that of the majority of delegates to the Amenia Conference, and the editor doubtless was tempted to support the Amenia proposals for improving Negro economic security by fostering the development of powerful black and white trade unions. Indeed, prior to 1930, Du Bois had worked diligently to advance the cause of labor solidarity. He had repeatedly insisted that union discrimination was no excuse for a blanket condemnation of the trade union movement, and he carried the union label on the *Crisis*, even though it meant that no Negro could print it. In 1924, when most Negro leaders were condemning unions, Du Bois proposed that the NAACP and the AFL sponsor a joint educational campaign against race prejudice.[6]

Du Bois never renounced his faith in the long-run efficacy of working class solidarity, but with the coming of the depression and the increasing competition for available jobs, he abandoned his tolerant attitude toward organized labor and, particularly, the AFL. Everywhere he looked during the depression, Du Bois saw the Negro facing "not his employer, but his white brother laborer who stands in the way of his getting a job." The American Federation of Labor was not a labor movement, he declared. It was a monopoly of skilled workers, who joined the capitalists in exploiting unskilled laborers. In his view, "the attitude of labor leaders, the lack of education and vision among laboring classes, and the monopoly of certain lines of employment made possible by excluding Negro labor, is rendering the present chance of raising Negro labor through trade unions improbable," and thus after having advocated working class solidarity for more than two decades, Du Bois announced in the midst of the depression that he would have nothing to do with organized labor "until the trade union movement stands heartily and unequivocally on the side of Negro workers." In his judgment, it was futile to continue making overtures for cooperation with labor; these efforts had been rebuffed in the past, and he saw no prospect for success in an era of massive unemployment and intense competition for every available job.[7]

Thus, Du Bois had come to believe that the NAACP's traditional emphasis on civil rights must be supplemented with a new attention to the economic needs of the black masses, but, unlike the Amenia delegates, his distrust of all white people—workers as well as employers and government officials—precluded opting for working class solidarity as the most viable strategy for immediately improving economic conditions in the Negro community. Instead, he insisted that if

Negroes were to survive and prosper in white America they would have to do for themselves what whites were unwilling to do. The American Negro, Du Bois came to believe, could best improve his position through self-help and racial solidarity. It was essential that black men and women band together to create for themselves the economic institutions and financial resources that would enable them to survive and ultimately prevail in the long struggle for equal rights.[8]

This thinking led Du Bois to place growing emphasis on the development of a separate black economy. He noted that to a considerable degree American custom and tradition had segregated Negroes in separate areas; and while much of the NAACP's activity rightfully had been directed toward breaking down the barriers of enforced segregation, Du Bois was convinced that segregation and discrimination would continue in America for the foreseeable future. Consequently, the practical problem that faced Negroes was "not a choice between segregation and no segregation.... The thing that faces us is given varying degrees of segregation, how shall we conduct ourselves so that in the end human differences will not be emphasized at the expense of human advance." While Du Bois believed that the NAACP should continue its unflinching fight against discrimination, he insisted that Negro leaders should also encourage racial self-help and self-organization "to supply those things and those opportunities we lack because of segregation." Negro leaders must do more than protest against segregation in an increasingly segregated world; they must assume responsibility for the development of the Negro community to the point where Negroes themselves could supply employment for large numbers of black workers and protection for Negro consumers.[9]

Throughout Du Bois's long career there had always been an

undercurrent of racial nationalism. To be sure, he was generally recognized, and rightfully so, as the leading spokesman for that group of black militants who uncompromisingly demanded fair and equal treatment for the Negro in every sector of American life. Along with the demand for civil rights, however, Du Bois also called for self-improvement, racial pride, and group unity—appeals which, when made by Booker T. Washington, smacked of abject surrender, accommodation and "Uncle Tomism," but which Du Bois believed were appropriate complements to agitation and self-assertion. Indeed, despite their differences, there were certain remarkable similarities between Du Bois and Washington. Each believed that black ignorance and lack of discipline were partly responsible for the Negro's condition, and Du Bois, no less than Washington, emphasized the need for self-help. While Washington is justly famous as the prime mover behind the National Negro Business League, it should be noted that Du Bois also advocated a philosophy of thrift and industry that would elevate Negroes to an independent entrepreneurial status; as early as 1899 his Atlanta University Conference was urging Negroes to enter business life as a "far sighted measure of self-defense." Just as a country could by tariffs build up its own economy to the point of relative self-sufficiency, so Du Bois believed that Negroes could create a separate economy that would enable them to survive in a hostile environment.[10]

It was to this emphasis on racial solidarity, self-help, and the group economy that Du Bois returned in the midst of the Great Depression. Convinced that the NAACP's civil libertarianism was not doing enough for the black masses, that it was futile to espouse the cause of biracial working-class solidarity, and that the New Deal would continue to ignore the needs of the Negro, Du Bois came to think that "the solution of the present problem of the American Negro is a matter of organizing

his power as a consumer." According to Du Bois, the time had
come for Negroes to make the best possible advantage of the
fact that they were racially segregated and would remain so
for a long time. It was unfortunate that Negroes had been
herded together beyond the pale in inferior neighborhoods,
but they should not "squat before segregation and bawl."
Instead, they should "use segregation. Use every bit that
comes [their] way and transmute it into power, power that
some day will smash all separation."

"Power is now needed to reinforce appeal," he declared,
"and this power must be economic power; that is, the nation
must be shown that the Negro is a necessary part of the
wealth-producing and wealth-consuming organization of the
country, and that his withdrawal from these functions in any
degree diminishes the wealth and efficiency of the country."
Du Bois estimated that the 2,800,000 Negro families in
America spent about $166 million each month on consumer
purchases—a tremendous power when intelligently directed,
and he considered it "nothing less than idiotic" for a group
with this leverage "to sit down and await the salvation of a
white God." Negroes, he insisted, must take care of themselves. They should buy at Negro stores, patronize Negro professional men, amuse themselves at Negro resorts and theaters.
Food grown on Negro farms, transported by Negro shippers
and processed in Negro factories ultimately would find its way
to intelligent and loyal black customers who patronized Negro
markets and restaurants. Du Bois claimed that by systematically developing their own resources Negroes would be able
to pull themselves out of the depression by their own
bootstraps. Only after establishing a solid economic foundation would it be possible for them to make meaningful
progress toward integration.[11]

Of course such a "Negro Nation Within the Nation" could

succeed only if all Negroes submerged their individual, selfish interests and joined together for the common good. Du Bois pointed out that cooperation, unity, and group pride had been essential prerequisites for such success as had been achieved by other ethnic groups in America, and he urged Negroes to learn from this experience: "Without the authority of the state, without force of police and army, a group of people who can attain such consensus is able to do anything to which the group aspires." If only Negroes would unite and work together they could create a cooperative commonwealth, but this would be difficult because so many members of the black middle and upper classes had rejected their origins and deserted their race. Du Bois repeatedly emphasized the existence of severe tensions and strains within the black community. This tension he attributed in part to the fact that the black middle class, in its desire to emulate white society, had come to reject the lower classes, whose behavior often was deemed responsible for the continuing rejection of all Negroes by whites; in part to the lower class Negroes who generally were not prepared to look to members of their own caste for leadership and instead looked toward the more potent white power structure; and in part to Negroes of all classes who forgot their group and devoted full attention to securing their own immediate interests. For all these reasons and others besides, there were, according to Du Bois, strong "centrifugal forces of class repulsion" within the Negro community, forces that atomized and weakened Negro society and undermined any sense of race loyalty.[12]

Du Bois believed that "the Negro problem" was twofold. On the one hand, there was the white man's Negro problem, the problem of white prejudice and discrimination. On the other, there was the black man's own Negro problem, the lack of internal cohesion and the absence of racial pride and self-help. It was difficult for Negroes to join together because, finding themselves suspended between the dominant white culture and their own subculture, many could not identify positively with their race. Most black men wanted to gain admission into the dominant white society, but the pattern of segregation had forced them to stay in their own districts and neighborhoods, with their own schools, churches, hospitals, newspapers, and businesses. Consequently, as Du Bois put it, "One ever feels his two-ness—an American, a Negro; two souls, two thoughts, two unreconciled strivings; two warring ideals in one dark body." Negroes would have to overcome this psychologically debilitating tension and learn to identify positively with their race before it would be possible for them to join together for effective community action.[13]

Positive identification with their own race would be difficult, however, as long as Negroes accepted the values of white society. Experience suggested that emulation could be effected only at the cost of anxiety, frustration, and disillusionment, all of which tended to undermine the self-reliance and confidence that Du Bois considered essential. Moreover, white propaganda to the effect that Negroes were inherently inferior, ugly, and immoral had insinuated itself in the minds of many black men and women. The Negro's self-esteem suffered because he was constantly exposed to an unpleasant image of himself; or as Du Bois put it, "It is a peculiar sensation...this sense of always looking at one's self through the eyes of others, of measuring one's soul by the tape of a world that looks on in amused contempt and pity."[14]

Du Bois was convinced that internal changes within the Negro community, the most basic being the restoration of self-esteem, must accompany an end to white discrimination, and throughout his career he had resorted to a number of expedients designed to combat the image of inferiority. On various occasions he had rented large stadiums such as the Griffith Baseball Park in Washington and the Hollywood Bowl in Los Angeles for the staging of great race pageants which not only celebrated dramatic events in Negro history (the fiftieth anniversary of emancipation, the one hundredth general conference of the African Methodist Episcopal Church) but also encouraged pride in Negro accomplishment and beauty. Similarly, he promoted a resurgence of American Negro interest in Africa, because he believed that white myths about the Negro past had contributed to self-hatred and that true knowledge of Africa could contribute significantly to Negro self-pride. But most importantly during the depression, Du Bois insisted that Negroes should work energetically to improve their own institutions, to make them so good that they could stand as monuments to Negro talent and enterprise. According to Du Bois, the purpose of "those persons who insist by law, custom and propaganda to keep the American Negro separate in rights and privileges from other citizens...is to so isolate the Negro that he will be spiritually bankrupt, physically degenerate and economically dependent." Against this it was "the bounden duty of every Negro and every enlightened American to protest." And in addition to protest, it was necessary for race leaders to organize the Negro's institutions and community so that "segregation does *not* undermine his health, does *not* leave him spiritually bankrupt, and does *not* make him an economic slave." To avert psychological destruction, Negroes must not only protest against segregation but also, while segregation remained the common practice, "use segregation...to make the very finest type of institutions the United States has ever seen." Only such institutions would rekindle race pride, and without pride it would be impossible for black folk to have the unity to build the separate economy that would provide the foundation for a successful long-range attack against discrimination.[15]

Of course the NAACP traditionally had opposed segregation, but Du Bois maintained that this opposition to segregation had been essentially an opposition to discrimination. Experience in the United States had taught Negroes that discrimination almost always accompanied segregation. Yet Du Bois insisted that segregation and discrimination "do not necessarily go together," and he argued that "there should never be an opposition to segregation pure and simple unless that segregation does involve discrimination." He claimed that the NAACP, while persistently opposing legal attempts to create a separate Negro ghetto, had "expressed no opinion as to whether it might not be a feasible and advisable thing for colored people to establish their own residential sections, or their own towns; and certainly there was nothing expressed or implied that Negroes should not organize for promoting their own interests in industry, literature or art." Moreover, in certain situations where segregation appeared to be inevitable, the association had no alternative but to face facts and make the best of the situation. Thus when the NAACP requests for admission of Negroes to officers' candidate schools had been denied during the First World War, the leaders of the association "saw no sense in tilting against windmills" and decided "there was only one further thing to do and that was to ask for a school for Negro officers." According to Du Bois, the NAACP had never officially opposed separate Negro organizations—such as churches, schools, businesses, and cultural organizations. "It has never denied the recurrent necessity of united separate action on the part of Negroes for self-defense and self-development; but it has insistently and continually pointed out that such action is in any case a necessary evil involving often a recognition from within of the very color line which we are fighting without."[16]

Du Bois recognized that some persons would interpret his emphasis on racial pride and self-help as a counsel of despair, as advice that Negroes should uncomplainingly accept the fact that they were segregated and would remain so for many years and should, therefore, make the best of an admittedly bad situation. Yet he insisted that he was still a militant advocate of full equality for the Negro, and he maintained that uncompromising agitation would continue to be an important tactic in the struggle for racial betterment. He rejected the pessimistic view that Negroes could never gain true equality in white America and therefore should give up and accept the inevitable. On the contrary, he insisted that "our business in this world is to fight and fight again, and never to yield." But it was necessary to fight intelligently, and Du Bois believed that while waiting for the walls of discrimination to crumble, Negro leaders should provide the institutions needed to preserve the morale and solidarity of black folk. He criticized some of his fellow leaders for thinking that "the fight against segregation consists merely of one damned protest after another, that the technique is to protest and wail and protest again, and to keep this thing up until the gates of public opinion and the walls of segregation fall down." Such a program, in his judgment, was physically impossible, psychologically demoralizing, and underestimated the staying power of the opposition. While he urged Negro leaders to "make the protest, and keep on making it, systematically and thoughtfully, perhaps now and then even hysterically and theatrically," he also demanded that they "go to work to prepare methods and institutions which will supply those things and those opportunities which we lack because of segregation."[17]

Beginning in 1930, Du Bois tried to work inside the association "for its realignment and readjustment to new duties." On several occasions he prepared memoranda for the board of directors urging that in a world order where "economic dislocation ha[s] become so great as in ours, a mere appeal based on the old liberalism, a mere appeal to justice and further effort at legal decision, [is] missing the essential need, that the essential need... [is to provide] such economic foundations as would enable the colored people of America to earn a living, provide for their own social uplift...and at the same time carry out even more systematically and with greater and better-planned determination, the fight that the NAACP had inaugurated in 1910."[18]

The board refused to move decisively in the indicated direction, however, and by the autumn of 1933, Du Bois had concluded that his efforts to work through channels within the association had been "almost totally unsuccessful." While some members of the board shared Du Bois's conviction that the association should place more emphasis on economic matters, they were only "a hopeless minority within a group of elderly reactionaries." The majority were firmly committed to the established techniques of public exposure, education, and legal action; for the most part, they were successful professional men who held to Du Bois's early belief that ignorance was the root cause of the race problem and that the essential prerequisite for reform was a focusing of public attention on the conflict between the nation's egalitarian principles and its discriminatory practices. Moreover, many members of the board were well-to-do white philanthropists who were cautious liberals motivated by a sense of fair play. It was

understandable that they would recoil "from any consideration of the economic plight of the world or any change in the
organization of industry," and Du Bois had long feared that
the board, out of deference to the opinions of the association's
white supporters, would be reluctant to address the organization to basic economic problems. Yet the editor was surprised
to discover in the 1930s that within the association "the
younger and more prosperous Negro professional men...were
clinging to the older ideals of property, ownership and profits
even more firmly than the whites," and he concluded that the
association had become dominated by "the higher income
group of colored people, who regarded it as a weapon to
attack the sort of social discrimination which especially irked
them rather than as an organization to improve the status and
power of the whole Negro group." With a few exceptions,
neither the whites nor the blacks of the NAACP realized "just
what momentous changes are taking place, particularly in
economic conditions." For them, "it was the same world with
the same problems to be attacked by the same methods as
before the war."[19]

It was at this point that the editor, believing that a new
orientation in NAACP tactics was essential, launched an important campaign to reorganize the association. Writing to
several score of progressive younger Negroes in February,
1934, Du Bois claimed that the existing Negro betterment
organizations were either reactionary, or unadapted to postwar conditions, or else so radical that they were out of touch
with the facts of American life. In his view, the NAACP
needed "fundamental and complete reorganization from top
to bottom" if it were to attack the economic problems of the
modern world effectively, and in a published statement he
openly proclaimed that he was "ready to unite with any

persons who think as I do in a determined effort to rescue this great organization and prepare it for a new and worthy future." Privately Du Bois contacted most of the young people who attended the Amenia Conference, and then he traveled through the Middle West and East personally conferring with many of the branch leaders whom he expected to sympathize with his new economic emphasis. From these meetings Du Bois concluded that criticism of the NAACP was widespread, that there was a growing awareness of the need to reorganize the association, and to George Streator, the managing editor of the *Crisis* and Du Bois's closest ally in the effort to reorganize the association, Du Bois confided that he was certain that reorganization could be effected. In the event that the attempt to modify the association's emphasis might fail, however, Du Bois acknowledged at the outset that he would resign rather than take responsibility for an organization whose program seemed inappropriate for the needs of the day.[20]

Yet while Du Bois had the prestige and intelligence necessary to lead an effort to reorganize the NAACP, he lacked the temperament and the administrative ability to see the endeavor through. Essentially, as Elliott Rudwick has noted, "Du Bois was not an organizational leader who could present a project to the NAACP Board, solicit ideas, translate the product into a working program, and weld individuals into a unit to administer it. The editor...thought of himself as a propagandist who stirred up controversies, commented on current events related to the race problem, provided arguments for racial egalitarianism, and formulated theoretical blueprints which other men were to bring into actuality." Moreover, Du Bois was sixty-six years old in 1934, an age that, he recalled twenty-six years later, "I regarded to be 'old' at that time," and he thought it was "time to retire to my ivory tower...and devote myself to study and give up propaganda." For this reason, and also because he wanted to ease the burden on the NAACP's depression-strained finances, Du Bois, while remaining as editor-in-chief of the *Crisis,* at one-fourth his regular salary, had taken a position as professor of sociology at Atlanta University. Thus, as the plan to reorganize the NAACP took shape, Du Bois was away in Georgia, and though he traveled to New York shortly before publication date each month, he was able to attend only two of the eighteen board meetings held between January, 1933, and June, 1934.[21]

On the whole, Du Bois was satisfied with his work at Atlanta, where most of his teaching was confined to small graduate seminars on topics such as "The New Deal and the Negro" and "Marxism and the Negro Problem," and where he was given the time to put the finishing touches on his magnum opus, *Black Reconstruction,* and to begin the systematic study of Marxism that would have such great influence on his later life. Understandably, he welcomed the opportunity to follow pursuits more in keeping with his scholarly tastes; having been a major protagonist in the important racial controversies for more than thirty years, the editor doubtless thought he deserved an opportunity for rest and repose. Yet this ambivalence—the conviction that the NAACP's strategy and tactics had to be reorganized if the association were to remain effective in a time of economic crisis, and the simultaneous inclination, because of temperament, age, and geographical location, to retreat to one's study in time of storm—was perhaps the central weakness that ultimately undermined Du Bois's attempt to inaugurate a new plan and program for the NAACP. Friends such as Professor Abram Harris of Howard University warned the old editor that "if this thing leads into a fight...you are going to have a much harder fight on your hands than you did against Booker T. Washington. The issues in that fight were drawn upon fairly simple lines of disagreement. The issues in the fight which might now be brewing are cut across by a thousand and one different interests." Yet Du Bois, while confessing the need for a new economic program, conceded at the outset that he was tired of the NAACP's intra-office factionalism, and he repeatedly confided to his close friends that he would resign if serious opposition to his proposals developed.[22]

Still another factor that may have militated against the success of Du Bois's efforts to alter the association's traditional emphasis was his disdain for intrigue and his decision to state his position to President J. E. Spingarn and Secretary Walter White and to take the case for reorganization to the public through the columns of the *Crisis*.[23] He had long thought of the journal as an organ of agitation that would lead "a liberal organization toward radical reform," and at this juncture he proposed to focus attention on the question of proper strategy in a time of economic crisis. In the September, 1933, number he clearly stated several of his premises in an article entitled "On Being Ashamed of Oneself: An Essay on Race Pride." And in January, 1934, he began a systematic public discussion of "Segregation"—a discussion that would occupy the editorial page of the *Crisis* for six months. While the editor solicited and printed all points of view, he made his own position unmistakably clear: "It is the race-conscious black man cooperating together in his own institutions and movements who will eventually emancipate the colored race, and the great step ahead today is for the American Negro to accomplish his economic emancipation through voluntary determined cooperative effort."[24]

Du Bois's decision to use the columns of the *Crisis* to discuss

and promote reorganization of the NAACP did stimulate
great controversy within the Negro community. Unfortunately, however, the decision to affix the phrase "voluntary
segregation," with all the emotional connotations of this word,
to the call for self-help and internal organization confused
many Negroes who thought of "segregation" as applying to
compulsory separations and as an evil to be fought and
condemned. Certainly many Negroes never properly understood Du Bois's new strategic emphasis. Noting that the new
program resembled that of Booker T. Washington in certain
respects, particularly in its emphasis on self-help and racial
solidarity, several commentators maintained, to take the editor of the *Norfolk Journal and Guide* as an example, that
"precisely what Washington stood for thirty years ago Du Bois
stands for today." This, of course, was far from the truth, since
Washington emphasized the importance of conciliating white
interests by renouncing any desire for social equality and
placed his greatest emphasis on the training of black artisans,
while Du Bois continued to agitate for full equality, insisted
on university education for academically talented black
youths, and thought that modern industrial technology was
rapidly displacing skilled workers—black and white. Moreover, Du Bois thought that his proposals for consumer cooperation were diametrically opposed to the petty capitalism of
Washington. He believed that "the old idea of accumulating
small capital by thrift and going into business" was unrealistic
in an age of oligopoly and financial concentration, and he
proposed a complete break with the "reactionary capitalistic
way of thinking." Du Bois was calling on the Negro to
organize a "cooperative and socialistic state within his own
group, . . . a collective system on a non-profit basis with the
ideal that the consumer is the center and the beginning of the
organization." Nevertheless, with the exception of the *Pitts-*

burgh Courier, the major Negro newspapers interpreted Du Bois's position as a renunciation of protest and an acceptance of Washingtonian petty capitalism and accommodation.[25] Similarly, syndicated Negro columnists such as Kelly Miller claimed that "after a quarter of a century of trial and failure," Du Bois had "openly acknowledge[d] the collapse of the NAACP program and virtually confirm[ed] Booker Washington's position." Even Negro leaders whose economic thinking paralleled Du Bois's had grave reservations. Thus, economist Gordon B. Hancock, whose program for the "Double-Duty Dollar" resembled that of Du Bois, claimed that the editor's new creed "is mild indeed and there is nothing that would disturb the most Mississippi-fied Mississippian. It is just about what Booker Washington would write if he were living." And William Hastie, a Washington attorney and a leader of the local "Don't Buy Where You Can't Work" campaign, an effort that was almost identical in purpose with the Du Bois program, disparaged the new Du Bois as another of the "abject, boot-licking, gut-lacking, knee-bending, favor-seeking Negroes [who] have been insulting our intelligence with a tale that goes like this: 'Segregation is not an evil. Negroes are better off by themselves. They can get equal treatment and be happier, too, if they live and move and have their being off by themselves.'" Later Du Bois would recall that "it was astonishing and disconcerting...that this change of my emphasis was crassly and stupidly misinterpreted by the Negroes. Appropriating as their own (and indeed now it was their own) my long insistence on self-respect and self-assertion and the demand for every equality on the part of the Negro, they seemed determined to insist that my newer emphasis was a repudiation of the older; that now I wanted segregation; that now I did not want equality."[26]

Certain critics, however, raised valid objections to Du Bois's new program. E. Franklin Frazier, who later would write a scathing analysis of the *Black Bourgeoisie* and who at the time was a professor of sociology at Fisk University, observed that "a militant organization like the NAACP must be militant," and Kelly Miller, noting that a protest organization "weakens its function and mission...the moment it begins to waver," suggested that while others should "analyze and compare and balance favorable and unfavorable factors," the business of the NAACP was to fight. Making the same point, the *Pittsburgh Courier* claimed that while "the Negro needs both Du Bois and the NAACP," it was possible that Du Bois could "analyze, criticize and instruct" more effectively as an individual citizen, while the NAACP as an organization should "continue to fight, defend and protect."[27]

Other critics claimed that by implicitly urging Negroes to deemphasize the struggle for civic and social equality, Du Bois was undermining the very race pride and initiative that were essential to the success of his new program. Ferdinand Q. Morton, a Negro member of the New York Civil Service Commission, called attention to "the evil psychological effects" that he feared would follow the adoption of Du Bois's new program: "The withdrawal to ourselves behind the barriers of segregation, as you propose, inevitably would be construed both by the Negro himself and by the majority group...as the voluntary submission on our part to the decree of segregation, and the acceptance by us of all the false implications of inferiority which that decree carries with it." J. E. Spingarn made the same point when he questioned the validity of Du Bois's distinction between segregation and discrimination. Spingarn noted that the latter almost always accompanied the former, and he reminded the editor that the distinction originally was made "by the Southern lawyers who wished to show that it was legal and constitutional to Jim Crow the Negro." Francis J. Grimke, the pastor of the Fifteenth Street Presbyterian Church in Washington, D.C., also maintained that there could be no such thing as nondiscriminatory segregation, and he insisted that "No race with any self-respect can accept the status of a segregated group for itself. To do so is virtually to admit its inferiority, to be content to have limits placed upon its possibilities by another race." Walter White reminded Du Bois of an earlier statement in which the editor had acknowledged that "there is no doubt that numbers of white people, perhaps the majority of Americans, stand ready to take the most distinct advantage of voluntary segregation and cooperation among colored people. Just as soon as they get a group of black people segregated, they use it as a point of attack and discrimination." According to White, segregation invariably meant inferior treatment for the proscribed group, and if the race failed to protest it would run the risk of "spiritual atrophy."[28]

White was particularly aggravated by Du Bois's approval of the use of government funds to support segregated relief and housing projects. The editor, claiming that he had "seen enough to know" that in certain cases the Negro would either "get a segregated development...or none at all," had praised the federal government when it funded all-Negro homestead colonies and slum clearance projects. He argued that it "would be nothing less than idiotic for colored people themselves to refuse to accept" such segregated projects, and he insisted that if Negroes made "these settlements model settlements of which anybody would be proud, they would do more in the long run to break down the Color Line than they could by any futile and helpless denunciation of race prejudice." White, however, believed that segregation of this sort eventually would mean that "less money will be expended for adequate sewerage, water, police and fire protection and for the building of a healthful community." It was for this reason that he resolutely opposed such segregation, and in a day when federal and state welfare projects were increasingly important to colored people, he insisted that "no self-respecting Negro can afford to accept without vigorous protest any such attempt to put the stamp of federal approval upon discrimination." White believed that "like cancer, segregation grows and must be...resisted wherever it shows its head." He feared that once some concessions were made, the way would be opened for others, and he complained that Du Bois's editorials were being used to strengthen the position of unsympathetic government officials.[29]

Still other critics, noting that the Negro community was badly divided, with little in common except skin color, doubted that the group possessed the unity that would be required for the success of a separate cooperative economy. Of course, Du Bois recognized this, and one of the major purposes of his new program was to combat group divisiveness; he was inviting unselfish, dedicated Negro leaders to join in a crusade for racial betterment. But critics such as George Schuyler, a columnist for the *Pittsburgh Courier* and a confidant of Roy Wilkins and Walter White, claimed that there was not enough racial loyalty and patriotism to sustain any such endeavor. Indeed, Schuyler thought Du Bois, with his calls for sacrifice and devotion to the cause, was asking more of Negroes than any but a handful of men could ever give. Moreover, if Negroes should succeed in constructing "a nation within the nation," Schuyler doubted that the long-range struggle for integration would be advanced; rather, there was the danger that certain Negroes would acquire greater vested interests in the segregated system and consequently would be reluctant to alter an order that gave them their advantages.[30]

It was this fear that the Du Bois program would dangerously divide the black community into working class and bourgeoisie that estranged many militant Negroes who shared the editor's conviction that the NAACP needed an economic program. Thus, E. Franklin Frazier dismissed the Du Bois strategy as a plan for locking the Negro "within his ghetto and there letting his petty social elite parade as the leaders and the upper class in the Negro group." Economist Abram L. Harris, a member of the NAACP's board of directors and a close friend of Du Bois, pointed out that the "nation within a nation" movement was "essentially the product of the revolt of the Negro middle class against the ever increasing restriction of their economic opportunities." While Harris believed that black businessmen did encounter unfair discrimination in the marketplace, he also claimed that the black entrepreneur, far from being motivated by any ideal of racial service, "wants most of all...to monopolize and exploit" the black market.[31] According to Harris, the Negro masses had no greater enemy "than the black capitalist who lives upon low waged if not sweated labor, although he and his family may, and often do, live in conspicuous luxury."[32]

As a long-time Socialist, Du Bois recognized the force of this criticism, and at times he could be scathing in his denunciation of the black middle class. Nevertheless, the number of Negro businessmen was so small that, in his judgment, conflicting economic interests were not nearly so divisive in the black community as in the white.[33] Moreover, Du Bois took care to distinguish his proposals from those of the Washingtonian National Negro Business League. According to Du Bois, the Negro Business League would develop the black economy on the basis of free competition and private profit, hoping thereby to enhance the power of Negro capitalists and their ability to provide an increasing number of jobs for black workers. Du Bois, on the other hand, perceiving that "in the future reorganization of industry the consumer as against the producer is going to become the key man," called not for petty capitalism but for the mobilization of black purchasing power by, on the one hand, organizing the masses into producers' and consumers' cooperatives and, on the other, using the boycott to force white concerns that had a large Negro market to employ Negroes in clerical and executive positions.[34]

To critics such as Frazier and Harris, however, the Du Bois program was essentially visionary. In the final analysis, they believed that the proposals of Du Bois and those of the Negro Business League shared a common middle class ideology and "shaded imperceptibly into each other." Both programs were impractical because with the integration and centralization of industry and capital that characterized late industrial economies it would not be possible for Negroes, or any other minority group, to establish a viable duplicate economy. Harris believed that the American economy had become "permanently cartelised," and thus "small industry whether individualistic or based upon racial self-help is going to have hard sledding." Moreover, he reminded Du Bois that "as long as capitalism remains...it is reasonably certain that the main arteries of commerce, industry, credit and finance will be controlled by white capitalists," and consequently it was "obvious that the independent black economy whether it develops upon the basis of private profit or of cooperation cannot be the means of achieving the Negro's economic salvation." Making the same point in more picturesque language, journalist Benjamin Stolberg asked the editor where Negroes would find the resources for building a separate black economy: "Is Wall Street colored?" he asked. "Is finance capital high yaller?"[35]

Militant Negroes such as those who had attended the Amenia Conference also looked askance at the Du Bois program because they feared it "would serve further to widen the breach between white and black labor." While they shared Du Bois's impatience with the association's failure to develop an economic program, they did not share his alienation from the white working class, and they perceived that the editor's work for racial unity ran counter to their own campaign for black and white working-class solidarity. According to the young militants, Du Bois was not only sabotaging every tendency among the black middle class to align itself with working class interests, but also was deflecting the natural militancy of the black masses into a feeling of solidarity with "their own people"—even when these people were exploitative black capitalists. The militants argued that it was basic inequities in the capitalist system that were primarily responsible for Negro unemployment and hunger, and they feared that the real forces behind these disabilities and discomforts would be obscured by the editor's new emphasis on race. If the confused masses accepted Du Bois's view, they would direct their energies toward the creation of a separate black economy and fail to see that their salvation in the long run depended on cooperation with white labor. Even if the "nation within the nation" were to become a reality, only a few thousand jobs would be opened for Negro clerks, salesmen, and managers, while the position of the hundreds of thousands of black workers who were employed outside the ghetto was inextricably tied up with the fate of all workingmen and could be improved only through the systematic development of biracial trade unionism.[36]

Of course, the Du Bois of 1934 could not accept the call for black and white working-class solidarity, for after more than two decades of espousing the cause of labor he had become convinced that most white unionists were hopelessly Negrophobic. Moreover, past experience with philanthropy and recent experience with the New Deal's economic recovery program had convinced him that significant help could be expected neither from capital nor from the government. Negroes, he believed, should "face the fact quite calmly that most white Americans do not like them, and are not planning for their definite future if it involves free, self-assertive modern manhood." Thus if Negroes were to weather the storm of the depression they would have to take care of themselves. Du Bois doubtless knew that the separate black economy was only a partial answer to the Negro's problems, that it was more valuable as a means of building a sense of community solidarity and pride than as a technique for dealing with the economic problems of the poor and unemployed, but he was convinced that unless Negroes organized for effective action they would be left out of the New Deal and the coming post-industrial order. He thought that his program would lead to more immediate economic improvement than any other, and, perhaps most important of all, it would give the NAACP the chance to address itself to the economic and psychological problems than confronted the masses of black workers.[37]

NOTES

1. W. E. B. Du Bois to the Board of Directors of the NAACP, 26 June 1934, NAACP Files; W. E. B. Du Bois, *Dusk of Dawn* (New York: Harcourt, Brace & Company, 1940), pp. 282-315; idem, *The Autobiography of W. E. B. Du Bois* (New York: International Publishers,

1968), pp. 289-307; Francis L. Broderick, *W. E. B. Du Bois: Negro Leader in a Time of Crisis* (Stanford, Calif.: Stanford University Press, 1959), pp. 150-179; Elliott M. Rudwick, *W. E. B. Du Bois: A Study in Minority Group Leadership* (Philadelphia: University of Pennsylvania Press, 1960), pp. 265-285; Charles Radford Lawrence, "Negro Organizations in Crisis" (Ph.D. dissertation, Columbia University, 1953), p. 138.

2. W. E. B. Du Bois, "The Anti-Segregation Campaign," *Crisis* 41 (June, 1934):182; idem, *Dusk of Dawn*, pp. 49-50, 56-59, 63-66; idem, *Autobiography*, pp. 183-235; idem, "A Negro Nation Within the Nation," *Current History* 42 (June, 1935):266. As Herbert Aptheker has noted, "a complete bibliography of Du Bois's published writings would cover scores of pages." Aptheker himself has prepared a good selected bibliography of Du Bois's more important publications, *The Autobiography of W. E. B. Du Bois*, pp. 431-437. Of course, the nature of Du Bois's role as educator was somewhat different at the NAACP than it had been at Atlanta. At the university he had been a social scientist, specializing in the preparation of sociological monographs. The association, on the other hand, was interested primarily in journalistic propaganda, a field that Du Bois quickly mastered. In this regard, it is interesting to note that while the condition of the Negro never was a central concern of most Progressive reformers, the leaders of the NAACP were firmly committed to the techniques of journalism and public relations that were so characteristic of Progressivism. Much as the muckrakers believed that significant reform could be achieved if men of goodwill were made aware of the existence of graft, corruption, and exploitation, so the NAACP assumed that many Americans would take steps to put an end to racial injustice if only they knew of the manner in which the American practice of discrimination contradicted the American principle of equal opportunity. To an extraordinary degree, the work of the NAACP focused on journalistic exposure. Specific examples of injustice were publicized in the hope that concrete information concerning the black man's plight would arouse decent citizens to take effective steps toward reform.

3. Du Bois, "The Anti-Segregation Campaign," p. 182; W. E. B. Du Bois, "William Monroe Trotter," *Crisis* 41 (May, 1934):134; idem, *Dusk of Dawn*, p. 296; idem, "Segregation in the North," *Crisis* 41 (April, 1934):115; idem, "Negro Nation Within the Nation," p. 266; idem, "Integration," *Crisis* 41 (April, 1934):117. Du Bois's early thinking with regard to the role of whites in the struggle for racial betterment was somewhat ambiguous. His emphasis on scholarship and publicity was based on the assumption that a significant number of whites would champion the black man's cause, if only they knew of his plight. Yet Du Bois's early emphasis on the need for university training for talented blacks grew out of a conviction that without such educated black leaders, the Negro masses would have to depend on whites who could never really be trusted to advance the interests of the race.

4. Du Bois, "William Monroe Trotter," p. 134; idem, *Dusk of Dawn*, pp. 194, 283-284, 296; idem, "Negro Nation Within the Nation," p. 266.

5. Du Bois, *Dusk of Dawn*, p. 194; idem, "Negro Nation Within the

Nation," p. 266. In the WEBD Papers, see Du Bois to Abram Harris, 26 December 1933; Harris to Du Bois, 6 January 1934; Du Bois to Addie W. Dickerson, 21 March 1934; Du Bois to Harry E. Davis, 19 July 1934; Du Bois to George Foster Peabody, 26 June 1934; Du Bois to Owen R. Lovejoy, 19 July 1934; Du Bois, notes for manuscript on "The Negro and the New Deal," 1934; Du Bois, memorandum on the Economic Condition of the American Negro in the Depression, 20 November 1934, NA RG 96; Du Bois, "The Negro and Social Re-Construction," (1936 typescript in WEBD collection, Amistad Foundation, Fisk University) p. 148. Some of the ideas in this paragraph may derive from a reading of the works of John Kenneth Galbraith, particularly *American Capitalism: The Concept of Countervailing Power* (Boston: Houghton Mifflin Company, 1952) and *The New Industrial State* (Boston: Houghton Mifflin Company, 1967). Yet it seems to me that Du Bois in the 1930s anticipated much of what Galbraith has said more recently.

6. August Meier, *Negro Thought in America, 1880-1915* (Ann Arbor: University of Michigan Press, 1963), p. 204; Broderick, *W. E. B. Du Bois,* pp. 97, 110-111, 140-142; Rudwick, *W. E. B. Du Bois,* pp. 252-254.

7. W. E. B. Du Bois, "The Negro and Communism," *Crisis* 38 (September, 1931):314; idem, "Marxism and the Negro Problem," *Crisis* 40 (May, 1933):103-104, 118; idem, speech at Howard University, 19 May 1935, reprinted in *Senate Miscellaneous Documents,* no. 217, 74th Cong., 2nd sess., 10016:26; idem, "Postscript," *Crisis* 37 (May, 1930):160; *Baltimore Afro-American,* 15 February 1936; Broderick, *W. E. B. Du Bois,* pp. 140-142; Du Bois to Martha Adamson, 27 March 1934, WEBD Papers; Du Bois, memorandum on the Economic Condition of the American Negro in the Depression, 20 November 1934, NA RG 96.

8. Du Bois, "Negro Nation Within the Nation," pp. 265-270.

9. Du Bois, "Integration," p. 117; idem, "Protest," *Crisis* 41 (June, 1934):183; idem, "Separation and Self-Respect," *Crisis* 41 (March, 1934):85.

10. Several scholars have called attention to the subcurrent of racial nationalism in Du Bois's thinking. See Meier, *Negro Thought in America,* pp. 190-206; Rudwick, *W. E. B. Du Bois,* passim; Broderick, *W. E. B. Du Bois,* passim and especially pp. 100-101. See also Charles Silberman, *Crisis in Black and White* (New York: Random House, 1964), p. 125.

11. Du Bois, "Negro Nation Within the Nation," pp. 265-270 and especially p. 269; idem, "New Negro Alliance," *Crisis* 41 (June, 1934):183-184; idem, "Boycott," *Crisis* 41 (April, 1934):117; idem, *Dusk of Dawn,* pp. 208-209; Broderick, *W. E. B. Du Bois,* p. 167; Wilson Record, *Race and Radicalism,* (Ithaca: Cornell University Press, 1964), p. 104; Du Bois to Will Alexander, 25 May 1934, NA RG 96; Du Bois, memorandum on the Economic Condition of the American Negro in the Depression, 20 November 1934, NA RG 96; Du Bois, "The Negro and Social Reconstruction," (1936 typescript in WEBD collection, Amistad Foundation, Fisk University) pp. 127-152.

12. Du Bois, *Dusk of Dawn,* pp. 173-220; Meier, *Negro Thought in America,* pp. 193-194; E. U. Essien-Udom, *Black Nationalism: A Search for Identity in America* (New York: Dell Publishing Company, 1964), pp. 26-27. John Dollard has noted that "white people tend to lump all Negroes together and to characterize the caste by its lower-class members. This behavior on the part of the whites is probably a form of resistance against status advancement of *any* Negroes." John Dollard, *Caste and Class in a Southern Town* (Garden City, New York: Doubleday and Co., Anchor Edition, 1957) p. 422. Charles Silberman quotes Du Bois to the effect that members of the black middle and upper classes "are curiously hampered by the fact that, being shut off from the world about them, they are an aristocracy of their own people, with all the responsibilities of an aristocracy, and yet they, on the one hand, are not prepared for this role, and their own masses are not used to looking to them for leadership." Silberman, *Crisis in Black and White,* pp. 121-122.

13. W. E. B. Du Bois, *The Souls of Black Folk* (New York: Crest Reprints, 1961), pp. 16-17; Silberman, *Crisis in Black and White,* pp. 68-161; E. U. Essien-Udom, *Black Nationalism,* pp. 22-25.

14. Du Bois, *The Souls of Black Folk,* pp. 16-17; Abram Kardiner and Lionel Ovesey, *The Mark of Oppression* (New York: W. W. Norton and Company, 1951), p. 302; Silberman, *Crisis in Black and White,* p. 109.

15. W. E. B. Du Bois, "Objects of Segregation," *Crisis* 41 (April, 1934):116; idem, "The New Negro Alliance," pp. 183-184; idem, "Negro Fraternities," *Crisis* 41 (June, 1934):184; idem, *Dusk of Dawn,* pp. 268-280; W. E. B. Du Bois to J. E. Spingarn, 16 July 1925, Spingarn Papers, Yale University.

16. W. E. B. Du Bois, "Segregation," *Crisis* 41 (January, 1934):20; idem, "The NAACP and Race Segregation," *Crisis* 41 (February, 1934):52-53; idem, "Separation and Self-Respect," p. 85; Du Bois to Walter White, 17 January 1934, NAACP Files; Du Bois to the Board of Directors, 26 July 1934, NAACP Files; Du Bois to J. E. Spingarn, 25 September 1917, and Spingarn to James Weldon Johnson, 27 October 1933, Spingarn Papers, Yale University; Spingarn to Du Bois, 23 January 1934, WEBD papers.

17. W. E. B. Du Bois, "Counsels of Despair," *Crisis* 41 (June, 1934):182; idem, "Protest," p. 183.

18. Du Bois's memoranda to the Board of Directors are referred to in the NAACP correspondence files (see, for example, Board of Directors, Memorandum for the Record, 9 July 1934), but I have not been able to find the original copies. The quotation is from Du Bois, *Dusk of Dawn,* pp. 295-297. See also Du Bois to J. E. Spingarn, 8 April 1930, Spingarn Papers, Yale University; W. E. B. Du Bois to James Weldon Johnson, 26 February 1931, James Weldon Johnson Memorial Collection, Yale University; Minutes of Meeting of Board of Directors, 13 April 1931, and 9 May 1932, NAACP Files.

19. Du Bois to the Board of Directors, 26 July 1934, NAACP Files; Du

Bois, *Dusk of Dawn*, pp. 288-291, 295-297, 313; in WEBD Papers, see Du Bois to Abram Harris, 26 December 1933; Harris to Du Bois, 6 January 1934; Du Bois to Harris, 16 January 1934; Du Bois, "A Negro Youth Movement," typescript, February, 1934.

20. Du Bois to Dear Friends, 5 February 1934 (printed in *New York Amsterdam News*, 21 February 1934); Du Bois, "A Negro Youth Movement." In the WEBD Papers, see Du Bois to George Streator, 1 February 1934, and 21 March 1934; Du Bois to Abram Harris, 22 January 1934, and 1 February 1934; Du Bois to Virginia Alexander, 1 February 1934; Du Bois to Maud Cuney Hare, 2 February 1934; Du Bois to George Foster Peabody, 26 June 1934; Du Bois to Wendell P. Dabney, 9 February 1934. See also Minutes of the Meeting of the Board of Directors, 11 December 1933, NAACP Files; Walter White, memorandum for *Crisis* Files, 8 January 1934, NAACP Files; Du Bois to J. E. Spingarn, memorandum, 13 December 1933, Du Bois to Spingarn, 14 December 1933, Spingarn Papers, Yale University.

21. Rudwick, *W. E. B. Du Bois*, p. 165; Du Bois, interview in the Columbia University Oral History Project, pp. 161-162; Du Bois to Harry E. Davis, 16 January 1934, WEBD Papers; Richetta Randolph to J. E. Spingarn, 6 July 1934, NAACP Files; Minutes of the Meeting of the Board of Directors, 9 July 1934, NAACP Files; Report of the Budget Committee, 13 November 1934, NAACP Files; Du Bois to J. E. Spingarn, 22 February 1933, Spingarn Papers, Yale University.

22. In the WEBD Papers, W. E. B. Du Bois to President Hope, memoranda, 28 March 1934, and 15 June 1934. See George Crawford to Du Bois, 1 October 1934; Abram Harris to Du Bois, 6 January 1934; Du Bois to Lady Kathleen Simon, 1 October 1934; Du Bois to John S. Brown, Jr., 16 January 1934.

23. Not all of Du Bois's supporters were above intrigue, and some of them plotted secretly to remove Secretary Walter White, who was generally thought to be the main obstacle to reorganization of the NAACP. Martha Gruening, who had been associated with the NAACP since its earliest days, and Helen Boardman, who had conducted several investigations for the association, prepared an expose of the manner in which White and Charles Houston handled the legal defense of a certain George Crawford. Their work was published in the *Nation*, and on the surface it seemed to be simply another trenchant example of that magazine's muckraking journalism. Yet privately the two authors urged their friends to see that "the beans are not spilt" prematurely, since they thought "there is dynamite enough in the stuff we have to retire Walter—and possibly Houston, too—to private life forever." Newsman Lester Walton secretly arranged "a plan for contacting people throughout the country who do not like Walter White," and managing editor George Streator toured the country, ostensibly to raise funds for the *Crisis* but actually to line up the support of those who favored reorganization and a change of leadership. Martha Gruening and Helen Boardman, "Is the NAACP Retreating?" *Nation*, 27 June 1934, pp. 730-732; Charles Houston and Leon Ransom, "The Crawford Case: An

Experiment in Social Statesmanship," *Nation,* 4 July 1934, pp. 17-19; Martha Gruening, "Reopening the Controversy," *Nation,* 18 July 1934, p. 75; Gruening to Du Bois, 14 May 1934, 21 May 1934, and 2 July 1934; Du Bois to Gruening, 27 June 1934; John S. Brown, Jr., to Du Bois, 22 April 1934; George Streator to Du Bois, 12 January 1934. WEBD Papers. George Streator to Leon Ransom, 6 June 1934. Walter White to Streator, 26 June 1934. Streator to the Board of Directors, 11 July 1934. White to J. E. Spingarn, 11 July 1934. Abram Harris to White, 12 July 1934. White to Harris, 13 July 1934. NAACP Files.

24. Du Bois to J. E. Spingarn, 21 April 1934, WEBD Papers; Du Bois to Harry E. Davis, 16 January 1934, WEBD papers; Du Bois *Autobiography,* p. 292; idem, "On Being Ashamed of Oneself: An Essay on Race Pride," *Crisis* 40 (September, 1933):199-200; idem, "Segregation," p. 20; idem, *Dusk of Dawn,* pp. 295-297.

25. The almost complete unanimity with which the Negro press denounced Du Bois's new program suggests the possibility that the editor's enemies within the NAACP were using the association's press service and contacts to inspire hostile editorials in the various newspapers. Both Du Bois and George Streator suspected that this was the case, but I have not been able to find any conclusive evidence on this point. For their views on this point, see Streator to Du Bois, 21 March 1934, and 18 April 1934, WEBD Papers. Of course most of the Negro editors were members of the black middle class, and since they were not suffering direct economic want, it is perhaps inevitable that many would be reluctant to see any diminution in the NAACP's traditional campaign for equal civil rights. Du Bois frequently criticized middle class black leaders for fighting their own battles in the name of Negro rights and failing to press issues of concern to the masses.

26. *Norfolk Journal and Guide,* 8 July 1933; ibid., 21 April 1934. For representative examples of Negro editorial opinion, see the *Sentinel,* 23 May 1934, and the *Chicago Defender,* 31 March 1934, and 14 September 1935. For a minority view, see the *Pittsburgh Courier,* 31 March 1934. See also Kelly Miller, "Kelly Miller Says," *Norfolk Journal and Guide,* 23 February 1935; idem, "Du Bois No Longer Eats Fire," *Baltimore Afro-American,* 8 January 1938; Gordon B. Hancock, "Between the Lines," *Norfold Journal and Guide,* 26 October 1935; William H. Hastie, "Du Bois: Ex-Leader of Negroes," *New Negro Opinion* (Washington, D.C.), 25 January 1934; William Hastie to Walter White, 17 December 1934, NAACP Files; Du Bois, *Dusk of Dawn,* p. 307; Du Bois, "The Negro and Social Reconstruction," (1936 typescript in WEBD collection, Amistad Foundation, Fisk University) pp. 85-87, 141-142.

27. E. Franklin Frazier, *Black Bourgeoisie: The Rise of a New Middle Class in the United States* (New York: Collier Books, 1962); Frazier to Walter White, 17 May 1934, NAACP Files; Kelly Miller, "Is the NAACP Reversing Itself on Segregation?" *Pittsburgh Courier,* 10 February 1934; *Pittsburgh Courier,* 16 June 1934.

28. Ferdinand Q. Morton, "Segregation," *Crisis* 41 (August,

1934):244-245; J. E. Spingarn, "Segregation—A Symposium," *Crisis* 41 (March, 1934):79; Francis J. Grimke, "Segregation," *Crisis* 41 (June, 1934):173-174; Walter White, "Segregation—A Symposium," *Crisis* 41 (March, 1934):80-81. In the WEBD Papers, see Morton to Du Bois, 7 May 1934; Du Bois to Morton, 17 May 1934; Grimke to W. E. B. Du Bois, 26 May 1934; W. E. B. Du Bois to Grimke, 27 June 1934.

29. Du Bois, "Segregation," p. 147; W. E. B. Du Bois, "Subsistence Homestead Colonies," *Crisis* 41 (March, 1934):85; Walter White, "Segregation—A Symposium," p. 81. In the WEBD Papers, see Walter White to Du Bois, 11 January and 15 January 1934; Du Bois to White, 15 January and 17 January 1934; John P. Davis to White, memorandum, 25 January 1934. See also memorandum of the conference of the Secretary with Mrs. Eleanor Roosevelt at her New York home, 1 March 1934, NAACP Files; Will Alexander to Du Bois, 17 May 1934, WEBD Papers; Du Bois to Alexander, 25 May 1934, WEBD Papers.

30. George Schuyler, "Views and Reviews," *Pittsburgh Courier*, 15 April 1933, 17 February 1934, 3 March 1934, 7 April 1934, 5 May 1934. See also Record, *Race and Radicalism*, pp. 72-73; and Broderick, *W. E. B. Du Bois*, p. 282.

31. As might be expected, Communist critics of the separate economy stressed this point. James W. Ford, the party's Negro vice-presidential candidate in 1936, claimed that Du Bois received his principal support from "a small Negro upper class which lives on the body of the segregated Negro community and opposes all efforts to wipe out segregation because it would mean destroying the basis of its wealth." Elanor Ryan, "Toward a National Negro Congress," *New Masses*, 4 June 1935, pp. 14-15.

32. E. Franklin Frazier to Walter White, 17 May 1934, NAACP Files; Abram Harris, *The Negro as Capitalist* (Philadelphia: The American Academy of Political and Social Science, 1936), p. 184; Harris to Du Bois, 6 January 1934, WEBD Papers.

33. Du Bois insisted that the position of the black business class was "peculiar." "They are not the chief, or even large investors in Negro labor, and therefore exploit it only here and there; and they bear the brunt of color prejudice because they express in word and work the aspirations of all black folk for emancipation. The revolt of any black proletariat could not, therefore, be logically directed against this class, nor could this class join either white capital, white engineers or white workers to strengthen the color bar." "Marxism and the Negro Problem," *Crisis* 40 (May, 1933):104.

Years later the editor recalled that he "didn't dream that the educated Negro class could themselves become exploiters. I thought of course the educated Negro was going to devote himself to the uplift of the Negro race, which of course was silly. They're human beings, and they're going to devote themselves—or a large part of them are—to uplift of themselves, and that's that. . .for a long time I argued that the Marxist doctrine doesn't apply to the Negro race in the United States because we have no classes." Interview in the Columbia University Oral History Project, pp. 187-188.

34. Du Bois, *Dusk of Dawn*, p. 208; idem, *Autobiography*, p. 291; idem, "Education and Work," *Journal of Negro Education* 1 (1932):64; Rudwick, *W. E. B. Du Bois*, pp. 245-246.

35. Harris, *The Negro as Capitalist*, p. x; E. Franklin Frazier to Walter White, 17 May 1934, and 15 June 1934, NAACP Files; Benjamin Stolberg, "Black Chauvinism," *Nation*, 15 May 1935, pp. 570-571; Harris to Du Bois, 6 January 1934, WEBD Papers.

36. Harris, *The Negro as Capitalist*, p. 181; Stolberg, "Black Chauvinism," pp. 570-571; Benjamin Stolberg, "Minority Jingo," *Nation*, 23 October 1937, pp. 437-439; Walter White to Stolberg, 31 August 1934, NAACP Files. The thinking of the young militants was in no way incompatible with that of Abram Harris and E. Franklin Frazier, and, indeed, Harris and Frazier had been prominent delegates to the Amenia Conference.

37. Du Bois, "Negro Nation Within the Nation," p. 266; idem, "Segregation in the North," p. 115; idem, *Dusk of Dawn*, p. 297; Du Bois to Harry E. Davis, 19 January 1934, WEBD Papers.

11

Rift in the NAACP

THE separate economy controversy aggravated tensions that had been developing within the NAACP for several years, tensions that stemmed in large part from the financial difficulties that plagued the association during the lean years of the Great Depression and from the personal hostility between editor W. E. B. Du Bois and secretary Walter White. During this time of economic distress, the organization was forced to cut the budget of its national office from almost $60,000 in 1930 to $38,000 in 1934. At the same time, the *Crisis*, which since 1916 had been paying all its own expenses, saw its income fall, and editor Du Bois reported that the journal could not survive unless the association was willing to give an annual subsidy of several thousand dollars. Under these circumstances, the chairman of the NAACP's budget committee warned that the organization would have to make "drastic reductions" in its expenditures or "face a disaster that might be irretrievable." The board of directors could see no way out of this financial morass except to ask all officers of the association to accept a 10 percent reduction in salary for the year 1932, and when revenue continued to decline during that year, the board voted an additional 5 percent cut for the last half of the year. Even these cuts did not enable the association to balance its budget, and in January, 1933, the board was forced to cut the already reduced salaries by an additional 16 percent. By 1934 all officers of the association except Walter White were earning less than $3,000 per year.[1]

As secretary of the national office, Walter White naturally bore much of the responsibility for cutting expenses. Under his direction a savings of more than $1,000 was effected by dispensing with two members of the secretarial staff, and another $1,500 was saved by reducing expenses for printing, mimeographing, and postage (during the depression, for example, all but the most confidential of the NAACP's communications were mailed at the low rate available for unsealed envelopes). Nevertheless, the income of the association declined even more sharply than its expenses, and White came to agree with those members of the budget committee who insisted that further savings would have to be made by reducing the number of executive officers. Although it was "exceedingly difficult to adjust these reductions to [the association's] sense of obligation to the men and women that have worked so faithfully," White and the budget committee concluded that "another six months of these conditions may see us virtually bankrupt and powerless. . . . We can't cut expenses without hurting somebody's feelings, but it is a choice between some individual's misfortune and the whole enterprise on the rocks."[2]

In these strained financial circumstances, White found that his own time increasingly was devoted to fund-raising, an activity for which he was well suited by virtue of a gregarious personality and persistent work habits. Understandably, he came to think that during this time of economic crisis all members of the staff should join in the fund-raising; and he believed that if the association had to reduce its payroll further, it should terminate those who during the course of the year failed to raise an amount equal to that of their salary. In this regard, it was White's view that a considerable savings could be effected by dispensing with the services of the director of branches, Robert Bagnall, and the field secretary, William Pickens. An elaborate office study, prepared under White's direction and comparing the amount of funds contributed by branches within two months after a visit from either Bagnall or Pickens with the amount contributed by branches visited by White or Mrs. Daisey Lampkin, indicated that the field work of the former was "carried on at a heavy expense and seems to produce a doubtful return." Specifically, White concluded that Bagnall raised only "a little more than his salary" and Pickens "did not raise his salary," while Mrs. Lampkin, who was brought to the organization for the specific purpose of raising funds, "has done very well." Acting on the basis of this report, the budget committee proposed to curtail expenses by "dispensing with the services of Mr. Pickens and his clerk," while Bagnall was to be instructed "not to give addresses on the Negro question" but to confine his field trips "to work specifically for raising money."[3]

In retrospect it seems inevitable that these recommendations concerning Bagnall and Pickens would arouse enmity and provoke a polarization of views within the national office. Bagnall had served the association for eleven years and Pickens for twelve, and each was popular with his colleagues. Moreover, the situation was complicated because White prepared his office study in secrecy, giving the other members of the staff neither warning of his intentions nor any chance to answer questions or provide additional information. All the executives of the national office, a small group that in addition to Bagnall and Pickens included only White, Roy Wilkins, Herbert Seligmann, and W. E. B. Du Bois, appealed to Du Bois as a fellow executive and as one of the incorporators of the association and a member of its board of directors to lead a protest against what they considered White's high-handed procedures and unfair recommendations. Though Du Bois generally avoided involvement in the concerns of the national office, he felt that he "could not shirk this appeal," and he wrote a letter, signed by all members of the staff with the obvious exception of White, in which the executive officers expressed their "deep sense of humiliation and wrong at the recent report of the budget committee," and especially at "the utter viciousness" of "a method which results in an unfair attack being made upon a person's record behind his back." While professing their willingness to do whatever was necessary to tide the association over its financial difficulties, the officers emphatically declared that they would not "sit down and allow the Secretary... to malign and traduce us without giving us a reasonable chance to answer."[4]

The officers of the association insisted that "the slightest disposition to deal fairly with us would have brought adequate answers to the charge upon which the proposed dismissal of one of our numbers was predicated." In their view the "period of two months upon which comparisons were based" was arbitrary and deceptive since it obscured "the results of meetings, campaigns, and contests, whose income is only available months after the visit." If the period of the entire year were taken as the standard, the income from field work amounted to more than $31,000 while expenses were in the neighborhood of $18,000, and this did not take account of the "thousands of dollars held in the branch treasuries for local purposes," money which "the Field Secretaries helped to raise and which in emergencies is available to the National Office." The average amount contributed by branches visited was almost three times as much as that yielded by branches not visited. Moreover, the officers believed it was unfair to compare the average revenue yielded by visits from Bagnall and Pickens with the average from visits by White and Mrs. Lampkin, since each of the former visited more than fifty branches, while neither of the latter visited more than ten, and these were the larger and more prosperous branches located in the major metropolitan areas.[5] According to the officers, facts such as these illustrated the unfairness of White's methods, and they concluded that while they had all had "considerable and varied experience," none had ever met "a man like Walter White who under an outward and charming manner has succeeded within a short time in alienating and antagonizing every one of his co-workers, including all the clerks in the office."[6]

Personal relations between White and Du Bois were particularly strained, and again much of the hostility grew out of financial problems. As early as April, 1929, when editor Du Bois had to borrow $3,000 for the *Crisis*, the journal had ceased to be self-supporting; and with each succeeding year the deficit grew, to the point where in 1934 the association had to contribute almost $7,000 in order to keep the journal alive. By 1933, the income of the *Crisis* had declined to $14,000, from a peak of $77,000 in 1920, and monthly circulation dropped from a high of 95,000 in 1919 to about 21,000. In large part these declines in circulation and revenue were the result of the desperate financial condition in which so many of the

Crisis's black readers found themselves. In addition, during the 1930s the *Crisis* no longer enjoyed the advantage of being the only nationally circulated journal of Negro opinion and instead had to face stiff competition from several Negro weeklies. At the same time, it had great difficulty collecting debts, as one agent after another went bankrupt or absconded. Had it not been for these bad debts, the journal might have weathered the period of economic crisis, but as things were, Du Bois twice was compelled to recommend either "that we cease publication of *The Crisis* magazine," or that the association be prepared to offer an annual subsidy of at least $5,000.[7]

As editor of the NAACP's official journal Du Bois had never enjoyed complete independence. He was obliged, for example, to publish official positions taken by the board of directors and the national office and to print all resolutions adopted at the association's annual conferences. Moreover, he acknowledged that the board had a right to censor material considered harmful to the organization. In 1914 he had recommended that a special committee be established to screen potentially damaging stories, and ten years later, when the editor's controversial stand in favor of Robert La Follette and the Progressive party had provoked considerable criticism, he somewhat reluctantly accepted a requirement that all news articles and editorials be sent to members of a *Crisis* advisory board at least five days before the magazine went to press.[8]

Yet Du Bois insisted that the *Crisis* had attained its popularity and effectiveness because it was essentially his own personal forum. With a certain amount of complacency and perhaps just as much accuracy, he considered himself pre-eminent over all his fellows in the ability to shed intellectual light on the problems of the Negro in America. Believing that no diverse group such as the NAACP's board of directors could express "definite and clear-cut opinions," he concluded that if the magazine had not discussed his own ideas "it would have been the dry kind of organ that so many societies support for purposes of reference and not for reading."[9]

Freely confessing that the *Crisis* was "the only work" in the association "which attracts me," Du Bois tolerated only token interference from the advisory committee and fought for as much independence as possible. He was convinced that the existence of an independent and fearless journal of Negro opinion would contribute enormously to the cause of racial betterment, and he thought of himself as the master planner who through the *Crisis* was charting the course which the NAACP would implement. Since no committee could "lay down for the NAACP a clear, strong, and distinct body of doctrine ...by majority vote," he insisted that the *Crisis* be organized independently of the association, with a separate budget, payroll and offices. Mary White Ovington, a founder of the association and a long-time member of its board of directors, summed up the unusual relations between the association and its journal when she observed: "Du Bois was a member of the Board [of Directors], careful in his judgment and scrupulous in never demanding his way in matters that pertained to the NAACP. On the other hand, he wanted complete freedom in editing the *Crisis* magazine."[10]

As long as the journal remained financially self-sufficient, Du Bois was able to proceed with only a modicum of supervision. But when the *Crisis* became dependent on the association for annual subsidies, it was inevitable that restrictions would be placed on the independence of the magazine and the freedom of its editor. During the period from 1929 to 1934 the association contributed more than $35,000 toward the publication of the journal, and Miss Ovington spoke for most board members when she maintained: "Now that *The Crisis* cannot balance its books and... [now] that the Association is responsible for all its debts...it is good business to put the business management in the hands of the people who are ultimately responsible." In 1930 the board officially declared that "in view of the new financial conditions... [the journal's] management should be more integrally correlated with the executive organization of the Association," and declared further that "*The Crisis* shall hereafter be managed by an Editorial Board of four persons, which shall have full charge of the editorial and business management of the paper, subject to the authority of the Board of Directors." Two years later, in a legal move designed to relieve the association from financial responsibility for the future debts of the journal, the *Crisis* was incorporated and the board took advantage of this opportunity to announce officially that "in order to relieve the Editor of unnecessary and onerous administrative duties," the editorial and business management of the journal would be divorced. While Du Bois was to continue as editor, the board assumed virtually complete control over financial matters, and even responsibility for editorial policy was to be shared with the recently established *Crisis* editorial board. Walter White, who increasingly was raising the funds which kept the association and the *Crisis* alive, understandably was appointed to this editorial board, and, as Du Bois later recalled, the secretary's ascendency soon created "an impossible position for me and a difficult one for White."[11]

The roots of personal hostility between Du Bois and White went very deep. Though White did have some colored ancestors, Du Bois insisted that the NAACP's secretary was in fact a white man. White had blondish hair and blue eyes and, according to the editor, "more white companions and friends than colored. He goes where he will in New York City and naturally meets no Color Line, for the simple and sufficient reason that he isn't colored." While Du Bois had nothing against white people per se, he had long believed that blacks should replace whites as determiners of their own destiny. Indeed, he had always placed great emphasis on the higher education of a Talented Tenth because he knew that "without this the Negro would have to accept white leadership, and that such leadership could not always be trusted to guide this group into self-realization of its highest cultural possibilities." Only those who daily and hourly experienced the insults and affronts that are meted out to black men in white America could truly understand the race problem. While the assistance of all men of goodwill was welcome in the struggle against prejudice and discrimination, Du Bois believed it was essential that the leadership of the National Association for the Advancement of Colored People be colored. Walter White, however, was not colored, and, moreover, Du Bois suspected that the secretary's opposition to segregation sprang from a desire to associate with white people. As one of White's biographers has noted, the secretary had developed virtually insatiable "tastes for fine food, good potables, frequent revelry, feminine beauty, and famous company." He lived, and no doubt enjoyed living, in intellectualized, reform-minded white circles, and Du Bois believed that as long as White remained ascendant in the NAACP's national office, the organization could never lead the campaign for voluntary separation and self-help that in his judgment offered the black masses a viable way out of their economic distress. The editor was convinced that "the problem of 12,000,000 Negro people, mostly poor ignorant workers," was not going to be solved by having the more educated and wealthy colored classes "escape

from their race into the mass of the American people." Quite
the contrary; racial pride, unity, and cohesion were the essential prerequisites for progress. And yet Walter White, in his
person and life style, seemed to symbolize "the absurd Negro
philosophy of Scatter, Suppress, Wait, Escape" that undermined group unity and condemned the masses to economic
poverty and psychic isolation. As long as white men like
Walter White headed the National Association it was inevitable that the primary work of the organization would be
directed toward tasks such as securing anti-lynching legislation, tasks that enabled NAACP leaders to associate with
prominent congressmen and the multitude of writers, actors,
and other celebrities who lent the prestige of their names to
ad hoc groups such as the "Art Commentary on Lynching" or
the "American Writers Against Lynching."[12]

In addition to this basic difference, the personalities of the
editor and the secretary clearly were in conflict. White was a
good mixer, with a ready smile, a sense of humor, and
charming manners. Du Bois, on the other hand, was austere
and dignified. He never gambled or consorted with women.
He drank sparingly and found it impossible to hail acquaint-
ances on the street or slap his friends on the back. By his own
admission, he "was not what Americans call 'a good fellow.'"
White and many others attributed the editor's reserved
manner to a certain arrogance and irascibility,[13] but Du Bois
was probably closer to the truth when he claimed that a
certain shyness was the real cause of his aloofness. Ever
sensitive to racial slights and rebuffs and alive to the need for
maintaining self-respect, Du Bois was "desperately afraid of
intruding where I was not wanted; appearing without invitation, or showing a desire for the company of those who had no
desire for me."[14] Volubility, emotionalism, and ostentation—

virtures in White's world of salesmanship and fund-raising—were considered vices by such a fastidious and shy Black Brahmin as Dr. W. E. B. Du Bois.[15]

Even before the *Crisis* had run aground on financial shoals, White and Du Bois had crossed swords on several occasions. In May of 1929, the NAACP's board of directors had passed a resolution to the effect that "the Secretary is the executive officer of this Association, and...all employees and all officers receiving a salary from the Association shall be subject to his authority." At that time James Weldon Johnson was serving as secretary, and since Du Bois's personal relations with Johnson were satisfactory, the editor offered no objections to the resolution. Two months later, however, Johnson asked for a leave of absence that would enable him to accept a year's appointment as professor of creative writing at Fisk University, and in 1930 Johnson unexpectedly decided to stay at Fisk and resigned his secretaryship. In the meantime, White, who had joined the national office staff in 1917 and had enjoyed outstanding success first as a field worker and later as an assistant to Secretary Johnson, assumed control of the national office. As noted above, within a year, White's aggressive and secretive methods had alienated his fellow executives, and Du Bois and his colleagues successfully demanded that the resolution of May, 1929, be rescinded. Years later Du Bois would recall that White "was one of the most selfish men I ever knew. He was absolutely self-centered and egotistical to the point that he was almost unconscious of it. He seemed really to believe that his personal interests and the interest of his race and organization were identical." At the time, the editor did what he could to reduce the authority of the secretary. In 1931, for instance, he proposed that "a larger element of democratic control" be attained by transferring certain powers then exercised by White and the national office to the annual conferences and the branches. Throughout the period, Du Bois used his position on the association's nominations committee to propose for membership on the board of directors men and women whom he thought would remain independent of White's influence. In 1933, Du Bois flatly declared that he would "not work under any Editorial Board of which Mr. White is a member, if that Board has authority which is more than advisory." The editor stated, "I can work with stupidity. I can work with open and frank dishonesty. But the combination of that with charm, double-crossing, and insincerity is something that I can't waste time on." On several occasions, Du Bois frankly told the board of directors that White was not the proper person to head the association.[16]

Du Bois particularly resented the secretary's efforts to have him assigned to fund-raising work in the field. At White's instigation, a special committee had been established in 1932 to "take up the whole question of Dr. Du Bois's relation to the Association," and White persuaded the committee that "if the Association gives Dr. Du Bois aid for the *Crisis*, he ought to do regular work for the Association." The editor claimed he was willing to do more work for the organization, but he "felt that a basis of cooperation should be worked out by which the association could get most from [*me*]." White was convinced that Du Bois's greatest contribution could be "in the field where the Association is most in need of stimulation," but Du Bois had long maintained that "raising money was not a job for which I was fitted. It called for a friendliness of approach and knowledge of human nature and an adaptability which I did not have." The editor knew that his forte was analysis; he had "knowledge of the Negro problem, an ability to express my thoughts clearly, and a logical method of thought." He was willing to write more and lecture more. To placate the importunate secretary, however, the editor promised to do four weeks of field work for the association. Yet the national office was "never able to arrange a schedule which met with Dr. Du Bois's approval," and the work was never done—a situation that led White to complain angrily that "during the incumbency of the present Secretary the Editor of the *Crisis* has never made one offer to help the NAACP."[17]

It was against this background of personal hostility that White by 1934 had come to think that subsidies for Du Bois's *Crisis* were an intolerable drain on NAACP resources. Noting that "we have cut our force and salaries, [and] gone practically without literature...to pay over to *The Crisis* during the last four years more than thirty thousand dollars," he concluded that "it is simply a question as to how much longer the Association...can continue publishing *The Crisis* unless there is a marked increase in income from circulation and advertising." To the secretary, it was clear that "the work of the Association has suffered severely because of the very large sums which we have had to pay for *The Crisis*."[18]

Yet White did not want to suspend publication of the journal. He knew that the *Crisis* contributed enormously to the association's national reputation, and he agreed with those members of the board who thought that discontinuation of the journal "would be construed among our susceptible people as a sign of weakness." According to the secretary, it was important to maintain the appearance of strength; otherwise "the Communists, the...segregationists and all the rest" would think they "have us on the run." As long as these groups thought the association was powerful they would "lay off," but if they realized the organization was in trouble "each one of them [would] hasten to give...an additional boot." Moreover, White believed that many of the *Crisis*'s economic problems could be solved if the national office exercised greater control over the journal's business operations. But all White's efforts in this direction were resisted by Du Bois, who, according to White, made it quite clear that *"The Crisis* would brook no interference under any circumstances and that he wished to maintain absolute control, wishing from the Association only money to make up whatever deficits occurred." For his part, Du Bois claimed that it was essential that he retain control over the business affairs of the journal: "In the first place, the Secretary has already more than he can do or at least do well; and in the second place, it would be fatal to the existence of *The Crisis* if *The Crisis* money was spent in the unbusinesslike way in which the general funds of the NAACP are wasted." Alluding to the secretary's extravagant style of personal life, the editor claimed that "the officers of this Association know exactly where the greatest chance to make our budget balance lies, and that is in a thorough-going examination of the expenditure of [the national office]. The Secretary has absolute domination of these expenditures and practically reports to nobody."[19]

If there had been no strained personal relations within the association and no serious financial difficulties, Du Bois might have succeeded in his efforts to modify the basic policies and tactics of the organization. In any event, had there not been these additional complicating factors it is quite possible that Du Bois and the association would have continued to work together, though as in the past there would have been certain differences of emphasis and opinion. Given the intensity of the internal strife, however, it is not surprising that Walter White took advantage of the controversy and hostility generated by Du Bois's separate economy agitation to launch a campaign aimed at forcing the editor to resign from the organization which Du Bois, more than any single person, had founded and fostered.

Shortly after the publication of Du Bois's first editorial suggestion that Negroes should "stop being stampeded by the word segregation" and should instead learn "to work with each other, to cooperate with each other, [and] to live with each other," White wrote to J. E. Spingarn, insisting strongly that the NAACP stand unequivocally against "the status of separateness which almost invariably in the case of submerged, exploited and marginal groups means inferior accommodations and a distinctly inferior position." While "not in any sense putting this as an ultimatum," the secretary frankly stated that he was "not interested in the Association" unless its attitude was one of uncompromising opposition to segregation. In White's view, the organization had "from the date of its foundation been opposed to segregation in any form, without any reservations whatever," and he called on the board of directors to "in no wise change [this] attitude."[20]

President Spingarn, however, recognized that the secretary's demand created a difficult problem. After all, he observed, "surely we cannot attack segregation in the abstract without attacking the Negro college, the Negro church, etc." Consequently, the board had "never 'defined' its attitude on this subject," but had "merely authorized certain concrete steps." While Spingarn had some reservations about Du Bois's new program, he acknowledged that in the past the association had tacitly accepted certain segregated institutions as better than nothing at all and on occasion had encouraged programs for Negro self-help and self-expression. Moreover, he reminded White that the association practiced as well as advocated free speech. Under the circumstances, Spingarn decided there was nothing the board could do since Du Bois "certainly has the right to discuss any problem freely and frankly, so long as it is made clear that the opinions are personal and not official." Of course, White was free to express his own views, but President Spingarn forbade him from making "any statement that indicates that you are speaking officially for the NAACP."[21]

Since Spingarn was the ranking officer in the association, his attitude with regard to the developing confrontation between White and Du Bois was particularly important. In most respects, the president clearly sided with the editor. The two men were close personal friends, with Spingarn eulogizing Du Bois at the editor's fiftieth and seventieth birthday celebrations (in 1918 and 1938) and Du Bois claiming Spingarn as his "nearest white friend." Spingarn, moreover, had for some time shared the editor's dissatisfaction with the way the association was operating. "When we started we had a programme that was revolutionary for its day," the president observed, but "now we have nothing but [legal] cases, and neither programme nor hope." Like Du Bois, Spingarn believed the association should place more emphasis on the economic problems that faced black people during the depression, and it was for this reason that in 1932 he had taken the lead in calling together at Amenia a group of young people whose ideas, as he put it, "have not hardened into conventional molds." He wanted these young people to discuss whether the association's program should "be changed or enlarged or shifted or concentrated toward certain ends"; and he hoped that "a new program suited to these terms may result." Yet when it came to making plans, Spingarn discovered that Walter White "was not particularly keen about the Amenia Conference of young people to be held next summer," and thus the project had to be postponed from 1932 to 1933, and Du Bois had to be placed in charge of arrangements. Declaring that he encountered this sort of frustration and lack of cooperation "every time I have tried to interest the Board in formulating a program," the president resigned his position in March, 1933, claiming that "someone who has the undivided confidence of the Board or the membership should take my place as President and Chairman." To be sure, when the members of the board and the officers of the association unanimously expressed their confidence in his leadership and declared that his departure "would be a serious detriment to the Association," Spingarn withdrew his resignation; yet the incident was an important indication of the president's basic sympathies with regard to reorganization of plan and program.[22]

Yet despite this substantial area of agreement, there were certain factors that made it difficult for Spingarn and Du Bois to work together for the reorganization of the association. On the one hand, Du Bois, who anticipated the evolution of an economic system dominated by noncompetitive cartels which would restrict output, maintain high prices, and exploit consumers behind the cloak of sophisticated advertising, maintained that Negroes had to protect themselves by organizing in countervailing power blocs. In his view, the depression only aggravated the Negro's economic plight, and the basic problem lay in the deeper fact that the present organization of industry was changing, and while the Negro never adequately shared American prosperity of the 1920s, his position in the developing new order would probably be even less secure. Yet Du Bois claimed that Spingarn, while poignantly recognizing "the dislocation of industry... [and] the present economic problems, still believed in the basic rightness of industry as at present organized. ...He was afraid

that I was turning radical and dogmatic and even communistic. . . ." To Abram Harris, the editor confessed that the basic
weakness of the association involved not only the "opportunism" of White but also "the reactionary economic philosophy"
of Spingarn.[23] For his part, President Spingarn had grave reservations about the wisdom of Du Bois's decision to campaign
publicly for the reorganization of the NAACP. He assured Du
Bois that his ardor for a new economic emphasis had not
changed and that "my plans for reorganization have been
based on having the advantage of your intellectual stimulus."
Yet the president believed that by publicizing the fight the editor was adopting a mistaken strategy that afforded critics the
opportunity to argue that it was rank insubordination for Du
Bois, a salaried employee of the board of directors, to call
openly for a thorough reorganization of the association's
personnel and policies, and he urged the editor to join with
him in a more cautious effort to pack the board of directors
with younger and more economically oriented men and
women. But despite this tactical objection, Spingarn remained
in agreement with Du Bois on substantial matters.[24]

With Spingarn evidently unsympathetic to placing con-
straints on Du Bois, Secretary White turned to other board
members, particularly those who in the past had either been at
odds with the editor or wanted to revise the fomat of the
Crisis. Charles Edward Russell, the prominent muckraking
journalist, for several years had believed that economy
demanded that publication of the *Crisis* be suspended. Carl
Murphy, the publisher of the *Baltimore Afro-American,* had
openly proclaimed that the journal could again become
self-supporting only if it were placed "under new and younger
management." And even Du Bois's old friend Mary White
Ovington was of the opinion that the editor's work was "of less

value than formerly." Secretary White discovered that these and other board members shared his conviction that discussion of Du Bois's new program was "analogous to the ancient theological discussion of the number of angels dancing on a needle's point," that it was a waste of time to devote board meetings "to ridiculous and acrimonious discussions of an issue which obviously has been raised as a smoke-screen," while in the meantime "the real work of the Association and the reason for its existence could not be discussed because so much time was given to the segregation discussion." (Miss Ovington, for example, complained that "as long as Dr. Du Bois has the *Crisis*" the board would be "obliged to spend a great deal of time...in defining its position," time that might better be spent in doing "work to advance the condition of the Negro.") Isadore Martin, a board member from Philadelphia, considered the editor's new proposals absurdly foolish and suggested that "the best way out of it...would be to say that when people begin to enter their second childhood days, they are not responsible for their utterances, and then laugh it off." Carl Murphy could see no alternative but to demand Du Bois's resignation; Miss Ovington agreed, but suggested that as a token of appreciation for the editor's long and valuable service he "be given the *Crisis*, together with its mailing lists [and] machinery."[25]

Yet many members of the board were loath to see Du Bois leave the association. Such evidence of internal dissension could only give comfort to the organization's enemies. Moreover, while most members of the board questioned the wisdom of any program of voluntary separatism, several believed that Du Bois was performing a valuable service in focusing attention on the question of proper strategy and tactics for Negro betterment organizations in this time of economic crisis. Harry E. Davis, a board member from Cleveland, maintained that "the officers of the Association, their work and the policies sponsored should always be subjected to a healthy and appraising criticism," and he opposed any effort to restrict Du Bois's editorial freedom. According to Davis, the value of the *Crisis* would be "almost totally impaired...if it degenerates into...a rubber stamp for the NAACP." Similarly, Field Secretary William Pickens was against all attempts "to set any limits upon decent expressions of opinion, especially in an organization like ours, whose propaganda is largely well-stated opinions."[26] Joel Spingarn doubtless spoke for many members of the board when he declared that Du Bois "is doing a service in trying to make the real meaning of the problem clearer than it has been." Rather than bemoan the fact that so much attention had been devoted to the question of voluntary separation, Spingarn maintained that "a hot controversy on the subject will help to keep interest in the NAACP more lively than ever."[27]

The controversy, which had been simmering for months, unexpectedly came to a head at the April, 1934, meeting of the board of directors. In March, Du Bois had summarized the essential principles underlying his new program, and he proposed that the board officially endorse the following statement:

> The segregation of human beings purely on a basis of race and color is not only stupid and unjust, but positively dangerous, since it is a path that leads straight to national jealousies, racial antagonisms, and war.
>
> The NAACP, therefore, has always opposed the underlying principle of racial segregation, and will oppose it. On the other hand, it has, with equal clearness, recognized that when a group like the American Negroes suffers conscious and systematic segregation, against which argument and appeal are either useless or very slow in effecting changes, such a group

must make up its mind to associate and co-operate for its own uplift and in defense of its self-respect.

The NAACP, therefore, has always recognized and encouraged the Negro church, the Negro college, the Negro public school, Negro business and industrial enterprises, and believes they should be made the very best and most efficient institutions of their kind judged by any standard; not with the idea of perpetuating artificial separation of mankind, but rather with the distinct object of proving Negro efficiency, showing Negro ability and discipline, and demonstrating how useless and wasteful race segregation is.[28]

Joel Spingarn, the most influential member of the administration committee which prepared the agenda for meetings of the board of directors, could find nothing that was fundamentally wrong with this statement, but he did not like the tone and knew that endorsement of such a statement would outrage Secretary White, and consequently he persuaded the committee to modify Du Bois's language and present a counterproposal for consideration by the board:

The National Association for the Advancement of Colored People has always opposed the segregation of human beings on the basis of race and color. We have always as a basic principle of our organization opposed such segregation and we will always continue to oppose it.

It is true that we have always recognized and encouraged the Negro church, the Negro college, the Negro school, and Negro business and industrial enterprises, and we shall continue to encourage them, so that they may serve as proofs of Negro efficiency, ability and discipline. Not merely external necessity but our faith in the genius of the Negro race has made us do this. But this does not alter our conviction that the necessity which has brought them into being is an evil, and that this evil should be combatted to the greatest extent possible.[29]

But this attempt to placate the editor with substance and the secretary with tone failed when White demanded nothing less than an outright repudiation of Du Bois's position. Aware of President Spingarn's great influence, though, White waited until the chief was called out of town and thus unable to attend the April meeting of the board, and then the secretary prevailed on his friends to introduce and pass as official NAACP policy a third declaration to the effect that the association

> is opposed both to the principle and the practice of enforced segregation of human beings on the basis of race and color. Enforced segregation by its very existence carries with it the implication of a superior and inferior group and invariably results in the imposition of a lower status on the group deemed inferior. *Thus both principle and practice necessitate unyielding opposition to any and every form of enforced segregation.*[30]

At the time this resolution was passed, Spingarn was traveling to New Orleans to meet his wife, who was returning from a trip to Guatemala. On learning of the momentous proclamation that had been made in his absence, however, the president altered his itinerary and made a point of stopping in Atlanta for a long conference with Du Bois. The editor naturally was aggravated by the turn of events and claimed he was "prepared to say some unpleasant things, even if it led to a quarrel," but there really was no opportunity, for Spingarn "was in his most agreeable and yielding temper. He wanted me [Du Bois] to understand that he agreed with me that the NAACP should be reorganized," and when Du Bois suggested that "Wilkins should be the first one to go and then White and Pickens," President Spingarn "agreed in general," although he saw "difficulty in letting either White or Pickens out unless they had jobs, and wanted especially to credit White for certain things he had done."[31] Du Bois was understandably elated by the conference, and he reported to his New York

lieutenant, George Streator, that all was well and valuable cooperation with Spingarn had been established. For his part,
Spingarn wrote a blistering letter to White, complaining that
the recent resolution was "weak and revolutionary": weak
"because it expresses disapproval only of enforced segregation,
whereas our historic attitude has been to regard all segregation as an evil, even though in some cases we were forced to
submit to it"; revolutionary because it committed the association to "unyielding opposition to any and every form of
segregation." Acknowledging that it was not always possible
to define "enforced segregation," Spingarn nevertheless believed "it is absolutely certain that the South enforces
separation of the races in schools and colleges," and consequently he interpreted the resolution to mean that the
NAACP now "must oppose every institution that is segregated
by force or custom, whereas in the old days we could say that
their segregation was an evil but we did not have to oppose
them." To emphasize the foolishness of this new position, the
president ordered that "in obedience to the resolution of the
Board, no officer of the Association should speak officially at
any Negro school or college in the South...that no money
received from any such school or college shall be officially acknowledged or used by us, until the Board so authorizes, but
shall be held pending such authorization in a separate
account; that no NAACP meetings be held in such schools or
colleges, and that communication with them be reduced to a
minimum." Only experience would indicate "what further
extension of this opposition should be taken," but in the
meantime President Spingarn "propose[d] to obey the resolution." "To do otherwise would brand us as hypocrites and that
is the last thing we can afford."[32]

The White group was too deeply committed to the anti-Du

Bois putsch to withdraw before the president's sarcasm. And when Du Bois continued to express his views on voluntary separation in the May issue of the *Crisis,* as everyone expected he would, White contended that the editor had challenged the board and that failure to meet this challenge would "properly, cause a loss of respect for the Board." Persuaded by this argument, the directors passed another resolution at their May meeting declaring that "the *Crisis* is the organ of the Association and no salaried officer of the Association shall criticize the policy, work, or officers of the Association in the pages of the *Crisis*; that any such criticism should be brought directly to the Board of Directors and its publication approved or disapproved." Spingarn, who was present at this meeting, found himself among the minority who indignantly grumbled that a "political intrigue" was afoot to muzzle Du Bois.[33]

At this point, to the surprise of neither Du Bois's friends nor his enemies, the editor submitted his resignation from the NAACP. While he did "not for a moment question" the board's right to take disciplinary action "whenever differences of opinion among its officers become so wide as to threaten the organization," he personally could not comply with the May directive. "In thirty-five years of public service," he observed, "my contribution to the settlement of the Negro problem has been mainly candid criticism based on a careful effort to know the facts." "I have not always been right," he admitted, "but I have been sincere, and I am unwilling at this late date to be limited in the expression of my honest opinions in the way which the Board proposes."[34]

Yet the resignation did not end the controversy, for President Spingarn had begun to rally several wavering and confused members of the board, and when the directors gathered for their June meeting they refused to accept Du Bois's resignation. Instead, a committee on reconciliation was appointed and instructed to intercede with the editor "in the hope that an understanding can be reached not incompatible with the Association's policy of unconditional opposition to segregation...nor with the right of Dr. Du Bois...to give full and free expression to his personal views through the columns of *The Crisis*." In the meantime, to prevent any of the editor's enemies from publicizing the fact that he had submitted a written resignation, "exclusive power to make statements for the Association" was vested in President Spingarn. Naturally, Du Bois's supporters were pleased, and George Streator reported to the editor that while the White faction had "mustered its full strength...without any attempt on the part of your friends to stack the meeting in your favor...the opposition was to all intent and purposes frustrated." Along with several others, Streator urged that "if it is possible for you to square your conscience with the proposals that the Board intends to make to you (of which I am not informed) I hope that you will be able to do so. Whatever you might feel about judicious silence, Negroes in America today do not need judicious silence, they need preaching to and hammering at. ...However much you have been annoyed by the situation, the colored people of the United States can not afford to have you rest in quiet in Atlanta." Striking a similar note, President Spingarn reminded Du Bois that while "I feel your criticism may to a certain extent be justified...I am no more convinced than before that your reasons for resigning are valid."[35]

At this point Walter White made it clear that the directors would have to choose between himself and Du Bois. According to the secretary, the editor of the *Crisis*, by ignoring the April and May directives, had "shown his utter contempt for the Board and put it on the defensive." Nevertheless, the board had refused to accept Du Bois's resignation and instead opted for reconciliation, a decision that "thoroughly nauseated" White because it could "only be construed as nothing more than a moral victory for Dr. Du Bois." Writing to President Spingarn, the secretary candidly explained that "when I left the Board meeting yesterday [June 11, 1934], I very definitely had the feeling that with the present constitution of the Board it is no longer possible for me to remain with the Association as its Secretary. Certainly the situation is at the point where my own self-respect will not permit me to do so."[36]

Had Du Bois known that White was on the verge of resigning, he might well have cooperated with the committee on reconciliation and attempted to forge a working agreement with the organization. Certainly he was convinced that White's leadership had been disastrous for the NAACP, and compromise was not out of the question, for Du Bois never doubted that the issue of voluntary separation could have been adjusted; he was convinced that whatever the board officially declared, the NAACP would continue its policy of protesting against segregation, and then if the protest failed it would bend every effort toward making black institutions as good as possible. Thus, "the only thing...that remains for us is to decide whether we are openly to recognize this procedure as inevitable or be silent about it and still pursue it." Under the circumstances, Du Bois believed that "the argument must be more or less academic, [and] there is no essential reason that those who see different sides of this same shield should not be able to agree to live together in the same house." Accordingly, he proposed a compromise that would have insured his freedom as editor while cooperating with a committee that would have exercised general supervision over the *Crisis's* business and editorial policies. The day after suggesting this modus vivendi, however, Du Bois reconsidered, and he informed Louis T. Wright, the chairman of the recently commissioned committee on reconciliation, that compromise was impossible. In his view, the board had "openly and defiantly sought to gag my expression," and therefore he had decided to "stand by my resignation no matter what the Board does or refrains from doing."[37]

A number of factors appear to have influenced this final decision. Away in Atlanta, the editor was not in close touch with developments in the national office, and he seems never to have suspected that Walter White's resignation might have been forthcoming if only he held on a bit longer. Yet the importance of this ignorance should not be overestimated, for Du Bois knew that White had the support of several board members, and thus the most the editor could hope for was a protracted struggle for power that would have involved personalities and lasted for months. At the age of sixty-six, Du Bois did not propose to get into anything of that sort, and, moreover, he so distrusted White that he may well have feared that the secretary, if defeated in a factional fight, would leave the association in a rage and consciously attempt to disrupt the organization. No doubt the old editor was also tired of the bickering and factionalism in the NAACP office, and the opportunity for solitude and contemplation in Atlanta must have seemed attractive. Yet perhaps most important of all, Du Bois thought he was "out of touch with my organization," and he believed that his efforts to reorganize the NAACP had failed completely. Thus there seemed "but one thing for me to do, and that is to make the supreme sacrifice of taking myself absolutely and unequivocally out of the picture,

so that hereafter the leaders of the NAACP, without the
distraction of personalities and accumulated animosities, can
give their whole thought and attention to the rescuing of the
greatest organization for the emancipation of Negroes that
America has ever had." To Spingarn, Du Bois confided that "it
is not easy. I am...cutting myself off from old and good
friends; but—*Gott helpe miche, ich kann nicht anders!*"[38]

Part of this premature defeatism must be explained as a
result of the editor's misunderstanding of the role played by
President Spingarn. While acknowledging his fondness for the
president, Du Bois later wrote that "Spingarn was skeptical of
democracy either in industry, politics or art. . . . He was afraid
that I was turning radical and dogmatic and even communistic, and he proceeded to use his power and influence to curb
my acts and forestall any change of program of the Association
on my part." The evidence presented here indicates that
Spingarn did nothing of the sort, that, in fact, his sympathies
and influence were definitely on the side of the editor. But
wrong beliefs are often as influential as correct ones. Some of
the confusion stemmed from the fact that Spingarn, while
agreeing with the editor on the major points at issue,
disapproved of the openness with which Du Bois criticized the
association. According to the president, Du Bois was raising "a
rather delicate question: Can the 'organ' of the Association
attack its policies and work and remain an 'organ'?" and he
warned the editor "that most members of the Board would
answer that question with a very vigorous No." Shortly after
their important conference in Atlanta, Spingarn wrote to Du
Bois that "what I said to you was based on the assumption, as
I tried to make clear, that you would 'play the game' loyally
from the inside." Du Bois may have interpreted these friendly
warnings as basic opposition—especially since his New York

informants were claiming that Spingarn was solidly in the camp of the opposition. Lillian Alexander, for example, telegrammed "Spingarn plans...another dastardly attack on Du Bois," and George Streator claimed that the president was "more than wrought up by your attacking the Board"; "Joel has given you the ≠ (doublecross). He seems determined to put you out." Yet Streator knew that Spingarn was also taking actions that "must have harried a certain blond young man [White] considerably," and after the president censured Streator for saying that he was at the center of the move to force Du Bois out, Streator conceded that he could not reconcile all the things he heard, and he finally concluded that "the thing is a puzzle." Away in Atlanta, Du Bois depended on his New York informants, and it is not surprising that he came to the same conclusion. This uncertainty concerning President Spingarn's position—the suspicion that he was trying to keep his power by talking against one faction to the other—no doubt contributed to the prematurely defeatist conclusions that played a major role in prompting Du Bois's final resignation from the NAACP. Writing to Streator six weeks after the event, the editor explicitly confessed his inability to understand Spingarn's role in the crisis, and he pointed to this uncertainty about the president's position as the major reason for his resignation.[39]

Of course it was not easy to resign. "To give up *The Crisis,*" Du Bois acknowledged, "was like giving up a child, to leave the Association was leaving the friends of a quarter of a century." On the other hand, staying apparently "meant silence, a repudiation of what I was thinking and planning," and a continuation of the factional strife, and thus the editor felt that it was best to leave "in order to see if without my sometimes irritating personality, other and younger men could not accomplish what I failed to do."[40]

NOTES

1. In the NAACP Files, see Reports of the Budget Committee, 1930 and 1934; Report of the Budget Committee for the Fiscal Year 1933 (December, 1932); memorandum from the Budget Committee to the Board of Directors, 13 June 1932; memorandum re salaries, 22 October 1936; Minutes of the Meetings of the Board of Directors, 18 April 1929, 12 September 1933, 13 November 1933; Charles Edward Russell to Mary White Ovington, 25 November 1931, 1 December 1931, 2 December 1931, 6 December 1931. W. E. B. Du Bois, *The Autobiography of W. E. B. Du Bois* (New York: International Publishers, 1968), pp. 291-293; Elliott Rudwick, *W. E. B. Du Bois: A Study in Minority Group Leadership* (Philadelphia: University of Pennsylvania Press, 1960), pp. 177-178, 267-270. Salaries for 1934 were as follows: Walter White, $4,021.87; William Pickens, $2,925; Roy Wilkins, $2,653.12; William Turner, $2,047.50; Daisey Lampkin, $2,193.75; Richetta Randolph, $1,947.37. Du Bois, who was on leave of absence teaching at Atlanta University but who continued to serve as editor-in-chief of the *Crisis*, was paid $1,200.

2. In the NAACP Files, see Minutes of the Meeting of the NAACP Budget Committee, December, 1930; Report of the Budget Committee, 14 December 1931; Report of the Budget Committee for the Fiscal Year, 1933 (December, 1932); Walter White to J. E. Spingarn, Charles Studin, and Louis T. Wright, 28 November 1930; White to Charles Russell, 10 November 1931; White to William Turner, 19 November 1931; Mary White Ovington to Richetta Randolph, 7 December 1930; Russell to Ovington, 25 November 1931; ibid., 6 December 1931; W. E. B. Du Bois, Herbert Seligman, Robert Bagnall, William Pickens, and Roy Wilkins to the Board of Directors, 21 December 1931; Pickens to White, 7 June 1932.

3. In the NAACP Files, see Report of the Budget Committee, December, 1931; Minutes of the Meeting of the Board of Directors, 14 December 1931; Walter White to Charles Edward Russell, 13 November 1931.

4. Du Bois, Seligman, Pickens, Bagnall, and Wilkins to the Board of Directors, 21 December 1931, NAACP Files; Bagnall to White, 5 December 1930, NAACP Files; Du Bois, *Autobiography*, p. 294.

5. As a result of this protest, the board of directors in December, 1931, decided to postpone action with regard to Bagnall and Pickens. Instead, Miss Edna Lonigan, former chief statistician of the New York State Labor Department, was secured to make an impartial investigation of the expenditure of funds by the national office and by the *Crisis*. Miss Lonigan reported that the method used by Secretary White to measure the cost and results of field work "was inadequate," but, according to the board, her "more elaborate study of all returns from all branches for three years is no more encouraging." The organization continued in the red during 1932, and in December of that year the budget committee, "at the behest of

downright necessity [and] ... with very great reluctance," recommended that Bagnall and two clerks be dropped from the staff. In addition, the committee recommended that Herbert Seligman be employed for only three and one-half days per week—an offer which prompted Seligman to resign. William Pickens remained as a full-time employee throughout the 1930s. J. E. Spingarn to Walter White and W. E. B. Du Bois, 5 February 1932; Minutes of the Meeting of the Board of Directors, 4 January 1932, and 8 February 1932. NAACP Files.

6. In the NAACP Files, see Du Bois, Seligman, Pickens, Bagnall, and Wilkins to the Board of Directors, 21 December 1931; Budget Committee report on "Estimated Cost of Branch and Field Work During 1931," 7 June 1932; Minutes of the Meetings of the Board of Directors, 21 December 1931, 4 January 1932, 8 February 1932, 9 January 1933; Report of the Budget Committee for the Fiscal Year (December, 1932).

7. Minutes of the Meetings of the Board of Directors, 18 April 1929, 10 June 1929, 14 July 1930, 10 April 1933, 12 September 1933, NAACP Files; Du Bois, *Dusk of Dawn* (New York: Harcourt, Brace & Company, 1940), p. 258; Francis L. Broderick, *W. E. B. Du Bois: Negro Leader in a Time of Crisis* (Stanford, California: Stanford University Press, 1959), pp. 173-174. Elliott Rudwick has noted that as early as 1925 and 1926 "*Crisis* losses were averaging about two thousand dollars a year." *W. E. B. Du Bois*, p. 266. Du Bois believed, however, that this early deficit was "not mainly one of demand or competition," but was essentially the result of "the failure of our business policy, especially in the matter of promoting sales and collecting debts." Minutes of the Meeting of the Board of Directors, 10 June 1929, NAACP Files. As late as 1931, Mary White Ovington maintained that "the situation every year with *The Crisis* is this. *The Crisis* people don't like to write off their bad debts. The Auditor doesn't believe they can collect what they think they can." Ovington to Charles Edward Russell, n.d., filed for December, 1931, NAACP Files.

8. Rudwick, *W. E. B. Du Bois*, pp. 151-183; Broderick, *W. E. B. Du Bois*, pp. 151-183, 173-174; Minutes of the Meeting of the Board of Directors, 9 July 1934, NAACP Files; Du Bois to Abram Harris, 17 July 1934, WEBD Papers.

9. Du Bois, *Dusk of Dawn*, pp. 293-294; Du Bois, *Autobiography*, pp. 259-261.

10. Rudwick, *W. E. B. Du Bois*, pp. 151-153, 165; Broderick, *W. E. B. Du Bois*, p. 98; Du Bois, *Autobiography*, pp. 257-261, 291-293.

11. Minutes of the Meetings of the Board of Directors, 14 July 1930, 8 September 1930, and 12 December 1932, NAACP Files; Mary White Ovington to Charles Edward Russell, 9 December 1931, NAACP Files; memorandum from the secretary re the NAACP and *The Crisis*, 12 March 1934, NAACP Files; Du Bois, *Autobiography*, p. 295. Du Bois maintained that the *net* contribution from the association was only about $15,000. He pointed out that the national office kept forty cents from every $1.50 subscription that was obtained as a result of the efforts of NAACP officers

or branches. This was the normal agents' commission, and Du Bois acknowledged that the organization was entitled to it. On the other hand, he thought it was only fair to note that over the years the NAACP had earned about $20,000 in this manner. Minutes of the Meeting of the Board of Directors, 10 April 1934, NAACP Files. See also Roy Wilkins to the Budget Committee, memorandum, 5 December 1936, NAACP Files. Unlike secretary White, president J. E. Spingarn was inclined to minimize the importance of the NAACP's contribution to the *Crisis*: "As to the *Crisis* figures, the way to look at them is that in twenty-three years of its existence, the Crisis has cost the Association about $45,000, or less than $2,000 a year, and that without what it did for the Association in most of those years, there would be no Association for you to be Secretary of or me to be President. But of course that does not mean that under present conditions we can afford to spend any more money on it." Spingarn to White, 10 May 1933, NAACP Files.

12. W. E. B. Du Bois, "Segregation in the North," *Crisis* 41 (April, 1934):115; idem, "A Negro Nation Within the Nation," *Current History* 42 (June, 1935):269; idem, *Autobiography*, pp. 236, 254. Nathaniel Patrick Tillman, Jr., "Walter Francis White: A Study in Interest Group Leadership" (Ph.D. dissertation, University of Wisconsin, 1961), pp. 76-77; Robert L. Zangrando, "The Efforts of the National Association for the Advancement of Colored People to Secure Passage of a Federal Anti-Lynching Law, 1920-1940" (Ph.D. dissertation, University of Pennsylvania, 1963), pp. 286-287, 292, 296; J. E. Spingarn to Walter White, 10 January 1934, NAACP Files; White to Spingarn, 15 January 1934, NAACP Files. White assured Spingarn that he was "not disturbed by the fact that there are Negroes who think that my opposition to segregation springs from a desire to associate with white people. If this were true I long since would have stopped living as a Negro and passed as white when I could associate exclusively with white people. As you of course know, I choose my friends and associates, particularly the former, not on the basis of their race but wholly on mutual points of interest."

13. According to Nathaniel Tillman, White was ever conscious of his own lack of intellectual depth—especially when dealing with men of Du Bois's caliber. This inferiority complex may explain why he interpreted the editor's aloofness as condescension. "Walter Francis White: A Study in Interest Group Leadership," p. 104.

14. Du Bois's New England upbringing also influenced his character. "It was not good form in Great Barrington," he recalled in his *Autobiography*, "to express one's thoughts volubly, or to give way to excessive emotion. We were even sparing in our daily greetings. There was on the street only a curt 'good morning' to those whom you knew well and no greetings at all from others. I am quite sure that in a less restrained and conventional atmosphere I should have easily learned to express my emotions with far greater and more unrestrained intensity; but as it was I had the social heritage not only of a New England clan but Dutch taciturnity."

This personal aloofness was later "reinforced and strengthened by inner withdrawals in the face of real and imagined discriminations. The result was that I was early thrown in upon myself. I found it difficult and even unnecessary to approach other people and by that same token my own inner life perhaps grew the richer." At Harvard College, for example, the young Du Bois "sought no friendships among my white fellow students, nor even acquaintanceships." Nevertheless, he found great satisfaction in embracing "the companionship of those of my own color...and forget-[ting] as far as was possible that outer, whiter world." The editor's "new" economic program of the 1930s obviously was deeply rooted in his own personal experience; in effect he was suggesting that the great masses of Negroes could overcome adversity by following a strategy that had been spectacularly successful in his own life.

15. Du Bois, *Autobiography*, pp. 93, 134-136, 139, 277-278, 293-294; Broderick, *W. E. B. Du Bois*, pp. 100-101, 116, 121; Martin Duberman, "Du Bois as Prophet," *New Republic*, 23 March 1968, pp. 36-39; Harold R. Isaacs, "Du Bois: A Contemporary Assessment," *The New World of Negro Americans* (New York: The John Day Company, 1963), pp. 197-200, 225-230.

16. Minutes of the Meetings of the Board of Directors, 13 May 1929, 9 February 1931, and 13 April 1931, NAACP Files; White to Lillian A. Alexander, 9 November 1933, NAACP Files; Rudwick, *W. E. B. Du Bois*, pp. 268-271; Broderick, *W. E. B. Du Bois*, pp. 173-174; Du Bois, *Dusk of Dawn*, pp. 312-313; idem, *Autobiography*, p. 293; Du Bois to J. E. Spingarn, 16 October 1933, and 13 December 1933, Spingarn Papers, Yale University; Du Bois to Abram Harris, 16 January 1934, and 17 July 1934, WEBD Papers; Du Bois to Harry E. Davis, 16 January 1934, and 19 July 1934, NAACP Files.

17. In the NAACP Files, see Minutes of the Special Meeting of the Board of Directors, 29 March 1932; Minutes of the Meeting of the Board of Directors, 11 April 1932; memorandum from the Secretary re the NAACP and the *Crisis*, 12 March 1934. See also Du Bois, *Autobiography*, pp. 257-258.

18. In the NAACP Files, see Walter White to Martha Gruening, 10 January 1934; White to G. A. Steward, 27 February 1934; White to James Weldon Johnson, 28 February 1934; White to James McClendon, 7 May 1934; Mary White Ovington to Louis Wright, 18 May 1934.

19. In the NAACP Files, see Walter White to the Budget Committee, memorandum, 10 October 1933; Charles Edward Russell to Mary White Ovington, 1 December 1931; White to Louis Wright, 31 May 1933; memorandum from the secretary re the NAACP and the *Crisis*, 12 March 1934; W. E. B. Du Bois, Herbert Seligman, William Pickens, Robert Bagnall, and Roy Wilkins to the Board of Directors, 21 December 1931. It should be noted that the *Crisis*'s financial difficulties continued throughout the depression, though after 1934 the national office exercised complete control over the business management. See Roy Wilkins to the

Budget Committee, memoranda, 27 April 1936, and 5 December 1936, NAACP Files.

20. Du Bois, "Segregation," *Crisis* 41 (January, 1934):20; Walter White to J. E. Spingarn, 15 January 1934, NAACP Files; White manuscript of article on "Segregation," January, 1934, NAACP Files.

21. Chairman of the Board to the secretary, memorandum, 10 January 1934, NAACP Files; J. E. Spingarn to Walter White, 12 January 1934, NAACP Files.

22. Du Bois, *Dusk of Dawn,* pp. 290-291; Ira De A. Reid to J. E. Spingarn, 15 January 1938, Spingarn Papers, Yale University; Spingarn to James Weldon Johnson, 26 June 1933, Spingarn Papers, Yale University. In the NAACP Files, see memorandum from Spingarn to Walter White and Du Bois, 22 December 1932; Roy Wilkins to Conferees, 16 July 1932; Spingarn to Board of Directors, 6 March 1933. Spingarn, memorandum on Amenia Conference, n.d. [Spring, 1933], Spingarn Papers, Howard University. Also, in the Walter White Papers, Yale University, see White to Johnson, 21 March 1933, 22 March 1933, 29 March 1933, and 3 April 1933; White to Spingarn, 14 March 1933, and 28 May 1933. In the James Weldon Johnson Papers, Yale University, see Johnson to White, 1 April 1933; Du Bois to Johnson, 17 March 1933, and 18 May 1933.

23. Spingarn was a white president of the association, and it has already been mentioned that Du Bois thought that the leadership of the NAACP should be black. Yet ironically in view of the editor's criticism of Walter White on this score, Du Bois never objected to Spingarn as president. In part this was because Du Bois, who was ever sensitive to condescension and subtle race prejudice on the part of white philanthropists, detected "no shadow of the thing [color prejudice] in your [Spingarn's] soul"; but it was also because Spingarn himself agreed with Du Bois concerning the desirability of Negro leadership. The editor and the president conferred about this on several occasions, and Du Bois went so far as to prepare a list of black leaders who "would command widespread attention and respect from the colored people." The more he considered the matter, however, the more Du Bois was "of the opinion that a time of stress, retrenchment, and criticism is not the time to make a change in the presidency of the Association. Later, when we are at the threshold of returning prosperity and there is some reasonable excuse, it would be a fine gesture to put a colored person in the presidency." Du Bois to Spingarn, 28 October 1914, Spingarn to James Weldon Johnson, 6 December 1932, Spingarn papers, Yale University; Dr. Du Bois to President Spingarn, memorandum, 9 December 1932, WEBD papers.

24. Du Bois, *Dusk of Dawn,* p. 290. In the WEBD Papers, see Du Bois to Addie Dickerson, 21 March 1934; Du Bois to Abram Harris, 16 January 1934; Harris to Du Bois, 6 January 1934; J. E. Spingarn to Du Bois, 27 March 1934, and 1 May 1934; Du Bois to Spingarn, 21 April 1934, and 2 May 1934; Du Bois to George Streator, 26 April 1934, and 2 May 1934; Du Bois, note for manuscript on the Negro and the New Deal, 1934. See

also Du Bois to Spingarn, 16 October 1933, Spingarn Papers, Yale University; Harris to Spingarn, 5 May 1934, Spingarn Papers, Yale University.

25. In the NAACP Files, see memorandum from the Secretary re the NAACP and the *Crisis,* 12 March 1934; Minutes of the Meeting of the Board of Directors, 12 September 1933; Carl Murphy to the Board of Directors, 17 May 1934; Mary White Ovington to Louis Wright, 18 May 1934; Ovington to Charles Edward Russell, 10 January 1934; Richetta Randolph to Ovington, 17 May 1934; Randolph to Walter White, 17 May 1934; White to J. E. Spingarn, 12 June 1934; Russell to Roy Wilkins, 29 August 1938.

26. The White-Du Bois controversy created a difficult problem for Pickens, whose position with the NAACP was not very secure. The field secretary could not afford to be on the losing side in this dispute, and he may have equivocated. (According to George Streator, "Pickens is riding the fence like a scholar and gentleman. I truly feel sorry for him in his dilemma.") Yet on balance I am convinced that Pickens sympathized with Du Bois and that he made his views known to President Spingarn and other members of the board. In the WEBD Papers, see Streator to Du Bois, 18 April 1934; Pickens to Du Bois, 10 April 1934, 30 May 1934, 16 June 1934 (copy to J. E. Spingarn) and 29 August 1934; Pickens to Spingarn, 10 June 1934.

27. Harry E. Davis to the Board of Directors, 9 June 1934, NAACP Files; William Pickens to Du Bois (copy to J. E. Spingarn), 16 June 1934, NAACP Files; Spingarn to Walter White, 12 January 1934, NAACP Files.

28. W. E. B. Du Bois, "The Board of Directors on Segregation," *Crisis* 41 (May, 1934):149; Minutes of the Meeting of the Board of Directors, 9 April 1934, NAACP Files; Du Bois to Louis T. Wright, 22 March 1934, WEBD Papers.

29. Du Bois, "The Board of Directors on Segregation," p. 149; Minutes of the Meeting of the Board of Directors, 9 April 1934, NAACP Files.

30. Du Bois, "The Board of Directors on Segregation," p. 149; Minutes of the Meeting of the Board of Directors, 9 April 1934, NAACP Files; Walter White to James Weldon Johnson, 11 April 1934, Walter White Papers, Yale University.

31. Du Bois believed that Wilkins was "intelligent and good-willed," but he objected to the assistant secretary because "Wilkins yielded to White in every request" and maintained his position in the organization by becoming "White's errand boy." W. E. B. Du Bois, *The Autobiography of W. E. B. Du Bois* (New York: International Publishers, 1968), pp. 294, 338; Du Bois to J. E. Spingarn, 14 December 1933, Spingarn Papers, Yale University; Du Bois to Spingarn, 10 April 1933, Spingarn Papers, Howard University; Du Bois to George Streator, 26 June 1934, WEBD Papers; Du Bois to Board of Directors, 26 July 1934, NAACP Files.

32. W. E. B. Du Bois to John Hope, memorandum, 13 April 1934, WEBD Papers; Du Bois to J. E. Spingarn, 14 April 1934, WEBD Papers; George Streator to Du Bois, telegram, 26 April 1934, WEBD Papers. In

the Spingarn Papers, Yale University, see Du Bois to Streator, telegram, 26 April 1934; Du Bois to Streator, 2 May 1934; Du Bois to Spingarn, 21 April 1934. See also Spingarn to Walter White, 25 April 1934, and 9 May 1934, NAACP Files.

33. Minutes of the Meeting of the Board of Directors, 14 May 1934, NAACP Files; Walter White to J. E. Spingarn, 12 June 1934, NAACP Files; White to Arthur Spingarn, 3 May 1934, NAACP Files.

34. Du Bois to the Board of Directors, 1 June 1934, NAACP Files; Du Bois, *Autobiography*, p. 298.

35. In the NAACP Files, see Minutes of the Meeting of the Board of Directors, 11 June 1934; George Streator to Du Bois 12 June 1934; J. E. Spingarn to Du Bois, 14 June 1934, and 7 July 1934; Harry E. Davis to Du Bois, 9 June 1934, and 2 July 1934; Dr. Du Bois to President Hope, memorandum, 11 June 1934.

36. Walter White to J. E. Spingarn, 12 June 1934, NAACP Files.

37. Du Bois to the Board of Directors, 26 June 1934, NAACP Files; Du Bois to Louis T. Wright, 25 June 1934, NAACP Files; Du Bois to J. E. Spingarn, 31 May 1934, Spingarn Papers, Yale University. In WEBD Papers, see Du Bois to Spingarn, 16 June 1934, and 25 June 1934; Du Bois to Mrs. W. E. B. Du Bois, 25 June 1934; Du Bois to Mrs. E. R. Alexander, 11 June 1934.

38. In the WEBD Papers, see Du Bois to Abram Harris, 17 July 1934; Du Bois to Mrs. E. R. Matthews, 14 December 1934; Du Bois to Lady Kathleen Simon, 1 October 1934; Du Bois to Mrs. Alexander, 11 June 1934; Du Bois to George Streator, 26 June 1934. Du Bois, *Dusk of Dawn*, pp. 311-312; idem, *Autobiography*, pp. 297-298. Du Bois to the Board of Directors, 26 June 1934, NAACP Files; Du Bois to J. E. Spingarn, 31 May 1934, Spingarn Papers, Yale University.

39. Du Bois, *Dusk of Dawn*, pp. 290-291. In the WEBD Papers, see J. E. Spingarn to Du Bois, 27 March 1934, and 1 May 1934; Lillian Alexander to Louis T. Wright, telegram, 3 April 1934; Alexander to Marion Cuthbert, telegram, 3 April 1934; Alexander to J. E. Spingarn, telegram, 3 April 1934; Alexander to Arthur Spingarn, telegram, 3 April 1934; Alexander to Rachel Davis Du Bois, telegram, 3 April 1934; George Streator to Du Bois, 12 January 1934, 15 January 1934, 2 March 1934, 2 April 1934, 9 May 1934, 11 May 1934, 16 May 1934, 28 June 1934, and n.d. [July, 1934]; Du Bois to Streator, 26 June 1934, 3 July 1934, and 17 July 1934; Du Bois to Harry E. Davis, 16 January 1934, and 1 February 1934; Du Bois to Abram Harris, 16 January 1934.

40. Du Bois to J. E. Spingarn, 31 May 1934, Spingarn Papers, Yale University; Du Bois, *Dusk of Dawn*, pp. 311-312; idem, *Autobiography*, pp. 297-298; Du Bois to the Board of Directors, 26 June 1934, NAACP Files. In WEBD Papers, see Du Bois to George Foster Peabody, 26 June 1934; Du Bois to Lester Walton, 12 June 1934; Walton to Du Bois, 21 June 1934; Du Bois to Francis J. Grimke, 27 June 1934; Du Bois to Owen R. Lovejoy, 19 July 1934.

12

The Harris Report

Of course, the departure of Dr. Du Bois did not solve the NAACP's problems. The organization remained without a modern economic program, and a growing number of Negroes were becoming impatient with the association's failure to integrate its traditional struggle for civil rights with a new economic policy. While the association organized twenty-three new branches in 1934 and claimed a membership of 85,000 scattered in 404 branches, many of its leaders feared that the influence of the organization was declining. After Du Bois's departure, circulation of the *Crisis* dropped to less than 10,000; only one-half of the 85,000 members could be counted on to pay dues; and a considerable number of young Negro intellectuals[1] were demanding that the association, as one delegate to the 1935 Annual Conference put it, "go to the masses...We must share common ground with the Negro worker. When we call a meeting on discrimination we have nobody, but when we call a meeting on bread-and-butter matters, we have a full house."[2]

Perceiving this discontent and no doubt fearing a continued loss of influence, several of the NAACP's directors and executives felt the time had come to consider possible changes in the association's structure, techniques, and goals. "There is no question that in some way we ought to democratize the Association," President J. E. Spingarn acknowledged. "We have just scratched the surface...we do not represent the masses," declared Roscoe Dunjee, the president of the association's branch in Oklahoma City. And Abram Harris, a board member with close ties to the young militants, noted that "as long as civil liberty and political rights were the main principles for which the NAACP stood, agitation and protest were naturally the best means of operating. Today, however, the problems are different...they are fundamentally economic. Sheer protests and agitation...do not bring out the fundamental maladies of economic society from which both the Negro and white workers suffer. If the organization is to continue its effectiveness it seems to me that it must go to the Negro workers and farmers with a program based upon knowledge of what is happening to them in the present economy. This program must show white workers that the problem of differential wages is their problem. It will seek through practical lessons to show white and black workingmen that as contradictory as it may seem they have a real identity of common interests."[3]

This call for black and white working-class solidarity was essentially the same formula that had been enunciated by the Amenia delegates in 1933. At that time it was rejected by the leaders of the association, who claimed that cooperation was a two-way street and that it was impossible to collaborate with workingmen who were as Negrophobic as most of those associated with the AFL. During the early 1930s, as we have seen, the leaders of the NAACP unremittingly censured labor unions that practiced racial discrimination and incessantly reproached the AFL for its lack of enthusiasm in organizing mass production workers. Of course the young militants were also opposed to trade union discrimination, but most of them continued to believe in the ultimate wisdom of affiliating with nondiscriminatory unions. While they sympathized with Roy Wilkins's statement that it was "not easy for an Association which knows so intimately the raw deals that have been given to Negro labor by the AFL to get out and shout from the housetops to Negro workers urging them to affiliate [with unions]," the young militants criticized the established leaders for devoting, as Frank Crosswaith, a Negro organizer for the International Ladies Garment Workers Union (ILGWU) put it, too much attention to "the unfair treatment meted out to Negroes in certain unions" and too little to "those unions wherein the Negro enjoys equality of treatment with his fellow tradesman."[4]

Aroused by the discontent among the younger black leaders and wishing to avoid any further loss of influence, the NAACP's hierarchy began in 1934 and 1935 to place greater emphasis on working class solidarity. Several of the younger militants were named to the board of directors, and the association's rhetoric became more pro-labor: the interests of black workers were declared to be "inextricably intertwined with those of white workers"; and Negroes were summoned "to union ranks as the only means of changing the low and unfavorable conditions of work imposed upon them." As W. E. B. Du Bois noted, however, such statements had "really no organic connection with the work and are not expressions of our real policy." The actual realignment of strategy had to await the emergence and phenomenal growth of the industrially organized and racially egalitarian new unions of the

Committee for Industrial Organization (CIO). When the egalitarian industrial unions took the field, the leaders of the NAACP at last felt that they could, in good conscience, implement the program for working class solidarity which Du Bois had advocated earlier in his career and which the Amenia delegates had espoused in 1933. After 1935 the opportunity seemed to be at hand for the NAACP to reestablish closer contacts with the alienated black intelligentsia and masses, and the association busied itself with the task of presenting the industrial labor viewpoint to the Negro community.[5]

To understand this shift in NAACP strategy it is necessary to know something about the character of these new unions, though the discussion here will be brief since others have already treated this subject in some detail. The young militants' abiding faith in trade union organization was largely the result of the favorable impression made by a handful of AFL industrial unions, particularly the United Mine Workers (UMW) and the International Ladies Garment Workers Union (ILGWU). These unions had learned that trade unionism could succeed in mass production industries only if it adopted the industrial form of organization. Unlike craft unions, whose bargaining power depended on the control of a few highly skilled and strategically located jobs, the power of industrial unions depended on their ability to organize all workers in a given industry. Thus, in industries such as mining and the needle trades, where colored workers were employed in substantial numbers, successful and effective unionization depended to a great degree on the inclusion of Negro workers.

No union took greater advantage of the opportunities offered by the NRA and the Wagner Act than the United Mine Workers. Under the able leadership of John L. Lewis, the UMW reached deep into its treasury for funds to finance a tremendous organizing campaign in the summer of 1933. An army of organizers was sent into the coal fields, and within three months more than 100,000 new members had joined the union. By the end of 1933 Lewis could announce that 90 percent of the nation's coal miners had been enrolled by the UMW. This campaign could not have succeeded without the support of the colored miners, for while Negroes were only 10 percent of the total number of workers in the coal industry, almost one-fourth of the southern miners were Negroes, and in the important Alabama field the percentage of black workers rose to more than half.[6]

Remembering the experience of 1927 (when the introduction of black strikebreakers had been one of the important factors responsible for the UMW's failure to organize the southern field), the union made a special effort to convince Negroes that they would benefit from organization. In the great organizing campaign of 1933-1934 the UMW employed Negro organizers in both North and South; local Negroes served on organizing committees, were appointed as picket captains, and were elected to the local union leadership. This use of Negro officials and the aggressive courting of colored labor helped to break down the suspicion and distrust which many black workers felt toward unions. Even more important, the UMW insisted that employers give equal pay for equal work, regardless of the worker's color.[7]

The racial policies of the International Ladies Garment Workers Union were even more egalitarian than those of the United Mine Workers. During its great membership drive of 1933-1934, the ILGWU employed Negro organizers in all major cities, and colored officers were elected in locals throughout the country. On several occasions when white employers threatened to fire colored workers rather than pay them wages equal to those paid white workers, ILGWU locals called shop strikes—insisting that Negro members be retained and paid equal wages. The ILGWU also refused to honor employers' requests for workers of a particular race or nationality. When locals had reason to believe that an employer was discriminating against members of one race or minority group, it was not uncommon for them to send only members of that group and thus force integration. In addition, Negro members were encouraged to attend the union's social events—dances, lectures, concerts, the summer resort in the Pocono Mountains, and various other activities.[8]

The racial policies of the UMW and the ILGWU were especially important because these two unions, along with the Amalgamated Clothing Workers of America (ACWA), formed the spearhead of the emerging Committee for Industrial Organization (CIO). The previously mentioned 1935 convention of the AFL (which saw the last-minute scuttling of the Committee of Five's forthright report on trade union discrimination and the substitution of the executive council's innocuous recommendation) was also the occasion of the final breach in the unity of organized labor. Led by John L. Lewis of the UMW, David Dubinsky of the ILGWU, and Sidney Hillman of the ACWA, the CIO renounced the AFL's traditional policy of craft organization and enthusiastically set about the task of organizing mass production workers in industrial unions. In so doing, it did not forget that black workers had to be organized if industrial unionism was to succeed.

While the CIO's egalitarian race policies were motivated primarily by considerations of expediency, it is nonetheless true that union members and officers were making significant efforts to modify old racial prejudices and lay the foundation for working class solidarity. In this respect the earlier experience of the UMW and the ILGWU served as models for many of the new industrial unions. For instance, when a CIO affiliate gained a foothold in the Armour Company's Chicago plant, it followed the example of the ILGWU and insisted that the company stop its practice of "tagging" the time cards of colored employees. At the Swift plant, the union insisted that the company agree to hire Negroes in proportion to their percentage of the Chicago population. In New York, several of the new unions called their workers off the job when employers refused to pay Negroes as much as whites who were doing the same work. Some unions, such as the United Automobile Workers, established their own fair employment practices department and carried on vigorous educational campaigns against race prejudice. There were similar developments even in the Deep South; in Birmingham, for example, several unions protested against the practice of classifying Negroes as "helpers" and paying them at the rate for common labor when in fact they were doing skilled work. Of course, actions such as these did not always succeed in changing deep-seated racial prejudices, but it would be a serious error to underestimate the extent to which the CIO improved the economic position of Negro workers and educated white workers on the color problem. Moreover, in the period after 1935, when AFL and CIO affiliates were often competing with one another for members, the egalitarian policies of the CIO frequently forced the AFL unions to adopt a more liberal racial policy.[9]

Although there were areas where Negroes remained skeptical about organized labor, most notably in the automobile industry and in the plants of Little Steel, after 1935 Negroes generally responded enthusiastically to the CIO's policy of racial equality and industrial organization. Exact figures on union membership are not available, but reports from various sections of the country indicate that after 1935 there was a substantial increase in Negro union membership. In New York City, for example, the number of Negro union men in unskilled work tripled, while Negro membership in the skilled craft unions remained negligible. In Birmingham more than 60 percent of the 50,000 new CIO members were colored. And for the North as a whole, the CIO's Steel Workers Organizing Committee reported that it "found no greater difficulty in organizing the Negroes in Northern steel mills than any other workers." Press reports indicate that organized black workers were loyal to their unions, that they would strike as readily, stay out as long, and picket as regularly as other workers. After 1935 and the emergence of industrial unionism, the divisive effects of race and nationality were no longer such potent obstacles to the development of a sense of working class solidarity. By emphasizing common problems, the CIO had given black and white workers a common sense of economic class-consciousness and united them in opposition to a common enemy.[10]

The transformation in organized labor's attitude toward the Negro and the subsequent change in the black worker's response to labor naturally improved the position of those militants who had contended for some time that biracial working-class solidarity was the best way to solve the economic problems that plagued the masses of Negroes. The developments on the labor front, when combined with the demands of friendly critics for a definite economic program, perhaps made it inevitable that the NAACP would begin to consider the possibility of changes in its future emphases and activities. Even Walter White, who had grave reservations about moving toward a more "mass-oriented" program and who felt that many of his colleagues were permitting themselves "to be stampeded by temporary or emotional situations and conditions," acknowledged that "it is essential that all organizations periodically take stock of themselves and of conditions which they face." Responding to this widespread sentiment, the board of directors in July of 1934 appointed a special committee to consider reorientation of the association's future programs and tactics.[11]

The Committee on the Future Plan and Program of the NAACP was chaired by Professor Abram Harris of Howard University and represented a judicious blend of the various views within the association. Representing experience were Mary White Ovington, one of the original incorporators of the association, and James Weldon Johnson, who had served as secretary for fourteen years; the prominent surgeon Dr. Louis T. Wright stood for the traditional civil rights orientation, and social worker Rachel Davis Du Bois[12] and literary critic Sterling Brown, along with Harris, were outspoken in their demands for a new emphasis on economic problems. President Spingarn and Secretary White were appointed to the committee as ex-officio members. According to Chairman Harris, who was given considerable latitude in defining the scope of the committee's operations and who himself did most of the preliminary work, the prime concern of the group was to formulate "a clear policy of what is necessary in the present, whether the type of strategy employed in these past activities can be used in the present period, and if it can't what must be the strategy at this time."[13]

During the summer of 1934, Harris traveled to New York and spent more than a week inspecting the records of the

NAACP, particularly as they related to past economic activities. From this study he learned that the association had a long history of protesting "against discrimination and segregation of Negroes in industry and against the refusal of the A.F. of L. unions to organize Negroes." More recently it had engaged in much needed "efforts to safeguard the rights of Negro workers in the...various national, state and local emergency agencies, relief projects, and in the legislation of the present administration." This activity, Harris acknowledged, was important and had led to "outstanding accomplishments... [that] cannot be easily dismissed."[14] As significant as past work in the economic field had been, however, Harris complained that it had been conducted "as an incidental phase of [the association's] civil liberty program." Essentially the work had been that of exposing discriminatory treatment in the economic realm, and like the rest of the association's agitation it was based on the assumption that once the truth were known, men of goodwill would see to it that the Negro secured "his rights as an American citizen under prevailing economic and social conditions."[15]

Harris and Sterling Brown and Rachel Davis Du Bois rejected the assumption that proper education would reform America, though their apostasy from the association's creed was unlike that of Du Bois in that it was based not on a despair of regenerating whites whose prejudices were perceived to be the result of age-long complexes, unconscious habits, and irrational urges, but on a belief that there could never be economic justice for workers—black or white—so long as the power of capitalism and private ownership remained unchecked. According to these young radicals, civil libertarianism under capitalism—no matter how militant—did nothing to improve the economic plight of the masses. The association had been attempting to secure equal rights and benefits for the black worker, but the basic problems of physical survival during the Great Depression had convinced Harris, Brown, and Mrs. Du Bois that even if "full citizenship rights and civil liberty had been acquired by the Negro, the real condition of the great mass of black men...would have been unaltered in its essential features." To be sure, the adverse economic condition that was the fate of most workers under capitalism had "affected a proportionately greater number of Negroes and...the impact of these changes upon the Negro was greater than upon the white man." Yet the three young committee members were convinced that the depression—which they considered the inevitable collapse of a fundamentally unsound system—had reduced "the white and black masses to a substantially identical economic position" and had shown that "the plight of these black peasants and industrial workers was inextricably tied up with that of white [workers]."[16]

Under the circumstances, equal treatment was hardly the answer to the economic problems of the black worker, and thus the young committee members called for "a reformulation of the Association's ultimate objectives." Instead of continuing to oppose discrimination in employment and the various manifestations of anti-Negro feeling among white workers, Harris, Brown, and Mrs. Du Bois urged the NAACP "to get white workers and black to view their lot as embracing a common cause rather than antithetical interests." In their view, the association should on the one hand "show the Negro that his special disadvantages are but the more extreme manifestations of the exploitation of labor; and, on the other hand...show white labor that the disadvantages suffered by Negro workmen and frequently supported by white labor not only perpetuate the historic hostility between white and black labor, but also place a reserve of cheap labor at the disposal of employers, serving as dead weight upon the effective unity and organization of labor."[17]

The rhetoric of the young militants doubtless contained revolutionary implications, but taken in the context of their actions it is clear that they were urging working class solidarity as the basis for effective, biracial trade unionism rather than as a foundation for proletarian uprising.[18] But even pro-labor convictions placed Harris, Brown, and Mrs. Du Bois considerably to the left of most NAACP board members, who remained true to the faith that ignorance was the root cause of exploitation and that meaningful progress would be achieved once men of goodwill became aware of desperate conditions. Thus, tensions between the young militants and the established leaders were inevitable, and an early indication was given when Harris, Brown, and Mrs. Du Bois refused an invitation to spend several days discussing the future program at President Spingarn's estate. According to Chairman Harris, "Discussion ought to be free and untrammeled," and he feared that "some of our members might not feel free to say some things they would ordinarily say. There are certain proprieties that some people can't ignore. I feel that this would be the case if we held our really important deliberations at Mr. Spingarn's home." Walter White, who doubtless welcomed the restraining hand of President Spingarn and who questioned the propriety of implying "that some members of the committee would be less outspoken and honest than they would elsewhere," attempted to persuade the young committee members to reconsider their decision, arguing that two members of the committee—James Weldon Johnson and Mary White Ovington—would find it much easier to attend conferences at Amenia, only a few miles from their homes in Great Barrington, Massachusetts, than in New York City. But pleas such as this only steeled Harris's resistance, and he called the committee to meet in the association's New York office late in August of 1934. Here the young militants were firmly in control, for neither Spingarn nor Miss Ovington, who admitted that she did "not really belong...because I feel that we have a large enough program as it is," was able to attend. Consequently, Harris won quick approval for his major ideas; moreover, he persuaded the committee to delegate parts of its authority to several advisory committees, a decision that enabled the young militants to involve other prominent dissidents such as Benjamin Stolberg, William Hastie, E. Franklin Frazier, and Ralph Bunche.[19]

The Report on Future Plan and Program that issued from the deliberations of the committee called on the association to place primary emphasis on fostering "the building of a labor movement, industrial in character, which will unite all labor, white and black, skilled and unskilled, agricultural and industrial." To this end, the committee proposed that the NAACP "lay the intellectual basis for united action between white and black workers" by systematically conducting classes in "workers' education." Political support was to be mustered behind "adequate legislation on immediate problems" such as old-age pensions, unemployment insurance, and lynching. Producers and consumers cooperatives were to be organized "as a means of furthering immediate economic relief...but not as a solution of the 'Economic Problem' or the basis of a separate Negro group economy, an ideal which the Association deems unsound." The traditional work to break down discrimination on the job and Jim Crowism in the union was to be continued.[20]

To facilitate this program of economic activity, the Harris committee recommended that the association "build up a literature adapted to the needs of workers" and "conduct a more systematic type of research and investigations in industry and agriculture"; for this purpose the committee recommended that the organization defray the expenses of the Joint Committee on National Recovery in Washington and that John P. Davis of the joint committee be added to the association's executive staff as economic adviser. To insure successful operation of this new program in its early stages, the Harris committee called for the creation of a five-member advisory Committee on Economic Activities, which would have responsibility for overseeing the work conducted under the new economic program. All five members of this advisory committee were to be "distinguished in some branch of economics, such as labor problems and cooperation, statistics or industry," and only the chairman, who was to have the prerogative of appointing the other members of the committee, was to be appointed by the board of directors.[21]

If enacted, the proposals of the Harris committee would have significantly changed the NAACP, for in addition to reformulating the association's basic strategy and tactics the report proposed to diminish the authority of the organization's board of directors by creating another and semi-autonomous power bloc—the Advisory Committee on Economic Activities. The constitution and bylaws of the organization vested "control and government of the Association in the Board of Directors who shall exercise all such power and do all such acts and things as may be exercised or done by the Association." In actual fact, effective control resided in a very small group of board members and executive officers who lived in New York, attended meetings regularly, and otherwise took an active interest in the affairs of the association. The NAACP, in short, was a highly centralized bureaucracy with decision-making centered in the national office in New York City; the influence of the branches and the mass membership was virtually negligible, and for years there had been complaints about this "NAACP dictatorship." Before leaving the association, for example, W. E. B. Du Bois had called attention to "a steadily increasing tendency...to conduct the policies of the NAACP without publicity or without the faintest shadow of democratic control," and he had insisted that "in some way, and very soon, the organized intelligence of American Negroes must be put in definite and complete control of this organization." Making the same point at the NAACP's Twenty-fourth Annual Conference (1933), Irwin C. Mollison, the chairman of the association's Illinois federation, charged that the "organization is run by a clique in the National Office," and even witnesses sympathetic to Walter White reported that "the idea prevails that the present set-up is a little too autocratic." Field Secretary William Pickens reported that there was considerable resentment against the existing "closed, inbreeding type of authority" and maintained that it was "imperative that the basis for membership on our national Board of Directors be changed, widened, at least in part, if we expect to tie our branches more closely to the National Office or even to keep the same devotion which they have shown under past conditions."[22]

Expecting that the well-to-do board members, secure and comfortable in their positions, would offer considerable resistance to any program whose goal was to create a new balance of power in the economy that had given them their advantages, the young militants attempted to take advantage of the grass roots demand for decentralization of authority.

They feared that their new economic program would not be administered effectively by the established NAACP leaders, and thus along with the demands for a new economic emphasis the Harris committee proposed a series of sweeping changes that would have drastically reduced the power of the secretary, the national office, and the board of directors. "For this program to function," they declared, "it is imperative that the local branches become transformed from centers of sporadic agitation to permanent centers of economic and political education and agitation," and to this end they suggested that the NAACP's branches be reorganized into several regional divisions, each supervised by a permanent and salaried regional secretary. The national office, meanwhile, would become merely "the central coordinating agency of the Association's activities." The board of directors was to retain supervision of the NAACP's civil rights programs, but responsibility for the new economic plans was to rest with the autonomous Advisory Committee on Economic Activities.[23]

In their private correspondence, the young militants stated exactly what they hoped to accomplish through these structural changes. Harris, for example, candidly admitted that "you are not going to get hold of the Negro masses until you begin to liquidate the influence of certain Negroes and whites who are now assuming leadership." In his view, most prominent Negro leaders, and the white philanthropists who supported their work, were hopelessly bourgeois, and he was convinced that "nothing is going to be done with the Negro and his special problems until we are willing to throw overboard certain political and social values that govern our thinking." "You can't rely upon the James Weldon Johnsons and the Walter Whites for any new program, for they represent just those values that I think stand in the way of clear thinking on the present relation of the Negro to world forces. As long as they . . . and others I might name are supported by the Phelps-Stokes [Foundation] and the Embree's [Rosenwald Foundation] and the Negro masses are taught to accept them and the things that they represent, you . . . will find that anything we plan will have to have their moral support or approval if we want it to succeed. Thus as important as a practical economic program is, we must have people behind us who are sick of the old intellectual rubbish. . . . This is going to take a lot of internal purging which we ourselves have got to do." Similarly, Rachel Davis Du Bois complained that while Walter White was a master at eliciting contributions from "well-dressed, handsome people of various hues," he did not represent "the labor point of view," and thus "Rome is burning" while the secretary was socializing with prominent philanthropists. Ben Stolberg caustically complained that "the Association not only has no program but it is intrinsically impotent to grasp one (as is the way with institutions in a menopause). For another thing, which is the same thing, there isn't the personnel."[24]

Thus, Harris and his colleagues not only called on the association to launch a more vigorous attack on fundamental economic problems but insisted that the masses of Negroes organized in the local branches play a larger part in future NAACP activities. According to Harris, it did not suffice "to say that the masses are uninterested [in the NAACP]; the truth is that the organization has been kept away from the masses." Granting that the association had been conceived by its founders and directors as an organization for and not of Negroes, the Harris group argued that "conditions have so changed in the past decade as to warrant decentralization and a more closely knit but democratic type of organization." In effect, they were declaring that the time had come when the black masses should play the leading role in the struggle for their own betterment. Implicit was the assumption that white liberals and philanthropists—however well intentioned—could not be expected to press issues which, if actually resolved, might endanger their own class position. Harris's Howard University colleague and fellow young militant, Ralph Bunche, summed up these sentiments when he wrote:

> The interracial make-up of the NAACP is an undoubted source of organizational weakness. There can be no doubt that the Negro leaders in the organization have always kept a weather eye on the reactions of their prominent and influential white sponsors. . . . These white sympathizers are, in the main, either cautious liberals or mawkish, missionary-minded sentimentalists on the race question. Their interest in the Negro problem is motivated either by a sense of "fair play" and a desire to see the ideals of the Constitution lived up to, or an "I love your people" attitude. Both attitudes are far from touching the realities of the problem. But the evident concern for the opinions of the white supporters of the organization, especially on the part of the National Office, has been a powerful factor in keeping the Association thoroughly "respectable," and has certainly been an influence in the very evident desire of the Association to keep its skirts free of the grimy bitterness and strife encountered in the economic area. . . . The liberal . . . recognizes and revolts against injustices, but seeks to correct them with palliatives rather than solutions; for the solutions are harsh and forbidding, and are not conducive to optimism and spiritual uplift.[25]

Related to this rationale for increasing the relative power of the black-dominated local branches were certain psychological considerations that doubtless influenced a good many of the young leaders but were stated most clearly by Professor E. Franklin Frazier of Fisk University. As noted above, Frazier (along with Harris, Brown, and Bunche) had been one of the influential delegates to the Amenia Conference of 1933, where he had argued that cultural nationalism and a certain amount of self-help were needed to restore race pride and ease the black man's identity crisis. In effect, Frazier and others were contending that blacks should not only do for themselves what whites were unwilling to do but should also provide even that which whites were willing to give. As long as white liberals were in the position of magnanimous benefactors, it was almost impossible for Negroes to develop the psychological attitudes that would enable them to control their destiny, for independence and initiative were not to be expected from members of a group that was powerless and subservient. Thus, it seemed that the problems of Negro personality and identity could be solved only if blacks gained control over the betterment organizations which played such an important role in their communities.[26]

The undercurrent of resentment toward old-line black leaders, who allegedly tried to advance their cause by becoming junior partners to wealthy white philanthropists, was manifested in the Harris committee's recommendation that thereafter the Spingarn Medal, the association's award to the outstanding Negro American of the year, should not be given to any persons "for achievement in the fields of interracial relations, religion, and social work." Explaining this position, Harris confided to W. E. B. Du Bois that "no program of economic welfare that is planned for the Negro is going to succeed until his so-called intelligentsia is emancipated. . . . If these intellectuals' thinking is done in the same grooves in which present leadership does its thinking, nothing will be accomplished." Except for Du Bois, Harris claimed there was hardly a Negro of national prominence who would attack dominant interests on grounds of broad social and economic policy; the great majority—particularly of ministers and social workers—wanted the Negro masses "to emulate the values which these interests represent." The association, he believed, should stop cultivating people simply because they were influential and should begin bestowing its honors on those who were working to give the black masses "a new set of values."[27]

The board of directors seems not to have recognized the depth of the young militants' resentment of their dependence on white allies, but even if it had been otherwise, most of the directors naturally looked askance at the sweeping changes proposed by the Harris committee. For the most part, the board continued to think of the association as an elite organization working for Negroes. Negroes in the mass, they believed, "were poorly educated, inarticulate, devoid of political experience and power, and...lacking in the financial and other resources that were necessary in order to develop and employ power successfully." The NAACP would not have been successful if it had ignored hard facts such as these, and members such as Roscoe Dunjee, of Oklahoma City, cautioned extreme care "in studying changes that possibly should be made in order that we do not destroy the institution which to date has meant so much to us." Reflecting the same perspective, Joseph Prince Loud, of Boston, "view[ed] with alarm the proposed changes in policy from that of claiming full citizenship rights for the Negro, to one of partisan and class appeal."[28]

As was to be expected, several members of the board had grave reservations about the proposed decentralization and the relative diminution of the board's own power. When the Harris report was first presented on September 25, 1934, board member Charles Studin questioned the wisdom of having only one member of the important new Advisory Committee on

Economic Activities appointed directly by the board; he noted that such a plan, by "placing the most important work of the NAACP...in the hands of non-members of the Board," constituted a "marked departure from the [traditional] NAACP attitude." In answer to Studin, Harris maintained that "this committee would be purely advisory; that its members would have to be approved by the board"; and that no present members of the board had the technical training in economics that would be required for effective service on the committee. Nevertheless, most board members remained skeptical. Walter White acknowledged that "the provision of approval by the Board of the other four members named by the chairman is something of a safeguard," but he did not think it was enough. "Should you be named as chairman of this committee," he reassured Harris, "your selection of the four persons to serve with you would, I am sure, be excellent. But suppose some years hence something happened to you and a less competent, or more conservative, or less well balanced person than yourself were elected chairman?"[29]

Granting that the traditional concentration of power in the hands of the board militated against efforts to increase the NAACP's popular following, most of the directors nevertheless believed, as Wilson Record has written, that "by experience, knowledge, personal dedication and long commitment to the NAACP they were the natural guardians of the Association's welfare." Harry Davis of Cleveland reminded his fellow board members that the NAACP placed great emphasis on agitation and education, and in his view "a survey of successful propaganda agencies will show that they uniformly adopt the principle of centralization." Other board members warned of the "ever-present danger of regional organizations getting into the hands of unscrupulous persons." Charles Edward Russell, for example, warned that "the Communists have disrupted the Socialist party and are apparently trying now to disrupt this Association," and President J. E. Spingarn was ever mindful that the party's chances for success would be improved considerably if the locus of policy were shifted from the board to the membership. Assistant Secretary Roy Wilkins, while believing that the NAACP should "tend to the left," warned that it would be dangerous "to adopt the radical left-wing philosophy as a group." Wilkins pointed out that the very white Americans who were always looking for reasons to justify their mistreatment of Negroes often had an intense hatred of economic radicalism, and he feared that if the Negro bcame associated closely with the far Left there was a very real danger that the prejudice against color would be compounded with the hatred of radicalism and thus release the forces of white fury. According to Wilkins, it was neither "practicable [n]or sensible...to ask the Negro, the most vulnerable, the poorest, the one most at the mercy of the majority, to embark upon...a political and economic revolutionary program."[30]

Even some of the most radical members of the board viewed the Harris program with suspicion. Thus, Charles Edward Russell, a long-time socialist who confided that "nobody hates the existing social system more fervently than I hate it," nevertheless insisted that it was not the association's function to remake society. In his view, the association had been founded as a reform organization working within the existing structure and composed of men and women of various political persuasions, and he did not want to see it "sidetracked into ways it was never designed to follow." Similarly, Mary White Ovington, another old socialist, observed that "while not using those terms, Dr. Harris preaches economic determinism, the class struggle, in politics, socialism or communism." "This," she noted, "is revolutionary doctrine to which I, for one member of the board, subscribe." But she cautioned that "those who want to bring it to the Negro will do best to bring it through socialist or communist organizations. A middle class organization like ours... would fuddle it." Moreover, Miss Ovington believed that the economic philosophy behind the new program was "held by very few Negroes," while the great majority supported the old NAACP emphasis on civil rights. ("They don't all say so, but they do in their hearts.") She feared that, far from drawing closer to the black working class, the association would "lose the mass of [its] support [if it were] to enter into the work that Dr. Harris suggests."[31]

Still other members of the association raised tactical objections to the proposed program. Isadore Martin of Philadelphia pointed out that "much of the work which [the report] suggests that we should do in the future is now being done by the Urban League." And journalist Percival L. Prattis contended that by implication the new program declared: "The Urban League has not done a good job. We know better how to do it. We'll show those fellows, and in doing so, jeopardize their existence because of duplication of effort. ..." Under the circumstances, Prattis predicted that the Urban League executives, rather than disband their organization, would "begin actively sabotaging the work of the NAACP." Of course, Prattis knew that "the economic clique" in the association was going to insist on action, but he reminded Walter White and the board that "in addition to a knowledge of economics one must have a sense of strategy in these matters." Moreover, like many middle-class black spokesmen, Prattis could see "no good reason for the NAACP attempting to take ALL the problems of the Negro race as work for it to do." He believed that "the big objective of the NAACP is the solution of all problems connected with all aspects of the civil rights of Negroes," and he insisted that far from having completed this traditional job, the association had "only scratched the surface." "If there is a desire to do more work," Prattis asked, "why not more along that line?"[32]

Since the power of their own national office would have been considerably diminished if the proposals of the Harris committee were put into effect, Secretary White and Assistant Secretary Wilkins not surprisingly shared the reservations of the board members. Yet the two leading executive officers generally refused to attack the Harris proposals directly and instead demonstrated their opposition in more oblique ways. Thus, in writing to William Hastie, Walter White insisted that he was "keen for practically all" of the new program, but he quickly added that Harris, "like many people who have excellent ideas but little practical experience in financing programs," had made no provision for funding the new work. The secretary repeatedly insisted that "our one need is money," and with considerable justification he maintained that "the wonder is not that we have not been able to do more work, but that the NAACP has been able to do so much on a mere pittance." White acknowledged that more time should be devoted to an attack on mass economic problems, but he claimed that this was impossible because "so large a percentage of our time and energy must be given to raising funds . . . [that] little time is left for actual execution of the program and for planning."[33]

Financial considerations were especially influential in shaping Roy Wilkins's opposition to the new program. Wilkins acknowledged that the committee had outlined "a splendid program," but he claimed there was "not a single item in it which will catch the emotional fancy of the people to such an extent that thousands of dollars can be raised," and he urged the board to consider the organization's financial limitations before accepting additional responsibilities. The assistant secretary was convinced that "to initiate even those items which [the Harris committee] designates for the first year would require at least $12,000 in additional revenue." Having succeeded W. E. B. Du Bois as editor of the hard-pressed *Crisis* and having himself narrowly escaped reduction to half-time status as a result of the association's desperate financial condition in 1933, Wilkins doubted that this sum of money was available. Nor did he think the black community would support activities such as those outlined in the Harris report. Wilkins claimed that in the past "the only occasions upon which it was possible to raise large sums of money were those occasions involving emotional upheaval over a specific injustice"; Negroes, he believed, "become excited about a lynching at the time it occurs, and then their interest dies down very quickly. They do not seem capable of persisting upon a program which requires long, careful work over a period of years." Of course, Wilkins recognized that "there still persists the idea that the Association is for the benefit of the 'upper class' Negroes," and he agreed with those who insisted that "more intensive work must be done upon the actual problems facing the majority of colored people." Unlike many members of the association, however, Wilkins believed "that the masses of Negroes in this country are concerned primarily with injustices [such as] lynching, discrimination, segregation. . . .Only a small minority is at all concerned with the question of integrating the race into the economic and political pattern of the day." While this "may not be as it should be," Wilkins was "convinced that this is what it is," and he feared "that if we go off too heavily on a theoretical social and political and economic program, we will find that we shall have cut ourselves loose from the support of the bulk of our followers."[34]

Most of the young militants thought that such economic criticism was purely captious. Thus Charles Houston and William Hastie, who sympathized with the Harris group while maintaining close ties with the established leaders, maintained that it was essential for the NAACP "to get lined up right on vital economic issues" if it were to "appeal to the man in the street and catch and hold his interest," and they believed that "if the [association] really feels the importance of the program... [it] could get the money." In their view, most of the talk about strained finances was merely rationalization for the leaders' personal reservations, and Houston exploded when White—despite the financial crisis—added Juanita Jackson, a prominent socialite in Negro Baltimore, to his administrative staff. "Personally... Juanita... is swell," he assured White. "But frankly, the thing that bothers me about your own set-up, and your personal thinking, is it is too white collar. What you need now is some strength on the industrial side; and frankly, you don't get it in Juanita." For his part, Harris complained that the association should not spend "almost $1,000 for an executive assistant when in view of the newly adopted program other types of work necessitate more important appointments. ...If the Association really believes in the economic program that we have worked out, it will have to use more and more of its resources for the appointment of people who will execute that program rather than for expansion of purely administrative personnel." As criticism of the report continued to mount, Harris became convinced that his program had no future in the hands of the board and national officers, and in March, 1935, the exasperated profes-

sor abruptly resigned from his position on the board of directors, claiming that "the NAACP should more speedily enter
the economic field, especially that it should more speedily
enter upon the work outlined in the report of the Committee
on Future Plan and Program." Harris was primarily an analyst
who mapped plans of action for others to follow; as Du Bois
noted, he was "fitted neither by temperament nor desire for
the kind of executive fight this thing calls for. . . . In times of
storm, he would rather be writing about Karl Marx."[35]

Given these reservations, it was to be expected that the
board would proceed cautiously with the Harris report. Four
entire meetings spaced over a period of eight months were
devoted to a consideration of the proposed new program, and
the question was raised briefly on other occasions. As a result
of these deliberations, three significant changes in the proposed program were effected. The most important revision
concerned the power and authority of the Advisory Committee on Economic Activities. In the original committee report,
this advisory committee, of which only the chairman was to be
appointed by the board, was to have responsibility for
directing the new economic programs; after the board's
revisions, however, the balance of power within the organization remained as it had in the past. "To insure the successful
operation. . . of the new program," the directors declared that
it should "be placed under the direction of the Board, with the
advice of an Advisory Committee on Economic Activities, to
be composed of not less than five members." The implication
clearly was that all five members of the committee were to be
appointed by the board of directors itself. In addition, the
board rescinded the Harris committee's prohibition of award-
ing the Spingarn Medal to those distinguished in the fields of
interracial relations, religion, and social work, and instead

provided that "the award is to be made to an American of African descent for real distinguished achievement in any field of human endeavor." And thirdly, the board revoked the provisions for taking over the work of the Joint Committee on National Recovery and adding John P. Davis to the executive staff. Instead it provided that "as soon as finances permit"—an extremely important qualification—the association should "cooperate with existing organizations in the [economic] field. . . and procure the most efficient person available to direct these economic activities."[36]

Yet in the final analysis the surprise was not that the board altered a few provisions but that it eventually approved so much of the report. Even in its final revised version, the Report of the Committee on Future Plan and Program retained most of the views of its original authors. In effect, the board placed its imprimatur on a program that pledged the association to "foster the building of a labor movement, industrial in character, which will unite all labor, white and black" and called for the laying of "the intellectual basis for united action between white and black workers." The rhetoric of the original preamble—claiming that the economic plight of black workers was not basically different from that of whites and that both were the inevitable victims of a vicious economic system—remained, as did the calls for workers' forums, systematic research on economic problems, and the reorganization of the association's branches in regional divisions "supervised by permanent regional secretaries." When this program was presented for debate at the association's Twenty-sixth Annual Conference (1935), it was quickly endorsed by an overwhelming majority of the delegates. On the surface, then, it appeared that the association had reached a turning point in its history. But in actual fact the authority of the board of directors ("who shall exercise all such powers and do all such acts and things as may be exercised or done by the Association") remained unchecked. The vote of the conference delegates was merely a recommendation that certain changes be made; everything would depend on the manner in which these recommendations were implemented.[37]

Given the conflicting cross currents within the NAACP—the young militants' demands for mass programs and the established leaders' preference for education, agitation, court-room activities, and congressional lobbying—decisive action was not likely, and perhaps it was inevitable that internal contradictions would be resolved by announcing one program and pursuing another. The association had been forced to give grudging endorsement to the proposition that the Negro question could be solved only through biracial, working class cooperation but, as Abram Harris had foreseen, the executives and directors had neither the inclination nor the resources to carry out the new economic work; the rhetoric of the association moved to the Left, but the program continued in the traditional civil-libertarian framework.

To be sure, under Walter White's leadership, the association moved to the left, but the program continued in the emphasized those aspects that were essentially educational and could be integrated easily with the organization's customary activities. Thus, White went enthusiastically about the work of making arrangements for the various syllabi that were to be used in the adult education classes (though he never abandoned his sophisticated middle-class tastes and confided to Benjamin Stolberg that "we have just got to find a better name [than] 'workers' education' "). At the secretary's urging, John P. Davis and Abram Harris agreed to prepare the course outline on economic activities, while James Weldon Johnson,

Rayford Logan, and Charles Houston prepared summaries on the Negro's cultural and historical traditions and his legal and political problems. By the early autumn of 1935, these course outlines had been completed, and many of the association's 404 branches were for the first time offering systematic instruction for black adults.[38]

At first, White was also enthusiastic about those aspects of the new program that called for thorough economic research and the development of literature on economic problems, and he agreed with Harris that to avoid duplication of effort it would be well for the NAACP to open negotiations looking toward the eventual absorption of the Joint Committee on National Recovery. Because of its very modest annual budget ($5,000 in 1934) and small office staff, the joint committee had concentrated on agitation and education; it had no positive program of its own, but attempted merely to focus public and official attention on the special problems Negroes faced in getting aid from the government recovery programs. Like so much of the NAACP's work, the activities of the joint committee were based on the assumption that an accurate picture of conditions was the essential prerequisite for corrective action; and as was the case with the NAACP, there were critics who claimed that for all its publicity, black workers had gained no real material advantage from the work of the committee. Yet Walter White and most other NAACP leaders believed that John P. Davis and his colleagues had done an enormous amount of work "under terrific handicaps as to finance, human endurance, facilities for getting the facts, etc.," and the secretary was convinced that "we cannot always measure effectiveness by things gained; we must also measure results by considering evils which have been prevented. Consider what *might have been* the Negro's plight had the

Joint Committee not been in existence." Given the essential methodologic similarity of the NAACP and the joint committee, White had no major objections to the proposed merger. Indeed, such a move must have seemed the ideal way to placate many of the young militants without basically changing the NAACP's traditional tactics and strategy.[39]

Even before the modified Harris report had been ratified at the 1935 conference, the board of directors had authorized White to "explore the possibility of the Joint Committee and the NAACP combining," and tentative agreement had been reached to the effect that the joint committee would permit John P. Davis to do economic research for the association and also allow the association to use the joint committee's files for the preparation of stories and pamphlets dealing with the Negro's economic status. In return, the NAACP pledged to pay half of Davis's $250 salary for six months, on condition that the other member organizations contribute $165 each month to cover office expenses and other costs. This subsidy, along with occasional gifts from philanthropists such as Mrs. John D. Rockefeller and Edwin Embree, enabled the joint committee to remain in operation during late 1934 and early 1935, though its existence was precarious at best. Yet in mid-1935, at the very time when the Harris program was allegedly going into effect, Walter White reported that "the budget of the NAACP has been strained to the breaking point," largely because of contributions to the joint committee and the expenditures involved in renewing the struggle for anti-lynching legislation, and White and Roy Wilkins claimed that it was "utterly impossible for us to continue paying $125 a month on John's salary." Small contributions of about $60 per month continued through August, 1935, but by November, White had persuaded the board to discontinue its aid entirely and to sever the NAACP's connection with the joint committee.[40]

White's reservations about affiliation with the joint committee were several. In the first place, almost everyone, including White, agreed that John Davis was an extraordinarily capable publicist and lobbyist and an indefatigable worker who had cultivated useful contacts with politicians on Capitol Hill and with prominent philanthropists and race leaders. Yet Davis had also maintained close contacts with those young people who were demanding that more attention be given to economic affairs, and thus he unquestionably posed something of a threat to White's position. Having so recently been under attack from W. E. B. Du Bois and Abram Harris, the secretary was understandably sensitive on this point, and from the very first he feared that under Davis's direction the joint committee might become a rival to the NAACP. Of course, one could argue, as Abram Harris did, that the association should parry this threat by taking over the joint committee and exercising control over its leader. Or one could urge, as Charles Houston did, that "the only way the Association is going to keep [Davis] from running off with the show—unless he breaks his neck in the meantime, which is always possible with John—is for the association to put on a bigger and better performance of its own." Yet White must have viewed both these suggestions with a good deal of skepticism, for it was doubtful if any secretary could really control as aggressive and talented a young man as Davis, and White must have doubted his own ability to surpass Davis when it came to publicizing and implementing an economic program. At the same time, Davis's existence as an independent rival for scarce philanthropic funds doubtless troubled White, and the secretary may well have decided that it was best to let the infant joint committee die a natural death because of lack of funds.[41]

Another factor that contributed to the NAACP's withdrawal from the joint committee, and the factor that White mentioned most frequently when questioned in this regard, was the national officers' personal distrust of Davis. White had for some time looked askance at what he called the "irritating and distastful quirks in John's nature," and it was because of these personal reservations that the secretary had rejected Abram Harris's suggestion that Davis be named as Du Bois's successor as editor of the *Crisis* and instead launched a successful campaign to have his own assistant, Roy Wilkins, named to the position. Davis' former membership in the International Labor Defense (ILD)—the left-wing legal organization that had tangled with the NAACP over the defense of the Scottsboro boys—was another source of tension, for, as Roy Wilkins has said, there was the fear that Davis was "a little too pink for us." From the inception of the joint committee, White was curious as to the source of Davis's funds, and in the fall of 1933 the secretary persuaded the YWCA to send one of his close friends, Frances Williams, to Washington, ostensibly to work gratis as treasurer of the joint committee but also to report back to the NAACP on the source of Davis's finances and the extent of his general plans and ambitions. With this inside information, the NAACP knew that Davis was not receiving any money from the far Left, but nevertheless there were board members who questioned Davis's sense of organizational loyalty and claimed he "would sacrifice the NAACP any time for his own more radical ideas." "He has seen the absurdity of the Social Welfare present method of relieving labor," Mary White Ovington warned, "and he knows that there must be something drastic. . . . The others are playing with [radicalism], but not he." Walter White eventually came around to this point of view, and by September, 1935, he was urging that "as a matter of protection of the Association, we should make a clean break as John may turn the Joint Committee over to the Communists, at least tacitly, if not openly."[42]

While withdrawing its support from the joint committee, the NAACP did not immediately drop its plans for research and publicity on economic problems; indeed, Walter White was simultaneously developing an ambitious proposal for a congressional investigation of discrimination against the Negro under the New Deal. White's outgoing personality and affinity for prominent people had combined to make him one of the nation's most effective lobbyists (as he had demonstrated on several past occasions, most notably in the 1930 struggle against Senate confirmation of the nomination of John J. Parker to the Supreme Court, and in the 1931-1932 investigation of Negro working conditions on the Mississippi levees). Believing that John P. Davis and others had already done sufficient research on New Deal discrimination and that the pressing need was for the development of protest machinery which would focus attention on such discrimination, White concluded that "the most effective means of doing this would...be through a congressional investigation of the plight of the Negro worker." His plan was to gather relevant information for introduction into the record, and then to call three groups of witnesses: government officials such as Secretary of Interior Ickes, Secretary of Agriculture Wallace, WPA Administrator Hopkins, and AAA Administrator Chester Davis; Negro experts such as Charles Houston, John P. Davis, Abram Harris, and A. Philip Randolph; and thirdly, black workers who would be presented as examples of the various groups that had suffered acutely. Of course, such hearings could be held only if proper legislation were introduced into Congress, and for a while the NAACP executives, knowing that "those who hate the New Deal might help us in showing its discrimination against Negroes," considered the possibility of using the "congressional forces against the President in getting [an] investigation of Negro discrimination." This unusual cooperation between the association and the right wing was not necessary, however, since White was assured by William Connery, chairman of the House Labor Committee, that if the NAACP could persuade Harlem Congressman Joseph Gavagan to introduce a resolution for an investigation of discrimination against black workers, the committee would give Negroes a hearing "and permit us [the NAACP] to put on record all the proof about said discrimination."[43]

The resolution that White prepared for Gavagan's introduction into the House called for a government expenditure of $25,000 in the course of the investigation, but White believed the inquiry would be ineffective unless the NAACP did considerable preliminary work, and he estimated that the cost of this might come to as much as $2,500. Unfortunately, the association did not have anything like this amount of unbudgeted funds available, and the board of directors, which during the depression had already drawn considerably on the capital reserve, was not willing to decrease capital assets again in order to meet current expenses. Thus White was forced to appeal to various foundations for the necessary $2,500, but no assistance was forthcoming though he addressed entreaties to the Falk Foundation, the Twentieth Century Fund, the Rosenwald Fund, the Rackham Fund, and the Carnegie Foundation. The foundations' lack of interest contrasted sharply with the enthusiasm of the potential witnesses White contacted; former AAA Assistant Consumers' Counsel Gardner Jackson, for example, replied that "your idea is swell... I'm always for as much publicity as possible...exposing the inequalities of our lousy system." Yet without the funds to support the preliminary work, White believed the investigation would be of dubious value, and he let the project drop, turning his attention instead to other areas where it was easier to secure financial support.[44]

During the 1920s and 1930s, the NAACP discovered that it was easier to raise funds for the campaign against legal discrimination and lynching than for any other activities, and the impact of this experience must have been forcefully underlined in 1933 and 1934 when, at almost the very time the major foundations were finding it impossible to raise $2,500 for the association's economic efforts, the American Fund for Public Service (Garland Fund) contributed $10,000 for the NAACP's fight against discrimination in schools and interstate travel. Moreover, the Negro community, as well as white philanthropists, seemed more willing to contribute funds for the fight against outrage and blatant injustice than for the attack on economic disability. Thus Roy Wilkins recalled that for several years the association had been able to raise large sums of money from the local branches only when spectacular cases arose in which individuals were victimized by racial hate—"to wit: the Sweet Case ($75,000)...the Arkansas peon case ($15,000)...the anti-lynching crusade built purely on emotional resentment; the Scottsboro case." And Walter White confided to Frances Williams that "knowing the 'brother' as you do, you have an understanding of how great a task it is to stir him up on non-dramatic issues even though they are so close at hand as the matter of jobs, food, shelter and the like." It may well be that the comments of Wilkins and White applied less to the black working class than to the predominantly middle-class members of the NAACP's branches; but it was the local NAACP people whom the national leaders relied on for financial support, and some indication of their predilections was given in 1937 when the association distributed 150,000 anti-lynching buttons to its locals, and realized $9,377.97 from their sale at ten cents apiece.[45]

These economic considerations were no doubt a powerful

incentive encouraging the association's leaders to abandon the Harris economic program and return to the campaign against lynching. Yet there were, in addition, several other factors also moving the NAACP in the same direction. After an encouraging decline in the late 1920s the numbers of reported lynchings for the period 1930 through 1935 totaled twenty-one, thirteen, eight, twenty-eight, fifteen, and twenty, respectively. Walter White no doubt felt that the association could not remain silent in the face of such outrage, and though it is questionable that he ever expected to break the southern filibuster and push an anti-lynching bill through Congress, White may well have reasoned that the national publicity and the fear of national legislation would prompt southern states to take preventive action.[46]

Equally important was White's temperament and personality. Under attack from radicals outside the organization and young militants within, the secretary responded by redoubling his efforts in the familiar field of congressional lobbying. Like most men, White was most effective when doing what he liked, and there can be no doubt that he loved his work as lobbyist and publicist—the consultation with prominent senators such as Robert F. Wagner and Edward P. Costigan, who sponsored the association's anti-lynching bill; the conferences with President and Mrs. Roosevelt; the petition campaigns organized in conjunction with leading writers and artists; the collaboration with nationally known legal experts—this was the world in which White's talents were most effective and in which he most enjoyed living. Yet there should be no question as to the sincerity of White's opposition to mob violence. One of the earliest memories from his youth in Atlanta, Georgia, was of the famous 1906 riots and of the White family armed with rifles to protect their home from invasion. This searing experience left its mark on White's soul, and in later years he often seemed preoccupied with mob violence; he rose to national fame as an intrepid NAACP investigator of lynchings (where he made good use of his ability to pass as a white reporter interviewing members of the mob) and chronicler of the subject (*Fire in the Flint, Rope and Faggot*). One of his friends of the 1930s later recalled that whatever the topic of discussion, the secretary generally turned the subject to lynching and famous instances of mob violence.[47]

All these factors—the need to outmaneuver critics within the NAACP, the practical problem of raising funds during the depression decade, and the personality and aptitude of Secretary White—led the association in 1934, and for the next five years, to devote the greatest share of its time and work to efforts to enact the Costigan-Wagner anti-lynching bill and its successors. Robert Zangrando has written in detail of the NAACP's fight against lynching, and here it is necessary only to say that by whatever standard one cares to choose—the amount of money expended, the amount of time consumed, the quantity of publicity given—it is clear that between 1934 and 1938 the association became increasingly concerned with the anti-lynching campaign, and this necessitated the de-emphasis of other activities such as the economic program mapped out by Abram Harris.[48]

Of course, the young militants were far from satisfied with what they considered White's excessive concern with the problem of mob violence. Ralph Bunche, for example, claimed that while the Harris program "contained the seeds for the revitalization of the NAACP...it has never been put into practice," and he insisted that the failure to implement the new economic program "must be explained mainly in terms of the narrow vision of the leadership of the Association in the

national office, the branches and on the Board of Directors."
Though Bunche acknowledged that "somewhat more lip-
service has been paid to the economic problems of the Negro
in recent years," he maintained that "the Association still lacks
an economic program and orientation; it continues to think
within the conventional framework of civil-libertarianism,
political and economic justice. Anti-lynching legislation and
the equalization of teachers salaries are now [1940] its main
pre-occupation. In an era in which the Negro finds himself
hanging ever more precariously from the bottom rung of a
national economic ladder that is itself in a condition of not too
animated suspension, the Association clings to its traditional
faith, hope and politics." W. E. B. Du Bois stated the same
view more succinctly when he lamented that "there's simply
nothing to be done so long as Walter White and Roy Wilkins
are running the Association." And even within the NAACP,
there remained a few officers such as the legal counsel Charles
Houston who believed the NAACP was not exploiting the
"vital economic issue," and thus was failing "to draw...a lot of
people who are somewhat lukewarm on the anti-lynching
bill." "Lots of us feel," Houston reminded White, "that [to]
fight for anti-lynching legislation without just as vigorous a
battle for economic independence is to fight the manifestation
of the evil and ignore its cause." According to Houston, "with
the activity of the national office centering so much around
the anti-lynching bill, there are not enough irons in the fire.
...From my view, this is bad strategy: There should be a
three-ringed fight going on at all times."[49]

But Houston's was a minority voice within the NAACP; for
by 1936 the major critics of White's leadership had left the
organization, and the secretary's power within the association
was dominant and virtually unchallenged. The militants were

convinced that their demise was largely the result of White's devious and unscrupulous tactics; thus Du Bois later claimed that the secretary "worked hard and went underground to accomplish many of his aims. Any employee who opposed him soon lost his job; but White never appeared as the cause." No doubt there was some truth to this charge, at least insofar as it related to the resignation of Du Bois; but equally important was the militants' temperamental aversion to factional strife and office politics. Du Bois resigned at a time when the militants had at least a fighting chance to oust the secretary, and Harris left the association before the real struggle over his program had begun. Of course White's skill as a fund-raiser was something of a trump card, especially in a time of economic depression, and there was much to be said for the view of those who claimed that "the NAACP ought not to be condemned too severely if it has ignored [economic] factors, especially when it is under-staffed, starved financially, and harassed by a multitude of irritations." But Du Bois's prestige, intellect, and close personal relations with President Spingarn were also factors of great importance, and it appears that Secretary White's victory was finally possible only because the militants abandoned the field.[50]

Yet however narrow the secretary's margin of victory, White did emerge from the factional battles of 1934 and 1935 as the dominant force within the NAACP, and for the next generation the association would continue to emphasize those civil-libertarian and public relations programs which the secretary and his assistant and successor Roy Wilkins considered important. For a while, the secretary's domination of the NAACP was obscured, largely by certain black militants who charged that the association's reluctance to enter the economic arena and develop a program for the uplift of the black masses should be attributed to the influence of the allegedly conservative white board members. Thus, the young Loren Miller, writing in the *New Masses* in 1935, claimed that "Walter White...is strictly a jobholder under the domination of Mary White Ovington and [J. E.] Spingarn. His real function is to please the Board on [the] one hand and make the Negro membership like it on the other. ...White stays because the Board wants him and because he is willing to do its bidding." This critique missed the mark, however, for by the mid-1930s the much discussed managerial revolution had begun to transform philanthropic organizations as well as business corporations, and even Mary White Ovington acknowledged in 1936 that the board of directors was acquiescing "in the rubber stamp attitude." Indeed, Miss Ovington lamented that middle management, in the person of Walter White, was virtually "the dictator" of the association, and she complained that the discussions of the board had little effect on the actual programs and policies of the NAACP. Making the same point in the early 1960s, W. E. B. Du Bois contrasted the democratic practices of the early NAACP with the later concentration of authority in the secretaryship. Though he acknowledged that the rank-and-file NAACP members were not "people of the highest education or widest experience," the old editor concluded that this was "no excuse for turning their most effective organ of protest and progress into a rigid dictatorship, virtually under the control of one man." He neglected to say that his own and other resignations from the NAACP in 1934 and 1935 were major milestones along the road to bureaucratic centralization in the association.[51]

NOTES

1. In the pages that follow, I will be using the phrase "young militants" to describe all those who believed that the libertarian-public relations and legal programs that carried the NAACP through its first quarter century were inadequate in a time of major economic crisis. Yet the phrase is not entirely accurate, for there were certain middle-aged and elder statesmen of the race who supported the demands for more emphasis on economic programs, and there was considerable variation in the degree of militancy. W. E. B. Du Bois, of course, stands out as an elderly "young militant," and younger men such as Abram Harris, while differing with Du Bois in certain respects, consulted the editor frequently and acknowledged that "there is hardly a single living man for whom I have greater affection and genuine admiration." Despite its limited accuracy, I have decided to use the phrase because most of those who demanded an economic emphasis were young, because they themselves used the term, and because I agree with Du Bois that the movement represented "not simply those who are young in years, but also those who are young in thought and adaptability, despite their years." Abram Harris to W. E. B. Du Bois, 6 January 1934; Du Bois, "A Negro Youth Movement," February, 1934. WEBD Papers.

2. Annual Report of the Department of Branches, 1934, NAACP Files; *Twenty-fifth Annual Report of the NAACP* (1934), NAACP Files; Loren Miller, "How Left Is the NAACP?" *New Masses*, 16 July 1935, p. 12-13.

3. In NAACP Files, see NAACP Press Release, 14 June 1935; J. E. Spingarn to Walter White, 20 July 1934; Report of the Committee on Recommendations, 27 June-1 July 1934; Abram Harris to White, 11 June 1934.

4. Roy Wilkins to Horace Cayton, 30 October 1934, Horace Cayton and George Mitchell, *Black Workers and the New Unions* (Chapel Hill: University of North Carolina Press, 1939), pp. 413-414; Frank Crosswaith, "Sound Principle and Unsound Policy," *Opportunity* 12 (November, 1934):340-342.

5. The most prominent young militants named to the board were Sterling Brown, Marion Cuthbert, Rachel Davis Du Bois, Lewis Gannett, and Abram Harris. Walter White and Roy Wilkins objected rather strenuously to the appointment of some of these new board members, particularly to Miss Cuthbert and Mrs. Du Bois, social workers who, according to White and Wilkins, did not enjoy the "influence, contacts ... [and] acquaintance with people of means and influence" that they considered important for effective service on the board of directors. See White to Lillian Alexander, 9 November 1933, NAACP Files; W. E. B. Du Bois to White, 16 June 1933, NAACP Files; Du Bois to J. E. Spingarn, 16 October 1933, WEBD Papers. The examples of NAACP rhetoric are from the Resolutions of the Twenty-fourth and Twenty-fifth Annual Conferences of the NAACP, 1933 and 1934, NAACP Files.

6. Herbert Northrup, *Organized Labor and the Negro* (New York:

Harper & Brothers, 1944), gives a good account of the racial policies of the UMW, pp. 154-171. See also Cayton and Mitchell, *Black Workers and the New Unions,* pp. 314-368; Arthur M. Schlesinger, Jr., *The Coming of the New Deal* (Boston: Houghton Mifflin Company, 1959), pp. 138-140.

7. Of course the UMW's record was not completely free from traditional discriminations. Regardless of how large the majority of Negroes in a local might be, it was a general practice to elect whites to the presidency and blacks to the vice-presidency. While meetings in the South were mixed, blacks generally sat on one side of the room and whites on the other. In many locals white union men were addressed as "Brother" or "Mister," while Negro members were addressed by their first names, though occasionally "Brother Sam Williams" or "Brother Bill Johnson" would be used. But Negroes had become accustomed to such conventional discrimination, and they did not complain. The problems created by technological displacement were more troublesome. The UMW did not oppose the introduction of labor-saving machinery as long as the benefits from increased production were shared with the remaining union workers. Since a high proportion of Negroes were concentrated in the hand-loading jobs and since many employers were reluctant to hire colored workers as machine operators, blacks suffered greater hardships from technological innovation than whites. The introduction of machinery in the South often meant that unskilled black workers would be replaced by white machine operators. Of course, these economic and racial patterns were established long before the UMW succeeded in organizing the southern coal fields. Yet it is noteworthy that during the New Deal period the UMW did not demand that employers make machine jobs available to all members, regardless of race. See Northrup, *Organized Labor and the Negro,* pp. 154-171; Herbert Hill, "Labor Unions and the Negro," *Commentary* 28 (December, 1959): 484; Cayton and Mitchell, *Black Workers and the New Unions,* pp. 314-368.

8. But even the ILGWU failed to achieve a perfect record in race relations. As was to be expected, the race problem caused more difficulties for the union in border cities such as Baltimore and Kansas City than in New York or Chicago. In Kansas City, Negro pressers and floor help were employed, but colored workers were not used as machine operators until the years of World War II and then they were segregated. In Baltimore at least one walkout occurred when black machine operators were brought into a shop, and even in New York there were union members who objected when Negroes were put to work making corsets and brassieres. Yet the vigorous efforts of ILGWU officials to bring local union practice into line with national union policy were more significant than these remaining traces of discrimination. Altogether Negro workers and leaders could not help but be favorably impressed by a policy as egalitarian as that of the ILGWU. See Northrup, *Organized Labor and the Negro,* pp. 119-138, and especially pp. 124-128; Charles Lincoln Franklin, *The Negro Labor Unionist of New York* (New York: Columbia University Press, 1936), p. 241.

9. David Brody, "The Emergence of Mass-Production Unionism," in

Change and Continuity in Twentieth-Century America, ed. John Braeman (Columbus: Ohio State University Press, 1965), p. 241; Franklin, *The Negro Labor Unionist of New York,* p. 241; Irving Howe and B. J. Widdick, *The UAW and Walter Reuther* (New York: Random House, 1949), p. 231; Cayton and Mitchell, *Black Workers and the New Unions,* p. 356; Northrup, *Organized Labor and the Negro,* p. 238.

10. Franklin, *The Negro Labor Unionist of New York,* pp. 160, 263; Cayton and Mitchell, *Black Workers and the New Unions,* p. 204; Lester B. Granger, "Negro Labor and Recovery," *Opportunity* 12 (July, 1934):190; idem, "The Negro Joins the Picket Line," *Opportunity* 12 (August, 1934):248; "Portents of the Future," *Opportunity* 12 (August, 1934):204.

11. Walter White to Percival L. Prattis, 4 June 1935, NAACP Files; White to J. E. Spingarn, 4 June 1935, NAACP Files; Minutes of the Meeting of the Board of Directors, 9 July 1934, NAACP Files; Rachel Davis Du Bois to W. E. B. Du Bois, 15 June 1934, WEBD Papers.

12. Mrs. Du Bois was not related to W. E. B. Du Bois, though she was a close personal friend and, like Abram Harris and Sterling Brown, she had been nominated for membership on the board by W. E. B. Du Bois.

13. In NAACP Files, see Minutes of the Meeting of the Board of Directors, 9 July 1934; Walter White to J. E. Spingarn, 11 July 1934; Spingarn to Richetta Randolph, 12 July 1934; Abram Harris to White, 14 July 1934.

14. "In 1912 [the association] assisted in the organization of southern Negro firemen and trainmen and caused the reinstatement of Negro fireman discharged as a result of contracts effected by organized white trainsmen; in the same year, it waged a successful fight against the adoption of the famous 'Full Crew Bill' by various state legislatures, especially Illinois; in 1913, it began its fight against the segregation and discrimination of Negro government employees, opposing the Aswel-Edwards Bill designed to make this a national policy; in 1917, when the railroads were under Federal control it successfully fought the discrimination against Negro railway employees; in 1919-1920, it obtained, in cooperation with the Association of Colored Railroad Employees, increased pay for colored trainmen; in 1919, through its branches, it furthered the organization of Negro steel workers at Pueblo, Colorado; in 1920, it fought the Ku Klux Klan and its attempts to force Negro cotton pickers and domestics into accepting lower rates of pay in many southern states; in 1921, it caused the United States Department of Justice to protect Negro trainmen from the violence and intimidation of white trainmen in the South; and in very recent years its efforts to safeguard the rights of Negro workers in the Mississippi Flood Control area, at Boulder Dam, and in the various national, state and local emergency agencies, relief projects, and in the legislation of the present administration are well known and too numerous for detailed citation." Revised draft of the Report of the Committee on Future Plan and Program, pp. 1-2, NAACP Files.

15. Preliminary draft of the Report of the Committee on Future Plan and Program, pp. 1-2, NAACP Files.

16. Preliminary draft of the Report of the Committee on Future Plan

and Program, pp. 3-4, NAACP Files; Walter White to Abram Harris, 13 July 1934, NAACP Files; Harris to W. E. B. Du Bois, 6 January 1934, WEBD Papers; Rachel Davis Du Bois to W. E. B. Du Bois, n.d.[1934], WEBD Papers.

17. Preliminary draft of the Report of the Committee on Future Plan and Program, p. 5, NAACP Files.

18. Perhaps Mrs. Du Bois best captured the groping and nondoctrinaire mood of the militants when she confided to W. E. B. Du Bois that "my private and personal subsconscious feeling is that the NAACP is a rather hopeless group for this day and age...Yet, I go and sit in...not knowing anything better to do—the truth is I'm growing more and more Left but can't see myself fitting into that role." Rachel Davis Du Bois to W. E. B. Du Bois, n.d. [1934], WEBD Papers.

19. In NAACP Files, see Abram Harris to Walter White, 28 July 1934; White to Harris, 30 July 1934; James Weldon Johnson to White, 31 August 1934; Mary White Ovington to White, 2 September 1934; White to Ovington, 5 September 1934; White to Irwin C. Mollison, Charles Houston, E. Franklin Frazier, A. C. MacNeal, Roscoe Dunjee, Daisey Lampkin, F. Katherine Bailey, Harry E. Davis, Felix Frankfurter, Ernest Gruening, and Benjamin Stolberg, 6-7 August 1934; Harris to Ralph Bunche, 28 August 1934. Stolberg to W. E. B. Du Bois, 3 October 1934, WEBD Papers; Mr. White to Miss Ovington and Mrs. Du Bois and Messrs. Brown, Harris, and Johnson, memorandum, n.d., White Papers, Yale University.

20. Preliminary draft of the Report of the Committee on Future Plan and Program, pp. 6-7, NAACP Files.

21. Preliminary draft of the Report of the Committee on Future Plan and Program, pp. 7-8, NAACP Files.

22. Constitution and By-Laws of the NAACP, Article II. (I have quoted from a typescript of the constitution that was in effect in 1934 and 1935.) For a perceptive discussion of the association's organizational structure, see Nathaniel Patrick Tillman, Jr., "Walter Francis White: A Study in Interest Group Leadership" (Ph.D. dissertation, University of Wisconsin, 1961), Part Three; W. E. B. Du Bois to "Dear Friends," 5 February 1934, WEBD Papers; Transcript of discussion on "Shifting Lines of Attack to Meet the Needs of the Day," 1 July 1933, NAACP Files; John C. Bruce to Walter White, 20 July 1933, NAACP Files; William Pickens to Abram Harris, 29 August 1934, NAACP Files. In his *Autobiography,* Du Bois generalized on the significance of bureaucratic centralization: "The hundred thousands of members of the NAACP are not people of the highest education or widest experience. But that is no excuse for turning their most effective organ of protest and progress into a rigid dictatorship, virtually under the control of one man. We see too much of this attitude already in current America, in the broad areas of business and industry; in the organized church; in social reform and uplift of every sort; in politics and government. It is the growing custom to narrow control, concentrate power, disregard

and disfranchise the public; and assuming that certain persons by divine right of money-raising or by sheer assumption, have the power to do as they think best without consulting the wisdom of mankind. It is the tragedy of the day that the democracy of which we prate so glibly is being murdered in the house of its friends, and in everyday life far more than in broad governmental decisions." (p. 337)

23. Preliminary draft of the Report of the Committee on Future Plan and Program, pp. 7-10, NAACP Files.

24. In WEBD Papers, Abram Harris to W. E. B. Du Bois, 6 January 1934; Rachel Davis Du Bois to W. E. B. Du Bois, 22 February 1934; Ben Stolberg to W. E. B. Du Bois, 3 October 1934; G. A. Steward to W. E. B. Du Bois, 23 February 1934.

25. The quotation from Harris is from an unsigned, undated, and badly torn memorandum in the NAACP Files, filed for September 1934. Internal evidence points to Harris as the author. See preliminary draft of the Report of the Committee on Future Plan and Program, p. 8; Ralph Bunche, "The Programs, Ideologies, Tactics and Achievements of Negro Betterment and Interracial Organizations" (Carnegie-Myrdal Manuscripts), pp. 147-148. Mary White Ovington, for one member of the board, reacted strongly against what she considered the racist undertones of much of the young militants' rhetoric. In her view, "There is one very noticeable change between the Association of twenty-five years ago and the Association of today—the proportion of Negroes to whites. At our first conference, held in 1909 in New York City, the number of white and colored was about even. Today the whites are not one in a hundred. *Only at the meetings of the Board do we have decisions that represent interracial discussion.* I shall not attempt to analyze why this is, but I believe it to have been a policy, unconscious perhaps, but nevertheless a policy of our Negro members. . . . it is not the white man who does all of the segregation. For twenty-five years I have watched the NAACP become more and more an organization manned by one race only." Miss Ovington insisted that there were thousands of whites who would gladly join the association, if only they were asked. See her typescript on segregation, June, 1934, NAACP Files.

26. In NAACP Files, see E. Franklin Frazier to Walter White, 17 May 1934, and 15 June 1934; J. E. Spingarn to White, 10 January 1934; Preliminary draft of the Report of the Committee on Future Plan and Program, p. 12. See also Charles Silberman, *Crisis in Black and White* (New York: Random House, 1964), pp. 192-200, 213-215.

27. Preliminary draft of the Report of the Committee on Future Plan and Program, pp. 11-12, NAACP Files; Roy Wilkins to Walter White, 19 September 1934, NAACP Files; Abram Harris to W. E. B. Du Bois, 6 January 1934, WEBD Papers.

28. Tillman, "Walter Francis White," pp. 46-50; Roscoe Dunjee to Homer Brown, 9 January 1934, NAACP Files; Joseph Prince Loud to Walter White, 22 September 1934, NAACP Files.

29. Minutes of the Meeting of the Board of Directors, 25 September

1934, NAACP Files; Walter White to Abram Harris, 14 September 1934, NAACP Files.

30. Wilson Record, *Race and Radicalism* (Ithaca: Cornell University Press, 1964), p. 81. In NAACP Files, see Harry E. Davis to Walter White, 21 September 1934; Charles Edward Russell to White, 14 June 1935; Roy Wilkins to J. E. Spingarn, 23 May 1935; Wilkins to Charles Houston, 23 May 1935. While this "fear of Communist infiltration of local branches . . . was an important factor in retaining the centralized organizational structure," Wilson Record has concluded that the danger, "though not wholly imaginary, was overdrawn." Record believes that the officers and directors of the association naturally felt that they knew what was best for the organization, and "in typical bureaucratic fashion, the incumbent officialdom identified its own interests with those of the organization." *Race and Radicalism,* p. 81. Roy Wilkins, memorandum of 12 March 1941, as quoted by Gunnar Myrdal, *An American Dilemma* (New York: Harper & Brothers, 1944), p. 834. (For stylistic reasons, I have transposed this quotation.)

31. Charles Edward Russell to Walter White, 14 June 1935, NAACP Files; Mary White Ovington to J. E. Spingarn, 23 September 1934, NAACP Files.

32. In NAACP Files, see Isadore Martin to J. E. Spingarn, 24 September 1934; Percival L. Prattis to Walter White, 10 June 1935, and 12 June 1935; White to Prattis, 13 June 1935, and 14 June 1935; Abram Harris to T. Arnold Hill, 2 January 1935.

33. In NAACP Files, see Mary White Ovington to Walter White, 2 September 1934; White to Ovington, 5 September 1934; White to Abram Harris, 14 September 1934, and 18 September 1934; White to William Hastie, 20 September 1934; White to J. E. Spingarn, 4 June 1935; White to Percival L. Prattis, 4 June 1935, 13 June 1935, and 14 June 1935.

34. Roy Wilkins to Walter White, memorandum, 19 September 1934, NAACP Files; Wilkins to J. E. Spingarn, 23 May 1935, NAACP Files; Wilkins to Daisey Lampkin, 23 March 1935, NAACP Files; Wilkins, interview, Columbia University Oral History Project, p. 59. On the proposed reduction of Wilkins to half-time status, see Walter White, to the Budget Committee, memorandum, 5 June 1933, NAACP Files; J. E. Spingarn to White, 7 June 1933, NAACP Files; Mary White Ovington to Spingarn, 11 June 1933, NAACP Files.

35. In the NAACP Files, see Charles Houston to Walter White, 24 September 1934, 9 February 1935, and 23 February 1935; William Hastie to White, 24 September 1934; Abram Harris to White, 17 September 1934, and 4 December 1934; Harris to J. E. Spingarn, 21 September 1934; Minutes of the Meeting of the Board of Directors, 11 March 1935. W. E. B. Du Bois to Rachel Davis Du Bois, 26 June 1934, WEBD Papers; Loren Miller, "How Left is the NAACP?" *New Masses,* 16 July 1935, p. 13.

36. Minutes of the Meeting of the Board of Directors, 25 September 1934, 8 October 1934, 13 November 1934, 24 November 1934, 11 March

1935, 8 April 1935, and 10 June 1935, NAACP Files; Comparison of the Preliminary and Revised Drafts of the Report of the Committee on Future Plan and Program, NAACP Files.

37. NAACP Press Releases, 7 June 1935, and 30 June 1935, NAACP Files; William Pickens to W. E. B. Du Bois, 31 August 1934, WEBD Papers; "Notes on the Twenty-sixth Annual Conference, 1935," WEBD Papers.

38. Report of the Secretary, 4 September 1935, NAACP Files; "Office Memorandum on Syllabi," n.d. [Autumn, 1935], NAACP Files; Walter White to Benjamin Stolberg, 30 August 1934, NAACP Files; Report of the Executive Secretary of the Joint Committee on National Recovery, 20 September 1935, NA RG 183, Oxley File; Mr. Wilkins to Mr. White, memorandum, 24 July 1935, NAACP Files; Mr. Houston to Mr. White, 25 July 1935, NAACP Files; Mr. Pickens to Mr. White, memorandum, 25 July 1935, NAACP Files.

39. Preliminary draft of the Report of the Committee on Future Plan and Program, pp. 7-8, NAACP Files; memorandum of conference between Walter White, Abram Harris, John P. Davis, and Charles Houston, 5 October 1934, NAACP Files; John P. Davis, "Report on the Joint Committee on National Recovery," *Senate Miscellaneous Documents,* no. 217, 74th Cong., 2nd sess., pp. 45-46; Statement of Receipts and Expenditure of the Joint Committee on National Recovery, 31 December 1933, NAACP Files; John P. Davis, "Two Years with the Joint Committee on National Recovery, 1933-1935," NA RG 183, Oxley File. For examples of the criticism of the joint committee, see Frances Williams to Walter White, 31 May 1934, NAACP Files; and W. E. B. Du Bois, notes for manuscript on the Negro and the New Deal, n.d. [1934],WEBD Papers. For White's defense of the joint committee, see White to Frances Williams, 2 June 1934, NAACP Files. See also Frances Williams to John P. Davis, 8 September 1933, NAACP Files; and Davis to Williams, 11 September 1933, NAACP Files.

40. In NAACP Files, see Walter White to William Hastie, 26 September 1934; memorandum of conference between Walter White, Abram Harris, John P. Davis, and Charles Houston, 5 October 1934; Minutes of the Meeting of the Board of Directors, 8 October 1934, and 13 November 1934; White to George Edmund Haynes, 23 October 1934; Haynes to White, 27 October 1934; White to Haynes, 30 October 1934; White to Frances Williams, 15 May 1935; Report of the Budget Committee of the Joint Committee on National Recovery, 17 January 1934; White to Charles Houston, 27 March 1935, and 8 May 1935; White to Richetta Randolph, 29 April 1935; White to Haynes, 10 May 1935, and 15 May 1935; White to Williams, 11 May 1935, 15 May 1935, and 24 May 1935; Minutes of the Meeting of the Board of Directors, 11 November 1935.

41. In NAACP Files, see Walter White to George Edmund Haynes, 14 September 1933, and 17 October 1933; Frances Williams to Henrietta Roelofs, 25 September 1933; Williams to White, 25 September 1933;

Abram Harris to White, 18 July 1934; Charles Houston to White, 23 May 1935; Haynes to White, 14 May 1935; Williams to White, 15 May 1935; Minutes of the Meeting of the Board of Directors, 13 May 1935.

42. In NAACP Files, see William Hastie to Walter White, 22 October 1935; Frances Williams to Elizabeth Eastman, 22 March 1935; Abram Harris to White, 18 July 1934; Charles Houston to White, 20 July 1934. Roy Wilkins, interview, Columbia University Oral History Project, pp. 65-66. See also, in NAACP Files, White to Henrietta Roelofs, 9 October 1933; Williams to White, 25 September 1933, 29 September 1933, 23 October 1933, and 11 December 1933; Report of the Budget Committee of the Joint Committee on National Recovery, 30 October 1933; Statement of Receipts and Expenditures of the Joint Committee on National Recovery, 1 September 1933, to 31 December 1933; Mary White Ovington to White, 6 October 1934; White to Mr. Houston and Mr. Wilkins, memorandum, 18 September 1935. As will be noted in the next chapter, Davis did turn to the left after 1936, but I have found no evidence that he took orders from anybody while he was associated with the joint committee. White's analysis may well have had the character of a self-fulfilling prophecy; having lost his support from respectable, progressive organizations such as the NAACP, Davis had little alternative but to take money wherever he could find it—even from left groups such as the CIO and the Communist Party.

43. In NAACP Files, see NAACP Application to the Maurice and Laura Falk Foundation Re: Appropriation for gathering and utilization, through a Congressional investigation, of material on discrimination against the Negro under the New Deal, April, 1935; memorandum on Proposed Congressional Investigation of Economic Status of Negro under the New Deal, 11 March 1935; Report of the Secretary, August, 1935; *Twenty-Sixth Annual Report of the NAACP* (1935), p. 5; Mary White Ovington to J. E. Spingarn, Arthur B. Spingarn, Louis T. Wright, Walter White, Charles Houston, and Juanita Jackson, memorandum, 18 November 1935; Houston to White, 23 February 1935.

44. In NAACP Files, see Resolution for Senate Investigation of Discrimination against the Negro under the New Deal (draft), n.d.; NAACP application to the Maurice and Laura Falk Foundation, April, 1935; J. Steele Gow to Walter White, 9 April 1935; White to Evans Clark, 4 December 1935; F. P. Keppel to White, 6 August 1935; White to Mother M. Katherine, 11 April 1935; Minutes of the Meeting of the Board of Directors, 9 December 1935; Gardner Jackson to White, 27 March 1935; Charles Houston to White, 6 May 1935.

45. Robert Lewis Zangrando, "The Efforts of the National Association for the Advancement of Colored People to Secure Passage of a Federal Anti-Lynching Law, 1920-1940" (Ph.D. dissertation, University of Pennsylvania, 1963), pp. 250, 351. In NAACP Files, see Minutes of the Meeting of the Board of Directors, 9 December 1934; Walter White to the American Fund for Public Service, 10 May 1933; Anna Marnitz to White,

5 November 1934; Roy Wilkins to Mr. White, memorandum, 19 September 1934; White to Frances Williams, 2 June 1934; Minutes of the Meeting of the Board of Directors, 4 January 1937; Report of the Secretary, 4 February 1937, and 14 April 1937.

46. Zangrando, "The Efforts of the NAACP to Secure Passage of a Federal Anti-Lynching Law," pp. 244, 347-348. Summary figures for the number of lynchings each year are given in the association's *Annual Reports*, 1930-1936. See also Roy Wilkins, interview, Columbia University Oral History Project, pp. 73, 75; Walter White to Frances Williams, 2 June 1934, NAACP Files.

47. Walter White, *A Man Called White* (New York: The Viking Press, 1948), chaps. 1, 6, 8, and pp. 67-69, 94, and 98; Zangrando, "The Efforts of the NAACP to Secure Passage of a Federal Anti-Lynching Law," p. 338.

48. Zangrando has written a good and detailed analysis of the various factors prompting the NAACP to place overwhelming emphasis on the fight for anti-lynching legislation. Yet it should be noted that his interpretation differs from that given here. Zangrando believes that three factors were primarily responsible for the association's new emphasis: (1) the rising incidence of mob violence; (2) far Left, and especially Communist, criticism of the NAACP as a do-nothing social fascist organization that was dampening the potential for black revolution by giving Negroes the false hope that reform was possible; and (3) the existence of a rising tide of liberalism, manifested not only in national politics but also in the South, where significant numbers of clergymen, journalists, academicians, editors, and community leaders were taking outspoken positions in opposition to mob violence—and in the process creating a condition that gave Negroes the optimistic feeling that it would be possible to push an anti-lynching bill through Congress. Thus, Zangrando concludes that "when . . . White and his Association decided to renew active lobbying for an anti-lynching bill, they did so in the face of increased lynchings . . .; they did so under pressure of visible competition and criticism from the far left; and they did so in anticipation that New Deal liberalism, the expansion of interracial co-operation throughout the South, and recent victories within the Senate all augured well for the attempt. Put more succinctly, the Association resumed its campaign for a federal anti-lynching law under conditions of necessity, apprehension, and hope." My own interpretation, in contrast, places much more emphasis on Walter White's temperament and personality and his efforts to outmaneuver critics from *within* the association. Zangrando, who endorses the association's overriding emphasis on mob violence, and I also differ in our evaluations of the significance and value of the anti-lynching crusade. He writes that "the failure to secure enactment of the [anti-lynching] bill . . . did not imply defeat for the NAACP's fight against mob violence or for its broader goal of equitable participation in American life for all citizens. Four years of intensive effort across the nation and in the halls of Congress had forced the American people to learn the worst about their interracial patterns; the lesson, though painful to absorb,

helped in significant fashion to prepare the country's conscience for the reforms that would follow in the next quarter century." "In long-range terms, the campaign against lynching helped significantly to educate the nation and its political leaders to the depressing conditions which existed in racial matters, and it thus laid a permanent base from which other interracial causes benefited. . . . By keeping the issue of mob violence before the public, the NAACP would never let them forget the wide gap between black America and its full integration into American society." There is, of course, a measure of truth to this contention, but I would maintain that by 1930 the association's major services in the field of educational propaganda had already been rendered; to an extraordinary degree the association had changed the nation's thinking with regard to race and discrimination, and the task of firing paper bullets at the American caste system had been taken over by well-endowed universities and foundations. If the NAACP were to remain on the cutting edge of reform, it might better have devoted its resources and intelligence to an analysis of the economic problems that were and are afflicting the great masses of black people. W. E. B. Du Bois, Abram Harris, and others recognized this, and attempted to adapt the NAACP so that it would be more relevant to modern conditions; Walter White and his associates, however, continued to emphasize the techniques of journalism and public relations. White's efforts were not without effect, but it may well be that other men and other tactics could have accomplished even more. See Zangrando, "The Efforts of NAACP to Secure Passage of a Federal Anti-Lynching Law," pp. 240-305, and especially 284-285, 376-377, 445.

49. Bunche, "Programs, Ideologies, Tactics" (Carnegie-Myrdal Manuscripts), p. 167; W. E. B. Du Bois to George Streator, 26 June 1934, WEBD Papers (copy in J. E. Spingarn Papers, Yale University); Charles Houston to Walter White, 9 February 1935, and 23 February 1935, NAACP Files.

50. W. E. B. Du Bois, *The Autobiography of W. E. B. Du Bois* (New York: International Publishers, 1968), p. 294; Harry E. Davis to Du Bois, 2 July 1934, WEBD Papers; Walter White to J. E. Spingarn, 4 June 1935, NAACP Files.

51. Loren Miller, "How Left Is the NAACP?" *New Masses*, 16 July 1935, pp. 12-13; Mary White Ovington to Walter White, 15 December 1936, 16 December 1936, and 21 December 1936, NAACP Files; Du Bois, *Autobiography*, p. 337.

13

The National Negro Congress

Defenders of the NAACP often claimed that the egalitarian American creed and the nation's legal system gave Negroes a strategic opportunity which the association was utilizing very effectively. Believing that the fight for civil rights was vitally important and knowing that the valuable support of many black and white citizens could be assured only if the organization steered clear of economic radicalism, apologists for the organization believed that it was necessary for the association's leaders to cultivate the goodwill and respectability that were so often ridiculed by radical young militants. Yet even defenders of the association recognized the need for organized efforts to ease the Negro's difficulties in earning a living and particularly in gaining entrance into labor unions. While believing that the NAACP should continue to emphasize the struggle for civil rights, many believed that the militants should establish other organizations specializing in different tasks and employing different tactics.[1]

353

Of course, most of the young militants of the 1930s did not accept the premise that the NAACP's legal work and anti-lynching campaigns were of transcendent importance, and thus they did not worry about alienating the support of economically conservative civil libertarians. But the militants knew their efforts to reorient the association had failed and that there was no alternative but to strike out on their own. John P. Davis, whose Joint Committee on National Recovery was virtually bankrupt after the NAACP contributions ended, took the leadership of this effort; and though he secured only qualified assistance from W. E. B. Du Bois and Abram Harris, Davis did win the support of many rank-and-file dissidents and some prominent leaders, and for a while during the late 1930s he seemed on the threshold of making his organization—reconstituted and rechristened as the National Negro Congress—a major rival to the NAACP. Yet the National Negro Congress never survived its infancy, and died an early victim of inadequate funds, too close an association with the far Left, and the changing mood of the nation as it moved from the depression to World War II and prosperity.[2]

One of Davis's first major undertakings was to implement Walter White's proposal for an investigation of the manner in which Negroes were affected by the New Deal. With less influence on Capitol Hill than White and with an even more strained budget, Davis did not hope for a congressional investigation, but instead he formulated plans for independent hearings at Howard University on May 18-20, 1935. Altogether some 250 delegates attended this conference on the "Position of the Negro in the Present Economic Crisis," and in general they represented the three categories that Walter White had anticipated: government officials, Negro leaders, and black workers.[3]

Though the government officials were by no means uncritical in their presentations, they naturally tended to defend and explain the position of the various New Deal agencies. Thus A. Howard Meyers of the NRA gave his view of the position of "The Negro Worker Under NRA"; M. L. Wilson of the AAA spoke on "The Government's Farm Policies and the Negro Farmer"; Charles Pynchon of the Department of Interior explained "The Policies of the Subsistence Homestead Division on the Negro"; and Frank Tannenbaum, a consultant to the Department of Interior, focused attention on the benefits he thought Negroes would receive from the Bankhead farm tenancy bill. Acknowledging the existence of some obvious but unavoidable defects in the New Deal programs, these officials argued that the government programs offered black workers the best possibility of improving their economic status, if only they would "organize themselves so as to take advantage of what is now offered."[4]

The tenor of these views, at least insofar as they minimized the discrimination that confronted Negroes, was sharply challenged by Negro leaders such as T. Arnold Hill, who described "The Plight of the Negro Industrial Worker," E. Franklin Frazier, who analyzed "The Effects of the New Deal Farm Program upon the Negro," and Abram Harris and W. E. B. Du Bois, who claimed that "New Deal Social Planning" was entirely inadequate as far as Negroes were concerned. To illustrate these contentions, several participants in an evening "Symposium of Negro Workers and Farmers" cited graphic examples of the inadequacy of the government programs. Thus a sharecropper from Lauderdale County, Alabama, described the manner in which local AAA committees were dominated by selfish and sometimes brutal landowners; a needle trades worker from Forest City, Arkansas, told how she lost her job when she lodged a complaint about NRA code violations; and a tobacco worker from Durham, North Carolina, claimed the effects of the New Deal on black industrial workers could be summed up in one terse sentence: "A fourteen cent increase in the price of fatback and a seven cent increase for cornmeal wipes out any wage increase NRA ever gave." Negro columnist Kelly Miller caught the mood of the conference when he reported that "the New Deal was criticized, denounced, and condemned. . . .Nothing good was found in it."[5]

There were a few radical delegates at the conference. Ralph Bunche, for example, claimed there would be no significant improvement in the Negro's condition until the nation accepted "scientific social planning" and "a single ownership of the means of production for use rather than for profit," and he condemned the New Deal as a futile "effort to refurbish the old individualistic-capitalistic system and to entrust it again with the economic destinies and welfare of the American people." A. Philip Randolph complained that the New Deal was doomed to failure because "it did not change in the least any essential aspect of the profit system," and, indeed, had been designed to perpetuate that system. Two unidentified speakers from the floor urged revolution through bloodshed, and one declared that "without shedding blood there could be no remission of sin."[6]

Yet Bunche and Randolph reflected minority views at the conference; most of the delegates believed that significant progress was possible within the existing socioeconomic framework, and John P. Davis represented the mainstream when he declared that "exploited Negroes must face and fight the present situation together with exploited whites." Several speakers insisted that workers could best improve their position by joining together to create an effectively organized pressure group which the government could not ignore, and the largest ovation of the conference was given to E. B. McKinney of the Southern Tenant Farmers' Union who, after describing the struggle of the sharecroppers in northeastern Arkansas in realistic detail, urged biracial trade unionism as the best strategy in this period of economic crisis.[7]

Most of the delegates believed that the Howard Conference was valuable insofar as it afforded government officials the opportunity to gain a firsthand acquaintance with Negro grievances and focused public attention on the special problems of black workers. Yet there were many who believed that it was time to supplement agitation and education with systematic organizational planning, and shortly after the final adjournment, John Davis and Ralph Bunche invited a select group of Negro leaders to meet at Bunche's home and discuss what could be done in this regard. Those in attendance at this meeting found themselves agreeing that Negroes were generally in the unfortunate position of protesting when others presented plans but having no constructive counterproposals of their own. Charles Houston of the NAACP, for example, reported to Walter White that "with all due respect, we have not worked out a solution, nor has any of the other organizations best known in the field." Several members of the group charged that no one had succeeded in "awakening...a response from the Negro masses," and Ralph Bunche claimed that "the NAACP does not have a mass basis. It has never assumed the proportions of a crusade, nor has it attracted the masses of people to its banner. It is not impressed upon the mass consciousness, and it is a bald truth that the average Negro in the street has never heard of the Association nor of any of its leaders." The consensus was that a new organization was needed to activate and politicize the grass roots of the black community, and it was hoped that this goal might be achieved by organizing a national Negro congress—a representative assembly of black Americans, with delegates elected from each state and county in proportion to the Negro population.[8]

After this meeting, Bunche, Davis, and A. Philip Randolph went to work making the necessary arrangements for such a congress. Knowing that the movement would arouse considerable apprehension among established leaders, Bunche publicly stated that there was no desire "to usurp the commendable work and programs of any one of the numerous interracial and Negro organizations already existing" and that the congress would merely determine "a minimum program of action upon which the representatives of the large number of Negro and sympathetic white organizations could agree." For his part, Davis claimed that the congress would simply provide the organizational framework that would enable "all Negro organizations and such other organizations as are friends of Negro rights [to] pool their strength to accomplish things of lasting benefit for the masses of Negroes." Working diligently and effectively, Randolph managed to secure endorsements from several prominent trade unionists, while Bunche and Davis enlisted the support of such black leaders as Lester B. Granger and Elmer Carter of the Urban League, James W. Ford of the American Communist party, M. O. Bousfield of the Rosenwald Foundation, and bishops James A. Bray, R. A. Carter, and W. J. Walls. Walter White, however, reported that within the NAACP "there was very bitter resentment" over Davis's efforts to secure an official NAACP resolution endorsing the congress movement. The doubts and uncertainties of the association's leaders were quite understandable, and so was their final decision to remain independent of the congress.[9]

The first assembly of the National Negro Congress was held in Chicago in February, 1936, only nine months after the original planning conference at Bunche's home. Altogether 817 delegates representing 585 organizations and 28 states were present, and the evening sessions were attended by as many as eight thousand persons. The delegates were a diverse lot, representing most shades of northern black opinion,[10] and yet Roy Wilkins was no doubt correct when he reported that on the whole the congress "differed from many other conferences, in that it enlisted great sections of young colored and white people under thirty-five years of age; the delegates were from the so-called working class and mass organizations, who came...committed to a militant fight for the Negro. It was not a congress of school teachers, college presidents and others." For all the delegates' differences, Wilkins discovered "a wide-spread feeling...that the Association is not a true representative of the aspirations of the race and is not attacking the problems as vigorously as they should be attacked; that its machinery is undemocratic and that much of its program is arranged from the top rather than being a response to the wishes of the people."[11]

Much of the first congress was devoted to establishing the necessary administrative machinery. Even before the delegates gathered in Chicago, the national sponsoring committee had found it necessary to abandon the original plan for apportioning delegates according to the Negro population in each state and county. Instead, it was provided that caucuses would elect delegates, with one representative for every five supporters if the organization was more than five hundred miles from Chicago and one for every ten if less than five hundred miles from Chicago. After convening the congress, the sponsoring committee dissolved itself and a presiding committee was elected to govern the conference, while a national council of seventy-five members would have responsibility for overseeing matters during the course of the year. In addition, there were fifteen national committees that would meet every six weeks and three elected national officers—President A. Philip Randolph, Executive Secretary John P. Davis, and Treasurer Marion Cuthbert.[12]

The deliberations in the congress's discussion sections covered a wide variety of topics, and ultimately more than a hundred resolutions were passed.[13] Because of its scope, the diversity of its composition, and the avowed intention of creating a broad program of minimum demands behind which all Negroes could unite, the congress was reluctant to emphasize the interests of any one group, and thus it is difficult to isolate one element as its central theme. Nevertheless, as Ralph Bunche has written, "in all the discussions there seems to have been a realization that there is a definite tie-up between better conditions on the one hand, with working class unity and mass pressure on the other." It is significant that A. Philip Randolph, the president of the Brotherhood of Sleeping Car Porters, was chosen as president of the National Negro Congress, and in his keynote address Randolph maintained that "no black workers can be free so long as a white worker is a slave, and by the same token, no white worker is certain of security while his black brother is bound." In his view, the only hope for effective relief from the prevailing economic distress lay in "the industrial and craft unions, with the emphasis on the former." "The industrial union," Randolph observed, "is important in this stage of economic development because modern business has changed in structure and assumed the form of giant trust and holding companies, with which the craft union can no longer effectively grapple." Randolph also noted that "the craft union invariably has a color bar against the Negro worker, but the industrial union in structure renders race discrimination less possible, since it embraces all workers included in the industry, regardless of race." Accepting these views, the congress itself resolved that "the industrial union offers a more effective solution of the problems of race discrimination in a given industry, skilled or unskilled." It formally endorsed "the movement in aid of industrial unionism" and sought "to secure definite cooperation of the Committee on Industrial Organization in the organization of Negro workers in mass production into industrial unions."[14]

The National Negro Congress got off to a good start in Chicago, and its reputation was enhanced in the months that followed. Drawing on support from many local CIO unions, the congress chartered fifty-six local councils in the four months immediately following the Chicago conference, and several score more were added over the course of the next five years. Some of these councils, to be sure, existed mostly on paper, but others carried on aggressive campaigns in their own areas. Thus in Oakland, California, the East Bay Council waged a determined fight against discriminations directed at black students at the University of California and registered a vigorous protest against the state bar's refusal to license an attorney because of alleged radical beliefs. In Washington, D.C., the local council carried on a boycott of a large department store that required Negro shoppers to use segregated rest rooms, and the Chicago affiliate launched a campaign to get Negroes more jobs on the public buses and streetcars. In New England, several councils succeeded in having books that unfairly characterized Negroes withdrawn from school libraries; the Baltimore council planned a vigorous campaign for the registration of voters; and when Gunnar Myrdal traveled through the country in 1939 and 1940, he observed that "the local councils of the National Negro Congress were the most active Negro organizations in some Western cities." The national leaders of the congress conducted an enterprising legislative campaign, mustered grass roots pressure on several bills, and testified at congressional hearings concerning the manner in which Negroes were affected by various pieces of legislation. It seemed for a while that the National Negro Congress might become the first mass Negro organization since Marcus Garvey's Universal Negro Improvement Association of the 1920s, and leaders of the NAACP were understandably worried. Roy Wilkins, warned that "Mr. Davis has certain qualities and certain freedom of movement not enjoyed by those who have called previous conferences. ...He has an excellent mind, a capacity for hard work, and a grasp of the economic and civic plight of the Negro second to none of his contemporaries. ...It would be a mistake to lump this Congress in with the other efforts which have been made, if for no other reason than that Mr. Davis is the organizer."[15]

Yet in the final analysis the efforts to make the congress the major organization of the masses ran aground. There were many reasons for this failure, but among the most important was the impossibility of appealing simultaneously to all black groups in the community. As Ralph Bunche has observed, there was a basic fallacy in "the assumption that the common denominator of race is enough to weld together such divergent segments of the Negro society as preachers and labor organizers, lodge officials and black workers, Negro business men, Negro radicals, professional politicians, professional men, domestic servants, black butchers, bakers and candlestick makers."[16]

From the very first, conservative Negroes were troubled by

the militancy and radicalism of the congress and its resolutions. Kelly Miller, for example, condemned "the spirit of radicalism [which] predominated throughout the proceedings" of the first congress. Everywhere, he declared, "the reds, the Socialists and Communists, were. . .in ascendancy, either in number or indominitable purpose, or in both. The conservative delegates, who constituted a considerable proportion of the conference were either outnumbered or out-maneuvered." And Lawrence Oxley, a Negro army lieutenant (ret.) who kept Secretary of Labor Frances Perkins posted on race affairs, reported that "religion, philanthropy, and patriotism, the three pillars upon which the life and hope of the Negro have been built, were either ruthlessly flouted or tepidly tolerated out of a sense of prudence." Not surprisingly, the first defection from the sought-after consensus came with the departure of important members of the black clergy. Shortly after the first congress adjourned, bishops Bray, Carter, and Walls complained that the program focused almost exclusively on economic and political matters and that the church leaders were "entirely ignored. . .with the exception of. . .making invocations and pronouncing benedictions." It seemed to the three bishops that they were being used to give just enough "alloy of religion to decoy the race" until the congress had captured their followers for secular goals, and they denounced what they called "this shrewd godless posing under the guise of giving us bread and protection." This defection was important, for the Negro churches, as the bishops noted, had "the largest following of any organized group among us," and their cooperation was important to the success of any mass movement. Yet the departure of the churchmen was only the first of many insurgencies; the years between 1937 and 1941 witnessed the steady erosion of support from Negro professional and civic groups, and especially from businessmen who wanted the congress to emphasize the development of black enterprise and who naturally looked askance at a leadership that stressed biracial trade unionism as the best hope for improving the economic condition of the black masses.[17]

The militancy and aggressiveness of the National Negro Congress also created doubts in the minds of many progressive but nonradical Negroes, such as those associated with the NAACP. As noted above, the NAACP had refused to endorse the congress in 1936 because, as Roy Wilkins put it, despite repeated official assurances that the "Congress is not for the purpose of supplanting any organization," there was considerable informal talk "of this movement replacing the NAACP and much question in the minds of many as to how they can carry out their plans if they stick to their promise not to form a new organization." Several informants from different sections of the country had written to the NAACP's national office complaining that in their areas, as Professor George M. Johnson of the University of California described the situation in the East Bay region, "the Congress began its operation through a small group of pseudo-communists and attracted principally those persons who have always felt that the National Association was not militant enough." Still others had objected to the congress's use of radical white clerks who were "not of the better classes," and warned that the movement might be "sold down the river" to the Communists.[18]

Yet many NAACP people were cooperating with the congress. Congress treasurer Marion Cuthbert was a member of the association's board of directors. And several local NAACP officers had played important roles at the Chicago conference, among them J. M. Tinsley of Richmond, Virginia, Henry D. Espy of St. Louis, Joseph Albright of Duluth,

Minnesota, Grace Wilson Evans of Terre Haute, Indiana, Helen Bryan of Philadelphia, Jerry Gilliam of Norfolk, Virginia, William Hastie of Washington, D. C., and Louis L. Redding of Wilmington, Delaware. Thus the national office found it impractical to condemn the congress, and Roy Wilkins suggested that the best way to make sure that the movement did not supplant the NAACP would be "to go in and have a voice in the making of policies."[19]

As the national leaders learned more about the congress, however, any enthusiasm for possible alliance was severely dampened. Wilkins reported that when he attended a meeting of the New York City council he found "all the old myths" about the bourgeois character of the NAACP "paraded...as truths," and he viewed the membership as a "heterogeneous collection of malcontents, eager to join any movement not so much for what they could do, but for the spite they can direct toward people and movements with which, for one reason or another, they have not hitherto been identified." Similarly, William Pickens persistently reported from the field that "John Davis and [the] Negro Congress [are] trying to displace NAACP in every way, everywhere they can do so."[20]

As far as Walter White was concerned, the most dire predictions were realized when Davis and the congress made the fight for anti-lynching legislation their top priority measure for 1937 and 1938. Like the NAACP, the congress had discovered that the crusade against lynching was the surest way to raise badly needed funds. Accordingly, John Davis had busied himself with a drive to arouse sentiment in support of the Wagner-Van Nuys-Gavagan bill: demonstrations were organized in several cities; thousands of telegrams were dispatched to Washington; a special conference of black leaders was convened; and Davis lobbied and testified on

Capitol Hill. Davis may well have thought that the congress was not duplicating the work of the NAACP, since it had connections with portions of the black community that were untouched by the association. Most race leaders, however, agreed with Elizabeth Eastman's assessment that "Davis is trying to take the leadership on anti-lynching legislation out of Walter White's hands." Certainly White resented what he called "John's attempt to capitalize on the fight for the anti-lynching bill and turn it to his own advantage," and he warned the association's branches and other groups that Davis's efforts "would not be as helpful as the conference which the NAACP plans to call at the proper time." To White it seemed that the efforts of the congress involved a "needless duplication of organization already existing," and he claimed that it was only "common sense to concentrate on the task immediately ahead of us, with the already well-established machinery now in existence...instead of starting out at this point to create additional machinery and to divide the already inadequate funds for the fight." Roy Wilkins agreed that Davis was "attempting in every way to cut in on our program." "He knows perfectly well that there is absolutely no chance, short of a miracle, for the anti-lynching bill to be put through at this session of Congress. Yet, he organizes this big ballyhoo for two reasons: to keep the name of his organization before the public, and to raise funds. No one will know how much or how little money is raised at his various anti-lynching meetings, but whatever is raised will go for the general work of the National Negro Congress, since there is nothing that can be done on the anti-lynching bill at the present moment." There was much truth to this analysis—perhaps more than Wilkins realized, for the argument partook of a double-edged sword that could be used quite readily to attack the NAACP's own emphasis on the fight for anti-lynching legislation.[21]

The loss of support from religious, civic, and reformist groups undermined the National Negro Congress's ability to secure funds from the foundations and well-to-do philanthropists that played an important part in financing the work of other betterment and welfare organizations. This loss of revenue would not have been crucial if the black masses had rallied to the cause, but judging from the financial reports it would seem that the lower classes were apathetic as well as impoverished, and the Congress's emphasis on economic reform evidently did not have wide appeal. During 1936 and 1937, the contributions to and expenditures of the national office, exclusive of the cost of preparing the annual convention, amounted to less than $6,000 annually, and this figure is striking testimony to the fact that the disadvantaged are frequently not interested in questions of economic reform. At the time, there were many rumors to the effect that the congress was financed by the Communists, by the Republican party, by the Liberty League, and others, but Roy Wilkins, who observed "the trickling in of money in small amounts and with great difficulty...(buttons and tags were sold; 25 cent dances were given; raffles were staged; programs were sold,)" was doubtless correct when he reported that "these rumors are wholly without foundation."[22]

Thus it would seem that financial necessity, in addition to the personal predilections of some leaders of the congress, ultimately paved the way toward closer alliance with the Left. Many of the congress's most enthusiastic supporters had come from the ranks of the CIO unions, and after 1937 the congress turned increasingly to these unions for support. Yet financial dependence on the CIO, though not so onerous for a militant organization as dependence on cautious philanthropists, was not without liabilities, for as the dependence on the industrial unions grew, it became all the more difficult for the congress to become the broadly based coalition the original program had envisioned. Even Philip Randolph, the most prominent Negro trade unionist of the day, recognized the danger of alienating the black middle class, and he vigorously opposed "the policy of tying up the Congress too closely with the CIO," because he believed that "wherever the Congress is tied up too closely with any organization it loses its mass character." In his view, "the Congress should be dependent upon the Negro people alone," but when the masses of black folk would not support the organization, there seemed no alternative to dependence on militant whites. Of course this was dangerous since, as Randolph put it, "wherever you get your money, you get your ideas," and the accuracy of this judgment was not long in being demonstrated; trade union representation in the congress grew steadily from 83 of 817 delegates in 1936 to 459 of approximately 1,200 in 1940, and by this later date the organization had become concerned almost wholly with taking the CIO point of view to the grass roots of the Negro community.[23]

The mass basis of the National Negro Congress was also jeopardized by the association of the congress with the Communist party. During the early years of the Congress's existence, from its inception in February of 1936 until the signing of the Nazi-Soviet Pact in August of 1939, this association was not a major liability. These were the years of the popular front, the years when the Communist party abandoned its traditional emphasis on the class struggle and the need for social revolution and stressed instead the need for cooperation with all elements that favored collective security against fascist aggression. After President Roosevelt made his famous "Quarantine the Aggressor" speech in Chicago in October of 1937, the party made a valiant and partly successful effort to move into the mainstream of American life and assumed a position as the left wing of the New Deal. In retrospect it is evident that the Communists were merely subordinating the doctrine of class struggle to the strategic needs of the Soviet Union, but this was not so apparent at the time, and the popular-front strategy enabled the Communist party to win a large measure of acceptance and respectability in the United States. Consequently, the association of prominent Negro Communists such as James W. Ford, Benjamin Davis, and Richard Wright with the congress did not automatically discredit the new organization. Moreover, while there was some Communist influence during these years, the party did not dominate the congress but was merely one of several groups joined together in a united front.[24]

Throughout its existence, the positions of the congress coincided with those of the Communist party, but this was not particularly significant until 1940-1941, since the party's position during the era of the popular front was only slightly to the left of the New Deal. The First National Negro Congress (1936) had taken an emphatic stand in opposition to fascism. In his keynote address, President Randolph had warned that the day was soon approaching when the world's democracies and dictatorships would be vying for supremacy ("Witness the march of Fascist Italy and Nazi Germany along their imperialistic paths of manifest destiny!"). The delegates to the congress heeded Randolph's warning and called for an economic embargo of Italy. Further, the congress went on record "as favoring a campaign by the Negro press and ministry and by other means to make American Negroes aware of the menace of Fascism in their midst." The congress itself established a special committee "to inform American Negroes of the disastrous menace of certain political combinations" such as those centered around William Randolph

Hearst and the American Liberty League who, it was alleged, were "allying themselves with the fascists in Germany and Italy and are responsible largely for the deplorable plight of the Negroes." Similar resolutions were enacted by the Second Congress (1937), after Randolph had criticized President Roosevelt for timidly hiding behind what he called "the sham of non-intervention and winking at the Spanish revolution, the Japanese in China, and the rape of Ethiopia by Italy."[25]

Yet in the spring of 1940, the American Communist party, in the wake of the Nazi-Soviet Pact, reversed its position on the need for collective security against fascism, and returned to the traditional Leninist doctrine that working people should refuse to fight in an "imperialist war." The party reminded Negroes that during World War I France and England, under the cloak of noble rhetoric, had extended their imperialistic control over colored peoples, and warned black people to oppose this second war, lest they be duped again. The party magazines and newspapers emphasized discrimination against Negroes in the American armed forces and defense industries, and the *Daily Worker* repeatedly editorialized on the connection between this and the "imperialist war."[26]

When the Third National Negro Congress met in April of 1940 it, like the American Communist party, executed a decisive *volte face* in its position on collective security. Ralph Bunche, who was a delegate to the convention, noted that almost every major speaker at the 1940 congress maintained that the war on the European continent was a struggle among imperialist powers, and that while it was raging, American Negroes should concentrate their efforts on an attempt to improve their social and economic position within the United States. He also observed that "the Soviet Union was never bracketed with the totalitarian states, and that Germany and

Hitler were carefully ignored. The attack centered upon imperialistic England and France and imperialist, undemocratic America." The principle resolution adopted by the Congress at this 1940 meeting clearly indicated that the organization's position on war and fascism had become indistinguishable from that of the Communist party:

> The National Negro Congress declares that the Negro people have everything to lose and nothing to gain by American involvement in the imperialist war and . . . further declares that the battle for democracy lies at home in the war against hunger and misery and for jobs, security, opportunity and prosperity and for full democratic rights. . . .[27]

It is obvious that by 1940 the Communist party had considerable influence within the National Negro Congress. Yet the Communists were not entirely responsible for the anti-interventionist position taken by the third congress. To a large degree the 1936-1937 statements in favor of collective security had been motivated less by adherence to interventionist principles than by emotional resentment growing out of the Italian rape of Black Mother Ethiopia. After 1937, as Wilson Record has observed, "Negroes in the United States were frequently quite apathetic about the issues involved in the European conflict. While they obviously opposed the race superiority doctrines of the Nazi regime and feared their extension, they could not embrace France or Britain as exponents of racial equality. Remembering the experiences of Negroes during World War I, they displayed a justifiable skepticism toward another great crusade for the democratic ideal." Moreover, most Negroes knew that discrimination in the American armed forces and defense industries was a real problem, not just the product of febrile Communist imaginations. Further, though the grass roots of the Negro community had not been thoroughly infected with the labor viewpoint, the pro-labor campaigns of the militant Negro leaders had not been entirely without effect, and thousands of colored workers had responded enthusiastically to industrial unionism. John L. Lewis and the CIO had assumed heroic proportions in the eyes of many black trade unionists, and the CIO's isolationism prior to the Japanese attack on Pearl Harbor doubtless carried great influence in certain sections of the Negro community— especially among the northern industrial workers who were so prominently represented at the National Negro Congress. It is interesting to note that the substance, though not all of the rhetoric, of the CIO's 1940 resolution on the "foreign war" was strikingly similar to that of the National Negro Congress.[28]

Regardless of whether the 1940 congress was dominated by Communists, the CIO, or both, President Randolph refused to stand for reelection, because he believed that control had passed from blacks to whites. Explaining his resignation to the assembled delegates (some two-thirds of whom walked out during the course of the remarks), Randolph insisted that he was still a militant trade unionist and in no way opposed to the CIO, but he stressed his disapproval of "the domination of the Congress...by any...white organization." Concerning the Communists, he was "not only opposed to...their rule or ruin disruptive tactics," but he considered their influence "a definite menace and a danger to the Negro people" because the Soviet Union, like the other great nation states, was "pursuing power politics... [and] what is in the national interest of the Soviet Union is not necessarily in the interest of world peace and democracy." There was, moreover, the practical consideration that most white Americans hated Communism and thus Negroes would be ill-advised "to add to the handicap of being black, the handicap of being red."[29]

Much of the responsibility for leading the National Negro Congress into close alliance with the Communist party rests with its talented executive secretary, John P. Davis. Davis's thinking went through three distinct stages during the 1930s, but the direction was steadily leftward. When he began the decade as a Republican, he was committed to the belief that agitation and education concerning the plight of the Negro would produce some amelioration. Working on shoestring budgets with the Joint Committee on National Recovery and the National Negro Congress, he had done more than any other black leader to bring the facts about the Negro's condition to public attention. Yet the government had repeatedly neglected the interests of poorly organized black folk, and by 1935 Davis, like many other young militants, had concluded that black workers could improve their position only if they organized themselves in a powerful political and economic interest group that the government could not afford to ignore. During the middle years of the decade, Davis frequently maintained that the future progress of the race was intrinsically tied up with ameliorating the condition of the entire working class, and he placed overwhelming emphasis on the importance of black workers affiliating with the egalitarian industrial unions of the CIO. His faith in the promise of black and white working-class solidarity was shaken late in the decade, however, partly because middle class blacks were reluctant to encourage trade unionism, but more importantly because he had come to recognize that the masses of poor and uneducated black folk were less interested in economic reform than in emotional crusades. (The exigencies of fund-raising had forced Davis to emphasize the admittedly sterile anti-lynching campaign, and the mass appeal of such emotional and largely irrational leaders as

Daddy Grace and Father Divine could not have escaped attention.)

The realization of the depth of black apathy and escapism forced Davis to question many of his basic assumptions and to reorganize his thinking. He had come to believe that there was no hope for the black man in white America unless there was significant change, and prior to the late 1930s he had refused to embrace revolution because he believed that necessary change could be effected by mass organizations working within the system. Yet once he concluded that the masses were indifferent to economic reform and thus unable to effect meaningful change, he was faced with the stark choice of either accepting an intolerable status quo or casting his lot with a revolutionary group such as the Communist party. "We have waited too long for reforms which never came," Davis declared. "Now we should know reform was never intended. Now we should be willing to challenge the old order with all the force we can command."[30]

After 1937 the position of Davis and the National Negro Congress on major public issues closely paralleled the twistings and turnings of the American Communist party. During the era of the popular front, as noted above, they heartily approved of President Roosevelt's "Quarantine the Aggressor" rhetoric and wished only that the president would take more effective steps to implement collective security against fascism. Yet after the Nazi-Soviet pact went into effect, Davis and the congress loyally adopted the anti-interventionist line, maintaining that the struggle was among rapacious imperialist powers and declaring that the Negro people would "refuse to fall victims to anti-Soviet adventures, [would] refuse to join American or world imperialists in any attack against the Soviet people." A few months later, after the German invasion of

Russia but before the Japanese attacked Pearl Harbor, Davis again reversed himself and expressed "full support of the President's foreign policy and the Government's program of national defense." On behalf of the National Negro Congress, he pledged that Negroes would "give their utmost support in the fight to preserve [the] country's independence even if it means giving their lives." On the domestic front, Davis, who had been so trenchant and perceptive in his criticism of the early New Deal, discounted the importance of discrimination in the wartime economy, pledged to support Roosevelt's "progressive administration," and repeated the cliché that "we Negro people who have suffered most during this depression" have good reason to be grateful for the president's "gallant fight to rid our nation of poverty and suffering."[31]

Certainly Davis must have known that when the congress allied itself with the interests of the Soviet Union and the line of the American Communist party, it would be publicly branded as a Communist front. No doubt he also knew that it was impossible to build a mass movement in the United States under the banner of the Communist party. It would seem, then, that Davis had abandoned hope of building a mass organization among apathetic black folk and concluded that he should do what he could to advance the cause of world revolution. Ironically, it was the decision to ally the Congress with the Communist party that, in effect, undermined its remaining influence in the black community. Writing shortly after the third congress (1940), Ralph Bunche had predicted that "the Congress membership will soon be reduced to devout party members, close fellow travelers, and representatives of the CIO unions," and Philip Randolph had warned that "until the stigma of Communist Front is wiped from the Congress, it will never rally the masses of Negro people."

Seldom have predictions been more accurate; Communist influence remained dominant in the congress throughout its few remaining years of life, and the organization never again exercised significant influence in the black community.[32]

NOTES

1. This line of argument has been effectively presented in summary form by Gunnar Myrdal, *An American Dilemma* (New York: Harper & Brothers, 1944), pp. 831-836.

2. Both Harris and Du Bois gave a certain amount of moral support to Davis's efforts, and each prepared a paper for the conference of the Joint Committee that will be described. Yet neither Harris nor the Du Bois of 1934 had the aptitude for administrative work that was necessary to organize an independent organization, and their contributions to the movement were only occasional. Du Bois, moreover, did not think the time was appropriate for the organization of as elaborate a congress as that planned by Davis. "When John Davis proposed a Congress to carry out the action of his Committee in criticizing and opposing the New Deal, he gave me the impression of having in mind such a representative assembly, and I opposed it because I did not think we were ready for the cost and trouble it involved.... To organize today a National Negro Congress with delegates distributed by States and counties according to the Negro population, and duly elected, to bring such delegates together and let them deliberate and take action, would be a tremendous undertaking, both in money and effort." Yet Du Bois did think that "sooner or later it must be done, and it ought to be done." In theory, a National Negro Congress might seem the inevitable political arm of the "nation within the nation" movement, but the orientation of John Davis's congress was so definitely interracial that even Du Bois failed to note its full possibilities. W. E. B. Du Bois, "Forum of Fact and Opinion," *Pittsburgh Courier*, 28 March 1936; Du Bois to Harrison S. Jackson, 22 August 1934, WEBD Papers.

3. Elanor Ryan, "Toward a National Negro Congress," *New Masses*, 4 June 1935, pp. 14-15; John P. Davis and Ralph Bunche to Leon Henderson, 23 February 1935, NA RG 9; Charles Houston to Walter White, 10 April 1935, NAACP Files; Program for conference on "The Position of the Negro in Our Economic Crisis," NAACP Files.

4. Slightly modified versions of each of these papers were printed in the *Journal of Negro Education*, vol. 5, January, 1936. A Howard Meyers, "The Negro Worker Under NRA," memorandum and speech notes, NA RG 9; Elanor Ryan, "Toward a National Negro Congress," pp. 14-15.

5. As with the papers of the government officials, a modified version of each Negro paper was printed in the *Journal of Negro Education* vol. 5, January, 1936. Elanor Ryan, "Toward a National Negro Congress," pp. 14-15; "Kelly Miller Says," *Chicago Defender*, 8 June 1935; U. S., Congress, Senate, *Senate Miscellaneous Documents*, no. 217, 74th Cong., 2nd sess., vol. 10016.

6. Ralph J. Bunche, "A Critique of New Deal Social Planning," *Journal of Negro Education* 5 (January, 1936):60-61; A. Philip Randolph, "The Trade Union Movement and the Negro," *Journal of Negro Education* 5 (January, 1936):54-58; idem, "The United States Supreme Court and the NRA," *Black Worker*, 15 June 1935; U. S. Congress, Senate, *Senate Miscellaneous Documents*, no. 217, 74th Cong., 2nd sess., vol. 10016.

7. Elanor Ryan, "Toward a National Negro Congress," pp. 14-15; Lester B. Granger, "The National Negro Congress," *Opportunity* 14 (May, 1936):151-153; "The National Conference on the Economic Crisis and the Negro," *Journal of Negro Education* 5 (January, 1936):1-2; "Kelly Miller Says," *Chicago Defender*, 8 June 1935, and 22 June 1935. At the other political pole, there were a few delegates such as Dean Kelly Miller of Howard, who claimed that working class solidarity was an idle dream since "the only components of the labor forces that are willing and ready to unite with the Negro are those of radical or communist leanings, and that it would be suicidal for the Negro to ally himself with any force intent upon upsetting the Constitution and promoting revolution." The radical speeches at the conference so disturbed Dean Miller that he wrote to Senator Millard Tydings, complaining that the "sessions were communistic in nature and that the overthrow of the United States Government by force was openly advocated." Miller specifically objected to the failure of Mordecai Johnson, the president of Howard and presiding officer at the conference, to rebuke those who advocated revolution, and he also noted that in the past Johnson had "pointed to certain features of the Soviet system as a solution to many of the problems found in the United States today." Other critics of President Johnson censured him for permitting radicals such as Norman Thomas and James W. Ford, the Negro Communist candidate for vice-president in 1936, to speak on the Howard campus. And a few others complained about the general state of the university: thus Perry Howard, a prominent Negro Republican politico who admitted that he was "very much annoyed" by the radical views of his son, who was a student at Howard, and Negro Congressman Arthur W. Mitchell, whose own son had "imbibed some radicalism at a middle western university," concluded that Johnson "should be censured for permitting radical remarks to be made in his presence at Howard University"; and Dean Miller had been a frequent critic of the university administration ever since Johnson had been named to the presidency.

The upshot of all this was a congressional investigation of "Alleged Communistic Activities at Howard University." Several of the government officials present at the conference discounted the charges of radicalism:

Robert Weaver, for example, stated that he did not observe any "advocacy
for the overthrow of the present Government"; Robert Strauss of
Resettlement could remember only that the speeches were "intelligent"
and "well thought out"; and J. Philip Campbell of the AAA claimed "there
was nothing radical in any remarks at the conference and...the conference
was held merely for the purpose of attacking the New Deal." Despite this
testimony, the government investigators recommended "that the president
of Howard University be advised that inasmuch as that institution is
supported in part from United States Government funds, he should not in
the future permit the university buildings to be used for meetings such as
those held at Howard University on May 18, 19 and 20, 1935." President
Johnson was outraged by the investigation, but he was not intimidated by
the experience, and radicals continued to appear on the campus. See U. S.,
Congress, Senate, *Senate Miscellaneous Documents*, 74th Cong., 2nd sess.,
vol. 10016, Document 217 ("Alleged Communistic Activities at Howard
University"); *Chicago Defender*, 1 June 1935, 8 June 1935, and 22 June
1935; *Baltimore Afro-American*, 30 May 1936; *Norfolk Journal and Guide*,
8 June 1935; Horace Cayton and George Mitchell, *Black Workers and the
New Unions* (Chapel Hill: University of North Carolina Press, 1939), p.
421.

8. Ralph J. Bunche, "The Programs, Ideologies, Tactics and Achievements
of Negro Betterment and Interracial Organizations" (Carnegie-Myrdal
Manuscripts), pp. 151, 319-320; Myrdal, *An American Dilemma*, pp.
835-836n; Charles Houston to Walter White, 23 May 1935, NAACP Files;
Charles Radford Lawrence, "Negro Organizations in Crisis" (Ph.D. dissertation, Columbia University, 1953), p. 296.

9. Ralph Bunche, "Programs, Ideologies, Tactics," pp. 319-320, 353;
John P. Davis to Mary McLeod Bethune, 25 November 1936, PPF 4266,
FDR Library; Wilson Record, *The Negro and the Communist Party*
(Chapel Hill; University of North Carolina Press, 1951), p. 154; Cayton
and Mitchell, *Black Workers and the New Unions*, p. 416; Walter White to
Charles Houston, 5 July 1935, NAACP Files; White to Maurice Hubbard,
3 February 1936, NAACP Files; White to Carl Murphy, 28 December
1935, NAACP Files; *Official Proceedings of the National Negro Congress,
1936*, p. 3. John P. Davis explained the purpose of the movement in a
widely circulated pamphlet, *Let Us Build a National Negro Congress*,
1935, NAACP Files.

10. Only 55 of the 817 delegates came from the South, while 729 came
from Illinois, Indiana, Michigan, Ohio, Pennsylvania, and New York. Two
hundred and twenty-six delegates represented civic groups and societies,
while other major representations were sent by trade unions (83), churches
(81), fraternities (71), political clubs (46), youth organizations (26), and
women's groups (23).

11. *Official Proceedings of the National Negro Congress, 1936*, pp. 3, 41-
42, NAACP Files; Cayton and Mitchell, *Black Workers and the New*

Unions, pp. 418-419; Bunche, "Programs, Ideologies, Tactics," p. 360; Roy Wilkins to the Board of Directors, memorandum, 9 March 1936, NAACP Files.

12. *Official Proceedings of the National Negro Congress, 1936,* passim; Granger, "The National Negro Congress," pp. 151-153; Cayton and Mitchell, *Black Workers and the New Unions,* p. 421; Roy Wilkins to the Board of Directors, memorandum, 9 March 1936, NAACP Files.

13. A partial listing of the resolutions enacted will suggest the scope of the delegates' concern. Negro housewives were urged to form consumers' leagues to combat "the high cost of living"; Negro groups and others were called on to support the Costigan-Wagner anti-lynching bill, to oppose "all legislation and practices designed to exclude Negroes from the constitutional exercise of the franchise," and to press for the enforcement of the Thirteenth, Fourteenth, and Fifteenth Amendments to the United States Constitution; the federal government was called on to increase the funds available under the pending Bankhead farm tenancy legislation and to provide a minimum wage for farm workers; direct relief was declared to be a responsibility of the federal government, a duty which could be discharged properly only by providing "uniform adequate relief to every unemployed and needy person"; the president and Congress were called on to "extend the present inadequate WPA program to the end that every employable person who is now unemployed may work on a WPA job at union wages"; the existing "so-called [Social] Security Program" was criticized as "inadequate and discriminatory" and support was pledged to the more progressive and comprehensive Frazier-Lundeen social security bill; city, state, and national governments were called on to place public employment on a nondiscriminatory, civil service basis and to abolish the requirement that photographs accompany job applications; the Hearst press was accused of being in favor of war and fascism, and Negroes were urged to boycott its advertisers; Negroes were also urged to oppose the enactment of "gag-laws" in the form of anti-Communist riders, criminal syndicalism laws, and teachers' loyalty oaths; the government was called on to aid Ethiopia by repealing the neutrality legislation and implementing an economic embargo against Italy; Negro ministers were urged to preach "an economic and social gospel as well as a spiritual gospel." See *Official Proceedings of the National Negro Congress,* 1936, pp. 19-37.

14. Bunche, "Programs, Ideologies, Tactics," pp. 323-353; Richard Wright, "Two Million Black Voices," *New Masses,* 25 February 1936, p. 15 (I have quoted from Wright's paraphrase of Randolph's speech); *Official Proceedings of the National Negro Congress, 1936,* pp. 10, 21.

15. Bunche, "Programs, Ideologies, Tactics, pp. 341-348; Myrdal, *An American Dilemma,* p. 818; Record, *The Negro and the Communist Party,* p. 159; Roy Wilkins, Supplementary Memorandum to the Report on the National Negro Congress, 10 March 1936, NAACP Files.

16. Bunche, "Programs, Ideologies, Tactics," p. 355. Cayton and Mitchell

have made the same point, *Black Workers and the New Unions*, p. 419.

17. "Kelly Miller Says," *Pittsburgh Courier*, 7 March 1936; Lawrence Oxley to Frances Perkins, memorandum, 5 March 1936, NA RG 183; Statement of Church Leaders in Opposition to the Program of the National Negro Congress, n.d., NAACP Files; Cayton and Mitchell, *Black Workers and the New Unions*, p. 420; Robert H. Brisbane, "The Rise of Protest Movements Among Negroes Since 1900" (Ph.D. dissertation, Harvard University, 1949), p. 78. Harold Cruse has focused attention on the contradictory class aims within the National Negro Congress. See his *The Crisis of the Negro Intellectual* (New York: William Morrow and Company, 1967), pp. 171-180.

18. In NAACP Files, see Roy Wilkins to Charles Houston, 15 February 1936; George M. Johnson to Wilkins, 3 April 1936; "Nuffie" to Walter White, 17 March 1936; White to A. Philip Randolph, 3 February 1936; Randolph to White, 4 February 1936.

19. Roy Wilkins to the Board of Directors, 9 March 1936, NAACP Files.

20. Roy Wilkins to John P. Davis, 11 March 1936, NAACP Files; William Pickens to Wilkins, 11 April 1938, NAACP Files.

21. In NAACP Files, see A. Philip Randolph to the National Officers, Regional Directors, State Directors, Local Councils and Officials of the National Negro Congress, 7 December 1937; Resolution on Program of Action—National Negro Congress Anti-Lynching Conference, 19 March 1938; John P. Davis to Walter White, 30 April 1938; Elizabeth Eastman to Henrietta Roelofs, 15 March 1938; White to Organizations Cooperating on the Anti-Lynching Bill and to all NAACP Branches, 14 March 1938; White to Davis, 1 April 1938; White to Roy Wilkins and Charles Houston, memorandum, 8 March 1938; Gertrude B. Stone to White, 24 March 1938; Wilkins to William Pickens, 19 April 1938.

22. Myrdal, *An American Dilemma*, p. 836; Financial Report of the National Negro Congress, 1937, as quoted by Bunche, "Programs, Ideologies, Tactics," p. 340; Roy Wilkins to the Board of Directors, memorandum, 9 March 1936, NAACP Files.

23. A. Philip Randolph, "Why I Would Not Stand for Re-Election for President of the National Negro Congress," *Black Worker*, May, 1940; idem, "Remarks Upon Resigning as President of the National Negro Congress," as quoted by Bunche, "Program, Ideologies, Tactics," pp. 367-368; Bunche, "Programs, Ideologies, Tactics," pp. 359-360; *Official Proceedings of the National Negro Congress, 1936, 1940.*

24. Irving Howe and Lewis Coser, *The American Communist Party* (New York: Frederick Praeger, 1962), pp. 319-386; Record, *The Negro and the Communist Party*, pp. 153-162; James W. Ford, *The Negro and the Democratic Front* (New York: International Publishers, 1938), pp. 73-76; Roy Wilkins to Charles Houston, 15 February 1936, NAACP Files.

25. *Official Proceedings of the National Negro Congress, 1936*, pp. 7, 28-29; Bunche, "Programs, Ideologies, Tactics," p. 351.

26. Wilson Record has surveyed this literature in some detail. See

Record, *The Negro and the Communist Party*, pp. 184-208.

27. Bunche, "Programs, Ideologies, Tactics," pp. 362-363; Resolutions of the Third National Negro Congress, 1940, as quoted by Record, *The Negro and the Communist Party*, pp. 194-195.

28. Record, *The Negro and the Communist Party*, p. 192. Richard M. Dalfiume has written a good account of Negro protest against discrimination in the armed forces and defense industries: "The 'Forgotten Years' of the Negro Revolution," *Journal of American History* 40 (June, 1968):90-106. Cayton and Mitchell have written the most complete account of the CIO's impact on Negro life, *Black Workers and the New Unions*. The CIO's 1940 resolution read as follows: "This Convention reaffirms its determination that this nation must not enter into any foreign entanglements which may in any way drag us down the path of entering or becoming involved in foreign wars...

"The Congress of Industrial Organizations and its millions of members...are determined to protect and defend this nation not only against foreign enemies who may dare to attack us directly but also against those forces within our nation who place the profits of their financial and industrial enterprises above the well-being of the millions of common people.

"Labor believes that national defense means the creation of a nation of strong, healthy, well-fed people employed at work at decent and substantial wages....Labor believes that national defense means the continued growth and expansion of powerful industrial unions which will protect and defend the interests and status of their members to achieve economic security. Labor believes that national defense means the vigilant protection and constant safeguarding of the exercises of all of our cherished civil rights of speech, press, assembly, and worship. Labor believes that ignoring these fundamental principles and limiting our nation's activities to the building of mere armories, of aeroplanes, tanks and guns will not serve but rather defeat the basic interests of national defense."

29. Randolph, "Why I Would Not Stand for Re-Election," *Black Worker*, May 1940; idem, "Remarks Upon Resigning as President of the National Negro Congress," as quoted by Bunche, "Programs, Ideologies, Tactics," pp. 367-368.

30. Though I have drawn on some factual material in Bunche, "Programs, Ideologies, Tactics," pp. 369-371, and the information listed in footnote 31 below, this paragraph is frankly interpretive and is based mostly on my own speculation concerning the course of John Davis's career. The quotation is attributed to Davis in an NAACP press release of 30 June 1935.

31. Randolph, "Why I Would Not Stand for Re-Election;" Bunche, "Programs, Ideologies, Tactics," pp. 361, 367-368; Record, *The Negro and the Communist Party*, pp. 192-197. In PPF 4266, FDR Library, see John P. Davis to Franklin D. Roosevelt, 11 November 1941; Davis to Roosevelt, telegram, 17 November 1941; Davis to Roosevelt, telegram, 8 October 1938; Davis and Charles Wesley Burton to Roosevelt, 30 October 1938.

32. Bunche, "Programs, Ideologies, Tactics," pp. 369-371; Randolph, "Why I Would Not Stand for Re-Election;" Record, *The Negro and the Communist Party*, p. 199.

Summary

As a result of the economic crisis of the Great Depression, the leaders of the NAACP were forced to reevaluate their tactics and goals. Generally it was admitted that new conditions demanded that the older emphasis on civil and political rights be supplemented with a new concern for improving the economic position of the black masses, but there was no consensus when it came to deciding which strategies and tactics were most conducive to economic betterment. A small group followed the leadership of W. E. B. Du Bois and favored the creation of a separate, cooperative economy as the best method for leading the black working class out of the economic wilderness. A larger group that included most of the prominent young leaders of the day advocated affiliation with the egalitarian industrial unions of the CIO. Believing that the future progress of the Negro race was intrinsically tied up with ameliorating the condition of the entire working class, these young militants rallied behind the report of the Harris committee and urged the NAACP to develop programs that would encourage the growth of biracial working class solidarity. They were convinced that black labor must be made conscious of its relation to white labor and that white workers must be brought to realize that

383

the goals of organized labor could not be achieved without full participation by the Negro worker. During the mid-1930s the NAACP itself paid lip service to this labor viewpoint, but Walter White and other powerful leaders of the association had grave reservations about the wisdom of any thorough reorientation of goals and tactics, and despite the growing rhetorical attention to the problems of black labor, the work of the association continued to focus on the struggle for black civil rights and against lynching.

In retrospect it seems that black people received less than a fair share of economic aid from some important New Deal recovery agencies and that there was much merit to the contention that black workers could improve their position only if they succeeded in organizing themselves as a powerful political and economic interest group that the government could not afford to ignore. Unfortunately for Negroes, the black community of the 1930s had neither the financial resources nor the internal cohesion, mass sophistication, and leaders with the ability and disposition to guide the race toward either effective self-help or working class solidarity. As a consequence, Negroes remained on the sidelines of American economic life during the 1930s, and they suffered the inevitable fate of a disorganized minority when they failed to participate fully in the recovery stimulated by World War II and maintained by massive postwar military spending.

Bibliographical Note
on
Manuscript Collections

MUCH of the information used in Part One of this study may be found in the records of the Agricultural Adjustment Administration which are in the National Archives (NA), Record Group (RG) 145. The files of the cotton section, the legal division, and the correspondence files of the individuals concerned with the sharecroppers' problems were most useful. The correspondence files of the various interested persons in the Department of Agriculture were also helpful; they have been collected in Record Group 16. In addition, the correspondence files of the leaders of the Farm Security Administration and the Resettlement Administration were of assistance; they are available in Record Group 96.

The records of the National Recovery Administration, including correspondence files and the transcripts of the various code hearings, have been preserved in Record Group 9. The files of Lawrence Oxley in Record Group 183 also contain much useful data on the situation in the NRA. The correspondence of the Department of Interior's advisers on Negro affairs and the records of the interdepartmental group concerned with the special problems of Negroes are available in Record

Group 48. The records of the Works Progress Administration have been kept in Record Group 69.

Throughout this study I have relied on correspondence in the NAACP Files at the Library of Congress. The extensive and valuable papers of W. E. B. Du Bois, in possession of Herbert Aptheker in New York City, were also very useful, as was a much smaller collection of Du Bois's correspondence and typescripts at the Amistad Foundation, Fisk University. The J. E. Spingarn Papers at Howard and Yale universities were helpful but not extensive, while the James Weldon Johnson Papers at Yale also contained a few useful documents. Less valuable for my purposes were the Walter White Papers at Yale, the Oswald Garrison Villard Papers at Harvard, the Emmett Scott Papers at Morgan State College, and the Alfred Smith Papers at Howard. The papers in the Franklin D. Roosevelt Library at Hyde Park were disappointing; only a few of the letters and documents in the Official File (OF) and the President's Personal File (PPF) were useful for this study. The files of the National Urban League are extensive but are temporarily closed while being arranged by the Library of Congress. Fortunately, many of the Urban League's typescripts and pamphlets dealing with various aspects of the Great Depression and the New Deal were made available to me at the league's national office in New York City. The valuable Carnegie-Myrdal Manuscripts, consisting of more than one hundred typescripts prepared by staff members assisting Gunnar Myrdal in the preparation of *An American Dilemma,* touch on many aspects of Negro life in the 1930s and are available in the Schomburg Collection at the 135th Street branch of the New York Public Library. The interviews with W. E. B. Du Bois, George Schuyler and Roy Wilkins in the Columbia University Oral History Project provided several useful bits of information.

Index